Hey, Waitress!

Hey, Waitress!

THE USA FROM THE OTHER SIDE OF THE TRAY

Alison Owings

UNIVERSITY OF CALIFORNIA PRESS

Berkeley · Los Angeles · London

The publisher gratefully acknowledges the generous contribution
to this book provided by the General Endowment of the University
of California Press Associates.

University of California Press
Berkeley and Los Angeles, California

University of California Press, Ltd.
London, England

Frontispiece: Katrin Wiese, *Wanza,* © 1999, acrylic on
wood, 12 x 15 x 5 $^{1}/_{2}$ in., collection of author

Photographs used by permission of interviewees. Ima
Jean Edwards photographed by *Greensboro News and
Record,* Wendy Levy by Peter Obermayer, Joanne
Mulcahy by Annie David.

Library of Congress Cataloging-in-Publication Data

Owings, Alison.
  Hey, waitress! : the USA from the other side of the
tray / Alison Owings.
      p. cm.
  ISBN 0-520-21750-0 (acid-free paper)
   1. Waitresses—United States—Biography.
I. Title.
  TX910.3 .O95 2002
  647.95'023'73—dc21   2002003614

Manufactured in the United States of America

11   10 09 08 07 06 05 04 03 02
10 9 8 7 6 5 4 3 2 1

The paper used in this publication meets the minimum
requirements of ANSI/NISO Z39.48-1992 (R 1997)
(Permanence of Paper).

FOR JONATHAN

CONTENTS

Voices from the Other Side of the Tray

Once, upon a short time. Howard Johnson's on the Pennsylvania Turn-pike, Valley Forge exit. Several of us girls from Conestoga High School—all gangly, giggly, gorging, and earning summer money for fall college—raced around HoJo's orange/aqua color scheme, a palette that extended to our uniforms. I was riveted, as outsiders are, by details: having to wear huge white shoes and a hairnet, getting to eat for free everything ill-advised for a teenaged complexion, from chocolate milk shakes to fried clams. The only items the HoJo powers forbade their staff were sirloin steak and fresh fruit, thus winning the latter a new, if passing, interest.

I was not a good waitress for at least two reasons.

First, despite being so nearsighted that I had worn glasses since third grade, I did not want to wear them now—not with that hairnet. Therefore I could see virtually nothing beyond my arm, including food, tables, or customers.

Second, I was embarrassed by tips. One man I forgot for close to an hour, mostly because he sat beyond my arm. When I bolted over to apologize, he thanked me for not rushing him, then pressed a quarter into my hand. A quarter was a friendly tip for lunch in 1962 on the Pennsylvania Turnpike. "There you are," he said. "Oh, no, that's all right," I said and gave it back.

Make her a cashier, suggested someone. I happily complied.

The above would have been the sum of my waitressing memories but for an incident a week later, an incident I believe was the impetus for this book.

While dashing through the employee break room, I suddenly stopped. Sitting in front of me was the one waitress who intimidated and fasci-nated me, a woman who acted more sure of herself than any female I knew, including cheerleaders. She was ancient (maybe thirty), wore makeup to work (I thought it was only for dates), and once had made me blush through my Clearasil. A certain assistant manager, she had muttered in a thrilling aside to me alone, "did not know his ass from a hole in the ground."

What shocked me now was her meal. She was eating soup.

"When you can have ice cream and fried onion rings *for free*," I blurted, "you have *soup?*" She looked up at me unbearably slowly, her eyes full of what I had never seen before. It was disdain.

I realized only then that she was eating HoJo soup because she had eaten enough HoJo junk, and that she had eaten enough HoJo junk because she was waiting tables not only for the summer.

Up to that moment, my view of the world had vaulted from my suburban front door to an unorthodox clutch of pen pals, including Saudi Arabia's Prince Khalid in England, a drummer in Nigeria, and a novelist in Bermuda. It had, however, skipped the wide American in-between— and the reality now glaring at me. Choosing soup means that some girls do not go to college.

If a myopic dork, internationally minded or no, could learn such a lesson about her own country from one silent waitress, I later thought, imagine what anybody could learn when waitresses talk.

By my calculations, at least 1,566,832 waitresses are working in the United States today.[1] Granted, a woman in Maryland may have thrown down her apron in mid-shift this morning and walked out, dropping the total to 1,566,831; or a woman in Iowa may have walked in, put on an apron, and raised the total to 1,566,833. The number is elusive. The women are not.

In virtually every inhabited corner of this country where food is placed for a price, a waitress works. Collectively, waitresses serve all of us, or almost all of us. Some of us, of course, find no reason to eat out and do not. Others are in one way or another incarcerated. Still others shore up economic extremes: so rich they eat in waiter-only places (where the glass ceiling covers the dining room) or so poor they barely can eat at all, much less out. Yet even homebodies and escapees, plutocrats and homeless sometimes belly up to a counter. When they do, chances are—especially at a counter—a waitress will serve them.

"Waitress." It is, in ways, a woeful word, a hanger-on from the days of the diminutives "stewardess" and "authoress," "Jewess" and "Negress," "poetess" and "sculptress"; but it remains current (sometimes concurrent) almost only with "actress." Because it is the only word that specifically means a woman who waits tables, I use it in these pages.

Why, I lately have been asked, did I start ruminating about waitresses? The answer may simply be that from childhood on, I have always talked to strangers. (Eavesdropping could and can be thrilling, too, but you don't get to ask questions.) As I got older, easily drawn by the lure of journalism, my interest veered from people who, justified or not, considered themselves noteworthy and instead focused on people who harbored no such notions. Their potential is being squandered, I recall thinking, and they are becoming others' self-fulfilling prophesies. One can hardly grow up as a woman (to name the state with which I am most familiar) without knowing that stereotypes maim.

For no further reason I can pin down—maybe it was a lot of traveling alone, chewing alone, looking up—waitresses began to hook me. At some point, I found myself watching and listening to them, to their customers, co-workers, bosses. In contrast to the frequent course of events involving male customers, I never struck up conversations with waitresses. They were busy, after all. Then, somehow, I thought of the woman who ate soup at HoJo's.

Soon the subject of American waitresses hooked me, too. I did not need to think hard to realize that waitresses were overlooked, underheard, underappreciated, and, unlike any other similarly large group of workers, understudied. They stand alone, I thought, even in rare moments when they sit down. Also, contrary to popular assumptions, waitresses are a diverse group, representing almost every stratum and age range of America, if mostly a white America. Many do fit into at least one of the predominant three stereotypes—college girl, would-be performer, or wise-cracking greasy-spooner—but many have little more in common with each other than an ability to serve food for money (or, that is, in the hope of money).

What, one may ask, about waiters? Although waitresses outnumber them about three to one, the two groups have much in common, from hearing "Give me a . . ." or "I'll try the . . ." (you'll *try?*), to being left a dismal tip (which, if I am a member of the dining party, I furtively up). The job is the same, and, if a unisex word such as "server," "waitperson," or "waiter" is used, the title is the same. Little else is the same, though—not at the low end, not at the high. Waiting tables, a job correctly (but incompletely) considered a woman's common remedy for financial desperation, becomes part of its stigma. When a job is thought to be common, it is dismissed. So are the women who do it. Let us not even address here the sexual implications of the work. Waiters, believe me, have it easier.

It is waitresses, en masse and alone, I realized, who signify upward and downward mobility within American democracy and capitalism. They are warning or hope. Some, as they wished, do become famous on stages wider than dining rooms, as actresses, as singers of opera or ballads or rock. Some raise children who become famous. Dan Rather's mother was a waitress. (He always tips well, he told me with a smile.) Al Gore's mother waitressed her way through nursing school. Writer Dorothy Allison's mother was a waitress, as was she. Wayne Thiebaud, painter of luscious pastries, grew up amid them in his family's coffee shop in Idaho, where his sister waited tables and his mother was cashier and hostess. ("Hostess"—another diminutive.)

Apart from national or familial claims to fame, though, most waitresses are so anonymous that not even their customers always recognize them, in or out of uniform.

In contrast, waitresses recognize everyone. As they are serving, so are they observing. They are there but not there, looking at us, gauging us, overhearing us. It is part of their job. Furthermore, because of their vast numbers, they observe much more than the minutiae of their employment. Through contact with co-workers, customers, friends, and families, they watch, witness, or are part of every upheaval, uproar, tradition, trend, debate, and issue that has blessed or bedeviled the experiment called America. *Everything* that happens in this country happens on a waitress's shift.

They are, however, surprisingly muted. At work, orders now are more likely to be written or entered into a computer than called out. With the exception of chatting with regulars, questioning an exceptional stranger, or uttering the trio of basic waitspeech—greet, take order, thank—waitresses do not necessarily talk much with customers. Exchanges among co-workers, depending on how shifts and side work are structured, do not necessarily last long either. One reason for after-shift drinks must be the anticipation of completing a sentence.

Muteness of another sort comes from the outside world. Waitresses know that the country they serve pays them little real heed, beyond, that is, cultural canonization. Anthropologists are not staked out beside dumpsters waiting to quiz women coming off lunch shift about their tribal customs.

I realized, as I began chewing a bit faster, that waitresses, stereotyped comically but ignored seriously, are the virgin chroniclers and commentators of our time. They know the U.S.A. from the other side of the tray. I knew they had a lot to say.

Wanting to reach as wide a range of women as I could, I began a multi-pronged search. Friends and relatives offered personal contacts. A "Reader's Query" in the *New York Times Book Review*, in which I asked to hear from "current or former waitresses of particular interest, insight, and/or volubility, or anyone who could recommend any," netted me a notice from my post office that I had excess mail. To track down women in more distant avenues, I applied journalistic training and upped my persistence. Over many more years than planned, I needed both.

As I began the travel phase of the work, a number of speaking invitations connected to my previous book, a study of German women during the Third Reich, came along. Coordinating carefully, I availed myself of airfare and honoraria, gave a talk at a university or a Holocaust studies center about what I consider the complexity of the Nazi era, hit the road in a rental car, and soon was asking a waitress how she got her job. There was never any choice but to interview in person; I wanted customers to see their waitresses.

Compromises came with each course. I did not find every type of waitress I sought, nor every individual. I rue the missed chances with those who got away: an elderly waitress on Maui who never had been off the island; a woman at Ponzio's Diner in Cherry Hill, New Jersey, who, a *Times* reader wrote, had been there thirty years on the same 5 A.M. to 3 P.M. shift *and* at the same area of the counter; a Las Vegas truck stop waitress in her sixties who answered to "Chicken Legs" and whom truckers voted "waitress of the year." The Maui waitress had to take her husband to the doctor the only time we could meet; by the time I could see her in action, the woman at Ponzio's was (small wonder) out on disability; and "Chicken Legs" split Vegas without a forwarding address.

Mostly, though, I lucked out. Given my interest, supplemented by the offer of a meal they did not have to serve, and given their trained ease with strangers, it is no surprise that the women, sometimes stressed, stiffed, stifled, or just off shift, agreed to talk. "Talk" indeed. They were like a coffee urn exploding on the countertop of life.

From Staten Island to Escondido, from Seattle to the Everglades and Memphis to Manhattan, when the tables were turned, the women dished it out. They told stories that impoverished fiction, offered insights that challenged tradition, and, through their economically arranged marriage (for better and for worse) with America, taught more about it than some of us might want to know.

A BRIEF, AND SUBJECTIVE, HISTORY OF WAITRESSING

*T*HE FIRST CLASSICAL WAITRESS, so to speak, was Hebe, daughter of the Greek god Zeus and the goddess Hera. Hebe's job was to pour wine for the gods. That is, in an irony perhaps relevant only to New Yorkers, the first known waitress worked in a Greek place uptown.

Yet even a myth has a mother. The notion of one person satisfying the thirst or hunger of another must have begun when woman first nursed child—a picture, say waitresses, that still informs some customers. (There are striking similarities between suckling and serving; breasts remain a factor, as does the urge to mollify as quickly as possible.)

Today's waitresses have inherited not only myth and the mirage of motherhood but history as well. None of these legacies has made the job easier.

The first American waitress—that is, the first woman from the European migration paid to hand over sustenance—is known neither by name nor by myth. She almost certainly worked in a tavern. Because English- and Dutch-style taverns, built by English and Dutch settlers, were part of the United States long before the States were United, she likely found work as early as the 1600s. Because country taverns typically relied on family members rather than hired help, she likely worked in a city—probably a northern one such as Boston, New York, or Philadelphia. The reason I deduce this is painfully simple. Thinking initially, illogically, that Colonial Williamsburg might be the place to find out about colonial waitresses (the cultural kin of English "serving wenches" appeared in my mind's eye), I called Williamsburg staff historian Patricia A. Gibbs, who brought me up short.

There were no waitresses in Williamsburg, she informed me. There were slaves. Most of those who served food, furthermore, were young men. In the South, she added, serving by slaves was so common that exceptions stood out. At Paxton's tavern in western Virginia, a visiting French marquis in the 1780s wrote in his journal that "breakfast . . . was served by Captain Paxton's daughters."[1] He would not have noted who served him, said Gibbs, had the occasion not been rare.

Considering the evidence, then, the first American waitress likely was a northern urbanite.

From the earliest days of the American pilgrims' progress, women more or less had a foot in the tavern door. As early as 1620 in New England, they were licensed to sell alcohol and (often in widowhood) became tavern keepers. Service was rudimentary. Drawings and diaries from the seventeenth and eighteenth centuries indicate that American innkeepers, men or women, often simply put punch bowl or platter on a table and let people help themselves.[2] A traveler in the Carolinas encountered less genteel circumstances: "Ten to one you had to cook the meal yourself."[3]

Serving food, however, was not the seed of American waitressing. Doling out spirits was. (If any colonial establishment served food without alcohol, I know not of it.) Local governments even ordered taverns to be built for the common good; alcohol was regarded as helpful in fending off diseases from air or water and in making people work harder. Unfortunately, alcohol also was known to encourage unseemly behavior. Taverns, by the nature of their product, not only tolerated unseemliness but attracted strangers. If taverns were dockside, propriety plummeted further. "They catered to transient seamen or day laborers, served beverages under the counter to servants and apprentices, and acted as houses of rendezvous for prostitutes."[4] The connection was fixed.

From the start, serving tainted the women who served.

Some women tainted themselves. A seventeenth-century Boston tavern keeper, Alice Thomas, was found guilty of admitting "Lewd Lascivious & notorious persons of both Sexes, giving them oppertunity [sic] to commit carnal wickedness." In the early eighteenth century, Mary Cook of Philadelphia was charged with allowing into her tavern "Whores, Vagabonds and diverse Idle Men."[5]

Among Williamsburg's tavern keepers was Anne Pattison (a widow thought to imbibe notably herself), known today less for keeping a tavern than for keeping the city's only surviving tavern account book. It shows she ran a thriving business (her inventory included wooden trays, pewter plates, and delft dishes) and offered meals based on meats, eggs, and breads, with vegetables from local gardens as side dishes. Actually, meals constituted a kind of side dish—Pattison sold four times more alcohol than food. Among her customers were slaves, who made up as much as 40 percent of Williamsburg's population. They had less significance to her as a customer base, of course, than as working property; she owned six.[6]

In New York, meanwhile, social concern attached itself to another serving-related matter. In 1750, a tavern launched the radical idea of offering businessmen an "ordinary," or meal, to spare them the long lunchtime trip home. Scandal! The restaurant was criticized for fomenting the breakup of the family.[7]

More than seventy-five years passed before the country's first formal restaurant, Delmonico's in New York, opened its doors. The date was December 13, 1827, and the reaction was, in a word, confused. A place to eat out for the heck of it? "People didn't know quite how to do it at first; they wandered in, read the menu, and wandered out again."[8]

Then they caught on.

The nation was changing. People traveled, by whatever contraption and for whatever reason, farther from home; human migrations originating from both within and without the country supplanted small-town societies; weather and war added to economic crises; and women, not for the first time, had to fend for themselves and their families. Restaurants thus soon served a range of needs. (They also served women, if those women were accompanied by men. Unaccompanied women still carried—and arguably continue to carry—the old tavern taint of prostitution. Susan B. Anthony, properly escorted to the dining room of an upstate New York hotel in 1859, had the nerve, though, to give her food order directly to the waiter. He tried to get her male companion to order for her, but the man "stumbled and stammered" until Anthony prevailed.)[9]

The occupation of waitressing must have been established by the middle of the nineteenth century, for not long thereafter entrepreneur Fred Harvey capitalized on it. While trying to build a restaurant empire at stops along the Santa Fe railroad, which was rapidly expanding westward, he became fed up with drunken waiters and followed a suggestion to employ women. They became his carefully chosen "Harvey Girls" (one of whom, Verna Welsh, was interviewed for this book). Harvey was so clever that he even knew not to call his employees "waitresses," a title considered lowlier than that of "maid."

At the end of the nineteenth century, the term "waitress," judging from two contemporary self-help tomes, often referred to a woman who waited tables in a private home. If *The Expert Waitress: A Manual for the Pantry, Kitchen, and Dining-Room* and *The Up-to-Date Waitress* are accurate, that woman had a full plate of work.[10] Not only was she required to serve courses competently ("Nothing but an unexpected extra should ever be asked for"), but she also had to clean up afterward. "Follow this rule: never pile dishes on a tray in a manner to look disagreeable to yourself or to those who sit at table." Get your pantry in order, too, up-to-date waitresses were urged; it will "conduce to celerity in serving and care of the table appointments."[11] The books gave cleaning instructions for everything from "salad plants" to wine-stained tablecloths, enjoined supposedly witless waitresses not to empty partly filled cups and glasses into dishwater, and offered rousing words about the job itself, claiming that a waitress "has a great field before her" that could compete with stenography, millinery, and teaching.[12] "The waitress with pleasant sleeping-room, and the use of a common sitting-room, whose duties are largely confined to a handsome dining-room and well-fitted pantry, enjoys her surroundings quite as much as does the owner thereof."[13]

The "up-to-date waitress," however, was not. Huge households were giving way to smaller ones, and many staff members were dismissed. Whether because of downsizing or a desire to escape, many a waitress decided that the "great field before her" was out the mansion door. These women washed their last salad plant, conduced the last celerity out of the pantry, packed their bags, and headed for a restaurant.

As the number of waitresses rose, their reputations fell—the usual blessing and curse of female mobility. Waitresses were, after all, often new to town, unescorted, and in contact with the unholy trio of men, money, and alcohol. (Prohibition did not go into effect until 1920.) They also were voteless and exploited.

One outsider became especially curious about them. " 'Why not find out about the waitress?' I asked myself, and the idea made a strong appeal to me. . . . These women represent the advance guard of working women who are marching steadily deeper and deeper into the world of economic competition, getting into new and dangerous contacts." The year was 1917. Chicago sociologist/teacher Frances Donovan decided to go undercover as a waitress. Alas, it was easier than she expected: "Throughout my experiences I had been chagrined at the success of my disguise which was no disguise at all. I had merely put on an apron and said that I was a waitress and immediately everyone accepted me as one."[14]

Donovan served nine months. Her experiences and observations, published as *The Woman Who Waits,* promised "an intimate, personal, and realistic account of the life of a waitress in Chicago restaurants."[15] In the slim annals of waitressiana, this volume is extraordinary because it exists. It is also remarkable for its resonance today.

The first striking corollary is Donovan's own perspective, The Woman Who Had Never Waited. "There was something terrifying about the idea of life so totally new, so absolutely outside the realm of my experience." Dressing by lockers in a damp basement for her first job, she saw about "ten girls" putting on makeup and "tossing back and forth to each other, apparently in a spirit of good-natured comradeship, the most vile epithets that I had ever heard emerge from the lips of a human being, and mingled with these were long oaths of obscene profanity. I felt dizzy, stunned . . . I was frightened, too. The musty-smelling little room seemed to take on an air of evil and of horror indescribable." Yet, on one busy lunch shift, "my fellow waiters and waitresses were very considerate and helped me in every way. They called me 'dearie,' 'girlie,' 'kid,' and 'kiddo,' and gave me whispered tips . . . to use a dirty glass if I couldn't find a clean one, but not to let anyone see me do it."[16]

Helpfulness aside, Donovan remained shocked by her colleagues' basement banter, at odds, she thought, with their looks. "They were very attractive girls with fresh-looking skins in spite of the rouge and the lip stick, and their chests and breasts were creamy white. . . . They seemed proud of their way of living and wished to flaunt it in everybody's face. They appeared to be happy, too, not cast down and ashamed of their degradation." When Donovan, still "sick at heart," felt she could not endure the language "another minute," it was time to work. In the excitement of filling orders, her heartsickness abated.[17]

On her fourth day, the manager, who walked up and down the counters yelling at the "girls" to step lively and snapping a napkin at them, fired her for questioning his command to take cream to a man who had told her he wanted his coffee black. The "girls" offered goodbyes in the basement with "kindness and sweetness."

Donovan's second job lasted two days. While attempting to enter the kitchen through the wrong door, she collided with another waitress. Boom! Fired. Later she confided that it was much easier to get a job than to keep it.[18]

At her third job, she met Lillie, Myrtle, and Flossie and herself became "Fannie." After a hard shift, "at half-past eight I descend to the basement dressing-room thoroughly exhausted" and "nervously tired," but "I did not want to go home. I was in a mood for anything, anything but home. One dollar and ninety-five cents in dimes and nickels, my tips for the day, jingled lightly in my pocket. The jingle added to my excitement. I was beginning to feel the fascination of the tip."[19]

Five days she toiled at this eatery, until an angry man screamed that she had not brought him coffee with his beer and stalked off. Fannie was fired again. The manager made a waitress give her the news. "I went down to the basement dressing-room in disgrace." The others, as usual, were dressing for an evening out. Flossie spoke.

" 'Ellen told me he made her fire you,' said she, 'she feels real bad about it,' and then she added, 'I'm awful sorry, kid.'

"I was exhausted and my nerves were raw. The tears began chasing each other down my cheeks. I could make no reply to Flossie. Finally I gave myself up to my grief and sobbed with uncontrolled ardor. The girls flocked about me and began to sympathize." One said the customer who screamed and stalked off was a dope fiend on morphine, and in vaudeville. Another said of the manager, " 'You don't want to pay any attention to him, he don't know what he's doing any of the time.' "[20]

Fannie kept serving, at a range of places, apparently a better journalist than a waitress. One co-worker took her aside: " 'Don't try another steady job until you are an experienced waitress.' " Another employer, a sage lady who sensed that Fannie was not what she claimed to be, told her, " 'Even though you may not have had to work for your living always, do not let the girls know that it is new to you. If they think that you fell above them, you will not get on well.' " An English waitress named Janet, whom Donovan visited in her small, dark flat and who looked as pale as many waitresses did for lack of sunlight, was wise to her, too: " 'As soon as I saw you, I knew that you had never worked much, you looked so fresh.' "[21]

Waitresses' hours, not unlike hours in other jobs, were grueling. Only ten years before Donovan donned an apron, Cleveland had passed a law reducing a waitress's work week to seventy hours.[22] In Chicago in 1912, the city's Juvenile Protective Association had issued a shocking report titled "The Girl Employed in Hotels and Restaurants," which was based on investigators' interviews with "girls" in seventy-two restaurants.[23]

The report claimed that most "girls" got into the work because it did "not require any skill," because it included meals, and because it brought them in contact with many people and some excitement. That was it for the good news. "There is much complaint that the work is very hard and that the girls can only stand it for a few years. The carrying of heavy trays and constant standing and walking causes ill health and trouble with the feet."

The greatest number of complaints, after health, were related to "bad treatment by the public." Among the remarks quoted in the report: "People think they can say almost anything to a waitress." "Another said she would rather not take the tips than have to listen to the remarks of the young men who gave them." One interviewer saw a male customer put his arm "around a waitress in a suggestive manner. She looked appealingly at the manager, but no protest was made." That was no surprise. "The manager often regards a pretty girl in the light of an attraction for his restaurant. In one place the pretty girls were put downstairs, where the men were served. The homely girls were put upstairs, in the room reserved for women customers."

Donovan saw the same: "Restaurants want women who are young and good looking; the advertisements announce it and most managers insist on it." Older, experienced women might get waitress work, "but for the most part the girl who is good looking has her pick of the jobs, for everywhere the waitress is playing a game. It is this which makes the life, hard as it is, fascinating to her. It is a woman's game, the sex game." A "dirty game," Donovan added. Even in restaurants where relations between waitresses and customers were "not actively sexual, there was the constant stimulation of dirty jokes and unclean conversation."[24]

Most women in the Juvenile Protective Association study (though fewer in Donovan's) were on their own. Ninety percent lacked what the study considered a home, some having come to Chicago to escape families, others to escape rural life. Two whom Donovan met had fled "waitress" work in private homes and told her they did not want to return. "It is the group life in the waitress world that makes the appeal and the lack of it is the strongest reason why girls are unwilling to work in private families."[25] Donovan said nothing about workload.

The Juvenile Protective Association study added, "Many of these girls, coming to know their own limitations and having no hope for a bright future, realize that they can expect but little in the way of wages and are therefore bent on having as good a time as possible while their youth and attractiveness last." Thus "it is no wonder that so many of them yield readily to temptation."

By 1912, the year of the study, work days were limited legally to ten hours. Many waitresses worked longer, up to thirteen hours. The usual working day was made up of a split shift that covered all meals: 7 A.M. to 2 P.M., and 5 P.M. to 8 P.M. The "girls" thus worked ten hours but were away from home for fifteen, from 6 A.M. to 9 P.M.

Midday breaks offered little relief, the investigators learned. If waitresses stayed in the restaurant to rest, they were expected to work. Some were so tired that they would "put pads on the tables and lie on them." Going home was not an option; it took too much time and carfare. "If they go on the streets they get little good from their walk, for at the best they go shopping, or look into the shop windows or go into nickel shows if they can find someone to invite them. Many young men loiter outside the restaurants to pick up an acquaintance with the waitresses during their leisure time."

The "improper attentions" from "evil men" led to many a moral fall. Investigators heard frequent references to such men suggesting how waitresses could supplement their wages. "The entire investigation revealed once more the hideous risks of the excessively fatigued and overworked girl who is able to obtain the rest and comfort she craves only through illicit channels."

The link between prostitution and waitressing became even stronger when sluiced by alcohol. "The waitresses who work in restaurants where liquor is sold are regarded as low-class by the other waitresses, and the excuse given by the former is that they receive larger tips."[26] Donovan also linked waitressing and prostitution, if from another view: "Because of the economic inefficiency of the men in her world, the waitress fails to realize her ideal of domesticity and so she takes on a life of semi-prostitution." With scant knowledge of birth control or money to raise children, such a woman was likely to become pregnant, and then "she resorts to the common practice of abortion."[27]

The Juvenile Protective Association had two major recommendations to make life better for waitresses. One was to abolish tips. Tips have a "pernicious effect," stated the report. "A young girl who under any other circumstances would not dream of accepting money from a man will accept it in the guise of a tip. In the hands of a vicious man this tip establishes between him and the girl a relation of subserviency and pa-tronage which may easily be made the beginning of improper attentions. The most conscientious girl, dependent upon tips to eke out her slender wage, finds it difficult to determine just where the line of propriety is crossed." Waitresses then "encounter that lack of respect which curi-ously attaches itself to one who accepts a gratuity."

The other recommendation was to offer shelter during the perilous midday break. It was "absolutely necessary that some place be provided where these girls can rest for the three hours they are 'off' duty." The Junior League of Chicago, said the report, planned to establish such a room, with matron and couches, so that waitresses could rest, read, or sew. The waitresses union already had a small room. (Waitresses unions had begun to emerge in the early part of the century, as described in the interview with Beulah Compton in this book.) The Juvenile Protective Association hoped that if the need for such refuges became known, "public opinion would in time become a natural safeguard and protec-tion."[28]

Good intentions on the part of the Juvenile Protective Association, the Junior League, and other high-minded persons aside, Donovan also implied that waitresses were not interested in a safe spot to rest during shift break. "The waitress," she wrote in her customary insulting sin-gular, "seeks constant amusement in her leisure time because the rush of her work keys her up to a nervous pitch where she demands more stimulation. But her pleasures do not make for efficiency, they have little or no stability and productivity and are a great waste." (One commodity not wasted was food. Whatever was left on customers' plates was "ea-gerly gobbled and choked down during the rush.")[29]

Frances Donovan's middle-class haven gave her all the seemly refuge and recreation she needed, but she was getting picky about where she worked. At the end of a week in one restaurant, she quit, noting, "I had never worked in a more badly managed kitchen." It was always running out of rolls. Mostly, however, her attention focused on the waitresses—"Here we have a feminist movement and ideals embodied in a class"—and how they interacted with each other and customers.[30]

She felt "the force of a discovery" upon learning that "the relation between the waitress and patron is a distinctly personal one. Eating in a restaurant is not exactly a sacrament, but under any sort of human conditions, it is something of a ceremony," and an especially intimate one with men. "The men who patronize the cheaper restaurants look upon the waitress as a social equal and any man who comes in other than the rush hour expects a little visit with her. These conversations are never particularly edifying," Donovan added.[31]

" 'You can't get along in any kind of restaurant,' said a girl to me, 'unless you jolly the customers.' " Fannie, readers will infer, was not a jollier. "Certainly the customers look for the jolly. Many times it is simply friendly and innocent but quite as often the man starts deliberately to explore. . . . If the waitress is too busy for jollying, the attitude of the patron is quite different. During the rush hour at a counter in a hash house, the waitress might as well be a machine as a human being for all the consideration she gets from the men she waits on. The busier she is, the greater her difficulties, the more impatient and clamorous become the men."[32]

Donovan noticed that male patrons differed by types: the old man "who always paid the waitress silly compliments, the grouchy, puffy, youngish fellow who clamored impatiently for food," the "boy with the restless shamefaced interest in women as represented by the waitress in her white apron," and "the father of a family who gratified a roving disposition for adventure by coquettish little jokes with the girl who served him." She recognized that a "lonesome boy" in the city "can get acquainted with the waitress probably easier than with any other woman; he can talk to her as soon as he meets her and call her by her first name as soon as he learns what it is."[33]

Frances "Fannie" Donovan, undercover waitress, swirled in a sociological stew.

The nicer the restaurant, she found, the wider the "social gulf" between waitress and patron, even with "nicer girls" who emitted "fewer oaths." If Donovan tried not to act as if she "fell above them," her face may have given her away. Randy jokes among waitresses made her muse: "I realized for the first time, how fragile a thing are the refinements of life." Because of their "easy familiar contact with men, these girls had acquired in regard to matters of sex (in which, like most women, they were mainly interested) the incredible candor of men."[34]

One exception was poor, pale Janet, who confided, " 'It's hard for a decent quiet girl to make tips anywhere.' " Donovan herself confided, "I was never very successful at working people for tips and never made over half what the other girls made."[35]

She learned who would not tip her: women "with bundles and babies" eating in a department store lunchroom. She also learned that "the poor man tips just as frequently as the rich man and that his tips are just as large."[36]

Donovan favored doing away with tipping, too, but knew the chances were nil. She speculated that managers did not want to end the practice, doubted that customers did, and knew that waitresses did not. Many told her the same: "I like to work where the 'side money' is good." (Such "side money" then made up a minority of a waitress's earnings.) Tipping, she concluded, "is the gambling factor in the life of the waitress. It redeems her work from dull routine and drudgery and puts into it the problematical."[37]

For all her empathy, Donovan was more condescending than admiring. "The waitress is a genuine Bohemian. Her life is spent in trying to escape definitions and to avoid suppressions. She has little idea of honor nor of personal obligation. She cannot be depended upon to keep her word." Furthermore, "there is not much that is complex about the waitress and her behavior can easily be reduced to the two fundamental appetites of food hunger and sex hunger. She is intelligent, efficient, industrious, dishonest, and dishonorable, loose in her sex relations, impatient of the restraints put upon her by the members of the group from which she came" and "inclined to set up new standards for herself and to make a new group life in which these standards are approved." Despite this new group, "the waitress is markedly individualistic in her attitude toward life." Her job fostered the same attitude.[38]

Waitresses are out for themselves, Donovan lamented. She had watched them steal each other's silverware and napkins. "Such a thing as team work among waitresses is unknown." For this she partly blamed employers, who "discharge" the "help at the slightest provocation." Waitresses thus "have no sense of security or permanence." She realized that waitress work "does not rank very high in the occupational scale. The waitress herself is ashamed of her job, and tries to conceal from her friends that she is a waitress." One waitress hid behind Fannie when neighbors unexpectedly entered the restaurant.[39]

Although all waitresses she met took the work "because it offers the most lucrative occupation open to untrained and uneducated women," Fannie seemed to sigh, they seldom save money. What the waitress needs is "education and a different attitude upon the part of the public towards her occupation." Donovan was blind to her own need for attitude adjustment. "The waitress is ignorant and coarse, but genial. She is often unwashed and her teeth are unfilled but she knows life and she is not afraid of life which is to her big, dramatic, brutal but vivid, full of color." Finally, she "does enjoy her freedom."[40]

After Donovan's investigation, "the waitress" did not receive much hardback attention for decades. Then in 1948 sociologist William H. Whyte produced his classic volume *Human Relations in the Restaurant Industry*. He was not concerned about vulgar language and off-the-job behavior; instead, his focus was on-the-job tensions. He saw restaurants as settings of complex human theater. "The customers begin to come in. The curtain goes up on the great American drama of food, hospitality, and personal service offered to the public every day by the restaurant industry."[41]

Whyte, for better and worse, reflected several forms of social consciousness. "The sort of behavior that is expected of waitresses will vary with the *social status* of the customers they serve." Echoing Donovan, he wrote that waitresses at modest restaurants felt free to handle customers as they wished, even with sass, but that "waitresses in high-standard restaurants face quite a different situation." Whyte implied that they wanted to climb the social ladder. "The waitress in a high-standard restaurant [has] unusual opportunities to make contacts with people of higher social standing, to observe their behavior, and to develop aspirations in that direction. It is then a very frustrating experience to have to put up with overbearing customers." Waiters, he felt, were more disturbed by this than waitresses were. "Men, growing up in a man's world, are not accustomed to the continual subordination that they face from customers."[42]

The occupational stigma Donovan had recognized in 1917 among her co-waitresses was still in effect in the late 1940s. Waitresses on vacation, Whyte discovered, never told "fellows" they met what they did for a living. If the fellows found out, "that cooled them off right away."[43]

In Whyte's opinion, the decisive factor separating server and served was not class but tips. "Many waiters and waitresses feel that some customers use their tipping power to demand a subservient attitude and special favors." He added, "In America, high-status people do not receive tips for their services, and tipping therefore tends to lower the status of the recipient." He suggested that managers "consider" an end to tipping. He did not buy the argument that without tips "waiters and waitresses would be careless in their work and become indifferent to their customers." A "false assumption," he wrote.[44]

For all Whyte's distaste for tips as a status separator, he remained remarkably status-conscious. The "girls" from farms and blue-collar backgrounds must "adapt themselves" not only to "middle-class behavior and standards" but also "to those of higher status. They must appear to subordinate themselves to customers and at the same time learn to manipulate the people and the situation to their own advantage. Girls who can absorb this sort of social learning find that their new pattern of behavior brings its own reward in enabling them to move up in the world." The "girl" of higher background, however, "finds herself taking orders from people whom she feels to be her equals and, in some cases, her inferiors" and "finds it exceedingly difficult to adjust to this unaccustomed type of subordination." He noticed that, in one restaurant, supervisors accorded college waitresses a higher status than full-time waitresses.[45]

Whyte, much more than Donovan, saw hostility in the wings, including that between waitresses and "countermen" (roughly equivalent to line cooks in today's parlance). One cook said he was glad for a counter area, where plates were kept warm, for it separated the kitchen staff and waitresses. "To him the important thing was that his counter protected him from the waitresses," who tended to yell at him. "We have ample evidence to show that many men who are in a subordinate role, or who feel anxieties over their position, gain a greater feeling of self-importance through sex domination. This would be one quite natural reaction to being on the receiving end of orders from women all day long."[46]

"The social role of the insignificant-looking spindle," today's "wheel" on which orders are clipped and spun around to face the cook, loomed large to Whyte. It too "serves to fend off from pantry people a good deal" of the "pressure exerted by waitresses." For anxiety-prone men, "the spindle makes the difference between a workable system and one that would blow up."[47]

Whyte noted a great need for workable systems. "When the waitress appears on the floor carrying food to her customers, she is taking the final step in the long and complicated process of production and service. All the steps are so highly interrelated and interdependent that a failure of coordination anywhere along the line can throw the waitress into difficulties with her customers." Then she cries, reported Whyte. "The case of the crying waitress emphasizes once more that the restaurant job can never be fitted into a pattern of routine."[48]

Whyte believed that control was the key to two parts of the great restaurant drama: waitresses controlling their customers, supervisors controlling everyone. "The well-adjusted waitress," to use Whyte's term, "tackles the customers with confidence and without hesitation. . . . There is never any question as to who is in charge. Most customers react favorably to this approach. It appears to give them a feeling of security when the waitress moves right in and shows that she knows how to handle her work." He also argued that most customers were willing to be controlled. The waitress must "seize the initiative in customer relations," by what she does, what she says, "the way she uses her voice, and the expression on her face." If she does not seize the initiative, Whyte warned, "the customer senses her uncertainty and seems to feel uneasy himself. This is likely to lead to trouble."[49]

In Whyte's opinion, a waitress required three things to shore up her self-confidence (and prevent her from crying): she needed "leadership experience" to help control customers; she needed to be "integrated into some group where she works and also in her life outside of work" to give her an "outlet for the tensions that arise in her job"; and she needed "security in her social position."[50]

Enter the "intelligent supervisor," who recognized that waitresses lack the "emotional security" found in factory jobs and must face "an ever-changing crowd of customers" and co-workers. Those co-workers were more important than supervisors realized, Whyte implied. "If a restaurant is not a good place for employees to make friends with each other, then it will not be considered a good place in which to work." Waitresses at one restaurant he studied were "not working just to make money"; they "got human satisfactions there—which meant, in large part, that they liked the girls they worked with."[51]

To Whyte, "the most important job" of the dining room supervisor was "maintaining or restoring the emotional equilibrium of the waitresses." (Read: no more tears.) This could be done by understanding that they needed "great skill" to "adjust to a wide variety of customers and fellow workers." Ah, but adjustment could go only so far, apparently. "The real problem then is how can we help the girl to feel like smiling, to enjoy her work?" Group meetings might be "particularly useful," Whyte suggested, especially if they helped a waitress "feel that something can be done about difficult customers." Once she knows whatever that something is, "her battle for adjustment is already won."[52]

A decade later, in *The Presentation of Self in Everyday Life,* Erving Goffman (who cited Whyte's views of waitresses) implied that adjustment includes faking it. "We know that in service occupations practitioners who may otherwise be sincere are sometimes forced to delude their customers because their customers show such a heartfelt demand for it." In other words, Goffman argued, we are all acting. "Whatever it is that generates the human want for social contact and for companionship, the effect seems to take two forms: a need for an audience before which to try out one's vaunted selves, and a need for teammates with whom to enter into collusive intimacies and backstage relaxation." Goffman's thesis was a general statement, but he could have been talking solely about waiting tables.[53]

The need for collusive intimacies and backstage relaxation has never flagged. Waitresses might have fled Victorian dining rooms, but they have not escaped servant status. In a study of waitresses at an unnamed chain restaurant in New Jersey, Greta Foff Paules wrote in 1991 that "the symbolism of service was simply transported along with the physical and social functions of the domestic from private home to private enterprise." As domestic servants a century ago did not dine with or near their employers, "so today waitresses are forbidden to take breaks, sit, smoke, eat, or drink in the presence of customers."[54]

Paules was outraged at how such segregation shores up "status lines" and conceals "the humanness of those whom one would like to deny the courtesies of personhood." She did observe, however, that one change had occurred over the years: the roles of server and served now are limited to the duration of the service and the boundaries of the restaurant (and, I would add, can be reversed the next day). She suggested erasing more boundaries—for example, getting rid of uniforms, separate bathrooms, and "the degrading term server."[55]

Anything that confines a waitress to a servant role, including being called by her first name, not only makes her adopt the role herself but also "encourages customers to treat, or mistreat, the waitress as they would a member of a historically degraded class." Consequently, many do. "Virtually every rule of etiquette is violated by customers in their interaction with the waitress: the waitress can be interrupted; she can be addressed with the mouth full; she can be ignored and stared at; and she can be subjected to unrestrained anger." She "is refused the most basic considerations of polite interaction."[56]

In response, the waitresses Paules observed did not cry. Instead, they turned things around to gain dignity: a bad tip was seen not as a reflection of their bad service but of a customer's cheapness.[57]

In an even more dour look at modern restaurant relations (not necessarily focused on the United States), another scholar seemed to suggest that waitresses, and everyone else involved in restaurants, should drop their roles, be true to themselves, and stay home. Joanne Finkelstein argued that dining out "reveals a barrier to civility" and is a sham from entrance and appetizer to dessert and departure. It is "a self-defeating activity, an entrapment in a style of life where desires are protean and satisfactions are made temporary and fleeting," and it therefore "promulgates incivility."[58] The customer has been deceived by owner, cook, and waiter and served up for consumption. The inference? Waitresses have become part of their own problem.

They certainly have become part of American culture. Indeed, they have become American icons.

Computers alone (and some computer games) confirm it. One Internet search engine offered about 250,000 Web sites containing the word "waitress." Most sites, it seemed, involved commerce. Wares for sale included "God Bless the Waitress" T-shirts; "The Waitress Is a Bitch" signs; a waitress angel pin; a waitress watch; an array of figurines, from Mary's Moo Moo Waitress and a pewter waitress clown to Coca-Cola waitress Barbie and taller statuary; and rentable waitress outfits, from standard to skimpy. The search also proffered Web pages belonging to waitresses (whew, do they vent!), listings for The Waitresses rock band (which includes men), and a plethora of visual and printed porn, aimed at gay women as well as straight men.

The women have become fodder in fiction, too. A further Internet search provided 14,000 listings that contained both the words "waitress" and "novel." After checking 400 or so entries, however, I had not learned much more than that many waitresses were writing novels, that an actress in a movie based on a novel had been a topless waitress, that journalists conducting lunchtime interviews of novelists sometimes mentioned the waitress, that Ayn Rand (!) had been a waitress, and that waitresses figure in a trayload of romance and science fiction, published on line and off.

Waitresses also figure in more literary fare, from W. Somerset Maugham's *Of Human Bondage* (though it's British and probably shouldn't count here) to Dorothy Allison's *Bastard Out of Carolina,* from short stories by Raymond Carver to Denise Chavez's enchanting *Face of an Angel,* the only serious novel I've encountered whose main protagonist is a waitress.[59] In the mystery genre, Erle Stanley Gardner offered a positive portrayal in *The Case of the Worried Waitress.*[60] (His heroine was waiting tables, it must be noted, because of nefarious goings-on in her life, not because she *really* wanted to wait tables.) Redoubtable attorney Perry Mason solved the case, of course. Although Gardner made her a proper young woman, an author has only so much clout. I doubt he wrote the book's come-on about a waitress "with more on her mind than the menu" any more than he designed the cover, which pictures a vixen in a strapless something stuffing money down her bosom.

Perhaps the farther waitresses stray from the written word, the worse they fare. In the movie *Breakfast at Tiffany's,* the rich Patricia Neal character is furious that her gigolo boyfriend has fallen for the Audrey Hepburn character, Ms. Holly Golightly. "What is she?" demands Neal, "A *waitress?*" Truman Capote's novel, on which the movie was based, contains no such line.

Mildred Pierce is a different story. The 1945 movie, which won Joan Crawford an Academy Award as the Depression-era homemaker turned waitress turned restaurateur, also underscores that waiting tables is a job scorned by the upper crust. The message is true to the character in the James M. Cain novel of the same name. "Only one thing worried me," says Crawford as Pierce, that "some day Veda [her bratty, spoiled daughter] would find out that I was a waitress." Indeed, Veda finds the horrifying evidence: a uniform. "My mother, a *waitress,*" she seethes to Crawford/Pierce, before asking how mom could "degrade" the family. Similar lines, including Pierce's comment that she cannot face her children "if they know I've been working all day at taking tips, and wearing a uniform, and mopping up crumbs," appear in the book.[61]

Cain's novel also provides an insightful musing on the subject of tips: "She had a talent for quiet flirtation, but found that this didn't pay. Serving a man food, apparently, was in itself an ancient intimacy; going beyond it made him uncomfortable, and sounded a trivial note in what was essentially a solemn relationship."[62] The reflection did not make it to the screen.

The most famous waitress scene in American movies undoubtedly is the one in the 1970 film *Five Easy Pieces.* Audiences howled at Jack Nicholson's put-down of the waitress, played by Lorna Thayer. "I'd like a plain omelet," he starts politely, and then lists his substitutions, including a side of toast. She points at the menu, which says no substitutions. The confrontation escalates, the waitress sticking to her manager's orders, until Nicholson makes his famous request for a chicken salad sandwich on toast—"hold the chicken, bring me the toast"—and adds that she will not have broken any rules. "You want me to *hold* the chicken?" Then comes the legendary shot: "I want you to hold it between your knees." I laughed along with the audience, then, and missed her next line. She tells him to leave: "I'm not taking any more of your smartness and sarcasm." With that, he swipes the filled water glasses off the table.

I am not the only person who hates that scene now. So does the working woman's friend, Studs Terkel.[63] "Elitist snob!" (or words to that effect) he raged to me over lunch one day. Putting down a waitress! At the time, though, few movie viewers seemed to consider the revenge that managers and cooks can wreak on waitresses who disobey the rules.

Nearly three decades later, in *As Good As It Gets,* Nicholson played another jerk customer, again sympathetically. This time, however, the waitress, acted by Helen Hunt, also was sympathetic. That must be progress.

Waitress characters starred or co-starred in a small clutch of other semi-recent movies, including—with varying results—Halle Berry in *Monster's Ball,* Susan Sarandon in *Thelma and Louise,* Jodie Foster in *Little Man Tate,* Goldie Hawn in *Protocol,* Michelle Pfeiffer in *Frankie and Johnny,* and Bridget Fonda in *It Could Happen to You.* Only the last two have much to do with waitress work, and in both the work plays a supporting role to romance. In its own category is the 1981 film *Waitress!,* composed of soft porn and hard corn. The sex (featuring waitresses' breasts) is not creative, but the pun-based jokes often are. Customer asks for wine; waitress whines. The filet of sole . . . is a shoe.

To my eye, better than most of the above, at least since *Mildred Pierce,* is a 1998 independent film, *Restaurant,* which explores staff relations in a Hoboken, New Jersey, restaurant.

Actresses also appeared as waitresses in television: "Alice Doesn't Live Here Anymore" spinning off from the movie; "Flo" spinning off from "Alice"; and rivals Carla and Diane serving at "Cheers." Waitresses can do better accuracy checks than I, but as a long-time "Cheers" viewer, I do not recall an issue being made, even comically, of real waitresses' daily concerns, such as tips.

Such concerns were very much the subject of a 1980s California performance group called the Waitresses. Co-founder (and former waitress) Jerri Allyn recalled that after the group did a weeklong job/art performance piece as waitresses, they collected enough material for years. "The waitress was and still is a metaphor for women's position in the world," she said in a later interview.[64]

Many, many poems, paintings, photographs, and at least two dozen songs have been rendered about waiting tables. The effect varies. "O-o-h, My Feet," sings Cleo in *The Most Happy Fella*, the 1956 Frank Loesser musical whose opening scene is closing time at a San Francisco restaurant. In contrast, in "The Waitress," Tori Amos sings about killing the "bitch" waitress she works with.

A song at least half a century old, written in the voice of a customer to his "purty little waitress," tells her to "git my order right." He wants not only beans and turnip greens but "a date with you tonight."

In attitude, it still is sung in some restaurants today.

Waitresses might as well take the heat. Nearly three hundred years after American waitressing began, work and worker still are often scorned. What indeed is so dismissible about a woman setting food on a table? Is it because millions do the same for free? Is it the tip? The old connection with loose morals, alcohol, and men? Is there something in the posture? Needs that customers do not want to admit? The vocabulary? (The phrase "take your order" comes to mind.) A chasm of class differences? The answer is anyone's guess.

With centuries of service behind them, waitresses entered the new millennium the worse for wear and ready for more. Some things have changed in the past decades, and some things have not. Tips have gone from being "side money" to being most or all of the money, many women being paid under the same table they wipe down. With the decline of waitresses unions, jobs are less secure. With the decline of feminist-supported lawsuits, top jobs in restaurants are less likely than ever to be filled by women. As of this writing, newspaper and magazine articles still cite the continued absence or near absence of females from the employ of the most expensive restaurants. Yet the basic job, if unsound in the specific, is quite sound in the general: barring a social cataclysm, there will always be waitresses in America.

As the work endures, so do waitresses. The National Restaurant Association estimates that in the year 2000 a typical American bought 4.2 meals away from home each week. Even though the phenomenon of take-out meals muddies the statistic, a conservative guess is that the estimated 1,566,832 waitresses serve 75,000,000 meals a day. That, all told, is a lot of work.

After her waitressing experience, Frances Donovan concluded, "Trying as it was and disagreeable as it was, I have come out of it with wider sympathies for all persons concerned, sympathies not only for the girls and for the men who conduct restaurants, but even for the patrons. The question is not one of persons but of institutions. These conditions have grown up naturally and inevitably out of the existing situation. If anybody is responsible it is society, and society ought to intervene to improve conditions."[65]

Why not, to quote Donovan, "find out about the waitress"?

Readers are advised, however, that, as the next pages make clear, "the" waitress does not exist.

Voices from the Other Side of the Tray

SLICES OF AMERICAN HISTORY

*W*AITRESS WORK EVOKES THE PRESENT. A meal is served *now,* minutes (if sometimes many minutes) after being ordered. Often within an hour it is eaten and paid for and its residue removed. The perception of waitressing as immediate, however, risks ignoring the deeper connections some waitresses have, in very different ways, with our common history.

Arleen Garcia

The Sonoran desert, the hottest in North America, spreads a scorch of earth from Baja California to Arizona. In its northern reaches, if winter rains are mighty, spring explodes with sparse lushness, in ascendancies of mesquite, yucca, bear grass, cholla, devil's claw, ocotillo, agave. The grateful people who utilized such bounty also planted seeds for squash, beans, and corn. Then they sang for summer rains, to make narrow rivers overflow onto the planted plains. If they failed to perform the rain ceremony, the Wi:gita, there would be no rains and no crops. That was the conviction. Soon the rains did come, the rivers did overflow, and crops did grow. After the harvest, the people left to spend winters by mountain streams and then returned each summer for the next song-through-harvest cycle.

Their prayers, songs, and speech were in an Uto-Aztecan language that is one of the most ancient spoken vocabularies. The people themselves may have been the most ancient of southwestern aborigines. Their descendants are the Tohono O'odham.

Their land, in Arizona and Mexico, totals 4,462 square miles.[1] (Only the Navajo have more.) The riches end with the mileage.

The Tohono O'odham Nation, boasting neither aggressive warriors nor turquoise jewelry, has a most unwarlike and uncommercial reputation, and has not prospered in the past century. A casino south of Tucson does draw gamblers, but, except for the annual rodeo, relatively few tourists head for the main reservation ("a graveyard of good intentions")[2] or auxiliary settlements. Furthermore, the land literally is not what it once was. Much was lost because the unaggressive Tohono O'odham—earlier called Papagos—indeed did not fight a great deal and thus were party to few treaties, for whatever good treaties might have done. The biggest property theft, however, was not land but water. Miners and cattle ranchers dug wells that took it away.[3] The Tohono O'odham were parched into place.

The tribal capital is Sells, about a one-and-a-half-hour drive southwest of Tucson. The landscape along the way opens to vistas of beige and gray, scenes that invoke the ages but do not invite stopping at dramatic, jaw-dropping overlooks. There are no dramatic, jaw-dropping overlooks. Nearing Sells, one sees roadside death sites made of crosses with plastic flowers, and then pre-fab houses, fences, and wires come into view. Then comes Sells. It is where some Tohono O'odham now spend all the seasons.

On the corner of a modest crossroads, with no sidewalks and almost no traffic, is a social center: a restaurant. It is a one-story wooden building shaded by a huge tree. Inside are metal and vinyl chairs, padded pink plastic tablecloths, a television on a refrigerator, a sign that says "Do not touch t.v.—thanks." The smell of cooking oil is pervasive. The featured menu is the diet that has turned a lean people into the stricken overweight: Indian fry bread, hamburgers, French fries, a scattering of meaty Mexican dishes.

After centuries of singing down the rains, of cyclical certainty, of self-sufficiency aligned with nature, the Tohono O'odham must be chagrined that there even is a Papago Cafe, or so thinks this outsider. One insider, a waitress, feels differently. Things are looking up. She has a job at last.

It is well after the lunch rush and slowing down. Slow is how Arleen Dora Garcia likes it. Rushing puts her off her pace. Her normal pace, notable as she walks from table to table, is a measured glide. Her back is straight, her face impassive. She could be the sister of the model on the so-called Indian head nickel, with sturdy features through forehead, cheeks, nose, chin. She has dark eyes and skin and shoulder-length black hair. She is forty years old, plainly dressed for work in a white blouse, pants, and sneakers, and wears no adornment of any kind.

When the tables empty for a while, Arleen sits at a sunny window to talk, her posture remaining the kind children are enjoined to emulate. Although semi–off duty, she is on the alert for door openings: customers in the front, the owner in the back.

When I asked her for a self-description, she hesitated. "I'm just an ordinary person," she said. "Being a Tohono O'odham, I guess you'd say. Grandmother." Does she call herself an Indian or a Native American? "Either way. Native American." No preference? "We used to [be] called Papago, but now we're Tohono O'odhams." Preference? The latter. She has always used it, along with a shorthand version, referring, for example, to the casino "run by the T.O.s."

Her words are often halting, her sentences sometimes fragmentary and spare, uninflected, filled with "mmm-hmm" and "mmm-mmm" for yes and no. The reason became clear. Arleen's native language *is* a Native language. Her English, whose sparseness contains archaic words like "naughty" or "a doings" (for a social event) that may be a legacy of missionaries, somehow seems not yet to fit her right.

"I don't know why I started talking English with my kids. Now my kids won't talk [O'odham]. They understand it, but they can't talk it." The tribe is not comfortably bilingual. The tribal newspaper *The Runner* published an article about the need for translators—"Applicants must speak O'odham and English"—in an upcoming election.

Arleen herself is a transition figure. She was born "not even in a hospital" but in "a little adobe house," her parents' home in a town named Ajo, at the western reach of the reservation. An exhibit at the University of Arizona museum in Tucson includes a replica of a Tohono "adobe house of mud bricks."

She seemed not quite of the present, either. At the cafe, several T.O.s—a chubby snack-buying boy who came in wearing his baseball cap backward, two elderly women in polyester dresses and tightly curled hair who chatted happily over lunch—appeared to be more contemporary than Arleen. So did a young Tohono woman, a Stanford alumna who ran a gift shop nearby and easily exclaimed, "Awesome!"

During one of many puzzled linguistic pauses between Arleen and myself, I commented on the cafe's brightly colored Indian-motif curtains. She said the boss's wife had made them. How nice, I chirped, glad for an easy subject. Arleen was unmoved by window treatment small talk. "Hopi design," she said flatly.

Despite the misunderstandings, she seemed willing and at times eager to talk, including about personal matters she later asked me to keep confidential. (I have omitted or changed many details of her life and have given her a pseudonym.) "I lived with my parents 'til I was in my teens. The way they are, you know, all teens get into being naughty and whatnot." For family reasons, she and her many siblings were sent to another site on the reservation to live with their grandparents when Arlene was about fourteen.

What was she doing that was "naughty"? "Really nothing much. We were just trying to be outside playing at night, and our parents didn't want us to be out there."

Her grandparents "talked to us about how we're supposed to be as we were growing up. It's like my grandma would tell us, 'This is how you'd fix . . .' when you cook something. She'd show us. That's how we learn. This is how we are right now; we know what to do. When you're off somewhere by yourself with a family, this is what you will be doing. By just looking at what she does, we learned it. And my uncles saying this and that, about how to be in life." She eluded my quest for examples.

Arleen started her own family early. "I'm a high school graduate, but I never went anywhere after I got out of school, because I had my kids." Her first child was born when she was "about twenty-one, I think," and another came several years later. She now has two daughters and two sons as well as two grandchildren. "I did try to work, but I couldn't. So I knew once my children are grown up, I finally thought, well, I'm going to get out and do something. Whatever I can come up [with]. I was on [welfare], and then at one point when I was by myself—that is, when my husband wasn't here—I decided I'm going to go find me a job."

She had, and still has, a small income from "things at home, like, I do arts and crafts. Basketry, crochet, beadwork. Sewing. But I wanted to do something that I could have money on the side for whatever I need, you know?" From her description, she does not seem to be an aggressive salesperson for her work, however. "Over at the church, there are usually some white ladies come in, and we have a little meeting, because they have a little women's organization. We say bring your arts and crafts, so we do. We sell it directly to whoever comes and [visits] our church."

One of the most active members of the church (it is Presbyterian) and a force in Arleen's life is the wife of the cafe owner. The owner himself is from the Iroquois reservation in New York State. His wife is Tohono. In Sells, it is a mixed marriage.

Long before Arleen worked at the Papago Cafe, the owner's wife invited her to join a church prayer group. "We have little prayer services here and there, at each [others'] homes." Arleen spoke of them earnestly. "That's how I learned, being a Christian, that you can come over things. Like a problem that you're trying to [solve]. It's a feeling I guess you get to know, learning about the Lord."

Arleen's early exposure to Christianity was to Catholicism ("we just take part in what they do"), which was the first missionary religion in the area. Rivalry between Catholics and Presbyterians caused enormous rifts in the tribe during the 1930s, sometimes splitting families,[4] but she mentioned none of that. If I inferred correctly, Arleen prefers the Protestant faith because it allows her to unburden herself without a priest as intermediary. "You can confess it to God and say, hey . . . when you're by yourself." Her main spiritual advisor, however, seemed to be the boss's wife. "She encourages me about how the Lord is supposed to work in your life and everything."

She also arranged Arleen's job.

"She told me to come in and talk to her husband. I got the paperwork. I just came in that following Monday. I've been here ever since. I worked as being part of the kitchen, cooking and everything. Preparing plates. Later on he was asking me, 'Would you rather stay back here, or you want to go out and wait tables?' I said I think it would be better if I get out and walk, because I found myself, being in there . . . during the summer, I get these headaches. The heat's too much for me." Summer temperatures zoom past a hundred degrees, and, judging from the cafe's other fixtures, its cooling system may not be the most efficient. To Arleen, though, who often walks the mile-and-a-half route between home and work, movement mattered more. "I have to keep going, keep walking around."

At the cafe, "my legs are too tired to be standing back there. What's good is me going back and forth, doing this. I've had [the job] for three years now." Her children "kind of missed me at one time, and it probably took them a while before they realized that I'm *working.*"

In Sells, a job is a precious commodity, but not one without cost. Arleen lost her benefits from Aid to Families with Dependent Children (AFDC). "Right now, I am just on what I work for." Her children are in a local health insurance program, but Arleen has no such coverage herself.

Her waitress training was minimal. "I was told to say hello as you're putting out your menus and treat them nice. That's all I've been trying to do. Other times when I'm in a bad mood, I don't feel like I want to say that." People understand when "I'm not in a good mood."

Some customers, she said with the trace of a frown, are "just picky people. They want you right then and there to bring whatever [they] need. Yet you have only got two hands. And you're waiting on other tables. You can't just leave and drop it. They have to wait until you serve them." The pickiest customers are older people, she noted.

Others simply "like to talk, you know?" Arleen got close to giving herself a compliment: "I'm the kind of person where I look at myself as being kind to everybody. And I'm a soft-hearted person, I guess, when they complain."

Almost all customers are Tohono O'odham. "Everybody knows each other around here." Sometimes, "I'm kind of jumping around." By "jumping around," she meant busy. "On one afternoon, me and [another waitress] shifted around our jobs. We rotated. I worked for her because I wanted to get off that afternoon. I just dreaded her job, because at noon this thing fills up." Then one man made a negative comment to someone about Arleen's work. "I didn't know what he said, and I didn't want to know."

Her usual late afternoon to evening shift is "not as bad, but I enjoy it. And the tips I get [are] a help, because what I get from my pay is not as much." Asked how well people tip, she said, "I'm beginning to notice sometime back that some people that has good jobs, are well-off, they don't tip you nothing. Nothing. [Other] ones that come in, they do, no matter a quarter, fifty cents, or a dollar. I noticed, and I told my boss."

He said he could have told her that the well-off ones do not tip well.

There are exceptions. "From last night, some people said, 'Oh, I like your food,' and I got a five-dollar tip. Very seldom I'll get a five-dollar, even more. A whole bunch come in for a meeting, like the veterans? We just give them coffee. We're not supposed to charge them. But they all put in their dollars. It's like eight dollars for eight individuals."

Asked about the Tohono chief, or chairman, she said evenly that he tips "all right."

Once in a rare while, tourists come through the door. They create diversions of more than one kind. At the reservation town of Covered Wells, I watched an elderly Tohono couple make tortillas at their modest outdoor restaurant, while retirees in pastel slacks circled with cameras, calling out instructions about when to smile. The woman of the couple later told me she gets annoyed at such behavior but does not object out loud—it is part of the restaurant business in Covered Wells.

Arleen claimed that picture-taking tourists did not disturb her. "Not really. If we have something like a doings next week, people come and take pictures or whatever."

What the tourists may not realize, as they snap pictures of Arleen or stare at her striking looks, is that she gapes at them, too.

"I'm amazed to see different ones come in, like from another side of the country. I enjoy talking to them, see. I say, well, I should have a book, let them sign that, and say, hey, I met this person from this [place]. There's still people I talk to at times. We get a conversation going and I go, 'Oh, I forgot I'm supposed to work.'" She came close to a laugh.

Other tourists disconcerted her. "Just the other day, some ladies came in, and I swear, I thought, well, my boss did think that they were"—she leaned forward over the tablecloth and whispered—"lesbians." They came back day after day. The first time, Arleen fled to the kitchen and consulted with her boss. "I said, 'God, this lady stared at me.' I was telling my co-worker and she said, 'No, they're not.' My boss said, 'Yeah, I could tell right straight out. They are.' Of course, I got curious, and I had to ask them . . . ," although she asked them not whether they were lesbians but where they came from.

"They were from Austria, and they were out here doing some whatever, research. They kept coming in for three days. God, I felt so uncomfortable. They were the *first* people that made me uncomfortable." Relief finally followed. "These ladies came in and were telling [the boss] about going back home because they were worried about their family and their children. So he said, 'Wow, they're not like that.'" Arleen seemed blind to the reason that anyone, much less Austrians, would stare at her.

Some local customers can make her uncomfortable for entirely another reason: they walk in the cafe drunk. They may simply stand around and order nothing. "We let them, and then they take off." Others eat. "We can't refuse services to anybody unless [they cause a problem]." Only one group misbehaved, "but I think they got picked up. I don't think they paid [for] what they ate."

She brought up the subject of alcoholism, as she folded and refolded a piece of paper at the window, the sun on her shoulder. "It's killing our people, alcohol, right now." She spoke about its effect on her own family but indicated that she has been free of the problem herself. "I tried it, but I didn't care for it. I won't. Up to now I just don't. And I'm trying to discourage my kids from that, because it's better to be sober than be in that."

It is ironic that once upon a time—but only once a year—alcohol was a respected part of the Tohono O'odham culture. Saguaro wine, or *nawait,* made from the fruit that grows atop the saguaro cactus, was dispensed as part of the Wi:gita ceremony to open the summer clouds. This was the only occasion when alcohol was drunk.[5]

As Arleen mentioned one of her grandfathers drinking, a new sound, perhaps just the back door squeaking from a gust of wind, came into the cafe. That instant, she sat up straighter, cocked her head a fraction toward the sound, and stayed utterly motionless for several seconds.

Ludicrous as it sounds, in those seconds before she relaxed (it was not the boss after all), I saw her in the Tohono desert landscape a millennium ago, standing stone still after hearing a twig snap. I shook myself back to plastic tablecloths, Hopi curtains, and Arleen of the present, whom I did not want to embarrass with foolishness.

She was speaking of how the modern curse of drinking puts children "through a lot. Things go on in the household. That's why the kids are the way they are right now."

The Papago Cafe serves no alcohol, part of an attempt to keep the curse off the reservation. "They're not licensed for liquor here, but we have bootleggers a lot."

Arleen Garcia also was concerned about her own future, as it related to the cafe and her life. She began to speak in unexpectedly intimate detail about her current circumstances and a decision about getting back together with a certain man. It was obvious she cared for him. They met "somewhere at a place that had a doings." She smiled as she reminisced, until mentioning that when he gets a job, he might want her to quit hers. It was obvious, too, that she does not want to give up financial independence.

She likes where she works, mostly. She gets along with her employer ("he's an all right boss"), although she does not like that he swears. "Because I don't talk like that. I don't want to change jobs. But if this place was closed down, I might need to start looking for something else. Somebody's offering me a job, trying to say come to the casino."

There is a long and benevolent tradition of gambling (part of a means of making scarcity seem like abundance) among the Tohono O'odham,[6] but the T.O.s Desert Diamond casino south of Tucson marks a departure from that tradition.

Inside a domed complex is a stretch of low lighting, the thickest cigarette smoke imaginable, rows of engaged slot machines, and continuous clangor: triple rows coming up, one-armed-bandit handles going down, clanky-toned payoffs, occasional screams of glee. Through the aisles, the women of the Tohono O'odham Nation, many with their straight black hair frizzed into coiffures of foreign tribes, push money change carts like ice cream dispensers.

Conversation is all but impossible, but one money changer shouted to me, after I shouted to her of Arleen's notion of working here, "You have to be sociable." I shouted, "She seems shy to me." She shouted back, "She won't be shy long."

At the cafe in Sells, I asked Arleen what she would like to happen in her life. As usual, she spoke softly. "I don't know. I just live a normal life. I'm thankful for what I get, even though it's not much. Yet *I* know I want more—if I was to have another job and get more pay, you know?" But "it's hard for me to leave this, because I've been so *in* it." She looked around her, and then she proved that, in one respect, belief in prayer has not changed for the Tohono O'odham.

"Being that my boss's wife is a Christian lady, when I joined that [church] group, at the end we'd say what we would ask for, a prayer. My request was, 'I want a job. I'm looking for a job. I'm praying for a job that I would some day have. I don't know what, but I want something.' My next time, later on, my prayers were answered."

Irma Jean Edwards

On February 1, 1960, in Greensboro, North Carolina, four teenage male students from a local college went downtown, entered the Woolworth's department store, bought a few items, walked over to the store's sizable and popular lunch area, and sat down at a counter. They assumed that the waitress who came over would say she could not serve them. She was white, they were black, and they were right.

Then they said they would not leave. That precise moment, at those four padded vinyl stools with metal tube backs along that long, cool counter, would take on enormous significance in the civil rights movement. It was the beginning of the first southern sit-in.

Ima Jean Edwards, who had been a Woolworth's waitress for seven years, was working at the combined bakery counter and snack bar a few yards away. "They came in that afternoon, late in the afternoon, and asked to be served. And of course at that time nobody in the South served a black person at the counter or otherwise. You might serve 'em in the kitchen, but you didn't serve them up at the counter with the other people." By "up at the counter," Ima Jean did not mean *her* counter, where she served food to customers, black and white, who ate it right there, standing up. No one objected to Woolworth's customers integrating themselves by eating while standing? "No."

That February day, co-workers later told her, the students ordered a piece of apple pie.[7] "The waitress who waited on them told them, 'I'm sorry, but I can't serve you.'" A manager stepped in. "They wouldn't move when the management asked them. They told them *then* they would be back the next day."

Ima Jean was among the employees who believed the students. "Some had said, 'Oh, no, they won't be back'; but they had definitely *told* us they would be."

While the sit-in began—"I knew it was going on"—she stayed at her counter, working. She had no need to get close to hear what management would say. "It really wasn't a definite policy, because it was ev-er-y-where. Nobody served a black person with the white people. It was the code of the South."

Ima Jean Edwards did not feel poised on the brink of history. "At the time, I didn't think much would come of it." Then again, she had been raised with lowered expectations.

A native North Carolinian, she grew up the eldest of six children on a small farm of meager output. Asked about her childhood, she said without inflection that it had been "really hard." If misfortune comes in threes, Ima Jean's first might have been poverty. The second came when she was eight. Carrying her baby sister to the post office while their parents were in the fields, Ima Jean collapsed, one leg buckling. She had polio. During a long convalescence at home, "I had to lay there with sand bags to my arm and my leg, to keep it from going crooked." The third blow came a couple of years later. Her father went to a chiropractor for a treatment and suddenly lost his memory. Diagnosed as insane, he was put in a mental hospital. "For four years, he did not know who *we* were, at all." The children who were old enough to work helped their mother keep the family's few farm animals fed and the corn and tobacco fields producing.

At the age of twelve, Ima Jean decided she could help best by leaving. She became a live-in babysitter for a local family in exchange for room and board. At fourteen, she made another decision to relieve her family's financial burden: as allowed under state law, she quit school. School and books were free, of course, but nothing else was. "If I had had the clothes and shoes and stuff I needed to go ahead to school, I would have. . . . I liked school. But I felt it was too much of a hardship on the family. I would be a-taking away from the others."

To earn her own way, she moved in with a couple who owned a small cafe, where she received room and board and also some pay in exchange for much labor. "I got up when they went to work and worked until they quit that night, and I worked as a waitress." The food was "just country cooking, like pinto beans, turnip greens, and chicken and beef stew." She liked waiting tables. "It gives you a chance to meet people, and I always liked people."

Ima Jean's pronunciation and speech patterns reflect her roots in the northwestern part of the state, a region known for fine fiddle music and proximity to the Blue Ridge Mountains. Her accent, however, can mislead the uninitiated. The Woolworth's building is not on "L" Street after all, as I learned after a fruitless drive, but on "Elm." If her accent and her slow, nearly swallowed, words took getting used to, she did not. A pale, hefty, white-haired woman with light blue eyes and a nice smile, she wore an appliquéd hot pink outfit more flamboyant than she was. She sat on a living room chair near her grandson's ex-girlfriend's unicorn collection, which she had ended up with, and answered all questions—except ones about the Ku Klux Klan—pleasantly and carefully.

With an abashed grin, she remembered her first waitressing job. "I was real proud of myself that year. I could go buy Christmas presents for all the kids." She bought each of her sisters "what I thought was a beautiful doll." A half century later, her pride still showed.

In the meantime, doctors at the mental hospital discovered that her father suffered not from insanity but from chiropractic malpractice: he had a pinched nerve. "When they straightened that out, he was fine. His mind cleared, and he was well." He returned home to farm life, her parents considering the episode "just another hurdle that they crossed over." Ima Jean, meanwhile, moved on.

She married at the age of sixteen. "Which didn't last but just a few months," she said, laughing. Her husband, a housepainter by vocation and a pool player and woman chaser by avocation, she learned, "was what I thought was the perfect man at that time. Tall and good-looking and all this." But "I don't think he ever considered himself really married. He was always a-running around." (They finally divorced some five years later.)

To avoid seeing him, Ima Jean worked out of town at another cafe, where she served food and gasoline. No matter the weather, waitresses ran outside in their white uniforms, pumped gas, ran in, washed their hands, and resumed waiting tables. Ima Jean happily reminisced that the waitresses could eat anything they wanted, even a T-bone steak, "because they didn't pay you much" and "tips wasn't much."

Her next move, to the big city of Greensboro, with a family member as companion-chaperon, had a dual motive: "Things wasn't really going like I wanted" in a new romance, she recalled, and she was also "wanting to move on to a better job." She set her sights on mill work, which paid better than restaurants. She failed a test at one mill (polio had left her "not real good in coordination") and waited to hear back from others.

"Finally, I picked up the paper, and I seen an ad for Woolworth's." The ad was for a waitress. "I said, 'I'll just go take that until I can get something else.'" She laughed. "'Something else' never did come along." Ima Jean worked at Woolworth's forty years.

She glowed with enthusiasm about the early days. "It was busy, busy, busy, that's all I can say. People *stood* all the way around the counter, all day long, from the time we opened up 'til the time we closed."

Prices were low, the food was homemade, and service was friendly. By more than one account, the integrated staff—white management and waitresses, mostly black kitchen staff—worked well together. "I can't remember not getting along with anyone as long as I worked." She listed waitresses, cooks, and other employees, fretting when she forgot a name. She recalled "a little girl that could not talk" who worked in "bake shop."

On February 1, when the store closed for the night, the four students—who had remained at the counter despite being unable to buy anything while seated—left. Woolworth's manager, C. L. Harris, who subsequently became well known for his role in responding to the sit-ins, called a meeting the next morning. Ima Jean attended.

"I don't remember the words," but she did remember the message. Harris instructed the waitresses that "in case [the students] did come in, to tell them that we were sorry, it was not *them,* particularly, but it was the policy of the South that we had to abide by until it was changed." Even though it was not a legal policy? "Right." She also remembered that she and the other employees were told to be calm and not to speak to the students.

Ima Jean had been right about the young people. "The next day they came back, with more added." This time they were on the early side of lunch, "probably about eleven o'clock. I think they stayed out of school." She paused and wondered out loud about that, about skipping classes in college. Her sacrifice of high school felt palpable. She continued, "Well, I seen them come in and sit down, you know, and they asked to be served, and then they just *sit,* they didn't move. [The waitresses] more or less worked around them."

Asked about the students' appearance, she said, "They were dressed fine. They didn't come in dressed like hobos would." And "they behaved in a good manner."

She observed from her post at the carry-out counter, where she was extremely busy. She did not recall talking about the sit-in with anyone, for she was "working just as fast as you can go," but she did sense a change in the air. "There was a difference. Yes, there was a tension. As the time wore on, it was *more* tension." She imitated bitchy voices: " 'Well, I wouldn't eat there.' I've heard a lot of that. 'I would not sit down besides one of them neither.' 'If you start serving them, *I* will not be back.' Stuff like this." Her reaction? "I thought, if you want to feel like that, feel like that. It's your privilege."

The students, of course, also had a logistical impact. "I think the general feeling was that they were taking away from the counters, [from] people that was trying to eat." As for the kitchen staff, "some of them was strongly against. Against changing. In fact, one or two had a few words with the students, about 'Why are you trying to cause trouble?' and all this."[8]

Asked how the waitresses felt about serving black customers, she paused a second. "Well, the waitresses. Some of them would have waited on them, some of them would not have. *Mixed* feelings, I guess you could say." Could she have guessed who would have been either way? "No. Because we were more or less friends with the blacks that we worked with. I mean, we talked to 'em, like I'm talking to you. I won't say socialized with them, but we treated them like they were one of the family, I guess. That's the word I'm looking for."

As for her own reaction about serving black people at the sit-down counters, she said, "I'm not sure what my reaction was there, because I served them all day long. My feeling was, well, I don't see *why* they have to be treated different, I guess."

That was her feeling then? Or now? "That was my feeling *then*," she said, with unusual forcefulness, and went on to recount that in the cafe where she had worked earlier a black man always had to eat in the kitchen and that she had disliked that there were separate waiting rooms at the bus station. "I don't know how I felt about it, but it didn't *seem* right. I felt like they should have been treated equally as we were. I guess that leads back to the Bible. How does it go?" she laughed some, trying to remember. "Treat each . . . Do unto others as you would have them do unto you."

As word of the sit-in spread, "it got so that [the protestors] were taking the whole counter, and there wasn't any place to serve the people. And of course, that was getting *them* mad, because most [were] on lunch breaks and so forth. They didn't want to go anyplace else." Some people came to Woolworth's to join the students, and some to harangue them, or worse. One photograph shows the students sitting in a row, neatly dressed, heads high, drenched with whatever had been thrown at them by onlookers. A mob of white people, mostly young men, screams inches from the students' faces. The photograph oozes hatred and impending violence.

Ima Jean painted no such pictures. Even during the sit-in, she kept her thoughts mostly to herself, she said. She never discussed the situation with her parents; she was not much of a letter writer, as her mother often fussed, and her parents had no telephone. Nor did she discuss the situation "a lot" with her new husband, a mechanic for the local utility company. She did remember one conversation, however.

"He wanted me to quit. Because he was afraid for me." Speaking softly, she said, "We didn't argue about it. I said, 'No, that's my job, and that's where I'm going to stay.'"

She did not talk much with her co-workers about the sit-in either, although she indicated that waitresses began questioning "the code of the South" more than before and that a majority favored integration. "I didn't hear a lot of argument about 'I'm not going to wait on them, if they start serving them' or anything." She added, "We couldn't work with them as close as we worked with them and be against them at the same time. I'm not sure that's *everybody's* feeling, but that was my feeling.

"In fact, a lot of [the waitresses] felt like if we had served them that day, all this other might not have taken place. It mushroomed from here all over the South." She also heard that the students had planned all along "to open up the South for serving" and that Woolworth's was picked first "because it was a name that was known."[9]

Every day throughout the sit-in, Ima Jean commuted to work as usual, boarding an electric trolley bus for the two-mile trip from her modest house (a block from where she now lives alone as a widow) to downtown and back. Twice a day, therefore, she saw another example of what the sit-in was about. "They had to go to the back of the bus. Later on, they [desegregated] the buses, too. They could sit anywhere." Her feelings about that? "My feelings about that would be, if you'd paid the price for the ride, why not sit where you want to?"

Looming over the sit-in was, of course, the Ku Klux Klan. It was "real active in Greensboro, and they got to heckling the students and so forth." She said, "I was not aware of the Klan until after I started dating my second husband. We went to a *rally,* out off of Market Street, in a field, just to see what it was. Not because we were interested. This was in the '50s. I didn't like it. I did not like the *hoods,* I did not like the fire. They had torches. Then as things went on, they burnt crosses in people's yards, different things that I did not agree with." Did her husband feel the same way? "Very strongly." Did the Klan give them any trouble? "A little." She elaborated only off the record. Her feelings about the KKK are "a whole 'nother story." As late as 1979, the Greensboro Klan and American Nazis massacred five demonstrators who were taking part in an anti-Klan march. Ima Jean said the Klan remains active in her neighborhood.

While tension and turmoil increased at Woolworth's sit-down counters, Ima Jean's stand-up counter was relatively calm and increasingly busy. It must have been the only prosperous part of the store. Woolworth's was losing a lot of money, she said, but its employees were not. For one thing, waitresses were not tipped. "At that time, we had up signs, 'No Tipping.'"

C. L. Harris, furthermore, reassigned any waitress whose counter was occupied by demonstrators. His feeling about the protesters, she said, was that "if he served them, he thought the rest of the restaurants should serve them also. It wasn't that he didn't want to serve them."

Day by day, while he worked behind the scenes, reportedly for city-wide integration, "everything was getting so out of hand" at Woolworth's. Klan members were "jeering the students and pushing. We felt like . . . it could be trouble."

The sit-in moved into the street, where protestors were arrested, although "it was still peaceful." What did she think of this strategy of nonviolence? "Well, I admired them for that."

A bomb threat forced the next move.

"That's when they made the decision to close the counter. Because they didn't want any disturbance to take place in the store." Also, "the customers were getting very irritated."

The counters received a kind of plastic flower funeral, culled from Woolworth's inventory of artificial plants. The managers "went over to the counters and told the waitresses, 'Clean your counter, put everything up. We're going to close it.' They covered the whole counter with wreaths of flowers and stuff. You couldn't even hardly tell the counter was there." The waitresses and kitchen staff then were put to work throughout the store. "They did not lose one penny or one hour," she said firmly. "They still had the baking and stuff to do." She emphasized, "Nobody lost their job at *all*."

As is well known, the students eventually won. It might be the only time that waitress work—or, rather, the nonperformance of waitress work—led to a change in federal law.

Hidden in the annals of the big story is a lesser-known one: the identities of the first African American customers. Even McArthur Davis, director of Greensboro's planned International Civil Rights Center and Museum, which is meant to occupy the old Woolworth building, was surprised. One afternoon, he unlocked the old store, which still stands near other elaborately fronted, high-ceilinged buildings, all now empty but glorious, in the old commercial heart of Greensboro. Once inside, he strolled along with Ima Jean and me, talking about the future and asking her about the past. The vacant, unlit premises were dim and dusty. The place looked forgotten. Some counter seats are missing. They are in the Smithsonian, not forgotten. Almost the only brightness came from pictures of advertised specials still lining the walls above the grill. Ima Jean saw them and smiled.

Earlier that day in her home, Ima Jean had related to me the information that so startled McArthur Davis: "Our first customers was the girls in the kitchen. When they opened that day, they had them to sit down, at the counter, to show that we were serving."

Woolworth's management had come up with the idea of asking three kitchen employees to be the first African American customers served at the counters. Geneva Tisdale, then twenty-eight, was one of them.

In a phone interview (thanks to the intercession of her old friend Ima

Jean), Geneva Tisdale talked not only about the drama of that day but also about the days that led up to it. She spoke almost without a southern accent, except for dropping some middle r's (so "board" was closer to "boad"), and was altogether faster and surer than Ima Jean as she described the moment the sit-in started.

"I remember these boys coming in, I'll say it like that, and they sat about middleways down. I was in the back working. Once in a while, you had to go up and down the counters for different things, so I happened to pass by, and I saw them sitting there. Well, kind of give me the chills at the time because, knowing it was an all-white counter, I was wondering why they were sitting there. Of course, I just passed by.

"I had this feeling it would cause problems, that's what I thought. We have had blacks come in and sit, and they would tell 'em that . . . it was all white. I don't know where they were *from,* but that has happened a time or two. I have seen 'em. So they would get up and leave. No problem there. When I saw these boys sitting there, I thought it could have been the same. Maybe they didn't know." When she realized they did know, and "it started increasing," she grew concerned. "I knew it was heading to something, I didn't know what, but that kind of shook me up. Because all you can think of is trouble." She added, "As long as it was just all white, you had no problem."

Geneva praised her then co-workers, from C. L. Harris ("a nice man") to lunchroom manager Rachel Holt ("a hard-working woman") to Ima Jean. "She and I got along together good. She's always been a good person." In a place where "there wasn't any, that I know of, hard feelings," Geneva sometimes helped out the waitresses with tasks such as taking and getting customers' orders, "because we'd be real busy."

Despite such occasions, she would not have been hired as a waitress; both sides of the counters were strictly white. "At that *time,* that's the way everything was. We were used to that. So we had no problem with that. It was all white waitresses. We did all the other work. Steam tables and fountain girl were black. Mostly. In the kitchen, we had all black. Once in a while, a white would come in, they would want a job, [Rachel Holt] would put them anywhere they could work. We had no problem with that. We all got along."

Asked whether she thought the waitresses might have served black customers, she said, "I feel like a lot of 'em would have. But they couldn't do it. I guess they felt they could get fired."

As the sit-in continued, Geneva's focus changed. "The more they got into it, I started thinking." She started wondering why black people could spend their money everywhere in the store but the sitdown counter. She confirmed they ordered "anything they wanted to" at the snack counter and ate it there, standing. "We all started thinking about it. The girls and I, we all talked about it, because we couldn't sit down there either. We worked there, and *we* couldn't sit at the counter. We were the ones fixing all the food for them to eat, but we felt we wasn't good enough to sit at the counter."

As her consciousness rose, so did her anxiety. "I didn't know *what* was going to happen, and I was carrying my third child then, and I really was scared." Her husband, a construction worker for the electric company, worked out of town a lot and kept track of the sit-in by listening to the news. He worried, too, but did not ask her to quit. "I was told to be careful." Like Ima Jean, "I didn't think about quitting, because I wanted the job." Rachel Holt—"Miz Holt" in Geneva's telling—moved her to work upstairs in the employee lunchroom, away from the activity.

She was hardly isolated upstairs, however, having to run outside during the bomb threat and realizing all too well that the sit-in had spread to the street. Protestors now included some of her neighbors' children, high school students. "In the demonstration they were in, they were loading them wagons up like I don't know what, taking those children to jail."

Rachel Holt approached her again and told her to go home. " 'Don't you come back until after you've had that baby.' So I had a break."

Geneva Tisdale's baby was born, and so was the first success of the sit-in movement. Woolworth's, in her phrase, was going to "open its lunch counters to everybody."

While she and others began preparing the counters for business on that day, Rachel Holt told her about the delicate ruse.

"She called three of us out in the hall. It was myself, Anetha Jones—she's deceased now—and Susie Kembler. She called us out and said, 'I want *you* three girls to be the first to sit at the counter.' Each one of us, spaced us out. She wanted to get the reaction of the public coming in. 'We're gonna see what happens.' She said, 'When you come in, bring a change in clothes,' so we wouldn't be in our uniforms, because she didn't want people to know who we *were*.

"We went in to work that morning like we always did." At a signal, the three were supposed to go upstairs, dress as customers, come downstairs, walk around as if shopping, and then sit at the lunch counter. "She said, 'Now, if you don't want to get in the papers' . . ." Geneva laughed. "She said, 'I got a feeling when the word gets out, they will have these photographers in there. Order something you can eat real quick, and get up and go upstairs and change back into your clothes and come back down on the counter to work. Let's see what happens.'

"I had on, I never will forget, a two-piece black-and-white little suit, and I had my black bag and some black shoes." No, there wasn't a double meaning in the black-white choice, she said, laughing high. "I didn't think of it like that. I just was trying to get into something that looked nice. Because I was supposed to be a customer."

Then came the moment to sit at the counter.

"Mabel Bozart, she was my waitress. They knew what was going to happen. Mabel did. When [we] went down[stairs], she tells me, 'You sit here in my station.' We were already close and good friends anyway. She had no problem waiting on me."

Geneva recalled not only what she wore but also what she ate. "Oh, I ordered an egg salad sandwich. I never will forget that. And I got a drink, a soda. I almost swallowed that sandwich [whole]." She added, "I don't think I've had an egg salad sandwich *since*!"

She did not wait to see whether photographers came in. "Being nervous, I didn't want to see *who* was coming in to do *what*." She laughed in apparent relief. "I got up and cut a beeline and we left the counter. We went on upstairs, back in our uniforms, came back down. Sure enough, here come the photographers. People coming in in droves. We stood around and looked. And blacks start coming in and sitting at the counter. So they started waiting on 'em."

Ima Jean remembered the new customers "didn't say anything. They just come in and ordered like it had always been."

Eventually, she was assigned the sit-down counter herself. "To me that was fine. 'Cause, I mean, [black customers] didn't bother me at all." Holt also asked the three sit-down pioneers whether they wanted to waitress. One said yes, but not Geneva. "I told her I would stay *right* where I was."

The customers changed in more ways than one. Some white customers left, as they said they would, recalled Ima Jean. "I thought, if that's the way you want to be, fine."

Geneva's recollections are similar. "We did have some of the whites get up and walk out. We went through that, too." She added, "You'd be surprised at, I guess I don't know whether you'd call it hate? Out of fear? I don't know what you'd call it, really, but I'd say *hate* in people, when you start into something like it. I've seen many [men and women] get up and walk out if a black person would sit beside 'em. For a while, anyway. I don't know if it was because they were scared, or if they thought they were too good to sit there beside a black person.

"After things settled down," she said, "you went to work. It didn't cross your mind right away. But then there was a time you would think about it, what a hard time they had to get that through." She never had another meal, not to mention another egg salad sandwich, at the Woolworth's counter. It was easier to eat upstairs in the employees' area, nearer where she worked.

"Many a time," though, she went downstairs "and just sat on the stool for a little while."

Geneva Tisdale worked the salad board and steam tables until 1993, when Woolworth Corporation, as part of a nationwide downsizing, closed first the lunch counters and then the whole store. She went to work at a Friendly's—where her old boss C. L. Harris visited her—until she retired.

Ima Jean Edwards was promoted to lunch counter manager in the 1980s and continued in that job until she retired.

Having known each other nearly fifty years, the two women stay in touch, mostly by phone. They come from two sides of the old "code of the South" but share concern about its staying power. Geneva said at one point, "Racism is not over *yet*. We all know that." Ima Jean, asked what she would like to have happen in the next ten years, did not hesitate a second. "I would like to see the people to get along together. That'd be my feeling."

Beulah Compton

She had no more desire to keep her opinions to herself these days than she did in more tumultuous times, and she was now ninety. Save for her snow white hair, one would not think her that old. She drove her car through the streets of Seattle skillfully ("I've got wheels!" she announced on the phone), her voice was strong, her creamy skin looked remarkably smooth, and her eyes flashed, especially when she talked about her adversaries.

Beulah Compton was a "union maid," as the phrase in the old song goes. She was not so much a rank-and-file member, however, as she was a union leader.

Waitresses unions, which started about the time the twentieth century did, are unique in the history of the American labor movement. They were so strong for so long and, in most cases, were adamantly separate from male unions. The spunky and gutsy "girls," as they generally called one another, wanted their own locals to fight their own battles, in an era when neither their sex nor their background was prized. Socially and financially, they were marginalized; but politically they organized. Imagine, waitresses—who did not even have the right to vote—going on strike! One early goal was a six-day work week. Another was a ten-hour work day. Over the years, their setbacks sometimes were as stunning as their successes, but by the 1930s they were a power.

So was Beulah Compton. From 1948 to 1956, more or less the peak years of unionization, she headed the country's oldest permanent waitresses union in one of the country's biggest restaurant union strongholds: Seattle. Her union, Local 240, was founded in 1900. In her last year in office, 90 percent of the city's restaurants were union, and nearly four thousand waitresses were in her charge.[10] As for her adversaries, the people who made her eyes flash, they included not only the usual foes but also some unexpected ones: certain union officials.

Beulah Compton first revealed her sentiments when I mentioned meeting her former cohort and contemporary Jackie Walsh, who had headed the San Francisco waitresses union. That union and Local 240 have long been part of the Hotel Employees and Restaurant Employees International Union (HERE).

"Oh, goodness, yes," said Beulah, upon hearing the name. "I always liked Jackie. We were a couple of rebels. Well, she got along with the international union better than I, but I was such an upstart, promoting minimum wage. Things like that were a no-no as far as the union was concerned. Getting a minimum wage—you close the door on unionism, [they'd say]. Afraid of a little floor to build on," she said mockingly.

She was sitting in her modest apartment in northern Seattle, surrounded by grief. One of her two daughters had recently died. It was helpful, she implied, to talk about something else. She fingered her string of costume pearls and let sadness surge into outrage.

"My union was and still is just full of crooked hierarchy." She raised her chin and laughed. "All men. The top echelon is always filled by men. They have a few women vice presidents, but I understand they sign a resignation form before they're hired. If they don't go along with the president's wishes, he can accept their resignation and say 'Goodbye now.'"[11]

Despite the praise of its supporters, HERE has amassed other notable detractors, too, including the federal government, which repeatedly investigated the union and put it under federal supervision during the 1990s.[12] Beulah Compton, in the meantime, amassed some detractors herself.

She was the child of an adventure. At the turn of the century, her family and several others climbed in a partitioned-off railroad car in Iowa and headed west. The trip and the tracks ended in Tacoma, near where her father had leased some timberland, to which the family then hiked. Beulah, named after a horse, she said, was born in 1905. According to family legend, she was such a beautiful baby that an Indian chief asked to trade an Indian woman for her. Beulah's father, not a man she grew to admire, refused.

She grew up in a log cabin he built. She later saw a photograph of him with the cabin windows strapped to his back. An especially strong friend named Olly carried the stove, joking that it would be less heavy if not for the sack of flour in the oven. The light-hearted spirit did not last. She portrayed her father as a domineering wanderer, her "absolute angel" of a mother as "very submissive."

Beulah then recalled an exception, a childhood incident that inspired her own later behavior. The family was in church. "Papa shot up and asked the congregation to pray for his wife, to make her a better woman. I remember her, with all the dignity in the world, standing up to her full five feet," and then she "swept out of the church. I wanted to clap. Papa left again shortly after that."

As a young woman, Beulah married a man named Ralph Compton, with whom she had her two girls. She was circumspect in describing him but gave the impression that his primary affections were directed toward himself. His family's social standing was more elevated than hers, but his work habits were not. Beulah soon had to get a job. She was living in Aberdeen, Washington. The year was 1929, and the Depression had just begun.

"I didn't realize what the Depression was, because I had been living in a depression off and on as a kid. I didn't realize there was any calamity going on. My husband would hop from one job to another." Beulah brought little hope to her search for work. "I didn't have any confidence. My husband didn't help give me any self-confidence, either. He was a compulsive gambler. It was at Christmas time, and we were living with my sister and her husband down the street. My mother cooked Christmas dinner, and we were all invited, and Ralph didn't show up. After dinner, I went home and I told him we were disappointed he wasn't at my mother's. He said he'd gotten his paycheck and gambled the whole thing. It was ninety-eight dollars a month. I said, 'Well, ninety-eight dollars. It could have been a hundred.' He put his arms around me and said, 'Oh, Beulah, I always felt I was much better than you, but right now I don't.' That was my compliment."

She and he soon parted company, and she supported her daughters on her own, waitressing one job full-time during the day, another part-time at night. On one nighttime job, in a place owned by Greeks (good, respectable family men, she recalled), she augmented her income by stealing seafood.

She put crab in one pocket of her apron and shrimp in the other, went home, woke her girls, and fed them "like little birds." Beulah pocketed seafood in part because she pocketed so few tips. "I didn't know how to promote tips. I really didn't like working as a waitress, to tell you the truth." She laughed heartily. "I probably showed it. An outgoing waitress could go right alongside of me and make more tips than I would.

"One time we were really short of help, and I went to work on the counter." It was huge—"almost a half block long," she said. She worked four to five hours a day, "and I think in six weeks I'd made one dime." The Depression, of course, was a big reason tips were low. "There wasn't that much money around." She remembered "a group of young lawyers that came in for coffee about ten o'clock every morning and sat at this long table. An old-time lawyer used to sit with them." They asked questions, he "held court," and they never tipped at all. At Christmas, however, they pooled their money and gave her red satin lounging pajamas, "just my size," she smiled.

Often management promoted her into other jobs. "I would either get to cashier or work as a hostess." Unfortunately, the salary often was even less than she made waiting tables. "I usually worked myself up to where I couldn't possibly make a tip. And I needed it."

In Seattle in the 1930s, working as a cashier, she encountered a policy about discrimination she never forgot. "If a black couple came in, the waitresses were told to . . . just let them sit there. Don't serve them. Discourage them." The people always left. "It made me feel terrible, but there was nothing I could do about it." As far as she knew, no one else protested, either.

Beulah began to accrue power to fight other fights. "The Bartell Drug Company in Seattle had fountains and tea rooms and cafeterias all over town. I went to work managing one of those and then worked up to where I was supervisor of the twenty-three food outlets. As such, I was the negotiator for management, and I had a lot of fun. You know, getting things fixed up for the help. I was maybe eight or ten years with the drug company [when] this one wonderful woman who was the head business agent for the waitresses union invited me to join her."

She was Pauline Newman, who also invited Beulah to accompany her to a union convention in Chicago. "She confided in me then she was sure she had cancer, but the doctors wouldn't tell her she did. She didn't think she was going to live long, and she wanted me to come to work with the union, because she didn't want to turn the union over to dirty hands. Meaning [her] boss, who was my boss later." Beulah identified the "boss," as she almost always called her, as Lillian Sandburg. Pauline Newman proved right about Sandburg, according to Beulah's account, and she also proved right about her own diagnosis. "She died, and it really broke my heart." Beulah then followed her mentor's wishes.

In 1947, "I got a job, paid job, as a business agent, and I *did* love that." Being a union business agent included traveling to restaurants in her territory and hearing what was on waitresses' minds. "I loved going from one to another and trying to correct grievances. Most all waitresses, as I knew them, particularly in those days, were forced into the [work]. One place you could get on-the-job training was become a waitress. And most of them had children and needed child care." For them, Beulah discovered a sympathetic and untapped resource. She went to "some of the older waitresses that were in their sixties and seventies and not working as waitresses, but maybe had lost their husbands and rattled around in a home big enough to share. I found a lot of places for working waitresses to leave their children with former waitresses.

"The boss"—Lillian Sandburg—"later heard about it and discouraged it. She said, 'I want you to know, Beulah, you're not a social worker, you're a business agent. You shouldn't have any real interest in what happens to that individual.' " (Sandburg, in Beulah's eyes, also committed the sin of being "uppity" to waitresses who served her.)

Beulah was not deterred. "I'm a strong union person. I believe in unions, and there's so much a union can do besides bread-and-butter issues." In her years as a business agent, she discovered that a common grievance was "harassment." She looked exasperated as she described the complaint of a fifty-five-year-old woman, "a really fine waitress working not far from a union hall, Sailors [Union] of the Pacific. She came in to see me and said the chef had fixed her tray for her . . . It was her [break] time, and she told him what she wanted for lunch. He had prepared that, but he put a note on it: 'This will cost you so many rolls in the hay,' or some silly thing. She brought the note in and showed me.

"I had a friend running the Sailors Union of the Pacific, [Max] Weisbarth; he was half Jewish and half Filipino. I called him and told him what was going on, and I knew he and his men ate there. He was built like a gorilla, a great big head and long arms and very muscular-looking, with a high little voice. He says," she piped her voice high, " 'Okay, what you want, Beulah? A broken leg?' I said, 'Oh, no, Maxie. I don't want anybody hurt. I just want him warned he has to treat the waitresses with respect.' " Maxie and "his following" kept going to the restaurant. "One day, sure enough, as the waitresses would come around the corner, this cook would reach out and grab them by the behind or did something right in front of some of Maxie's men. [Then Maxie] says, 'He's in the hospital now.' 'What?' 'Oh, he'll live okay. He got broken up, but he won't tangle with any more waitresses.' "

Beulah smiled again.

She had great admiration, too, for the union's top boss, whom she met during one of her first convention trips. She was "fairly new," but "very popular with the membership" and had been elected a delegate early on. Hugo Ernst, "the president at that time, was a dear old Jewish man from Czechoslovakia. Oh, my, he wore spats, and he walked with a cane, and there were no flies on him. A sweet, dear, honest old man." Ernst was more progressive than his times. Despite a racist enmity held by rank-and-file members toward Asians (Chinese and Japanese in particular), Ernst tried for years—and in vain—to bring them into the union. Two waitress orators at the convention, who had earlier spoken eloquently against the condescension of "helpful" bourgeois women (who disapproved of waitresses serving alcohol, for example), helped to trounce Ernst's attempt.[13]

A person for whom Beulah had no admiration was Lillian Sandburg. "The female sex is not a passport to heaven. I found *that* out." She charged, among other things, that Sandburg "was in up to her neck in kickbacks" (all allegations I was unable to verify).

Beulah decided to fight Sandburg for the leadership of Local 240. "I either had to get all the way out or all the way in, so I ran against her and got [up] a slate of some of the misfits with me." Then "I had to pick executive board members to run with me and . . . made it." In 1948, Beulah Compton became the leader, the executive secretary, of Seattle Local 240.

She now was in charge of some three thousand women, and she got to work. She hired business agents from a variety of places, one "from a banquet group and one on a working men's counter and one from a fine hotel," and watched how well they did their initial jobs. Then, "when I got better acquainted with them," she expanded their duties. "One, in addition to having her territory to cover, called on the sick and ran errands for ill waitresses." Beulah also promoted health lectures for members. "At the union meeting I invited doctors in with different specialties, particularly oncologists. Any waitress interested could go get breast exams, and there were seventeen or eighteen small cancers found. All but a couple of them were small enough that they could be taken care of."

She also fulfilled a campaign promise: she set up child care centers at union halls so that waitresses could more easily attend meetings.[14] And she made "a lot of headway" with African Americans as union members—"putting them on committees, making them feel part of the union."[15]

During her first three years of leadership, she not only went beyond her expected tasks but also set about achieving a major goal: to get Seattle waitresses a good contract. After efforts she did not describe, but which must have been mighty, she became the head of a negotiating team of five unions, representing cooks, bartenders, waiters, waitresses, and hotel maids, and got very close to settling a contract. The year was 1951.

"The [old] contract was expiring at midnight on the thirty-first of May, and we were all set to strike." Then came an unexpected blow. The international union by that time was no longer headed by Ernst, and Lillian Sandburg was still in the picture, having been promoted within the union after losing the election to Beulah. "The international sent a wire to continue negotiating, pull off the strike, and sent a copy to the union boss, Lillian Sandburg, with a copy to the head of the restaurant association, saying we couldn't strike." Beulah's tone took on outrage.

"[Sandburg] brought this wire up to the lawyer who was the president of the [restaurant] association, and he read it to his associates. We were in negotiations. It was *on* the thirty-first, around noon. He said, 'You couldn't strike if you *wanted* to.' " She pounded her dining room table. "He called his group of negotiators out and left us with egg on our faces."

Some on the negotiating team "were scared to death of the international." Beulah was not scared but was furious about the betrayal. While those who "had whipped us went out for a banquet," she and a friend, who headed the hotel maids union, went off "to talk it over."

Inspiration struck during dinner. "One of the employers was by this time running the Bartell chain restaurants. I had been his boss and was a good friend when he came out from New York to work on one of my counters." Beulah now called him. "I said, 'Fred, there's no way we can stop this strike from going on. We've got a tiger by the tail, so you tell so-and-so and so-and-so to meet us in the basement meeting room of the cooks union hall before midnight, or the strike is going to go on and there's no way we can stop it.' It was all a bunch of *lies*. I could have called it off just like that."

She knew she was in defiance of the international. "So we were in this meeting hall, and just before midnight who comes in but the head of the hotel chain [and the] head of the restaurant chain and about four or five restaurant owners, almost with their tails between their legs. They came in and wanted to talk. I had left one door open, showing all the picket banners, so they could see we were ready to go, and something happened. Suddenly in that hall was hammering, hammering, hammering, banging around, 'Strike!' 'Strike!' 'Strike!' These kids were going to strike. Somebody had put them up to doing this, but it wasn't me. I never did find out who did it. Well, it *really* scared the employers to death. They started talking business.

"We stopped the clock at midnight, and by quarter after midnight, literally, we had a contract all wrapped up. This was the good contract with the health and welfare plan and the dollar and thirty-five cents [per day raise]." She looked ready for a celebration.

The next step was to offer her hard-won contract to the members. (According to her daughter Dorothy, only San Francisco's contract then had comparable health and welfare benefits.) When Beulah presented the contract at a big meeting to be voted on, however, she said, she made another horrifying discovery: the union opposed it.

The person voicing the dissent was none other than Lillian Sandburg. "My boss got up and tried to talk the waitresses into turning it down." Beulah then realized her boss had become an enemy from within. "She hired me, and I was the fair-haired child until I got this good contract." Why would Sandburg, among other officials, not want a good contract for the workers? The reason was simple, according to Beulah: union officials were in secret league with restaurant owners. "You see, [restaurant] employers would pay union management to keep the wages down. That's why we were three dollars a day below San Francisco waitresses."

Sandburg's speech burned in Beulah's memory. "One thing she said was that I had accepted the health and welfare in lieu of wages." The editor of the international's publication, "who *knew*" that was false, said so. "He was at this meeting, and he took the mike away from the executive secretary and explained what I had accomplished." The workers voted for the contract. "I dropped to my knees up on that stage. It had been such a struggle."

If the union did not support the contract, restaurant owners soon did. "They realized how good it was for them to have their employees able to get this service. If [employees] started getting symptoms of a cold or the flu, they'd have it taken care of right away, where if they didn't have the health and welfare plan, they would really get sick. It was preventive measures."

Beulah knew she had won big, against the orders of HERE headquarters, then in Cincinnati. She did not know there would be repercussions. "At that point, there was nothing the international could do, except they were going to finish *me* off.

"They decided I was a communist. They spread this word. It was the most un-American thing you could imagine. I was investigated by the FBI. My poor little son-in-law in Kentucky was investigated. My other union friends shied away from me as though something was going to rub off on them. I remember [being] in the central labor council, where I was compulsive about being there on time. I always sat in the same seat. There was room for about four hundred members. Friends would come and ask my advice and chat with me. Well, when that story broke that I was a communist, you could have shot a cannonball around me. *Nobody* sat near me. It was a horrible thing to go through."

As soon as she learned about the investigation (through a former boss who said he had been questioned), she called the local FBI office herself and went with a sister to see an agent. When he refused to tell her who had reported her, her sister got so angry that "she jumped all over him like a little wet hen. Finally he said, 'Miss Compton, if your conscience is clear, your record is clear.'" Just in case, "I called a lawyer who had been a busboy under me," and he told her that the coming Christmas holidays "might dust this whole thing off." They did.

Among the only people who never wavered in their support of her were the rank and file of Local 240. "As far as me being called a communist, those waitresses couldn't have cared less. They knew I had been running a good union."

Along the way, Beulah learned the identity of her putative betrayer.

She said, eyes flashing, that it had been Gertrude Sweet, "the international union vice president, head of the northwest region." Beulah called her "a very sweet-looking woman who had always been lovely to me."[16] She also claimed Sweet was merely "the hatchet woman," who had spread the rumors because the international ordered her to. The hatchet man? "I'm sure, the president of the international union," whom she identified as former Kansas City bartender Ed Miller, adding sharply, "He's dead, and the world is better off because of it."

She all but spat that "the liquor industry" had first put Miller up to run for secretary-treasurer and had "told [Ernst], this dear old man, to endorse him or he would find his older brother and nephews floating down the Ohio River." While relating further allegations of hardball tactics implicating Miller, she added, "Nothing against unionism, but . . . the individuals that get in there are so crooked."[17] Union members "had no way of knowing."[18]

As executive secretary of Local 240, Beulah Compton prided herself on keeping accurate books, on going beyond the issues of hourly pay, child care, and health care. She also challenged tips.

When an old boss started his own restaurant and came to see her about staffing it, she told him that if he would pay "above the scale and discourage tipping," she would assign him the best waitresses in Seattle. He agreed. Menus featured a large lettered announcement about the arrangement. "That place took off like wildfire. The customers *loved* it." She said the owner "was a great manager, and he knew how to buy." Ever since, contentions that restaurants will go under if good wages are paid are hogwash to Beulah Compton. "I would like to see [waitresses] paid a living wage without depending upon tips." Tips, she said, give waitresses no "dignity."[19]

When Beulah Compton retired from leading Local 240, she was barely into her fifties and not about to quit working, especially on behalf of other working women. She got a job helping to administer Washington state's labor laws. Concerned about tray weight at Seattle's Olympic Hotel (now the Four Seasons), "I called a waiter down there to find out what that tray weighed to serve four people in silver service. He filled one up and he weighed it, and it was twenty-two pounds." Beulah got to work. "I put out a notice—and I had no authority to do this—recommending that [weight] be the maximum a tray could be loaded for a woman to carry." She grinned. "It went over just fine."

Beulah still had clout, but unions were losing theirs. In addition to reverberations from the McCarthy era and from the Taft-Hartley Act (which limited picketing and seriously curtailed other powers of unions), factors particular to waitresses unions weakened them. A new generation of restaurants began dotting the country's nonunion regions such as the South, the Southwest, and the suburbs, making organizing difficult. Fast-food franchises appeared, owned by corporations resistant to unions. Waitresses changed, too. More worked part-time, and newcomers challenged older leaders on matters such as protective legislation. Union sisterhood gave way to individual saleswomen. Finally, waitresses and waiters locals merged, begetting unions unresponsive to the issue of job equality and other feminist concerns.[20]

Beulah herself moved on, from the state to the federal Department of Labor, becoming regional director of labor standards for western states. According to a resume she wrote in her seventies, she proposed the first Washington State Governor's Commission on the Status of Women, helped draft and lobby for the state's 1959 minimum wage bill, and organized women workers in the pulp and paper industry "to eliminate inequitable wage rates and discrimination in promotions."

The resume led to Seattle's city hall. "This last job I had was in the mayor's office for senior citizens," she said happily. Who would not hire a septuagenarian who listed her current hobbies as painting, swimming, and auto mechanics?

Another "hobby" was eating out. Beulah lamented, though, as she drove to a restaurant she liked, that it was nonunion. "Very few restaurants are unionized any more in this area. I just gave up trying to find one."

Verna Welsh

She was part of a legend, although it took her a while to realize it. She was a Harvey Girl.

The Harvey Girls, sometimes known as the women who "civilized" the Wild West, were young Americans (well-groomed, well-behaved, single, and white) who left family and friends to head west as waitresses for the Fred Harvey restaurants along the Santa Fe railway. Their heyday was the turn of the twentieth century; their territory covered an area from Illinois to California, with a concentration in the Southwest. Their boss was an entrepreneurial genius.

Fred Harvey, an immigrant from England, perceived in the 1870s that railroads were transforming the western United States. He also realized that, despite very long journeys, passengers and crews had little more for food than private picnic baskets or public slop. Harvey convinced the Santa Fe management to let him open eating establishments of superior quality wherever the trains stopped. In exchange for his making Santa Fe riders happy, the railway would provide free coal, free ice, and free freight for anything Harvey's establishments needed, from fresh fruit to fresh employees. Harvey would reap any profits. Agreed, in a handshake.[21]

The handshake had significance beyond the future empire of Fred Harvey and family. Some contend he started America's affair with fast food: no Harvey's yesterday, no McDonald's today.

Another touch of Harvey's genius was knowing that his vision of superior and spotless restaurants in the hinterlands would be aided by superior and spotless waitresses.

He advertised for young women "of good character, attractive and intelligent" to become "Harvey Girls," a term he used to signify that "they were more than simply waitresses."[22] He also knew the importance of constructing safe living environments. In 1905, upstanding girls from upstanding families (most from small towns or rural areas of the Midwest) could not be expected to take off to unknown spots like Rincon, New Mexico, or Guthrie, Oklahoma, without proper accommodations, especially given the social stigma that could be attached to working in general, and waitressing in particular. So, as Harvey Houses went from one trackrolling success to another, he arranged group dwellings for Harvey Girls, complete with curfews and other proprieties.

The waitresses' virtue was paraded in the ridiculous 1945 movie *The Harvey Girls,* starring Judy Garland. (The real star is Angela Lansbury as a befeathered showgirl of dubious morality, who would not be caught dead in the silly—and unauthentic—hair bows the fictitious Harvey Girls wore on the silver screen.)

Harvey Houses soon gained a reputation as being as pristine as their waitresses. Photographs and menus from the era bespeak dazzling feasts, with a backdrop of starched linen, monogrammed plates, and polished silver, all presided over by women who were impeccably trained and immaculately frocked, no matter how their uniforms changed over the years.

In the middle of *nowhere,* gushed Santa Fe customers, in the middle of the *desert,* look at what there is to eat! One menu from 1929 listed fresh shrimp cocktail, mangoes, Blue Point oysters, broiled live baby lobster, avocado salad, Camembert cheese, frozen eclairs, and lemon sherbet. That free ice helped.

If most passengers were lured by the victuals, most waitresses were lured by the prospect of a job, not (as legend holds) an adventure.[23] Among the job seekers was Verna Northcott, who was leaving Newton, Kansas, for Winslow, Arizona.

"I packed my things in my two suitcases, got on the train, and headed west." The trip was 1,200 miles; the year was 1938, or perhaps 1939— "I never did write it down." To supplement her memory, she later penned an account of the trip itself. "First I was very excited as I watched the rolling hills of Kansas go by," she read, "and then we climbed higher as we reached Colorado and traveled through the mountains. Going into New Mexico, we soon came into the barren desert and the Indian lands. I could see a hogan here and there, but that land looked so dry and desolate I thought to myself, 'What have I done? Where am I going?' " The only creatures she saw were sheep. "It was too late to change my mind. My ticket was only one way."

She related her tale from Winslow, where she has lived since 1938, or perhaps 1939. She is an affable, buxom woman, a few months shy of eighty, with curled hair, spiffy glasses, and a pastel outfit. One boon of the westward rides, including returning from visits to Kansas, were the sunsets. "One of the most beautiful sunsets I *ever* saw" stayed with her. "I can still remember how kind of awed I was, because the sun came down through the clouds and the rays came down, just as if Christ was coming back *through* that."

Verna had no celestial welcome when she first arrived in Winslow. She was twenty, give or take a year, and she had been hoodwinked.

She never meant to wait tables for Fred Harvey. In Newton (coincidentally a Harvey terminal), she had waited tables for a few months at the Harvey House and at a hotel owned by a relative and had also been a private waitress serving dinner parties at the home of a well-to-do couple. She attended college one year "with the limited funds I had saved," in the hope of eventually being a schoolteacher, but she quit to earn more funds before going back.

To that end, she was working in Topeka at a job she liked, as a clerk in the Hotel Registration Division of the state government. Then she was voted out. "The Democrats were defeated" in Kansas, as her old Harvey House boss, a Mr. Wright, had predicted, and Verna found herself jobless. She recalled Mr. Wright saying that if she wanted to work at the place he was going to help run—La Posada, in Winslow, Arizona—he would help. She wrote to ask whether he needed a hotel desk clerk. His answer was a one-way ticket. Her parents felt that Arizona was a long way to go for work but that it was her decision.

In Arizona, Verna arrived at a virtual oasis that was a monument of architectural grace. La Posada, the last grand Fred Harvey hotel (now on the National Register of Historic Places), was built in 1929 by his major architect and designer, Mary Elizabeth Jane Colter. La Posada, which took up eight acres by the Santa Fe tracks, was meant to recall the colonial Spanish ranchos of the area. It has elegant archways and long halls, a tile roof and stucco walls, and was decorated by Colter in her customary blend of roughly hewn local furniture and imported antiques. Even today, after decades of use as railroad offices before being abandoned (although it was being renovated as a hotel when I visited), it exudes coolness and serenity, amid seemingly perfect proportions. La Posada was said to be Colter's favorite creation.[24]

Verna happily walked through it with me, admiring carved bedroom doors, wall crannies, wrought iron fixtures, the sweep of it all. On her first trip, though, she was not in a mood to admire anything. Mr. Wright told her there was no job available on the hotel desk. She could be a waitress, he said.

In other words, he had brought her there under false pretenses! He had snookered her. "He did. He did," she agreed. "I was really upset at first. But I had a ticket one way. There was no going back. And I had worked for him in Kansas for a couple of months and he knew my folks. He was a nice gentleman. But," she sort of laughed, "it wasn't what I wanted to do at the time." She may have said nothing. "We were taught to respect our elders."

Before long, "I guess I just accepted it for what it was. And the other girls, the waitresses and everybody, were very nice, and it was a job, and I was out on my own, and I was getting to see the West."

Bound by the rules, she lived in a dormitory and had a dorm mother. She said her room, long vacant and layered in red dust and dirt (many of Winslow's streets were then unpaved), held only a bed, a dresser, and a chair. She went to J. C. Penney as soon as she could, bought yards of cretonne in a green print, sewed a curtain and pillow covers, and eventually had a place she called "homey."

Although uniforms were less cumbersome in the late 1930s than in previous decades and standards less rigorous (the Depression changed some rules, as World War II would later change others), it is notable that Verna skipped the once-mandatory month of training. Neither at the Harvey House in Newton nor the one in Winslow did she ever learn the famous Harvey coffee cup placements her predecessors used to show the coffee pourer whether, or how, customers wanted their brew (for instance, an upside down cup meant no coffee).

On Verna's first day, her "most outstanding recollection" was that one of the railroad men, "a smart aleck" named Brian, used insulting language about her. He was "talking about the new waitress" and "this and that." She still looked pained during our interview and would not reveal specifics. "I was pretty young and innocent."

A major difference between Harvey work and other restaurant work was that Harvey Houses were always open, to accommodate the trains. "As a Harvey Girl, we worked shifts, and the shifts were round the clock; six A.M. to two, and then two to ten, and then ten to six. We rotated. I preferred the two to ten. Then I could sleep late. I didn't care for the night shift."

Verna remembered clearly the rush of serving the Santa Fe's crew and passengers during the standard thirty-minute stops. "The passenger trains that came through stopped for breakfast, lunch, and dinner. And the preparations were made [by the kitchen] before the train arrived . . . so they had food they could get out in a hurry. Usually they would tell them they had thirty minutes to eat, [but] it went a little bit longer than that. If people were still eating or if there were more people and they couldn't get waited on in that particular amount of time . . . the train wouldn't go off and leave them, is what I'm trying to say."

It helped to be prepared. "Before the trains would arrive at a station, the conductor or brakeman would go through and ask the people how many wanted to eat, and they'd send the message on ahead so that the different Harvey Houses would know how many people to prepare for." No matter how fast the rush, "as far as serving the guest, we had to do it properly; serving from the left, picking up the dirty dishes from the right. We were to anticipate any extra needs. If people needed more water, more coffee, more bread or butter, we were to serve that without them having to ask." The trick was "to have a keen eye and keep an eye on what's going on at the tables that you're waiting on."

As far as she recalled, her customers never needed to cry out. She might have, however, from fatigue. La Posada's stunning proportions meant waitresses had to carry food long distances. Furthermore, as in other restaurants, the work called for more than serving. "We were re-

quired to do what we called side work, which was polishing the silver,"
probably silver plate, she figured, "but it all had to be polished. And, of
course, they have the counters and all underneath there were shelves.
We had to keep those clean. The coffee urns had to be washed every
day, which was a job that we didn't any of us relish. And there was
always the folding of the napkins." They were large, white, and linen.

"You probably have read what they said about the Harvey Girls coming west," she said, picking up notes she had written earlier to refresh
her memory. "They brought culture, refinement, and romance." Refinement indeed. "We also had to serve finger bowls." Yes, with a slice of
lemon in them, exactly as she had served them in Newton. Harvey Girls,
she continued reading, "were required to serve friendly, extraordinary,
and perfect service to hungry, friendly, or grouchy train travelers."

A famous and frequent customer was La Posada's own architect,
Mary Colter. "When I knew her, she was a very elderly lady. She had
gray hair, and she pulled it back, kind of poofy like, on the sides. She
wore glasses, and we knew she had false teeth because she always clicked
her teeth," she laughed. "You would remember something like that.
Mary Colter thought that she owned La Posada. That was her baby, see,
and she thought everybody should cater to her, so to speak. I hate to tell
you, but you know how things stick in your mind: she would never tip a
waitress. So we didn't care whether we waited on her or not."

She was also demanding or, in Verna's word, "precise," about her
food. "She always had soft-boiled eggs for breakfast, but you didn't dare
break the yolk. If it was broken one little bit, back to the kitchen it went.
She knew what she wanted. But she was a smart woman and very tal-
ented." She paused, smiling. "I can still see her sitting at the table on
the south side, right by the window."

The Harvey organization was almost as strict about the waitresses' time
off the job as it was about on-the-job behavior. "As Harvey Girls, we
were not permitted to really visit very much with the guests, and when
we were off duty, we had to leave the premises. Occasionally we did go
into the gardens and walk around, but they really didn't want us doing
that, either. By the time I came along, the rules and regulations were not
as stiff. They didn't lock the door at ten o'clock like it tells in the books."

Discouraged from socializing with guests, Harvey Girls' romances
centered on Harvey boys—that is, the male employees—and on railroad
workers. It was a railroader, L. D. Welsh, who won Verna's heart. In
Winslow to visit his grandparents, he spent an evening at a cafe, where

a mutual friend introduced him to Verna. "I wasn't too impressed." She hesitantly revealed why: "I never did care for a man with a mustache." Once he shaved it off, they started dating.

Harvey Girls "didn't have any place to entertain our gentlemen friends or anything, and L. D. and I still laugh about how he'd get my attention." When he arrived for a date, he would throw rocks up on the roof of her dormitory room. "That's how I knew he was there. We laughed that by the time I quit work, there were quite a few rocks up on the roof."

Both she and a Harvey Girl friend, Virginia Graff, married railroad men who also became friends, working the Santa Fe's Winslow to Gallup run. The friendship among the four is approaching sixty years, thanks to Fred Harvey.

The empire started by the clever, gentlemanly entrepreneur drastically changed when World War II broke out. The Harvey House staff went from opening fresh oysters for tourists to dishing out far meaner fare to thousands upon thousands of U.S. troops. (The staff, more integrated than it had been, served both white and black segregated units equally.)[25]

Winslow, later popularized in the Eagles song "Take It Easy" (". . . standing on a corner in Winslow, Arizona . . ."), became a major stop of troop trains heading to California and the Pacific. Verna Northcott Welsh, who married L. D. in January of 1941 and had their first daughter by December, was no longer a Harvey Girl by then, but her longtime friend vividly remembers serving the troop trains, two to three hundred young soldiers at a time.

"My heart ached for 'em," said Virginia Graff, for the "boys." One reason was the not-up-to-muster Fred Harvey service. Silverware and china were gone, as were linen tablecloths. So were the good cooks, she said, all gone to war. She cringed that the soldiers had to use paper plates and "horrible tinware." Also, the "food was not desirable. Powdered eggs."

She remembered a Harvey Girl named Jenny Sterling, a "Polish woman with a sense of humor," who cracked up a dining room full of soldiers. Jenny took one young soldier, a "little red-headed guy," by the ear and said loudly, "Does your mother know you're here?"

Then the little red-headed guy was gone.

Verna Welsh never again waited tables at La Posada, which closed in 1957, as travel by train lost favor to travel by car or plane. The closing was part of the gradual demise of the Harvey empire, whose economic remains and name his heirs later sold.[26] The reason Verna Welsh quit work, however, was her husband. "After we were married and we started our family, he did not want me to work. He felt he was the breadwinner and he was to take care of his family." Verna did as he wished. When the couple wanted to enlarge their small home, though, "I finally talked my husband into letting me go to work, to make a little extra money so we wouldn't be too much in debt." She found a job waiting tables in another Winslow restaurant, to which the two of us headed for dinner.

It was so un-Harvey-like—from Muzak playing "True Love" to a waitress asking us, "How you guys doing?" to slapdash service—that Verna began getting a little giddy. She managed to talk some about Harvey House etiquette. "We always were required to pick up a glass to refill it with water." Demonstrating, she showed that picking up a glass not only deters spillage but also helps the person pouring, who doesn't have to stretch as far. Then a large fly began assaulting us and our food. When it persisted, and she jokingly asked the waitress for a fly swatter, and the waitress returned to the table, set a fly swatter down, and walked away, Verna started laughing so hard she could barely stop.

The élan Fred Harvey brought to town has gone. Here, as in other such railroad stops, though, Harvey Girls or their descendants remain. Verna Northcott Welsh, for one, now realizes she was part of a significant institution in American history. "For years it was nothing. To me, being a Harvey Girl was just another job."

Marguerite Schertle

Having "always" been in good health—"until I fell, I never had an ache or pain"—Marguerite Schertle was mightily annoyed to need a steel walker while her broken foot and fractured hip healed. She shoved the support as if it were to blame as she made her way into the kitchen of her son and daughter-in-law's split-level suburban Maryland home, where she was recovering.

In truth, she missed her job, waiting tables in the tea room of the Women's Exchange in Baltimore. She had not planned to stop working this young. "I fell five days after my ninety-fifth birthday. Tripped over the breakfast girl's foot."

The "breakfast girl" would be Charlotte, who is about eighty-five.

Until the premature layoff, Marguerite woke at 7 every weekday morning and at 7:50 got a ride to work with her sixty-two-year-old son, Ken, an "assistant vice president whatever," whose office was nearby and whose plans for retirement hinged on not quitting before his mother did.

At the tea room, Marguerite worked her own shift, and more. "I didn't have to be at work until ten-thirty, but I helped the breakfast girl. I'd clear tables and fix coffee [or] toast for her, pull up the dumbwaiter, take the food off. Anything I wanted to do." The waitresses had lunch at 10 A.M., and "we were on the floor" from 10:30 until 2. "We really didn't get busy until eleven-thirty. But downtown has dropped off. Even the Women's Exchange. It was *nothing* to have two hundred people. We're lucky if we get ninety now. It's a shame."

After work, Marguerite took a bus home, then walked two blocks to her apartment. "I didn't mind it. I loved it." With her job, the walk, and her housekeeping errands, she likely had more daily on-the-hoof exercise than other ninety-five-year-olds. That is, until Charlotte's foot. "She was standing by the door. She shouldn't have been there. She had a foot back, and I came out the door. I always walk very fast. My doctor said, 'Take it easy.' He used to say, 'Don't walk so fast. You'll get there.'" Charlotte must feel terrible, I wagered. Marguerite had me turn off the tape recorder for her reply.

All is not tomato aspic, chicken croquettes, and vanilla cupcakes at the tea room of the Women's Exchange.

"A Baltimore tradition for over 115 years," as the menu states, this and other Women's Exchanges were opened along the East Coast in the 1880s by Quakers. The menu quotes the nonprofit's constitution, noting that Exchanges aimed "to encourage and help needy women to help themselves by procuring for them and establishing a sales room for the sale of women's work." According to lore I had long heard, Exchanges began as outlets for destitute Civil War widows to sell discreetly whatever items they still had or could make.

Baltimore's Exchange, in a lovely red brick building on Charles Street, has a handiwork room in the front, with crocheted baby sweaters and quilts and baked goods for sale. The tea room, visible through the door, is an economic evolution.

It hardly feels evolved. The most notable aspect is quiet. No music plays. Customers speak softly (although one deaf older man loudly states of his army career, "If you don't have to go into combat, it's a darn good life"). Mostly, a visitor has the sense of being in a pastel parlor.

The Baltimore Exchange is unique in that it is the only branch still in its original building. Marguerite Schertle is unique in that she may be the oldest waitress in the United States. She may, in fact, be the oldest in the world.

"I never think about my age, hon. No, never do." A niece is going to put her in the Guinness Book of Records, she laughed. " 'The oldest waitress in the world.' Oh, dear." Marguerite claimed not to take the idea seriously. "I don't take anything serious, hon. Take one day at a time."

She is slender, with short reddish hair, penciled eyebrows, and a prominent nose. Her hands are agile, her fingernails long, strong, and polished pink. "I was brought up the right way," she announced, erect at the kitchen table. She was one of five children of German immigrants who settled in Baltimore. Her mother, a whiz at baking, sewing, reciting American poems such as "The Village Blacksmith," and singing American folk songs, loved her new country so much that she managed to lose her German accent. Marguerite keeps her Baltimore ("Balmer") one, and the local endearment "hon" is never absent long.

Being "brought up the right way" refers not to how Marguerite was raised but how she was taught to be a proper waitress. The Dutch Tea Room, the first place she worked, catered to leading figures of city society. Among those she served was Wallis Simpson. "She married the Duke of Windsor, whatever. He gave up his throne for her. That was [known] nationwide, I guess."

Marguerite began working there at fifteen, in 1915, following the intervention of her mother, who made altar cloths for priests of St. Mary's Seminary. Knowing that one priest ate lunch at the Dutch Tea Room, she asked him to help get summer work permits there for Marguerite and Anna, her twin sister, now deceased. Soon Anna was helping make the ice cream (strawberry, banana, raspberry, vanilla, and chocolate, Marguerite easily recalled), while Marguerite served lunch in the dining room and worked mornings in the pastry kitchen. For the pastry job, she first had to make a test cake for the bosses. "I was a nervous wreck." But Marguerite Klaus, granddaughter of a Nuremberg baker, passed the test and was hired.

"Then I started making pies and cakes and nut bread. I was in the pastry kitchen about thirteen years. I went down there six o'clock in the morning, made big crocks of icing." It was "a lot of work. Work never hurt you, hon, never hurt."

Marguerite's baking became so well known that she developed a private clientele among Baltimore's leading families. "They called me up and asked me if I'd make a cake and get the chauffeur to pick it up. I made it at my mother's house."

As carefully as she baked for the prominent, so did she serve them food. "They taught us how to wait on customers at the Dutch Tea Room, yes, ma'am. We weren't allowed to wear any nail polish, we weren't allowed to wear any drop earrings. We had to wear a hair net. We had to learn how to be courteous, serve from the right side, never from the left side. To this day, they serve from any side, and I don't do that. I served from the right side until the day I left the Women's Exchange. You don't reach over people." (It is now standard, of course, to serve from the left and remove from the right.)

Waitresses were treated almost as delicately as customers. "We did not have to carry any food." Others brought it out on trays, "put it on the bus stand, and we served it from the bus stand to the customer. We were not allowed to clear tables. We had a girl that cleared the tables, set them up, put on a clean tablecloth. That was a much, much more refined place, 'cause we waited on"—her voice dropped—"very, very rich." She named names, from "the Black and Deckers" to "Wallis Simpson and [her] Aunt Bessie" to many others. "Oh, I could sit here and mention dozens and dozens of people that became *my* customers because they liked the way I served them."

Baltimore's society ladies dined tidily. "We had assorted sandwiches, we had sandwich and a half" (six pieces cut in cubes). "One was a minced chicken, one was an egg [salad]. In the summer, it was a lettuce and tomato, cream cheese and jelly, and a minced ham. We sold a lot of those. I used to go in the morning and help make them. We used to have big trays full, and they'd put a wet cloth over it, because they went—you wouldn't believe. They ate light, much lighter than they do now. People are eating too heavy. It's surprising the amount of lunches we serve to people . . . and then," she grimaced, "they'll get a dessert."

The Dutch Tea Room also offered a more baroque diet. "We used to have sweetbreads under the glass, kidney stew and waffle, giblet stew, Smithfield ham and poached eggs, vegetable platter, which Mrs. Decker always got because she never ate meat. And never would wear a fur coat, you know. Mrs. Decker was a lovely person. She introduced me to her friends when she brought 'em in. She called me over and put her arms around my waist and [said], 'I want you to meet Miss so-and-so, I want you to meet my best friend, Marguerite.'" An uncharitable question gave Marguerite only slight pause. Did she and her "best friend," whose husband co-founded Black and Decker, see each other away from the restaurant? "No. Off the job, no." A moment's silence followed.

While employed at the Dutch Tea Room, Marguerite married. "I made my own wedding cake—three tiers of pound cake with white seven-minute icing" and decorations of "leaves and what not" she crafted with a pastry tube. The tea room donated the ingredients, and the ladies who lunched showered her with wedding presents. "Miss Wexter gave me my place settings. Came from Longer's. Still have them," she recalled, as she listed gifts by giver, item, and store.

She praised all the ladies, from Wallis Simpson to a Mrs. Bauerschmidt, the brewer's wife. "But you got to be careful how you wait on 'em. I mean, every . . . I wouldn't dare make a mistake." Table settings were meticulous. "Cup and saucer on the right side. They were very fussy about how the silver was placed. You had to put it down just so," she demonstrated at the table. "Now, down at the Exchange, they put the napkin like this," she said grimly, placing one under a fork. "I was never taught that. What I do," she showed, is to place the napkin "alongside of the fork, 'cause you're not supposed to pick up the fork before you pick your napkin up."

She recently chastised a younger waitress, Loretta, eighty-one, for putting forks on napkins. "'I don't *like* them like that, please?' 'Everybody else . . . ' [Loretta started to say]. 'I don't care what the other girls do, honey. I'm not doing anything disrespectful to the Exchange, I just like my napkins on the outside.'

"I couldn't stand seeing a fork like this"—askew—"when you can, very easy, do it like this," she again demonstrated. "Even here at the Women's Exchange, when we had Miss Warfield [as] hostess, she was very strict about how the tables were set in the morning, the salt and pepper shaker and the ashtray. I thought everything was just so, but with Miss Warfield, nothing was ever just so. She would find a little tiny flaw, and she would say, 'Marguerite . . . ,' and here I thought, perfect, right? I wasn't. But it was good she was like that. She kept us on our toes. I wish we had more hostesses like that.

"That's gone now, that era, when people used to be meticulous about things, about the tables and the flowers and everything. Why? Why is that gone?" The question hung in the air.

In the Dutch Tea Room, Marguerite also was schooled in pronunciation. "I've always said 'to-mah-toes.' The kids made fun of me when they were little. A lot of my customers do, too. I said, 'I'm sorry, I'm not really putting on, hon. I was taught to say "to-mah-toes" at the Dutch Tea Room.'"

There and at the Exchange, Marguerite learned her lessons well enough to become head waitress. "Every waitress that came in I trained." By her account, there is much to impart. "You'd be surprised at the amount of people that *do not know* how to set a table." She crumpled up her demonstration napkin. "Napkins not even folded." Even the tea room's tea was served improperly. She shook her head. "Towards the end I said, 'Nope, take me off as the head waitress. Forget it.'"

In Marguerite's unwritten training manual, proper customer service includes a proper finale. Do not "clear the table before the customers get up. Makes them feel they should get out, you know what I mean?" When she points out to "some girls" that they are rushing customers, "they don't like it."

There have been many tempests in the tea room. "I tried to tell the girls . . . '*Do not serve [only] one customer* when you have three at that table.' Keep it back, keep it on the side, because that makes the other ladies say, 'Well, where is mine?' You don't do that. But they'll do that *time* and *time* again."

Marguerite tells them not to complain about management either, but they do, she grumbled. "No need to say you have a nasty boss or you don't like her. There's no such thing as that. You're the one that creates ill feeling. If you do the right thing, you won't have no ill feelings with your boss. I never had problems, hon, with mine. The same way with the customers.

"When a customer comes in, if you're busy or something, you'll say 'Hello' or 'Good morning, I'll be with you in just a moment,' but you don't gush over people. Some people like it, some don't. You have to *know* your customers." She served cherry pie to Mr. Dow only if it was "fresh and runny." If it was "thick with corn starch," she would not. "You pretty well know what your customers won't like," she laughed some, "after all them years."

Strong fingernails drummed the kitchen table, as she fumed about certain waitresses who gossiped so loudly that customers could hear them. "Tone it down," she told them. "Maybe this is why they didn't like me, because they thought I was bossy or what. But somebody had to control them, right?" She fumed, too, about waitresses who complain about their tips. "I've had people leave and didn't tip me and mailed it to me. *Mailed* it to me. They knew as sure as I'm sitting here, I did not work for that tip."

When the Dutch Tea Room era ended ("they closed up, hon"), Marguerite "went down to Lovely Lane where Carrie, Loretta's sister, worked. They're no more alike than the man in the moon," she added. The Lovely Lane "was more of a restaurant. They used to serve four and five hundred people a day. It was a very quick place." Forks were not laid carefully to the left of the napkin. "I think the silverware was rolled up in the napkins, like you see in a lot of places." Her face harrumphed.

She disapproved of the change in standards but had a more important matter on her mind at the time. Her husband, a fireman, "wasn't making a big salary," and they were buying a house, "so I really had to get to work to do something." She also went to night school, "taking up millinery and dressmaking." She would have loved doing that as a career, but waitressing paid more.

After eight years at Lovely Lane, it too became history, and Marguerite began working at the Women's Exchange, a place that held its own history and eventually would hold hers.

"When I first started there, oh, I thought maybe I was going to last one day." She did not know where anything was, and an embarrassing early moment almost did her in. She had taken a glass of iced tea to a male customer and upset it "down the front of his pants." The man asked whether she was going to wipe it off. "He was only kidding, and I thought he meant it. I went back and my face was blood red. I died a thousand and one deaths."

Revived, she learned her way around and got "into it after a while." "A while" became fifty-two years.

She became, indisputably, the Exchange's in-house perfectionist. Take the famous starched white organdy sashes, tied (by her) in a huge back bow, which waitresses wore over their robin's egg blue uniforms. She put on a clean sash every day. "Sometime they didn't take theirs home for a week. I said, 'I'm not tying it anymore. It looks like a rag.'" (Loretta told me a sash could last her all week, and spot cleaner worked fine.) Who tied Marguerite's? Who else? "I'd bring it in the front and tie it and then put it back. Where there's a will, there's a way, hon."

Somewhere along the decades, Marguerite's reputation grew beyond the small square tables and sky blue walls of the Exchange. "I had so many write-ups and so many books. A monthly magazine or what, I was in there, picture of me. Hah! I think it could be a little jealousy. Of the girls. But no reason why they should be, because I never act any different towards *them*." She said management wanted to have an enlarged picture of her in the hall. "I said no way, I don't want it."

The cap to Marguerite's fame, and cause for even more public interest, was moviedom. She spent seconds in *Sleepless in Seattle*. The Rosie O'Donnell and Meg Ryan characters are eating lunch in the (unnamed) Women's Exchange and talking about the Tom Hanks character, "Sleepless in Seattle," whom Ryan had heard on the radio. As O'Donnell speaks the sentence, "Now two thousand women want his number," Marguerite walks by. She is wearing glasses, white button earrings, and the Women's Exchange uniform. She is moving quickly (no acting skills required there) and carrying food she places on a table. "That thing never did die down. Now they're playing [it] tonight. I'm going to get a check for that. I've gotten so many checks, you wouldn't believe."

All the Exchange waitresses were invited to be in the film, she said, and to get paid by the producer and double-time by the restaurant. Only she accepted. "They couldn't give up their Saturday," she said, mockingly. "They had to do this, they had to do that. I had a lot I had to do, too, and I had a hard time getting down there." Finally, a granddaughter drove her. "They treated me like, oh, my, I was royalty. Anytime I do something, they'd holler, 'Hip, hip, hooray, Marguerite.' I thoroughly enjoyed that day, from nine in the morning to nine at night. I didn't know I was there."

She knows her part was modest ("you don't see much of me, hon; you got to look fast") but is not letting anyone forget the decision to stay away. "Every time I got a check, I took it down to the Exchange. 'See what I got?' I did do that. I shouldn't."

Publicity from the film brought more Marguerite-watchers. "*Oh, yes.* Even to this day, when they come from out of town, 'Where's the lady who was in *Sleepless in Seattle*?'" Some wanted an autograph, which Marguerite gave. Some wanted to chat, but the working waitress drew the line. "I'd say, 'I'm sorry, I can't talk to you. I'm busy now.'"

Marguerite Schertle's longer roles, of course, have been behind the scenes. She is concerned about "one of the new girls" who told one cranky man he had to wait his turn. "Now see, she should have *never* said that. I would have said we were a little short today, but I'll make up for it, I'll see that you get even better service than if I had waited on you ten minutes ago. I do, even if I'll let somebody else wait that is not in a hurry. Now I got another customer, right? Tipwise, it doesn't bother me. I work for the benefit of the Women's Exchange. That was my second home, and I loved it."

If anything prevented her from going to work over the half century, she said, she cried. When she missed her bus by working late, which she did "many a time, [I] didn't get home until five o'clock. But it was my job and I had to do it."

She could not and cannot imagine life otherwise. "Now, when this foot gets well and I . . . I don't know what I'm going to do with myself." Months after the accident, she did go back to work, but only for two days; her hip was not ready for her. Those two days were long enough to impress the new thirty-seven-year-old manager, Lucy Weiss, and to convince her that Marguerite's memory surpassed hers. Lucy impressed Marguerite as well. "A round bucket where they have the dirty silver, she put it underneath the bus stand. I was for that one hundred percent. The girls didn't want to do it." They, she scoffed, "didn't want to stoop a little bit."

Marguerite, edging toward her ninety-sixth year, was hopeful about returning to the Exchange. The possibility of not going back made her uneasy. "I haven't started to think about that yet." She had, though. She planned, she said, to get rid of her walker and do more needlework, from embroidering to crocheting to knitting. She also wanted to bake and sell her date and nut bread for five dollars a loaf and to volunteer at a nearby hospital, maybe its gift shop. "Anything," she said.

It would take a lot of work to replace the Women's Exchange.

Cathryn Anita Smith

The time of the battle, the mid-1970s. The battle site, a legendary castle of haute cuisine at 5 East 55th Street in Manhattan. Unaware of the gathering armies, old customers enter easily, while new ones contend with crossing many a moat: name, nerve, wallet, wardrobe, and French. Once inside, however, all who enter are rewarded. Glorious sustenance is delivered with exquisite attentiveness, amid sumptuous decor.

Nothing is more important to some customers, however, than simply being seen or else perusing the crowd for those who have come to be seen. Ill-at-ease newcomers or the couple on a splurge, behind menu shields, shoot glances furtive or bold toward the glitterati. Eyes skim the not quite recognizable (the king of Belgium, for instance, or women who populate small photographs in society columns), then snap in recognition at Richard Nixon and Sophia Loren (not together) in one corner, the shah of Iran and his retinue (with accompanying bodyguards seated in less desirable areas) in another, and—the most prized sighting of all—Jacqueline Kennedy Onassis. She never looks around.

The legendary spot is La Côte Basque. The name misleads. Neither within nor without East 55th Street (the restaurant has since moved across town) is a "Basque coast" conjured. Only one Basque dish, an honored chicken entree, is served. The decor does incorporate the Basque trio of red, green, and white (subtly altered to off-white for a warmer look); but the cuisine, she is French. Presiding over it all is Madame Henriette, a one-woman *ancien régime* who refuses to let any woman enter her domain wearing trousers. Legend has it that among the well-dressed ladies turned away was Mrs. Onassis. But she came back, the legend goes on. They all come back.

At any given hour, for example, one might see returnees from *the* scandal—Truman Capote's shocking and salacious story, published in *Esquire* magazine, about the sexual dalliances of those animated society women with whom he used to dine. It was unclear to readers which anecdotes he made up, overheard, or was told; but it was clear he aimed to wound: several women are named, and the story is titled "La Côte Basque." Capote is persona non grata in extremis to his former dining companions, but he is back. They, in slim suits and perfect pumps, are reeling and furious; but they are back, too. Separate tables, please.

The battle to come, which will provoke its own headlines, is being waged behind the scenes. While La Côte Basque's customers may have been consumed with their own concerns, and while the restaurant may have considered itself an oasis *extraordinaire* within the vast desert of America, a new revolution has stormed right past the maître d'. It is feminism.

La Côte Basque has just been sued for sex discrimination in hiring. *Mon Dieu!* Madame may have cried. What brought this about? The answer: an act of friendship between two waitresses.

Before becoming an inadvertent revolutionary, a young woman named Cathryn Anita Smith was waiting tables at the Blueprint, a restaurant many blocks and worlds away from La Côte Basque. She had grown up on a cattle ranch in northern California, moved to the southern part of the state while her parents were divorcing, and for a while attended college with the dream of studying music (one of several "dreams" or "dreams come true" she would mention). She dropped out, in part for lack of emotional and financial support from her parents. Then, in what she now considers an act of rebellion, she began waitressing.

The work led to a pattern of toil, quit, and travel, whenever mood and tips added up. Every time she quit, "I would throw away my aprons and swear I was never going to go back to waitressing. *Every* time I did, I had to go back and be a waitress."

Then came the battle to be more of a waitress than she had planned.

She chronicled it in her small, packed Upper East Side apartment, which I reached after ascending five flights of stairs. Her welcome beamed, but she had nothing of the elegant look I had seen one other evening. Today, her hair was lank, she wore bulky clothes and slippers and looked like someone recovering from an operation. She was. She had developed a hernia from toting boxes of floor parquet up the five flights for her latest home improvement project. A glance downward reveals that the project is not finished. But who would notice? Her small foyer is so crammed with objects—for example, a drum set (she plays in two community orchestras)—that the floor is barely visible. In the miniature living room is a grand piano, next to it an ornate metal cage containing a strident parrot. Prowling nearby is her cat, meowing a counterpoint to the squawks. A piano bench serves by default as a table. La Côte it ain't; home it is.

After years of bicoastal waitress rambling, by 1974 Cathryn had settled in New York and found a boyfriend. She partied nights at clubs and worked days at the Blueprint. There she became friends with fellow waitress Jeanne King. "[Jeanne] was trying to get another job at night, so she could go on this cruise through the Panama Canal in this catamaran with a bunch of people. She couldn't get a night job because all the Upper East Side places"—Cathryn spoke so slowly that each word stood by itself—"would not hire women." The "places" Jeanne sought out were modest. No matter. "All the little *bistros* would not hire women."

Landlocked on Manhattan, Jeanne was getting discouraged. "She had tried and tried. Someone had said to her, 'Why don't you go to the New York State Civil Liberties Union and, you know, Title VII.'" One of the best-known parts of the 1964 Civil Rights Act, Title VII essentially says employers cannot refuse jobs to people based on matters not of their choosing, such as sex or skin color.

"So she did. The woman said, 'Why don't you go to the national office and speak to Kathleen Peratis, who was working on the women's rights project? I think we can do something a little more interesting with this on a national level.' So Jeanne did. Kathleen said to her, 'Find another woman who can do this with you. You both are going to need to say you looked for these jobs, and you're going to have to stand up in a court of law and say, yes, I was with her when she went in there and she was refused.' "

Jeanne asked Cathryn to be the other woman. Cathryn, "a silly, timid, little twenty-five-year-old," agreed.

In ensuing strategy sessions, it was decided that Jeanne King and Cathryn Smith should not try to get work at sex-discriminatory bistros but rather at sex-discriminatory haute cuisine restaurants. "We basically targeted the top ones. You have to choose."[27]

The two waitresses, pumped for victory but primed for rejection, set out to gather evidence. "We took turns," recalled Cathryn. Jeanne "applied to the 21 club, I applied to Lutèce, I applied to La Côte Basque. We alternated." They mostly met maître d's, who were "very brusque. Several of them flatly said, 'No, we don't hire women.' " In response, the women offered their practiced guise of nonconfrontation.

"We said, 'Thank you. But may I leave my resume?' " Jeanne, meanwhile, "managed to get the money together and took off on her little sailing trip. And I had to keep calling these places every month to see if they had any openings."

Cathryn began to sense she was involved in more than a gesture of friendship. "There was something instinctual that made me realize you have to make things better in your own way." She also liked the idea that "the little fish in a little pond in California is somehow going to make a splash in New York."

In the course of evidence-gathering, she also studied French. The ACLU, not wanting to risk its plaintiff being unqualified, sent her to the Berlitz language school. Cathryn had taken French in high school and college and thus knew basics, but she would need much more in an all-French kitchen. She certainly had time to study. Soon after she agreed to be part of the case, she and her boyfriend, a teacher-turned-bartender, broke up. "He was totally appalled. That I should presume to sue a restaurant."

In May 1975, presumption paid off. A sex-discrimination lawsuit was filed against a number of restaurants, including 21 and La Côte Basque. The suit also named the restaurant workers union, for not trying to alleviate sex discrimination.

Cathryn soon had to face La Côte Basque's lawyer. "He cross-examined me eight hours in discovery. I knew I could put up with anybody after that. I learned how to answer, and I learned how *not* to volunteer information."

In November, a top target caved. Jeanne King, back from her sailing trip, was hired by 21 as its first female waiter. The four-star restaurant's capitulation made the front page of the *New York Post*.

The next summer, La Côte Basque abandoned its separatist stance—Cathryn Smith had won, too. Under the terms of the lawsuit, she was to receive a cash settlement close to twenty thousand dollars, which she got "in dribs and drabs," as well as entrance into the inner French realm.

She still seems enchanted by the restaurant, describing it from memory, the front door bar area leading to "that huge entry hall called the *royale*, where all the people who wanted to be seen sat, the celebrities and those who could pay the maître d' enough money to buy a table. Manhattan real estate," she laughed. In the rear was *la salle*, a "very beautiful room with beautiful murals." She spoke of an area where coffee was poured and of the stairwell that led down to the kitchen, which, she said, was clangingly loud, busy, and steaming from "unbelievable heat, especially in the summer. That kitchen had to be a hundred and ten degrees."

Cathryn's professional entree was picked up in the *New York Times* and on local and European television. "I got a kick out of it." Yet, La Côte Basque had not hired its unwanted woman to be a waiter. Cathryn was to spend a year as a "busgirl." The reason, she said, imitating a French accent, was that "no woman could possibly know how to be a French waiter."

When Cathryn began working in her litigated but humble role, Madame Henriette and almost everyone else on the otherwise all-male staff welcomed her with closed arms. Cathryn does not seem to be a whiner, but she leaves no doubt that her colleagues' intention from the start was to make her life miserable. "They did everything possible to make me quit. I could never do anything right, blah, blah, blah. They were supposed to fill out a monthly report on how my 'training' was going on, my learning how to carve and how to do things in the French manner. Of course, none of that went on." She again affected a French accent: "'We are too busy, Cat-reen, to teach you zat kind of stoof.' I said, 'Well, I'll come in on my day off, and you'll teach me how to carve. Is that agreeable to you?' I would go in on my day off. At that point, they pissed me off, and I was not going to let them get away with it."

She struggled mightily. "They were going to give me a test on French wines and sauces. I remember going to the New York Public Library, being so overwhelmed by *Larousse Gastronomique*. I got depressed, and I started falling asleep. The cop is coming over, he hits me with a club— 'Miss, Miss, you can't sleep in the library,' like I was a bum," she laughed. "But I'm looking at all these sauces and trying to learn what comes from what."

Months before her busgirl year ended and waiter status loomed, unexpected obstacles appeared. "Girard [the maître d'] said, 'Cat-reen, you don't know enough about wine.'" Cat-reen was ready. "I said, 'Why don't you give me two months off with some money to go to France to learn?' I had been reading about it, and I was truly interested in the whole history, the romance . . . I loved that stuff. So I called all the big importers and said, 'I'm the new person at La Côte Basque, and I want to learn about wines. Is there some place you can recommend I go to?'" They arranged a two-month trip. The powers that be at La Côte Basque gave the busgirl their blessing.

"They thought I wouldn't come back. I did everything legally through the union, everything from La Côte Basque, so they could not screw me, and I went to France July ninth."

Her face lit up. "I was treated like a *queen* in France. I was picked up in chauffeured limousines. I stayed in the finest chateaux. White glove service." She "drank cognac from the time of Napoleon. A cask of 1812 cognac," stored in *la cave de paradis* of her host's wine cellar, was tapped for her to taste. At night, a butler turned down her bed and put out her nightgown.

One reason for the treatment was investment, she thought. "They had no idea where I was going, what I was going to do, and I'd made the newspapers. Who knows, must have touched something in these peoples' minds." She liked the experience so much that she signed up to learn more about wines the next summer. (During lunch at the West Side reincarnation of La Côte Basque, Cathryn rolled a sip of chardonnay in her mouth and remarked that the flintiness indicated the grapes were from southwestern France.)

When she returned to New York, royalty became reality.

Not only was she treated as shabbily as before, but her promised promotion seemed to be stalled. In an interview in *Cosmopolitan* years later, she is quoted (in words that now embarrass her) as saying, "It's a bunch of baloney that women don't have enough class. Women should have these jobs, damn it!"[28]

In response to the stalling, Kathleen Peratis called for arbitration. Cathryn's assigned arbitrator was Ruth Bader Ginsburg, with whom she recalled having a lively dinner. The future Supreme Court Justice was appointed to a court of appeals, though, and Cathryn was assigned someone else, a law professor, who made the terms of the settlement stick. Thus, after a quest of nearly three years, Cathryn Smith began waiting tables at La Côte Basque.

Day one in the new position was "very stressful. The men refused to work with me." Cathryn's temporary reign as a queen in France, however, had given her confidence and knowledge. She now knew her sauces, her favorite being Perigourdine, "a demi-glace sauce, which is a meat sauce with veal bones in it, then they put black truffles in it and Madeira or Porto. Yum, yum, yum." She also had learned about her co-workers.

"I realized what I ended up getting involved in was a clash of two cultures and the war between the sexes. I was a woman who had gone to college, not that I graduated. They all left school when they were thirteen or fourteen. They couldn't make it in France," she added scornfully, "so they came to America. So there you had poorly educated men—it's a typical stereotype—whose position and earnings are being threatened."

"Little things" pointed out the basic truth. "Raymond [a waiter], who really hated me, told me he was my sworn enemy and he would do anything to screw me up. He was the first one who refused to work with me. When I realized he sold the man who was eating fish a half bottle of sauterne because he didn't know he was giving him a sweet wine, I brought it to the captain's attention." The captain sold the man something else.

Cathryn also began to recognize that the French staff made many mistakes in French grammar. "These other clowns I was working with who knew nothing" could "barely speak poor French. You start picking up the differences. Understanding *grand bourgeois, petit bourgeois, paysan* [peasant].

"There was *one* waiter who went to hotel and restaurant school in Nice, and he was the one I would always try to emulate. He really knew about service, he really knew about the sauces, and he [was] always impeccably dressed. And he refused to work with me." The waiter's nickname was Josie. "He was working with this guy named Phillipe who always had dirty nails. He was like a big horse. I said to Josie, 'I don't understand why you will work with Phillipe when I'm the much better waiter. I'm clean, I'm . . .' He almost started to cry"—she imitated his flustered voice—" 'I cannot work wiz a *woman.*' I literally thought the man was going to break down in tears, he was *so* emotional!" She laughed. "I said, 'Okay, Josie.' But part of it was because I was upstaging him, too."

The French restaurant system did not promote cooperation. The serving staff had specific job titles, such as the *chef de rang* and the *commis de suite* ("the one who ran to the kitchen"), fostering "real definite delineations, which is sort of revolting. My idea is, if something needs to be done, we have to help to get it done." Some waiters had "a humanistic approach, who would help people out. Other ones . . . thought their shit didn't stink."

Cathryn had one important ally: Jean-Jacques Rachou. "The chef happened to like me, so I never had any problems with the kitchen. One time, one saucier was arguing with me. The chef was standing right there. It was this young smartass kid who'd just come over from France and saw the others giving me a little bit of a hard time, so he was going to do it. I said to him in perfect French, 'Excuse me, André, but have I said something to offend you? Please tell me what it is, and I will apologize if I've done *anything*.' The kid couldn't say anything. 'Cathryn, *ce n'est rien* [it is nothing].' I said, '*Merci, merci.*' "

Sometimes harassment behind the scenes verged on dangerous. "In the period when they refused to work with me, they hired another waiter to work with me. He hit me once. We were having a little confrontation about a check. I told him the table needed a check, and he hadn't put it down. We were in the stairwell, and I had a tray, and he went like . . ." She mimed a smash to her stomach. "He hit me right here. It so happened that one Italian waiter saw it. He stood up for me. I ran to the men's locker room, and they were trying to get him to say he hadn't seen it. But, 'I'm sick of it. I saw it. He hit her.' "

"Eventually they got sick of harassing me." Behavior that had been hostile became nearer playful. Once while the staff set up, Josie took a serving cart, a *guerridon,* and pointed it at Cathryn. "He was going to run me down, and I didn't move. He started pushing at me, and he realized I wasn't going to move. I said, 'Josie, say *excusez-moi.* Are you looking for a fight?' 'Zees is not zee battleground where I fight zee women.' I said, 'I get to choose the terrain.' 'Ah, *mademoiselle,* I have zee choice of weapon!' " She roared.

Her shift, like that of other waiters, started at 10 A.M., six days a week. Everyone was suited up for "service" in the same outfits: "functional" black shoes, pants and cummerbund, a white shirt, "a white modified waiter-dinner-jacket thing," and a black bow tie. She laughed, recalling the reaction of one customer, actor Tony Randall: "Oh, you look so darling in that outfit!" She liked it, too. "I felt absolutely comfortable. Having grown up on a cattle ranch, I wore completely functional clothing." Her daily school clothes had included cowboy boots and jeans.

Some customers envied Cathryn "the pants thing," for Madame Henriette's stricture had not changed. "One of the old, really rich women said to Madame, 'She has to wear pants, and you won't let any of us in in pants.' Madame turns around and says"—a growly female French accent ensued—" 'She want to work like a man, she can dr-r-r-ress like a man.' " Another laugh. "She was in her eighties, perfectly coiffed every night, immaculate."

Cathryn's outfit did partially disguise her figure but not other differentiations. She hennaed her hair a reddish brown and "used to wear it up in a modified French twist. And I could afford to have a facial every week, so my skin was beautiful. I was in the bloom of youth then, too." Furthermore, at 5 foot 8, "I was taller than most of the men." She added, smiling, "I was fifty pounds thinner then. I weighed one hundred forty. I was all muscle." Male waiters resented that "I actually could run up and down those stairs and carry heavy trays."

The serving staff's first task was to prepare dining areas for lunch. "I usually ended up filling and cleaning all the salt and pepper shakers and doing the condiments, because I was naturally neater and cleaner. Men hate doing that kind of stuff." At 11:30 A.M., the staff had lunch. "In the beginning, there was not much conversation. But after a while, you start talking and laughing and telling jokes. The human nature has to share."

At noon, when the ceremony of lunch began, so did the hard work. "I would assist the captain, or I would be running up and down to the kitchen getting the plates and the hors d'oeuvres and the main courses and the desserts, except if it was a soufflé or a hot prepared dessert." To my surprise, her jobs never included taking a person's order. She did not, I asked, recommend dishes? Did not need to know all those ingredients in *Larousse Gastronomique* sauces? Anything about wine? "Of course not. Neither do these people, as I came to find out."

As in most such establishments, the captain took customers' orders. Lower-ranked waiters, including Cathryn, merely delivered. "You just say, '*Bon appetit*,' and move on." First, though, they had to consult a copy of the food order and set the table accordingly. "Making sure all the proper place settings for the fish course or the salad course or whatever it was that people ordered were *on* the table for them, so as soon as the plates were down, they would be ready to eat. Each course is set separately. That's the time-consuming thing. [If] one person would have asparagus [and] the other person would have the cold salmon appetizer, you would have to make sure the person that had the fish had a fish knife and fork, and the person who had the asparagus had a knife and fork." A fish fork has more tongs on the sides for flipping out little bones, she explained, whereas the fish knife is not as sharp. "Then everything is cleared away after they've finished, and a whole new setting is put out.

"If somebody had a shrimp cocktail, you'd bring the stupid little thing with the oyster crackers and the Tabasco and horseradish. Nobody should ever have to ask for anything." Not for anything French, that is. For ketchup, "they would have to ask. It's an American condiment." Cathryn brought it in a "little silver condiment holder" as if the request were culinarily correct. The goal was to make customers comfortable. "They're paying a lot of money for their food, and if they want to doctor it up with ketchup, more power to them. But in the back, there would be, 'C'est Shee-cah-go [Chicago]'. It's like mobsters from Chicago—no class."

In one exception to the comfort commandment, a couple of rich regulars ("he was head of Bristol-Meyers or something") were asked to leave their *royale* table and take coffee at the bar so that someone "very glitterati" could be seated. "I thought it was horrible." So did the couple. But they too came back.

Someone who never got bumped was Jacqueline Kennedy Onassis. "I remember Jackie coming in with [her companion Maurice] Templesman. She always sat very close to whatever man she was with and gave him her un-di-vi-ded attention. The woman knew how to make a man feel like a man. She had that ability." She also had the undivided attention of the captain, who delivered the food himself. She "knew what was going on."

She also knew about Cathryn Smith's battle. Cathryn recalled a day when Jacqueline Onassis dined with Pia Lindstrom, a New York television celebrity and daughter of actress Ingrid Bergman: "I remember . . . Pia Lindstrom saying to me, 'Mrs. Onassis finds it wonderful you're here.' " Could Mrs. Onassis not speak for herself? "No, she never did." But "she always smiled. She was very nice." Cathryn added, "Almost everyone took care of everything for her. She almost never spoke to anyone. She was in her own little world."

In his own little world within the *royale* was Capote, whom Cathryn often saw. She reread his "La Côte Basque" at my request and reported that he evoked wonderfully the visual sense of the restaurant, but she claimed no knowledge of conversations he quoted or made up. Other than overhearing one man tell another that he had never masturbated ("Yeah, I bet," she recalled thinking), she rarely heard anything. "I was too busy trying to do my job, stay out of everybody's wrath." Her fellow waiters "had no opinion" about Truman Capote, she said. "I mean, they didn't read."

Cathryn was more taken by movie star celebrities. "I remember the time Sophia Loren came in. Everybody was very nervous. We didn't want the busboys near the table because they might knock something over, so only the waiters were supposed to take care of it." She laughed. "No picture has *ever* done this woman justice, let me tell you. She is so beautiful, and she was wonderful." Cathryn's friendly admirer won her praise, too. "Tony Randall was wonderful. You could [sit] him anywhere and he wouldn't care. He never made a fuss. I adored him. He was a pleasure to take care of." She had another celebrity supporter in British film director David Lean. "He said to me, 'My dear, you have handled this with great dignity.'" She laughed again.

In contrast to her reception from colleagues, that from her customers was generally positive. "Most of them were terrific. I had my real champions. [But] there were some who were totally offended by it." Who? "Men. American men. Generally, there would be a hostile feeling coming from them," as if, she said, she could not put a plate of food in front of them properly. "Not ever look at you or thank you."

As for the types of women Capote parodied, "they were just wonderful. They had no real worries. Noblesse oblige. They had the time to be gracious, they had the time to enjoy. All of them are well educated. They went to women's schools, they married well, which is sort of what they're supposed to do."

Lunch ended as late as 3 P.M. Capote wrote, from his point of view, that "it was an atmosphere of luxurious exhaustion."

Servers felt differently. They had a break and then had to return to work, dressed and ready to go, for the staff dinner at 5:30, before being back on the floor at 6:00 for dinner service, which could last more than six hours.

"I usually got home between one and two o'clock in the morning, and I had to be back at work at ten. It was a killer. All I did was work." On her single day off, "I'd sleep to one in the afternoon and then go out to dinner. Come home, get ready, wash my shirts and [iron them], ready to go work the next day."

Cathryn's days were not only hard and long but also lonesome. After she and her boyfriend parted, she keenly felt the lack of a lover. "Every young woman wants to have a significant other. [Then] you've chosen to do something you believe in and they don't. It's very hard. It's just not negotiable." She never got involved with a Côte co-worker, she said, aghast at the suggestion. "No, no! How could you get romantically involved with someone who didn't treat you nicely at your job?" The only one she was interested in was the chef, "but he was married, so I . . . you know." Her friends married, too. "All my friends married and had children. Without exception."

Her work did have two silver linings. She could take long breaks during the restaurant's winter and summer slow seasons, and she was paid well. Waiters' tips were pooled and divvied fairly. Co-workers apparently resented only her presence, not her earnings. She spent hers on rent, getting "my first own place" (where she still lives), and on indulgences. "I bought good china"—an eight-place setting of Lenox's Autumn pattern is packed in a cabinet—"I bought good crystal, I went to Europe twice a year. I pissed it away, but I had a good time."

By the fall of 1980, after three and a half years at La Côte Basque, Cathryn Smith decided nothing compensated for the work or the hours. "I didn't want to keep going on like that anymore." With no plans, she decided to quit. Asked whether her decision had been gradual or sudden, she laughed loudly. "I never wanted to stay the day I walked in the door!"

When the time came to inform Jean-Jacques Rachou of her decision, she surprised herself by crying. "We gave one another big hugs. I said I felt like I'm getting a divorce, like I've been married. I didn't want to say I felt battered."

The news of her decision "went through the restaurant like wildfire." Her colleagues wished her well and took her out for a drink after work. "They did do that." Did any ever apologize? "No," she answered crisply. "I knew it wasn't going to happen. Men don't like to apologize to women, I don't think."

Times had changed, though. By then, La Côte Basque had hired other women waiters and a woman pastry chef. "There was not a woman in the kitchen when I started, either."

When Cathryn left, one of her contacts at La Côte Basque, a wine importer, got her a job as a captain at Windows on the World, the well-known restaurant in the World Trade Center. "The view was incredible," she sighed when I spoke to her weeks after the view plunged to earth in the September 11 terrorist attack.

At the time of the attack, Cathryn was on her way to a temp job at a law firm nearby. She spent her efforts getting a "visibly shaken" man from the Midwest on an uptown bus and therefore did not see the building's collapse. But amid the common aftermath of horror, she has been thinking of the many restaurant workers who died in the attack. Breakfast, she said; Windows began serving breakfast years after she left. When she worked there, in the lunch-and-dinner-only days, the busboys were from Pakistan and Bangladesh. They had asked what they should call her, and she had laughingly suggested Begum Fatima, after one of Muhammad's wives. They had laughed, too. She wondered which immigrants had replaced them, and died.

Cathryn Smith recalls her days at Windows on the World as "ancient history" and says that she has no "what if?" thoughts about what her own fate might have been had she continued working there. Similarly, she considers her fight at La Côte Basque "like a dust speck" in women's history. She opened doors, but who cared to enter them?

"It's hard, brutal work" for women and men, and women face the unspeakable behavior of co-workers. "They make it *so* difficult. There are other ways to earn a living."

The fight, though, was more than a dust speck for her. "How it changed *my* life is what was important, I think now," she said. "In its own weird way, it made certain dreams come true for me" and taught her to "stand up for myself."

About fifteen years later, in 1995, La Côte Basque closed its 55th Street doors. The reason was another form of New York real estate: a Disney store got the lease. "Disgusting," Cathryn said cheerfully. Just before the closure, she and a friend went by for a farewell lunch. "They all came over, they were giving us food, they were giving us wine. They were so happy to see me."

Something did not make her happy, however. She looked around and walked around, and she realized that no woman, not one, worked there any longer.

"WE SHOULD BE RESPECTED"
Professionals

WHY DO PEOPLE who have a "career," as opposed to a "job," have the careers they do?

I suspect that the reasons for any particular career choice are many and that the reasons for staying with the choice are usually as much a matter of satisfaction as of money. I also suspect that many professionals believe that career waitresses are different, that these women did not choose waitressing and do not stay in it because they want to.

Such people are often wrong, on both counts.

Meet the pros.

▬▬▬ Margie Watson

"Let me tell you just a little bit about myself," wrote Margie Watson in rounded letters on a lined yellow pad. "I grew up on a farm. After School I left and went to [the] big City of Memphis Tenn. That is when I began my career as a waitress. Yes I love it dearly. I meet all kinds of people from everywhere. I am a big talker. Waitresses not only serve food. But they are Consider[ed] . . . Match Makers Nurses Friends Community workers. You name it and that is what we are." She went on, "I love the power of seeing into a situation. I love making someone happy. I always like to see the results of what I do. I love the Nature of things."

To the letter she mailed me she had stapled the take-out menu of her employer, the Audubon Cafe. "An Old Fashioned Family Restaurant" it read, above a drawing of two ducks (the restaurant's sole nod to nearby Audubon Park) and the motto "Your

Satisfaction Is Our Reputation." One of the priciest breakfast offerings on the menu was the LYB, for $5.99. It included two eggs, bacon or sausage, grits, gravy, hash browns, Belgian waffle or short stack, and toast or biscuits. LYB stands for Loosen Your Belt.

The Audubon Cafe, on Park Avenue in central Memphis, shares a gray stucco building with Chuck's Alterations and the Tennessee Card Company. Across the street is part of Memphis State University. A short drive away is the arresting sight of a sign for The Chatter Box Speech Clinic, and still farther (but never too far for Margie) is Graceland.

One blazing Saturday afternoon, toward the end of her 5 A.M. to 2 P.M. shift, Margie was behaving as if she had just begun. In Audubon-prescribed black, from knit top to thick-soled shoes, she stood, if rarely still, about 5 foot 3. She was doing what needed to be done, and doing it well. At the cash register, she handed back change with a "Y'all have a good day" or a "Come back and see us." On her way to a table, she greeted a bare-armed tattoo-covered man by name. When her next customer ordered a vegetable plate, an economical southern tradition, she exuded approval with every choice made from the Audubon's twenty-three menu items. Spinach casserole: "We sell so much of that," she commented, quickly writing on her pad. Pickled beet slices: "My favorite," she said.

She exuded pride of appearance, too. She was in her late fifties, her short brown hair perm-curled and her smooth, pale skin and thin lips carefully made up. Cloisonné earrings dangled. Strong-looking glasses whose side pieces dipped into a decorative downward swoop magnified unwavering brown eyes.

Her voice is loud, a boon to anyone shouting food orders. In Margie's experience, "Drop me one!" meant that the kitchen should start cooking a chicken-fried steak. "Pig walkin'!" meant putting together a pork barbecue sandwich to go. Her volume asserted its own pronunciations, encompassed in her strong rural Tennessee tones. The word "floor" got two syllables. The word "believe" got one. She referred to her regular customers as her "reggers." She has many. Anyone with a lick of sense would know why.

"To me, being a waitress is something you've got to want to do. I've been in the restaurants where I've seen them come and go by the droves. They've got to have their heart in it. To me, it's really helped me in my lifetime. I've become acquainted with a lot of people in all kinds of work all over the world. People on vacations. When I come home and I get a letter out of the mailbox, I know these people cared—because they done traveled, they've went back home, and they done sit down and took the time to send me a postcard or a letter. I felt there is something I have done inside to make these people happy while they're on vacation.

"The main thing that I get out of [work] is helping older people. It brings tears to my eyes, it does something *to* me, when I see old people out trying to get the door open and, bless their heart, they ain't even got the strength. I enjoy going out and helping these people in. They *thank* you for it. Stuff like that, I guess, has really inspired me more than anything."

Margie has been a waitress for "thirty-something years." She thinks "sometimes I'm getting ready to retire, like my husband right now wants me to quit. [But] I have no desire to want to quit. I will miss my customers. I've gotten into it so much that I don't even think about the money part. I think about the love and the joy I get out of it. When someone tells me they think they would have done been dead a long time ago if it hadn't been for me, that means something. This lady Miss Norton tells me that all the time." Miss Norton told Margie that another waitress, who has since retired to Arkansas, was "grouchy and hateful-like. You'd have to laugh to hear her tell about it. It would crack you up."

The idea of a joke, much less cracking up, comes as a shock. In days of talks at the restaurant, at Margie's home, and in the car to and from Graceland, Margie Watson smiled seldom, laughed less, and seemed a stranger to irony. She would not even josh about the glutton-friendly LYB, commenting only that she had sold a few.

Her career began with a kindly gesture. "Really, I was just nothing but a teenager. We had an older-like guy that owned a cafe in the little small town where I worked at, and I used to go in and hang out like all the kids did. He would get behind, and I would feel sorry for him, because he couldn't get them waited on and they'd be hollerin'. I got up and lent a little helping hand, free of charge. This went on from time to time, and all of a sudden he said one day he couldn't pay me much, but he'd give me a dollar a Saturday to help him out when he was busy. That really is what got me into it."

That dollar meant a lot. "I came from a very poor family, I sure did." The family farm, where her parents "raised cotton and corn and soybeans," was about eighty miles northeast of Memphis, in Crockett County. "To me, even though we didn't have much, there was more love, I b'lieve. Everybody had more time for one another. On weekends, we'd look forward to visiting the neighbors and going to the kinfolk's house, for a Sunday dinner." The six children—three girls and three boys—were taught to work hard, not to use a certain word ("I was raised up to say 'colored folks' "), to make do with little, and to share.

"We went barefooty because we wanted to save our shoes. When our soles started coming off, we used hog reams to keep [them] on." (Hog reams are metal C-shaped clamps.) When socks wore out, Margie took "a needle and thread and you'd whip them holes up and turn 'em back out. You couldn't hardly get your foot in them, they'd been whipped up so many times."

The girls shared their one toy, a "plain old naked rubber doll" they treated "like gold. One time, me and my sisters was down in some chest of drawers, and we seen some little old receiving blankets and baby clothes, and we were just *excited*. We knew mama had bought us some baby clothes to go on that old rubber doll." The girls barely contained their excitement through Christmas. "All of a sudden, after Christmas comes, the blankets and stuff was gone because there was a baby brought home. The baby got the blanket stuff, and our doll still didn't get any." It was news to Margie that the doll had competition. "[You] didn't know back in those days that your mother was pregnant or anything." Her baby brother was born when she was twelve.

Margie did know that brothers were favored. "Daddy gave them five acres apiece of cotton, and whatever that cotton brought, they got money. Us girls never did get any." She also knew that food was scarce. Even as a farmgirl, she "didn't have much to eat."

She gladly gravitated toward restaurants.

Her first Memphis boss was known as Daddy Ray Gammon. "Daddy Ray, he always told me, 'The customer's always right. Whether you think so or not, you've got to let them think they're always right. Don't stoop down to their low and be like them. Smile and say I'm sorry, walk away.' He was the best teacher I ever had.

"It's like when somebody is gripey. A man came in the restaurant one day and he ordered spaghetti. I went by and I noticed he wasn't eating his spaghetti. I said, 'Sir, is something wrong with your spaghetti?' He said, 'Don't worry about it,' and knocked it plumb across the table up against the wall. I reached over and I was just going to get it out of the way. He said, 'Don't touch it!' So I said, 'Oh, excuse me,' you know?

"I went to [Daddy Ray], and I told him what had happened." He told Margie not to charge the man anything if he would not take a replacement meal. "When he came to the register to pay his ticket, I said, 'Sir, you don't owe me a dime.' 'Yes, I do, yes, I do.' He was real hollerin' now. I said, 'Your spaghetti is on us, because you didn't eat it. Undoubtedly there was something wrong with it.' He said, 'I insist on paying the bill,' and I said, 'I insist that we don't take the money from the customers if they're not satisfied. That's our policy.'" The man left.

Two hours later, Margie felt a tap on her shoulder. "I had done forgot about the incident, because I had been so busy. He come back and he said, 'Ma'am, you went out of your way to be extra nice to me. You apologized. You tried every way under the sun to make me happy.' And he said, 'I was so rude to you it's pathetic. My conscience is bothering me. I've come back to pay for that spaghetti, because it cost y'all money. To begin with, it wasn't nothing wrong with it.' He said, 'Me and my wife had just had a fight when I came in here, and I come in and took it out on y'all's spaghetti and on you.'"

The next thing Margie knew, the man not only paid for his spaghetti but also tipped her three dollars, "just for *one guy*."

An even more memorable occurrence took place at Daddy Ray's on August 16, 1977: the electrifying news blew in that hometown hero Elvis Presley was dead. "They cut the programs off and they come in live, on the TV, the radio. It was a standstill. Everybody was coming through the doors listening. 'What's on the TV? What's on the radio? Listen, listen . . . ' Couldn't nobody get nobody waited on, 'cause everybody was standing there trying to get all the answers. It was about like it was when Martin Luther King got assassinated here. *Here* they do anything. The South, they was always against it." Margie ended her switched story—her "it" surely meant what Dr. King was striving for—with uncharacteristic softness, decibels lower than when she began.

When Daddy Ray decided to retire and sell the restaurant, Margie made a shrewd career move. Rather than finding another job, she found another owner—a man who had no idea that this was her plan for him. He was an employee of Sears and a regular customer. "I started out at him in a joking manner about buying the restaurant. Finally, he said he wanted to talk to me." She got him. "He was an easygoing person, and I thought this was something I could work him into." She was right. "It wasn't nothing he wouldn't tackle. You'd tell him you was busy and needed this, he'd be right in there with all hands, feets, everything."

Only when the property itself was sold some time later did Margie go to the Audubon Cafe. When a new owner, a food salesman with no restaurant experience, later took over there, along with his wife, again Margie did the training. She thought they worked out so well that she had a plaque made:

Congratulations to Robert and Jill Conklin
For 5 years of hard work and devoted service

During Margie's early years at the Audubon, her round-trip commute was 115 miles. Home, where her first husband, their two sons, and her in-laws lived, was the in-laws' farm in "Missippi," as she pronounced it. "I took care of them when they got down sick and waited on them hand and foot, because they didn't have a daughter." They willed the farm to her, not their son. "After they died, my husband—my ex—he starting running around. He got worse and worse and worse, and, um, he chose another woman."

The Audubon assumed renewed focus in Margie's life.

The dining room—"old-timey," she called it—features wooden chairs and tables, vinyl booths, and a hodgepodge of local calendars, baskets, artificial plants, and framed testimonials from appreciative civic groups. (Margie herself actively volunteers for the Optimists Club.) Below a huge board that lists specials is the window where orders are shouted to the kitchen and then clipped to burned wooden clothespins dangling from a wire. Smells radiating from the kitchen, where a massive steel dough machine helps cooks turn out hundreds of rolls and pans of cornbread daily, are entirely enticing. The cafe's clientele ingests not only massive amounts of carbohydrates. The drink of choice, iced tea (known, of course, simply as tea), is served in plastic tumblers the size of oil drums. The Audubon, with its menu rich in regionalism, reflects its southern history—as does its staff: an almost all African American kitchen staff, mainly white servers, and white ownership. In a way, then, the Audubon meets expectations.

Around Margie Watson, however, expectations take flight.

At 2 P.M., when her shift is over and she is walking more slowly, it is apparent she has a limp. It is more apparent she is displeased that her replacement has not shown up. The young woman, cheerfully apologetic, will be ten minutes late—an hour in waitress time. In those minutes, Margie does allow herself to sit and then begins rolling napkins to help the next shift.

She also catches up with her friend, fellow waitress Marie Coats, who has the distinction of having gone to school with Elvis. "O-oh, he was fine!" exclaims Marie. Her friend is more circumspect on this subject. When I asked whether she was an Elvis fan, Margie's browns remained steady. "Yes. I am."

Margie is solemn about the demands of her job, too. She will say,

"It's hard work. 'Cause it's all standing on your feet and legs. It's a lot of liftin', it's a lot of totin', it's a lot of puttin' up with, listening to." It is a lot more than that. Taped to a wall is a list of handwritten cleanup commands. Margie and a waitress named Rene are to clean the pick-up windows, the rack, the tea table (including under it), the microwave and breadwarmer, the shelves by the water buckets, the salad bar, the steam table, and the jelly, syrup, and honey containers as well as clean the "condiment containers" and wipe the tables in their own stations.

There is an equally long list for prep work, which Margie summarized. She and Rene "set up everything for breakfast. [Then] we tear things down from breakfast, turn around and set it back up for lunch," including the salad bar. After lunch, they "sweep the floor, fill up our condiments on the table, and do our side work." For all that, plus waitressing, hostessing, cashiering, and busing tables, five days a week, nine hours without a break, Margie is paid $2.13 an hour.

"It's chicken feed," she said, tersely. At the time (1995), federal minimum wage was $4.25 an hour, but the law includes a provision that employees who receive tips can be paid less than minimum wage. A number of states, and thus many of their restaurants, decided that less was better. Margie was also earning half of minimum wage, however, for nontipped work. "From five 'til we open at six-thirty—an hour and a half—we're going ninety miles an hour, trying to get all the stuff done. For two dollars thirteen cents an hour. And there's no tips involved there. We can mop the floor at one-thirty to two-thirty. There's no tips involved *there*." The clincher: Margie is so good that Robert Conklin promoted her to be the Audubon's manager. He did not pay her a penny more.

Audubon waitresses, moreover, are customer-rich but tip-poor. "Now, I got one customer I really get irritated at. He comes in every day, and he's going to sit in my station. I don't car-r-re [what]," she trilled, "he's going to sit in my station. He brings a newspaper in, he gets a plate lunch, and he drinks water. He sits there the *whole* lunch hour. See, I can't get any more customers because he's held up my whole booth. And the highest I've ever seen him leave was forty cents."

Low tips deliver a double whammy. Since passage of the 1987 federal law tightening the requirements for reporting of taxable tips, employers and employees are under more scrutiny. Tax laws require restaurants to report all their food and beverage sales as income, and servers are supposed to report all their tips as income. Obviously, if the Internal Revenue Service audits a restaurant, it can use the restaurant's sales figures to estimate tips to servers (not to mention other employees such as busboys, who are tipped by the servers) and can charge back taxes.

In Margie's interpretation of low tippers, she loses all around. First, she gets a low tip. Second, the IRS may assume that she was tipped more than she was. She also seemed to be operating under the old rule of thumb of declaring tips (as taxable income) based on 8 percent of her sales. Thus, the more she sold, the more she would be taxed, no matter how poor the tip.

"A lot of people knows, these reggers that come in [here], they don't tip." The Audubon staff is not anxious to wait on the low-tipping regulars anyway—"and if they do, they're not going to go and encourage them to get dessert, because the more you add on that bill, it's the more taxes you're going to have to pay. If you really think about it, it's discouraging."

Discouragements abound. During the same lunch hour in which she often waits on the forty-cent man, "two little coffee drinkers" hold up another of her booths. "Now, these two guys don't work," she fumed. "One day I did get irritated. I was so busy. I walked by, and he said, 'Margie, can we have some more coffee?' I looked at him and said, 'This ain't no coffee shop during lunch hour, do you understand? You done had four cups, and you ain't getting any more.' " Another man, who ignored her recital of the breakfast specials, including "a choice of grits, gravy, or hash browns," caused her to make eight trips to his table. She recited each encounter in detail. "Liver over creamed potatoes," who comes in every Friday, does not tip very much, but, she said grimly, she has to make only two trips for him. Elderly "Miss Betsy," who sits in Margie's station daily, counts among the time takers. "She wants me to listen to her problems. I'll listen for a while and then I'll say, 'Miss Betsy, I've got to go. I've got customers to wait on.'

"The bad ones . . . takes away from your good ones, [so you can't] do for them like you would want to do. I've had regular customers I've known for thirty years that were probably empty on tea, and I was knowing I needed to get a tea pitcher and get right back up to 'em before they had to go back to work. I have seen 'em get up and leave before I could get a chance, because of the bad ones running me to death.

"Back when I first started being a waitress, everybody dreaded waiting on a woman. Nowadays, the women tip better than the men do. I think this all happened when the women got out and went to work. If you give women real good service, some of them will double-tip you, just to show the 'preciation. Men—to me, they don't care whether you go out of your way or how much you have to run. I've got one man, he's not going to leave but a dollar," whether he comes in alone or with a party of twenty-five.

If he put a penny on his buck, Margie would have inferred another message. "That means good service. Two ones and two pennies, that means *double* good service." Margie has been thus rewarded, but such rewards add up only emotionally.

"Somebody ought to do something, because if my husband wasn't retired and drawing a check, I couldn't make it with what sometimes I make . . . a day." She added a line that could work in a country song: "Some times are better than others, but you never know when those better times are going to be."

Margie was in a livelier mood that evening, following a visit to the Graceland souvenir shops. We had dinner at a mall, where two wait-resses, formerly of the Audubon, embraced her, gushed that she was such a whiz at organization that she could do in two minutes what took them ten, and then scolded her for going back to work so soon after her angioplasty. To my alarm, she confirmed that, yes, she had had the procedure three weeks earlier. (Every night Margie takes pills for her heart and puts nitroglycerine patches on her chest.) And one of the wait-resses chided her: Margie "came up there hobbling around on one foot" after a hip operation. Several hip operations, it turned out, including a total replacement. (She almost hurt her hip again recently, by tripping while running at the Audubon to answer a phone that turned out to be a customer's cell phone.) Furthermore, the two waitresses chorused, Robert Conklin does not appreciate Margie.

Driving home later, her face in the dark, Margie's voice became un-commonly light as she described someone who does appreciate her.

Clyde Watson had phoned the Audubon one December to see whether it would be open over Christmas. At the time, he had been a widower for two years.

It was Margie who told him no, the Audubon would be closed. When he asked what an old man like himself should do for something to eat, Margie had a frisky reply. "I was in a good spirit, you know, Christmas time, and I said, 'Sir, the onlyest I can suggest is you find you a young good-lookin' blonde to come and cook for you.' He said, 'I don't know if you're a blonde or not, but you sound like a young, good-lookin' woman,'" and promptly invited her out for dinner. Margie informed him that she saw enough food as it was. Clyde was not dissuaded.

A World War II veteran—he had barely survived a German torpedo attack on his ship during D-Day preparations[1]—and a retired railroad engineer nineteen years Margie's senior, Clyde suffers from obesity and emphysema but not shyness. After the Christmas holidays, he showed up at the Audubon. "He said, 'I'm looking for that young, good-lookin' girl.' I tried to wiggle out, that I didn't know nothing about no phone call." Then Clyde recognized her voice. "I probably turned every color in the *book*." He asked her out again, and again, but still she refused. He then made a smart move: "He started being a regular."

Clyde's courtship by now was the talk of the Audubon. Staff opinion was unanimous: have dinner with the man. Margie did. Soon, "I got to wondering" whether he was married. Margie had known a lying husband before. So, on one date, when Clyde stopped by his house to put his dog out, Margie decided to follow him inside. "I thought, this is my chance. I'll walk through and see if there's a woman here. You can spot women's stuff." And? "There was no indications." She remained skeptical, though, until he made another smart move: he showed her his wife's death certificate. Reassured and lonely, she melted. "His kindness is what made me fall in love with him. It happened just about over nothing."

After work, Margie goes straight home to Clyde, driving up to a ranch-style house whose front yard whirls with oversize plastic flowers. The house, where Clyde lived alone after his first wife's death, has, under Margie's attention, been decorated to a fare-thee-well, with every frill and bow imaginable. "Oh, I changed it from one end to the other. It was plain Jane."

Nursing a glass of tea in the den (which had escaped some, but not all, frills), she leaned back in a Barcalounger and allowed that, over the decades, some things have changed in the restaurant business.

She is no longer sticking to all Daddy Ray's maxims, like the customer always being right. "I tell Robert, 'The customer is not going to curse me. If he don't want me to curse him, he's not going to curse me.' Me, personal, say maybe ten or fifteen years ago, I would [have been] scared to death to say anything back. But today, no, ma'am." Marriage to a man who collects pensions has made the difference.

There has been no change, in her telling, about the legacy of racism. "We've got one waitress that hates waiting on blacks with a passion, and she makes it well known. The kitchen help has caught on, and they'll call her racist." Margie pronounced the word as though it seemed new to her. She agrees with the staff and has confronted the waitress. "I said,

'We don't pick customers in here.' " Margie now added, "I have found out it takes a lot longer to get a black person's order, because they want to change their order all the time." Although African American customers also seemed to want an array of extras—straws, a lot of napkins, lemons in their water—many such customers have become her regulars. "I love 'em. Sure do." Also, they "tip real good."

She seemed uncomfortable when talking of integrated construction crews who came in as customers, ate together (their back-pocket screwdrivers sometimes punching holes in newly covered vinyl seats), and used the common slur when talking to each other. "You always having some of the whites or some of the blacks saying, 'You better get to work, nigger,' and this kind of stuff." One day she spoke up to the recipient. "I said, 'You gonna sit there and take that off of them?' He said, 'I'm used to it.' " She believed him. "It goes on in business down here all the time." The businesses include the Audubon; an African American man in the kitchen had used the word to Margie the day before while telling her a tall story.

She paused. "I had an incident this week with one of the black guys that was serving food from the steam table." She recalled, with the same detail she used for all encounters that touched her emotionally, that while serving a table, she had seen that her tray was short an order of pinto beans, and she went back for it. " 'George, I need a side order of pinto beans. You forgot and left it off my ticket.' 'Get it in a minute.' You're standing there, and you're losing time that you could have . . . took that and been getting somebody else's order or somebody else's drink." After asking George for the beans "about four times" while he stood there "running his mouth," she said, "I did call him a name."

Margie put down her glass of tea. "It wasn't nice." Yes, she said, it starts with *n*. George's reaction was to laugh. "He looked at me sort of funny, and I said, 'I said it, and I meant it.' " He laughed more, and the next day he was still laughing. She exploded. He gets paid no matter what, she told him, but she does not. Think about it, she demanded. If customers leave for lack of pinto beans, the Audubon will close, and he and she will both lose their jobs. "The next day he started being extra nice to me."

One day—Margie being Margie and racism being a more sociologically intimate event in the South than elsewhere—she held forth right there in the Audubon kitchen on the topic. "I said, 'I wasn't here during slavery time. I didn't have anything to do with it. If any of my ancestors did, God's not going to make me pay for what they did wrong. The day of the Judgment Day, I've got to answer to the good Lord myself.' I said, 'I get tired of being blamed because I'm white. I don't know no more about what happened back then than y'all do today. Y'all wasn't there, I wasn't there, we don't even know what went on. So *why* have we got to have hard feelings between us when it was something we didn't even know anything about?' They said, 'Well, you're right.'"

In contrast to her thoughts about black co-workers (almost every anecdote she told was serious), she seemed mostly bemused about white co-workers. If anything notable involving them goes on after she leaves, she learns about it from Marie, who works until closing. "When she gets home, she'll call me and tell me about so-and-so getting into it, mouth-wise. [Waitresses] crying or getting mad, or Cliff the little night manager getting on to them about what they *wore*. I call it nit-pit stuff." She does, spelling it out, *n-i-t p-i-t*. In a recent nit-pit drama, Robert ordered Cliff to tell "the little racist girl" she needed a doctor's note after calling in sick. (Word had spread that she was really going to a concert.) Her angry boyfriend thereupon threatened Cliff: "'I'm going to close y'all up.' He tells Cliff he's some kind of a li'l ol' marshal." Cliff was so upset that he hung up the phone. Soon the boyfriend stormed in, yelling, "Man, you ain't gonna hang up no phone in *my* ear!" Cliff ran to the office, the boyfriend followed, Cliff threatened to call the police. . . . Marie reported it all.

Margie could laugh at escapades the waitresses initiated, but actions directed toward them were another matter. She shot up in the Barca-lounger, riled, when recalling an upset young waitress who had recently confided in her that a customer wanted her to go out with him for "wrongdoings."

"They think because [a woman's] a waitress, [she's] not dedicated to a family home. I feel like people don't want to respect waitresses. They think we're nothing in life. But I've come a long way with being a wait-ress. I'm a churchgoer," Margie added. She is "not knocking anybody" who does not go to church and likewise thinks nobody should knock anyone who serves food for a living. "Deep down inside, I really feel like we should be respected, just like any secretary, any factory worker. We're as important in life as anybody working for Federal Express, or Holiday Inns, or whatever."

Réka Nagy

With "my European background," she said, "I have an idea of what serving means. I was raised with 'how to serve.' I saw how my mother dealt with her [servants]. There is a way. Europeans know this. Although in America we don't have classes, supposedly, of course we do. There is something to be said for . . . classes. Everybody knows their place and how to behave in their level."

Réka Nagy was born in Hungary. Shortly after World War II, she moved with her family to London, where her father worked in the foreign service. When the Soviet Union invaded Hungary, he resigned both diplomacy and homeland and took the family to a parish in Canada (he was also a minister) and later to Ohio. By then in her teens, all Réka wanted to do was to fit in and be an American. It was while waitressing, to earn money for school, that her memory of old-world class systems returned.

"There are responsibilities that belong to each class," she continued, "and there are benefits. Of course, in an ideal world, aristocrats would behave nobly and the happy peasants would enjoy being happy. It doesn't work that way, really, because people are imperfect, and so they have revolutions and we have America."

She was speaking in an egalitarian setting she had chosen, a busy self-serve muffin shop in lower Manhattan. Clad in fuchsia and lavender from head to toe, including earrings (a gift from her daughter), she stood out by hue alone. Even her short hair was tinted magenta. The color was a choice, but the style was not: her hair was growing back after chemotherapy. End of subject, she said.

The idea of serving, she went on, in a precise manner that indicated British cadence, "does have this effect that people are very uncomfortable [with] in America. [They] don't know how to deal with a servant or service people." Even the term "waiting on me" causes uneasiness. "If you're the waitress, though, it's your job to overcome the problem for both you and the customer. It *is* a problem for both. We're all 'equal' here."

Such supposed equality leads to the horror, she shuddered, of name exchanges. "Every once in a while you get, 'I'm Joe and this is my wife Sally.' 'Lovely to meet you.' This is what I mean—people's discomfort. Are we supposed to be friends? What are we here? You're guests, but not at my *house*."

Similarly, when a customer is asked, "Would you care for something at the bar?" and does not want a drink, the answer should simply be no. "We don't need to discuss your medical condition [or] your moral strictures about the consumption of alcohol. I want to know what you drink and I'll get it. Period." Maybe customers want her to understand they are not being cheap? Réka looked ready to hurl her muffin. "You never explain to a servant why, or what the master or the mistress wants. They've spoken. That's it.

"I dream of opening up a school to teach people, because I think nowadays it's so poorly done." Servers do not know to serve from the left with the left hand and take from the right with the right hand, Réka lamented, before explaining why the system made sense to her. "Most people are right-handed, so if they're having a drink, they're liable to reach just when you're serving, so you put it from the *left* and curve your arm around so they don't have the elbow." She sighed. "In Europe, you don't walk in and say, 'I'm going to wait on tables.' You have to learn how. It's considered a profession."

The professional who taught her more than anyone was her late husband, Charlie. Their union was a restaurant love story. Hungarian waitress meets Greek Cypriot chef/boss after both make their way to Manhattan. She is twenty-four, he is forty-five. He has the years, she has the height—when she wears heels, his head reaches her chin. Among their first adventures was working together during the city's famous 1965 blackout.

"We were one of only four restaurants in all of New York City that served complete meals. He was something else. The minute the power went off, he sent out the guys to corner the market on candles, on dry ice. They made a lot of candles with glasses. You fill them with oil and undo a paper clip and stick it through string, and they make wonderful flickering romantic lights. On every table we had several of these." The staff quickly made some to illuminate the kitchen, too. The stoves, which were gas, worked. The dishwasher, which was electric, did not. Réka washed dishes by hand. "My hands were covered with cuts. I was bleeding," she laughed. "Everyone was so busy, they simply threw the plates in the water." That night was one of the best in her and Charlie's quarter-century together.

With his encouragement, she learned "about the business" by buying books, including the *Encyclopedia of Wines and Spirits,* and by subscribing to *Gourmet* magazine. As she read, "Charlie cooked all kinds of food. Sauces, stocks. We ate out, read about herbs, spices, California wines, all kinds of ethnic cooking. We had friends in the business with whom we got together and had experimental dinners, some of which were fabulous and others not." He, of the "old guard," conveyed more lessons.

"My husband believed you should know how to make" or at least know every ingredient in "every sauce on the menu." He also believed you can teach "the mechanics" and much about food and wine, but "you can't teach people personality. People know if you resent coming to their table and resent bringing them their food."

After hours and after customers, Réka and Charlie kept the personality going. "God, the entire crew used to get *stoned*. Drinking, cocaine. You're like this"—she made a crazy face—"if it's really busy and tense, and you need to relax and unwind. I had a drinking problem for a while. Go out every night until four or five in the morning." Often the night ended with Charlie making breakfast for everyone back home. His poor health ended up saving hers. After he had heart surgery, the couple explored moderate behavior.

About 1970, she and he moved from Manhattan to "a real small town" in food terms: Chicago. The only variation from daily orders of steak and potatoes, she said, was lake perch on Fridays. "That was it. 'Tail piece well done,' " she laughed.

She and Charlie went as upscale as they could, she as waitress, he as chef or maître d'. When Chicago eventually moved beyond lake perch, Réka was ready, even if the public was not.

"You have to teach people what this food is, and how to eat it, and how to enjoy it, and [to] try the wine." The most sophisticated customers, she said, asked questions.

Réka waited tables for one of Chicago's traditionalist restaurateurs, Bill Mallick, who hired waitresses, she said, because he found that waiters stole. She benefited from her gender again when a newcomer, Rick Melman, arrived and decided to use costumed women in notable roles. "We had the female captains who were dressed in black long skirts, slit up to here, and a cream-colored dickie, very elegant and ladylike." The men "were strictly the waiters and the busboys."

As she acquired more experience, she also learned logistics—for example, figuring out seat numbers. "Number one is traditionally the seat closest to the kitchen door. The other numbers follow clockwise, but this can vary according to the peculiarities of a given restaurant. With round tables, where the number of seats can vary, you often have to tell your team members 'lady in red is number one.' Can you believe some restaurants don't number their tables? In that situation, I always assigned my own numbers, just so I could work. The numbering of individual seats became automatic also, and busboys quickly learned. It makes it so much easier to be able to say 'Number two on six needs a napkin.' Pointing is *out*."

Some of what Réka learned appalled her. In the bar of a restaurant owned by a former Playboy club manager, she was told to put the mix (such as club soda) into a highball glass, "then the bartender was supposed to float a little booze on top. If you asked for a Scotch and soda, you would get that first taste of Scotch and then a lot of water." At a "trendy, popular" place, she was told to refold used napkins, for serving wine. "I found this disgusting and tried to sneak clean napkins, but sometimes the owner was watching and I couldn't. One day, I shook a used napkin open to dry a bottle from the ice bucket and saw to my horror a big wad of phlegm clinging to the napkin. Luckily, it was on my side, and the customers did not see it."

Her complaints at both places got her fired.

She took on customers, too, with mixed results. One man who (among other outrages) summoned her with a loud "Pssst!" was "impossible." When she happened to see him leaving the restaurant after she finished her shift, "I felt this is my own time now." She told him there was something she had wanted to say all night, delivered a Bronx cheer, and walked away. "You so seldom get to do *anything*," she said, beaming over her muffin crumbs.

A customer at Chicago's Tango restaurant got a written version of Réka's wrath. "This man should have known better. He was a businessman; he had three people he was entertaining. I saw what he wanted, and I provided superb service. They had a great time, and they ate and drank up a storm." After her four hours of work, he tipped barely 10 percent. "It was the insult of not appreciating what I had done. I made his customers very happy." In a fit of pique, Réka wrote "amateur tipper" on the man's American Express form—and again got fired.

She was always flabbergasted if her skills were not rewarded. One night the host of a party of twelve ordered a certain wine with dinner. When she realized that four bottles would be needed, but only one was chilled, she rushed into action to prepare the other three bottles. "I had to quick-chill it with the salt, packed in ice, twirling it and all that, and run around and keep pouring, never mind the rest of the meal." The host later told her that he never tips on wine.

What people like him do not realize, she said, is that tips keep meal costs down. If employers paid servers "decently," equivalent to a 15 percent tip, they also would have to pay taxes and Social Security fees and tack those on to meal costs too.

Réka nonetheless likes the tipping system. "If I'm better at pleasing people and taking care of them and they tip me accordingly and I make more than you do, I feel good."

One of her "money-making tricks," as she called them, was memorizing orders, "which was particularly effective with conventioneers." They even placed bets with each other on whether she would get their orders right. Her trick then commenced. "It was like a mental tape recorder. Click on, stare into the person's face—prime rib MR, baked with sour cream, butter, and bacon, creamy garlic dressing—click off." Twelve orders was her limit. "When I brought the food, I'd look at their faces, and the playback would click on." In congratulation or compensation, both winners and losers then tipped her more.

"My nicest tip, my favorite ever" came from a child whose family Réka waited on at a Jewish deli in Montreal. "The littlest girl was about five. The father paid the check. It must have been she saw him putting money beside his plate, because when I came to the table to say goodbye, she said"—Réka imitated a child's voice—" 'There's a surprise for you under my plate.' I said, 'Really? Can I look?' So we looked and there was a nickel. She had obviously taken her very own money. Now, when you're five years old and you have a nickel and that's all you have and you give it to somebody, that is a truly generous tip."

At the peak of her career, Réka landed work at Chicago's Pump Room. It was a "wonderful period" in her life, she smiled.

One evening there, an especially "handsome, tall" manager named Bill, wearing the requisite black tuxedo, knelt to check a loose corner of the brown and black carpet. "I'm coming out from the kitchen with my cocktail tray with two drinks on it, a Bloody Mary and a glass of red wine. I don't see him, and all is dark—the lights are dim, atmospheric. I walk right into him and go flying. My hitting him sent *him* flying. The two of us are full-length spread on the floor. He is holding one side of the tray because, as I hit him, he turned around and saw me coming and grabbed the tray. *I* had the tray on the other side. And the drinks did not spill!"

She began laughing. "We are lying there, and all the tables start applauding. Bill jumped up, held his hand, pulled me up—I still have my tray in my other hand—and we took a little bow. That was a moment you could do a thousand times and never [have it] happen again. It was wonderful."

She also was a captain at the Pump Room, again partly because of her gender. "Their gimmick [was] to have female captains." She did "all the talking with the customer" and oversaw a waiter in the front of the house, one in the back of the house, and a busboy. "You really have a team of four people." Her skills were important, she added. Women "have to concentrate on knowing more, doing more, being more, the best of whatever you can be. And that's what opens the doors." Soon she was promoted to training captain and "trained all the waiters, all the busboys, all the captains. When I was doing the training, I used to say, 'Grab them by the balls before their ass hits the chair.'

"The idea," she said, grinning at my rather rapid blink, "was that you have to get control. Then the customers can relax and enjoy themselves. They know they're in good hands."

At the Pump Room, her maxim faced constant tests. One evening, a family was honoring an older woman "who was a real termagant. We were barely getting started and she started giving me orders and completely interfering with what I was trying to do to make it work." Among her orders was that the tables be moved. Réka took her aside and, "lightly enough, but very definite," explained that she got paid to worry, not the customer. She asked the woman to signal if something was not right, but otherwise to sit down, get everyone else to sit down, and "start enjoying yourself." The woman "had something to do, ordering everybody else around, not me." The family sat down and started talking, and before long "she had a wonderful time."

Nobody was happier than the son-in-law ("this guy must love his wife a lot"), who overheard Réka telling his mother-in-law to behave. He gave a big tip of appreciation, then his wife slipped Réka a tip, too, although Réka protested she had been paid. Finally, so did the guest of honor, despite further protest. "I know, but I want you to have this from *me*." Réka thus netted a "triple hit."

She estimates servers have thirty seconds to read and grab. "It can be a hot romance. It can be old marrieds. It can be he's gay and she's married, but they're friends. It can be brother and sister. It can be business. She's selling him, he's selling her. You have to know the difference, and it's in the body language. As I get to the table, I look at everyone but focus on the head of the party. I am seeing and sorting a lot of information: ages, hairstyles. Facial hair on men tells a lot—vanity, illusions, affectations, poses. Clothing, shoes, grooming. I listen to *how* they talk, as well as what they say."

Body language was never more important than when Réka was assigned to wait on the Karmapa whom she described as the "highest teacher" to Tibetan Buddhists, and dozens of other non-English-speaking Tibetan monks who would be dining with him. Just before their arrival, she went to the Pump Room's special dining room to make sure everything was in order for their meal of steaks and soft drinks. Instead of calm, she encountered American Buddhist organizers who "were running around like maniacs. 'Karmapa's coming! Karmapa's coming!' They're frantic. 'You have to serve everybody in the right order.' "

Réka had no idea what the right order was. Suddenly the Tibetans came "sweeping in. Young ones, old ones. They seat themselves. Apparently *they* knew." All she knew, by easy observation, was which diner was the Karmapa. "I'm thinking, 'How do I know [who's next] after I serve him?' " The answer was to read the group.

After serving the Karmapa, the next person to be served sat up with a certain posture: she raised her chin, as if she were a notable. " 'Right here.' " When Réka finished the first table, chins at the next ranking table went up, and she found the head person there. "It was the body language. I knew exactly who was next and who was next [after them]." Not a word was ever exchanged.

She leaned back in her chair in the muffin shop. "The thing about eating, it's the only basic function that is socially sanctioned to be performed in public. You shit in private, you make love in private. But eating—it's the most revealing thing people do publicly. I'll tell you about Jesse Jackson. I took care of him one night. He came in with a gorgeous, gorgeous blonde. I approached the table, and just getting his attention—forget it. Finally he deigned. 'Would you like anything from the bar?' 'Do you have any fresh-squeezed peach juice?' Come on. That was how it started. It was like pulling teeth to get him to look at me, answer me, give me an order. He came here presumably to eat and drink, but [did not] want to order." Once he finally did, "he ordered for himself first."

Two other celebrity customers were the opposite. Vernon Jordan "was sophisticated, charming, knew his food and wine, ordered beautifully, was gracious, and was a twenty percent tipper." Yul Brynner was with "a gorgeous female, who he was obviously interested in, but each time I came to that table, his total attention focused on me." In fifteen seconds, "we got the proper wine, we got the fresh fish cooked the way he liked it, everything. When Yul Brynner focuses on you with those burning eyes and that deep voice . . . how deftly he handled it."

Réka observed, patting a last crumb from her lips, that if she ever does open a school to teach waiters and waitresses, she would also have to teach customers. "Really good service is always a collaboration."

Patty Devon

"Going out after work was the *best* thing. We would talk about the *food,* we would talk about 'That guy, did you hear him? Oh, I thought I was going to have to slap him.' Endless. We would rehash that night for five hours and get plastered. One night, we invented a resort where waiters could go." The fictional haven featured a room with a punching bag. "I have *long* advocated this. Every restaurant needs a punching bag. I used to go in the walk-in [refrigerator] and scream and scream. All it got me was a sore throat." Sometimes she went in the walk-in not to exhale but to inhale; it was a safe place to smoke dope.

Patty Devon, a tall, pretty woman of delicate features, with many tiny earrings traipsing up her ears' sides, leads a cleaner life than she used to. Her home, part of a converted house in one of New Orleans's famously charming, raggedy neighborhoods (although not one of the safer ones), is furnished with visible care, thrift, and evidence of overcoming her past. A card congratulates her on an anniversary of sobriety.

While patting her companion, a large dog, goodbye, she paused to explain some puzzling decor. An exuberance of drapery—voluptuous swoops and swags bedecking every window—is out of keeping with the modest dwelling. Her father, she said, had been an aeronautics engineer in Washington state who found a less stressful calling as a draper back here in his hometown. Everywhere she moves, he does this, she smiled, gesturing. He and her mother run the drapery company. Earlier, her mother had been a waitress.

Patty picked up the thread of the story in my burnished hotel room in the French Quarter. Sounds of outside revelers split the night, while she sipped ice water. All but enfolded within the wings of an old armchair, she looked weary from her day waiting tables at an Italian restaurant in the suburb of Metairie, but she talked with animation about her first connection to the job.

"My mother told me stories, the whole time I was growing up, about waitressing. I'm sure she did glamorize it. In the forties, when she was rooming with other women, they would [have office jobs], making fourteen dollars a week, and she'd be making a hundred and forty dollars.

That had some influence. I was your basic, unskilled person." After high school in Washington, when "I came back to New Orleans, there was a restaurant job open through a friend of my mom's. It was fine dining and *all* women, which was very unusual." As Patty knows too well, New Orleans glories in its near-sacred restaurants, legendary in part for their obsequious male waitstaffs. "Fine dining is locked up. That's men." She paused. "I don't know why people like being waited on by men so much. Maybe it's a societal attitude that women are *supposed* to serve you. 'Gee, my mom served me food my whole life, and now my wife serves me food. Why should a woman [be paid to] serve me food? That's nothing.' "

The all-women restaurant, a curiosity named Roje's, started Patty as a busgirl, "invisible" and silent. "You could go a whole night without saying a word to a customer except, 'May I help you with your coat?' " Patty's mouth may have been closed during her introduction to restaurant work, but her eyes were wide open.

She was "in awe" of how one waitress (a future insurance agent) increased tips. "She walked up to this table of two couples one night—the women were dripping in diamonds, the men had on thousand-dollar Italian suits—and said, 'I'm sorry, I'm going to have to ask you all to leave. We do have a dress code and you are underdressed.' I was petrified. Oh, my God, this is horrible, why is she doing this? I wouldn't even attempt that. Of course, they went like"—Patty mimed someone flipping bills from a wad—"whoosh, whoosh, whoosh, peeled off the money because she was so amusing."

After a month as a busgirl, "they *promoted* me," Patty said with theatrical self-deprecation, "to a waitress. It was fabulous. I still rate that as one of the best jobs I've ever had."

On her first day waiting tables, she realized being a silent busgirl had not been good training. "I was like, g-g-g-o-o . . ."—she mimed someone too choked by fright to speak. "I had to *talk* to these people! I was terrified. 'They're looking at me!' It was very nerve-wracking, but I got over it *really* fast. You know why? Even though I may not have very good self-esteem, there's a ham in there dying to entertain. I believe that's the part that came out to save me, because before long it was like I had been doing it all my life."

Roje's was several rungs down the social ladder from the places that would have refused to hired her, but during Louisiana's boom of the late 1970s, Patty Devon made too much money to care. "Oil was big. It was trickle-down economics, and it *really* did trickle down. Everyone got some." Conspicuous consumption was in. "That was women and furs and double martinis and eight-course meals." The excess included tips. It became "traditional," she said, for waitresses to receive tips amounting to "a hundred percent of the bill." A modest meal of sixty dollars? " 'Here's sixty for you.' "

"Through the restaurant grapevine, all the waiters in town knew about the place and knew how much money we were making, so male waiters would come in to apply and the maître d' would say, 'I'm sorry, we only hire women.' " The reason was sex. "We dressed like French maids. That was *real* big. French maids, only it was about this short." She pointed to her mid-thigh. "Actually, they were kind of tacky-looking."

Between shifts, Patty had a perfect audience in her mother. "She got a vicarious thrill out of talking with me. I would come home and talk about *people*. Wearing that stupid French maid's uniform, there was some flirtation going on, especially when a tableful of men would come in. We would wait on all the Mafia." Everyone knew who they were, she said, imitating a friendly shout between waitresses: "The Mafia's here!" To her, the mobsters, except for one "scary-looking" man, were "big goofy guys" who talked about grocery stores and the race track.

At Roje's, Patty Devon made a major decision: waitressing would be her career. "When I had that first job, I knew right away this was something I wanted to do. I loved it. We used to take an *hour* to set up, and when it was time to open, the lights would go down. It was very show business-y. That really stuck with me over the years."

The oil boom did end, however, and with its demise Roje's ended, too, but Patty kept working in upscale restaurants, priding herself on professionalism. "Every place has at least one 'star waiter.' I've even been that star waiter. I don't know why." One owner gave her several hundred dollars " 'for your great work.' That is *unheard* of," she smiled. "No matter where I worked, I was well received, and I was okay inside, knowing I had chosen to do something and I was good at it. I don't know what else human beings look for in their work.

"Meanwhile, seventeen years go by." In that time, she worked in about a hundred restaurants, she estimated. The major reason she left any of them was "not enough money. New Orleans is *very* seasonal, except for some of the established [restaurants]," which would not hire her anyway because of her gender.

The more professional Patty became, the more upset she became with co-workers who did not share her standards. Staff put-downs of customers pained her. At one restaurant, "their favorite phrase was 'peasants.' 'I've got peasants at table [six] . . . ' Waiting on stuck-up people made the waiters be really stuck-up." At the well-known Mr. B's, Patty worked "with some of the crappiest waiters I've ever worked with in my life." She shifted in her chair. "Here's a small personal peeve. I don't believe in saying the *same* thing to every goddamned table like a machine, treating every table like they're cattle. Shabby service, real perfunctory. I was shocked at how much they didn't care."

She did develop another peeve: uniforms. "We have jokes about it. [A customer will] say to this other waitress, 'Did you get that glass of wine?' I'm at the bar picking up the glass of wine. The girl he asked is five foot four with a long blonde ponytail, and I'm five foot eight with short brown hair. They don't *look* at us, which is one reason it's so frustrating when [owners want] to make you look a certain way. I guess you're an extension of their *ego*—'You're presenting my restaurant.' "

Still, she knew she "wanted to stay in the restaurant business for the rest of my life." Then came an incident that left her so shaken and unsure that she asked me not to use her real name in these pages.

Anyone who has read in the past decade about the "new breed" of New Orleans restaurants—high on style, low on gumbo—may know of the "renowned" spot with "a very good name" where Patty landed a job. "It's one of those places within the business that waiters talk about. Out of the blue, I was unemployed and they weren't advertising. . . . I went there, put in an application. I spoke to the owner briefly. He said he was impressed with me. He called me back to do an interview. I did, and I got hired. I was *ecstatic*. The job turned out to be . . ." She trailed off.

"After he hired me, he seemed pleased with my work, for this little while. Then he started to pick me apart. It started with how I looked. He wanted me to take off my jewelry. That's not unusual that people want their waiters to look a certain way. I took my jewelry off, except I didn't take these bracelets off." She extended a wrist dancing with slim silver circles. "He said I looked too bohemian. I looked over to my right and there's a *man* waiting tables wearing Birkenstock shoes, a ponytail halfway down his back. I thought, *he's* not bohemian? I said, 'All right, I'll go along,' 'cause I really wanted this job. The money was very good. And it was kind of prestigious.

"The owner used to stand at the podium, right by the door. That was his web, and he was the spider in the web. He would be up there looking at every breath I took. I can remember him standing up there one evening and we were talking. He says, 'There's fifty million dollars in this room right now, I bet. That's Mr. Texaco, that's Mr. Blahbity-Blah, that's Mr.

So-and-So.' That was a big insight into his character. That's all he saw. 'He's a millionaire, he's a multimillionaire, *she's* a millionaire . . . ' inherited, of course.

"Places will have a clientele," she said, over beery male whoops from the street below. "When I worked at [that restaurant], I hated that clientele. They were *tough*. They were really hard to wait on. Kind of ironic—the clientele sort of matched the management." Customers were "real unreceptive. If you [are] going up to a table, you're kind of vulnerable. I don't bounce up to the table and go 'Hi!' especially working somewhere like that. I might come up, very dignified, say 'Good evening.' The response I would get would be, 'Anyway, Cozumel was *divine.*'

"Then [the owner] started criticizing my service, which, I'm telling you, it's just not common. So I . . . I started to get self-conscious. It went on and on and on. And the kitchen was *really* bad about sexual remarks. *Man*, I used to go in there and hear stuff that would make my hair curl. Believe me, I'm the *last* person in the world to be a prude, but I cannot even repeat what these guys said. It's not even printable."

Most comments came from a cook. "The waiter more would be like, 'Look at the tits on this woman on table five.' The restaurant business is full of innuendo, which I've dealt with for a long time. I'm also very . . . I'm a feminist. I don't like hearing my gender trashed. That started coming up. The owner didn't like that I was making a fuss. I told the people directly: 'What you're doing is wrong, it's not legal. It's called sexualizing the workplace.' I tried to explain it to them in this rational way, and they looked at me like, 'What are you talking about?' "

Then the set-to increased. The remarks became "more directly personal, like someone commenting on my anatomy. I said, 'Really, that's it. I'm going to the Labor Board if you don't stop.' " At the same time Patty was hearing about her body, the owner was complaining about her service.

"It's an old adage that's true," she laughed in an unlaughing way, "if you look for mistakes, you're going to get mistakes. Sure enough, I would be like"—she blew air through her lips—"bumbling, when in actuality, I'm an excellent waitress. I've been *told* I'm an excellent waitress. So. I had a very bad night one night. I had customers complain about their food taking too long and their meat was too rare. He fired me.

"It felt like shit," she whispered. "It felt horrible. He told me I was inefficient. 'I can't afford to have people like you working here.' It was *really* awful." She had been at the restaurant four months. "Everybody took him with a grain of salt, but he was so nasty to deal with. When he was sitting there in that chair, he was like *venom* shooting out of his eyes."

Patty reacted in a way that startled her. "I cried. I cried in the *office* when he did it. It was a yucky situation, 'cause I didn't know what to say at first. As he went on and on, when he said I was inefficient, that was too much for me. I said to him in this *really* little voice, like a little kid's voice, 'I *am* efficient.' He said, 'No, you're not.' He shot me down completely. But I have a theory about this guy, too. I think he's gay, but he won't admit it. I don't think he likes women very much, period."

That night, "I crept away with my tail between my legs and fell apart for a little while. Then I regrouped. I went out and got another job." She also availed herself of help. "I was in therapy at the time, and I talked to my therapist a lot about it. I tried to *heal* that incident. I'm still trying to do it." A friend of Patty's who is a chef responded as friends do. "She brushes him off completely. She kind of reassures me that it was him and his problems, and it did not reflect on my ability. She also reminds me that there's more of a sum total of a human being than our work. There's much more to me than being a waitress.

"Since then, I feel kind of doubtful of my, you know, adequacy on the job. I find myself taking these jobs that are nice little places, nothing demanding, not very good food, nyah, nyah, nyah kind of places. When in actuality, I would like to march into Bayona and say, 'I want to work here.' " Bayona was another "new breed" restaurant with a female chef, Susan Spicer. "I would walk on my *knees* to serve Susan Spicer's food, because over the years I've developed this incredible interest in the foods, not just putting it out there.

"I don't want to serve spaghetti and meatballs, but that's what I'm doing because I'm scared if I go into Bayona and *make* them hire me out of sheer desire to work there, I'm not going to measure up. I'm afraid that's going to happen again. From *one* guy doing that to me."

Patty knows it is "important" to get back her confidence as a waitress. "That's where you get all your *presence* from at a table." She shook her head. "I'm trying to put it in perspective, and I'm trying to do that inner work, that healing that needs to be done. Sitting there in his office, part of me felt everything he said was true. I have to start rallying around and come back and mentally shout at him, 'That's a goddamned lie. You don't like me, is what it is.' "

Later, a valet and a waiter from the restaurant got in touch with her and sympathized, for which she was grateful. "That really meant something."

Patty leaned back in the wing chair as if spent, then laughed. No matter the insult, she is free of a mean boss, "rich, stuck-up" customers, and a raunchy cook. "I'm *glad* I got fired! I didn't even like it anyway!"

Now she works at Mali D's, a none-too-thriving Italian restaurant. The location is good, but, she admitted, she does not like it "a lot." The reason by now is obvious. "I feel I'm capable of much better. I'm not realizing my potential as a waitress there. It *is* what I chose to do as a profession."

Yet the incident at the restaurant where she was so insultingly fired also made her question her professional choice. She has begun noticing most customers are not as "kind" as they were but instead are "discounting." She added softly, "Maybe I'm over-sensitive, but sometimes they talk to me like I'm not very intelligent. [So] I might say a word that'll put me in a different vocabulary bracket than they think I should be in." She sees their faces change. "I'm supposed to be dumb and I'm maybe not dumb, so they try to *make* me dumb." Other customers are less subtle. "Something I've seen a lot of in recent years is what I call a waiter-baiter. They know I am not allowed to fight back or say what I really think."

While some customers have become less civil to her, she also notices that she herself has become less civil to them. She has been "pretty darn snappy," saying things such as, "I *heard* you the first time"—"not attacking," she explained, "but more like parrying."

She joked about instituting "mandatory retirement" for waitresses after fifteen years on the job. " 'Cause your temper's not going to hold out, your love for the human race is not going to hold out, your bod's not going to." She ran her hand through her hair. "Also, I feel we're kind of a dying breed," she said, stretching the word into two syllables. "I know that sounds dramatic, but people that do it just for the doing of it? Those of us that really love doing it? Kind of rare."

Melinda Rubke

When Melinda Rubke the customer goes to a restaurant, Melinda Rubke the waitress is witheringly alert. "I train myself on how to work there in five minutes. I find where everything is, I find out who's quick and who's not by the looks on their faces. I see who's important and who's a small potato, and I see their system and how it works. I look at their back, just from what you can see from the table [of] their little side station."

The more expensive the restaurant, the more exacting the wither. "I look and see if they've polished the silverware, if they've polished the glasses. I do this because I've spent so much time doing that little behind-the-scenes thing that nobody sees me doing, that takes an enormous amount of time. [Automatic] dishwashers don't wash off lipstick if it's red—you have to wipe it off with a napkin. If you [want] to walk into a restaurant and see the glasses sparkling in the candlelight, you have to polish them an hour before the people see them. Polishing them yesterday wouldn't do it."

We were having dinner in her place of employment, the exquisite (now closed) Pirosmani, nestled within a converted Victorian house in the Queen Anne section of Seattle. The food is Georgian—the Georgia whose capital is Tbilisi. (Melinda draws maps for the geographically challenged.) Here glasses did sparkle in the candlelight. The food, including such condiments as Nigvzis da Brotseulis Tsveni, a pomegranate walnut sauce, was spectacular. Not all waitresses spend a free evening eating where they work, but Melinda's readiness to do so is as understandable as her disdain of places that cost more than they deliver.

She spoke in scathing detail of eating recently in San Francisco's expensive Aqua restaurant with a small group of "restaurant people" and being "*mortified*" by the "snobby" and "shoddy" service, despite an eight-hundred-dollar tab. "They weren't waiting until everyone was done to bring the next *course*. They were rushing our courses like there was a fire in the kitchen." The "very last straw" was seeing an old gum wrapper on the plate holding the cream and sugar. "I wanted to stand up and scream."

Melinda was not always this exacting. She grew up in a hippie commune on the California coast south of Mendocino, with her three siblings and their mother. The source of income was welfare. "It seemed like circumstance. *Sometimes* I was embarrassed for being poor in school, but I [didn't] think of it as government money versus anything else." Melinda did envy classmates who got to travel to Europe. "That was something I noticed [that separated me] from them, the haves and the have-nots."

Now an attractive woman of thirty-five, Melinda could be a model for hippie backlash. She is wearing a simple outfit as conservative as her vocabulary, her hair is neat, her even features lightly made up. She began leaving the commune mentally when she was barely a teenager, and her world unexpectedly widened.

A woman who ran a "teeny little cafe" attached to the local post office left a message that she had "heard about me," Melinda smiled. "I was very mature at thirteen." The woman wanted to teach Melinda "how to prep cook" at her cafe and how to wait tables there.

"I would go in early in the afternoon and do all the prepping and then quickly change at five-thirty and go out and do the waiting." The wage was 75 cents an hour to prep; for waitressing, she earned nothing but tips. "I was a clever kid and I learned well. She was a horrible, mean, awful, spiteful, menopausal bitch," Melinda half-laughed, "but she taught me everything about the classic basic French cooking. I made all the sauces, I prepped all the stocks and the vegetables, and I made every-thing ready, the *mise en place*." Melinda referred to the ingredients and implements which are all prepared, like a tableau, for the chef to turn into meals.

"She taught me all that in a month. She taught me how to wait tables as well. She taught me how to carry things. How to present myself. How to speak clearly. How to be professional." That meant, Melinda said, altering her posture. "How to make yourself minimal when it's impor-tant and to bring yourself out when it's important. When the attention is on you, you're supposed to stand up straight and be seen. When the attention is not on you, you are supposed to—not slump, but . . . dis-appear." The cafe owner also taught Melinda a basic rule: "Make pri-orities."

Melinda became priority's child. "The most important element of waitressing, no matter if you're in the most fine dining or the tackiest little coffee shop, is a matter of prioritizing every move you make. Every time you do something, the list changes.

"I wasn't great, but"—she put on a mock bragging tone—"I made twenty-five dollars a night" in tips in the summer of 1973, twice what her mother received in welfare "for all five of us." Praise from home was minimal, however. "I knew people ten and eleven [years old] scrap-ing by on their own. I don't remember getting any kudos for having a job."

By the age of nineteen, Melinda had worked in "countless restau-rants" in and around Mendocino and trained other waitresses. She refused to train two types of would-be waitresses: those who considered the work "an interim job" and did not "take it seriously" and those with no "sense of urgency."

Urgency is a "behind-the-scenes thing" that "goes hand in hand with priorities," she said, leaning over the table. "It doesn't matter what kind of priority list you have, if you have no sense of urgency, you won't ever be able to do it well.

"You are always evaluating the entire room and changing. There's also the attitude of the [customer] that plays into it. You have nice people, and then you have something in between, and then you have jerks. You have to prioritize according to how those people are going to see you. I go up to a table and the first minute I am standing there, I make a value judgment about whether they are well-bred or not. It has nothing to do with money, because sometimes the wealthiest people are the most wonderful and other times are the worst jerks, and it's the poor people that only spend a teeny bit, but they'll be gracious."

Jerks "take more maintenance than others, more time, more cajoling." They also "want to show how much they know about the wine list, so they ask pointed questions, which is very time-consuming because wine talk is really wearisome."

Melinda's face is no mirror. "I never look annoyed. Never, ever, ever, ever." She stopped for a bite, then told me of an exception. "One time when I was working here, I said something to a table I wished I hadn't." A man had wanted dessert but could not eat "something basic," like sugar or flour. "I was trying to make suggestions. 'There is nothing on the menu you can have, but maybe we can put together' this, that, or the other thing. I was trying to help him out. He *laughed* at me really loudly," when she suggested a dessert based on fruit. "Then everyone at the table laughed at me. It made me mad. Instead of saying, 'Okay, sorry,' I said, 'Don't laugh at me. I'm trying to help you.' As soon as it came out of my mouth, I was *so* mortified. It was completely against what I trained myself to do."

The man "felt embarrassed," but his discomfort worsened hers. "You don't try to shame your people. . . . [It] means that he won. Once you lose your composure, they've got you."

Two weeks earlier, another customer had challenged her to an especially tough round of the same game. "I went to the table and said, 'If you're finished reading the menu, I would like to tell you about the specials tonight.' It was a man and a woman. The woman had some papers she had pulled out of her purse and was spreading them all on the table." After Melinda waited for a signal to indicate whether either of them wanted to hear the specials, "he looked up and said, 'What do you want? Eye contact? Do we have to look at you?' "

Melinda was "aghast" for a second. Then she recited the specials "with some sort of serene happy look on my face, because I was easily winning."

"I have always tried to win. It's always been, can you rise above this? If it makes you mad, you lose. That sort of splits apart the professionals from the amateurs."

If she can "get to be the better person," something else comes into play. "In that way, I can be a waitress and feel I am a really good person, as opposed to being a waitress and thinking I'm a failure."

While still a teenager, Melinda was thinking less about work than about her fear that she "might be really different all my life" because of her commune upbringing. To widen her horizons, she headed to Atlanta, where her father lived. There, she reeled from culture shock, tried un-successfully to become a travel agent, and all the while earned money by waiting tables. She also had an epiphany.

It happened on her twentieth birthday. She got "ragingly drunk," dragged a girlfriend into a bar near the visiting circus, and soon was spending most of the next two weeks on the fifty-car circus train with an animal trainer. She came to realize that the "entire perspective" of the five hundred circus people flowed "from within" the circus itself. "The trainers, the keepers, the clowns, the tall skinny guys, and the short fat guys . . . it was like an entire city." Circus people varied ("there's people that watch 'General Hospital' every day" and people who do not), but "they're all colored by this circus experience. The same as restaurant work. You can leave it for a period of time, but most people end up going back at one point or another in their life."

In Atlanta, a place where initially "everything was different" to her, including the terrifying traffic, Melinda realized that waiting tables "was actually the thing that was kind of the same. It was probably the *only* place I felt confident. All the social graces of living in the city and living in the South were so alien to me, a hippie kid from Mendocino. . . . I felt out of place just about everywhere but work."

She knew she "had experience way beyond my age," and quickly accumulated more. She became a shift leader and trainer "for a *very* prestigious semiprivate dining club" and even fulfilled part of her travel wish by working in Belgium for "a bigwig" who wanted to start American restaurants there. When she returned to Atlanta, she married impulsively, ran a group of restaurants known as Aunt Charlie's, and got "wonderful managing experience" in an "upscale fine dining place" called Atkins Park. (One customer, former president Jimmy Carter, "a nice guy" who "tips well," upset the French busboys by asking for a doggie bag. "They thought an American president should do better." Her opinion of another celebrity, CNN founder Ted Turner, was less favorable.)

Then Melinda reached the end of her endurance. She was "basically a well-dressed waitress" managing a restaurant "that had a hundred employees. It was a lot of benefits, a lot of cushy things, and I worked seventy hours a week." She also seethed. Her "incredibly sexist" boss let her manage because she was pretty and because he was "good buddies" with her husband. "I did a really good job. You could take the paperwork and the sales before I started—they *doubled*. I made him a *lot* of money, but my job still rode on how good a wife I was to his buddy."

She did not stay the buddy's good wife long. They separated, and she raced back to Europe, had an affair with a young Frenchman, returned, and got divorced. She moved to Key West to learn to sail and pay off the debts her husband had accumulated in her absence. There, she finagled a job cooking on "a five-million-dollar boat owned by the richest man in Spain, Mario Conde, [King] Carlos's good *buddy*." She experienced much trauma and mixed success on this job, but toward the end of the trip she met her current husband, Hans, a Dutchman whose captain knew her captain.

They moved to Seattle for a personal reason: to be near her brother, who had AIDS. "I'm his bitch. Other people say I'm his advocate." While casting about for work, she heard of Pirosmani. Arriving for the first interview thinking Georgian food meant piroshki, Melinda did poorly. Again, it was time to prioritize. She went to a library, "took out videos and books, and [at] my second interview I was quoting old wives' tales from Georgian folklore. That's what you do, right?" She got the job.

The owner and chef is a woman, and how she is treated makes Melinda boil. "When people come in here to eat and ask about the chefette or the chefess . . ." The put-downs remind Melinda of Atlanta, where she sometimes was called "the manageress."

Melinda also boils about bad tippers. "Medical professions in my estimation [are] the absolute worst, second only to teaching. I have theories on both. Teachers spend their whole life [saying], 'What do you want to be, a waitress? Or do you want to have a career like me?'" Doctors, who usually part with 10 percent, she said, are cheap because they had teachers for so many years. "They also consider [waiting tables] the polar opposite of their higher calling." Her efforts not to show emotion are especially tested, she said, when AIDS experts make jokes among themselves, as she serves them, about the futility of their efforts.

All in all, Melinda likes waiting on Europeans best; they bring out the professional in her. "They don't like having to make a lot of choices. 'How do you want that done?' 'What kind of dressing do you want?' 'How's everything?' They consider interruption to be more than annoying—they find it *so* intrusive. Don't ask them how they want their meat done. They want it done however the chef wants it done. They don't want to be asked about coffee. They want it, but after dessert."

The little hippie girl who once wanted only to visit Europe now feels she knows its people well. She knows exactly what to expect from them and knows they will never ask whether they have to look at her.

Tamara Thompson

On a busy avenue in northeastern Tucson, where stores tender carpet remnants and used VCRs, stands a restaurant so misnamed—the Village Inn—it must be corporate. Confirmation comes inside: pastel walls and neckerchiefs-on-waterfowl knickknacks. This late morning, business is slow and friendly, and the visible staff members look calm. There is one exception: a middle-aged man in glasses bolts from table to table, greeting customers.

It must have been Don, said Tamara Thompson at home that afternoon. She is twenty-three, stick-thin in jeans and a blouse, and her carefully teased blondish hair is offset by circles under her eyes. A glamorized portrait, taken by a photographer at the urging of her Mary Kay cosmetics consultant, hangs in the hall. The consultant suggested the beauty products for the portrait but did not apply them; Tamara cannot stand to have anyone around her face. Next to her portrait is one of her two dark and beautiful daughters, five-year-old Meagan and two-year-old Luz Maria, both playing noisily in a bedroom.

Tamara swung her mind to Don. "He's this unbelievable manager," she said, shaking her head. "He knows a lot of our regular customers.

He gets into their daily lives. We are supposed to know names. 'Go learn some names.' I'm not going to walk up to somebody that's trying to eat and say, 'Can I know your name?' Yeah, right. They're going to look at me like I'm *crazy*."

It is Friday, Tamara's day off. Sniffling with a cold, she is sitting at her dining room table, an ear cocked for the girls. If she can afford child care (a big if), she spends Friday hiking in the nearby Santa Catalina mountains or stays home, listening to a CD of Indian flute music and trying to relax. Usually she spends the day doing chores, like driving around to pay bills.

Don does not make that easier. When he schedules "the back of the house, you have cooks leaving at one-thirty and no one coming in until three." He forgets to order pies, she said, forgets to order honey. Tamara literally does his job two days a week, for fifty cents an hour more. "I'm 'server in charge.' That just means I've got more work."

For her basic job title, she prefers "server," she said quickly. Waitress "seems more lower-class. A server sounds more professional."

For Tamara Thompson, professionalism may be as much a mental refuge as her home seems a physical one. From outside, the house appears to be a shabby structure on a parched lawn, but inside birds chirp in cages and plants stretch above a faded couch. A corner of the living room holds a clay fountain, a present from "my fiancé," a generous-sounding man (although Tamara is concerned about his beer intake) who works in his family's construction firm. She says "my fiancé" often, as if the phrase is amazing to her. She has never been married, wears a diamond engagement ring, and told a police officer she waits on that she does not know how she could be so lucky.

"I have a real hard problem with messed-up men," she said, sort of laughing. "I think it stems from my father being an alcoholic and a beater." Matter-of-factly, with a few shrugs and not an ounce of self-pity, she described a short life so long on drama that her attention to her work was almost startling.

During a "navy brat" childhood, during which she dreamed of being "a mechanic or a truck driver," Tamara grew up with five sisters (including two stepsisters). She moved mostly back and forth between California and Texas, depending on her parents' fractious relationship. Even her name is a divide. Her mother's family, which came from Mexico and included a "great-great-aunt" from Spain, pronounces "Tamara" with the stress on the second syllable. Her Texas "hillbilly" father (with whom she has not spoken in years) always called her Tamara with the stress on "Ta."

At seventeen, living in El Paso, she worked at Peter Piper Pizza as a cashier, "decided I wanted to be a psychologist," and took as many courses on it as she could in high school. She still reads books on the subject. Diverted from that goal, she got pregnant, had a fight with her mother, left home, moved in with a female teacher who "basically adopted me," quit school, took and passed her GED, and had Meagan.

The fathers of Meagan and Luz Maria are both Mexican Americans with notable shortcomings. Meagan's began "shooting up heroin" after Tamara got pregnant, once put a loaded gun to Tamara's head (it seems clear why she does not want anyone around her face), and is thought to be up to no good in Mexico. With Luz Maria's father, who is "supposed to be getting out of prison March the fifteenth," Tamara put up with "a lot of affairs, a lot of drinking, a lot of out-all-night-longs." He robbed a bank at seventeen, after his mother killed herself, and has been back to prison often. Tamara takes the girls to visit him monthly. "I care very much for him."

Luz Maria poses other difficulties. "She had fifteen ear ruptures before she was one. Not ear infections, *ruptures*. She would hit me, she would bite me, she would literally beat Meagan up." Meagan, in turn, has become a little parent, getting her baby sister dressed, changing her diapers, and telling Tamara after a hard day at work, "I think you need to be by yourself. I'll watch Luz Maria."

Between the two births, Tamara had a horrific pregnancy, one "where the placenta drops and it's right there on the opening, and you continue to bleed." For six months, she rushed to the hospital nearly every night, hemorrhaging, before finally miscarrying. She left her boyfriend (Luz Maria's future father) in El Paso and, "still bleeding to death," moved to Waco to help a sister care for her own young son and to get a job.

Tamara's summary of this time in her life—"I worked graveyard shift, and she worked days, and we helped with the kids"—proved typically, misleadingly sunny. Within a week of the miscarriage—and indeed still bleeding—Tamara began hostessing at the International House of Pancakes (IHOP). The job kept her on her feet from 3 P.M. to 6 A.M. At home, she was too tired to pay much attention to something a glance away: the Branch Davidian cult. She returned to El Paso before the FBI standoff at the cult began, but the fire that destroyed the complex spewed ashes on her sister's house.

After her sister and family moved back to El Paso, too, her sister began working at what Tamara said, grinning, was "one of the best Chinese restaurants in El Paso." One busy night she telephoned, and Tamara's melodrama shifted focus.

" 'We're in need of a waitress.' I said, 'I've never waitressed before.' I could cashier, I could hostess, but I can't waitress. She said, 'We *need* a waitress. You're a quick learner. Get your butt down here. Leave the kids with Carlos.' That was her husband. She said, 'There's a tuxedo shirt in the closet, there's some black pants. Put 'em on and get in here.' I was like, 'Fine, fine.' " Tamara's smile is beautiful.

"I went into work not knowing anything. By the end of the night, I was doing my own tables. Boom! It happened *so* naturally."

That first night, "I looked over the menu for ten minutes" and began. "A lot of things I kind of breezed right through." The boss told her, " 'You be here tomorrow.' They didn't hardly speak any English. 'Okay, I guess I got a job.' "

One of the best Chinese restaurants in El Paso, however, was no match for what Tamara smilingly referred to as "my hormones." She soon was pregnant with Luz Maria. This pregnancy was complicated emotionally. Luz Maria's father was about to return to prison for violating his parole, after flunking a urine test. Then, "the nicest parole officer I've ever met" offered a reprieve. He would not rearrest her boyfriend until after the baby was born, and he also allowed him to accompany Tamara out of state to a place her boyfriend wanted her to go.

It was a place Tamara had sworn she would never go: her mother's home in Tucson. She told her boyfriend, "I will live in the Salvation Army before I move to my mother's." Then she realized that homelessness was truly the alternative.

Thus, the two-bedroom, one-bath apartment where Tamara's mother lived with her four youngest daughters now held eight people and countless resentments. "Me and my mother hadn't spoken in six months to a year before that. My mother chooses men over her kids on a *lot* of different things, which makes me angry. I'd give my life for my children."

From day one in Tucson, Tamara focused on earning money to rent her own home. She summarized briskly: "I worked at a Greek restaurant when I first started out. It was dead. You'd sit half the night without a customer. That's when I started hounding Village Inn. Put my application in and called once a week, then got the job." Tamara borrowed a

menu and "learned everything on that menu, so I would not be in training for over one day." She was assigned to follow another waitress, a
"drill sergeant type"—indeed, a former army police officer named Connie. "She showed me one table. I made her over a hundred dollars the
first night." Connie "sat down in the back and smoked cigarettes. I took
the whole section by myself. I wanted *out* of my mother's home."

Under similar circumstances, a trainee might get a share of the tips.
Connie gave Tamara not one dollar. "She told me, 'I'm very impressed,'
and walked off."

The next day Tamara was on her own, working nights so that her
mother or sisters could watch the girls. "I know how to waitress. That's
not a problem for me. The computer was the only thing I thought was
going to worry me, but it's very simple. Your server number and then
your table number and guest count. You have to do beverages first and
then whatever else."

There was a problem at home, however: mother-daughter relations.
"She told me I was a bad mother, and I exploded." Tamara moved out
"as quick as possible," into her present home.

She does everything she can to keep it. "All the time" she tries to
increase a check. "It's called suggestive selling. You go up to a table.
'Buttermilk pancakes.' You ask them, 'Would you like bacon or sausage
with that?'" She suggests drinks. "If they just want water, fine. You
make sure that water is continually refilled. A lot of waitresses will leave
their iced tea until somebody asks them. I am not like that. Iced tea's
constantly refilled. A lot of times I don't ask, I just refill.

"If you give them good service, even though you couldn't suggestively
sell something to raise that price to get a better tip, if you make sure
they get good service and over, they are going to leave you more. That's
the way I've made it to now, you know? Another waitress might get a
dollar, I might get three, because of the way I wait on my tables."

Spanish-speaking customers are a separate challenge. "Luz Maria's
father speaks to me in Spanish and I answer him in English." She un-
derstands more than she speaks, she said. "I'm afraid I'm going to say
the wrong thing. I need to learn all the words in between 'is' or 'the.'
At work, whenever people come in that don't speak English, they'll sit
and talk amongst themselves, and I'll tell them, 'You want this,' and
they'll look up at me—'Oh, you understand Spanish.' '*Poquito,*' a little
bit. Then they try to give me these big old long sentences real fast. 'I
understand your eggs, okay? Let's not get into everything else.'"

Tamara keeps everything she can under control. "Everybody at one point gets 'in the weeds.' Everybody gets stressed. As they tell me at work, when they see me stressed, they look at me like, *shock*. I'm the one that's very calm, very easy-going." She stays calm by focusing. "You don't think about too much other than the things you need to accomplish. Everybody else, they think the cook's messed up the eggs three times, these people are ticking me off, this table won't quit sucking down the iced tea, and this other waitress went over and stole my table. Or the cooks are mad. You fly over it." Of one cook, she said, "It makes his day if he can make a waitress cry."

Sunday mornings at the Village Inn are singularly trying. "I go in at five-thirty, we get slammed around eight o'clock, and we don't stop until after lunch. So I smoke. You have to run in the back, then your manager's screaming at you, 'You just got a down. You're smoking too much!' On Sundays, a lot of the slower waitresses, they flip." She wailed theatrically, " 'I can't take this! He keeps slamming me!' " The "he" who "keeps slamming" the waitresses by seating more customers than they can serve is Don.

Tamara reaches high stress "once every six months," she estimated. One time, she exploded. The incident started when a cook did not follow her philosophy of restaurant relationships, which is to please the customer, no matter how difficult a request might be. "The way that I see it, they're my customers and I'm the cook's customer. So cook the food and shut up, you know?"

When the cook screamed and carried on because her customer wanted bread grilled without any fat, and Tamara told the cook to do it anyway, he retaliated by holding back all her orders. She told him off; he told her to fuck off. She summoned Don, who responded as he usually did, she said, by trying to take over in the kitchen and getting the orders wrong but saying nothing to the cook. That led the cook to mock her for going to Don at all. "I'm getting shaky now, I'm fuming mad." She threw her order pad, "and I said, 'Fuck you!' I looked at Don. 'Fuck you, too! *You* go take out all my food.' I walked out." After receiving Don's phone apology, she was back the next day.

The walkout was an exception. Usually when stress mounts, "I stop, and [say,] 'You guys need to cut the floor' "—in other words, stop seating so many people. "I go in the back, I smoke a cigarette, I come back out, and"—another snap of her fingers—"boom. I change my thoughts." Tamara's version of stress management is one of her two keys to being a good waitress. The other is "common sense. That's what a lot of waitressing is. Common sense and organizing your thoughts, which I've always been very good at."

She is so good that she trains all the new waitresses, if with mixed success. "There are some people that are not meant to be waitresses. I'm sorry, but they *cannot* organize their thoughts. I've just had to put one back into retraining." The young woman under discussion cannot handle three tables at once, Tamara said, shaking her head. She is "getting As in school, but she can't seem to figure out how to organize everything. She stresses out. Once you stress, you're basically screwed. You think you're doing bad *before* you stressed?"

She put on a soft voice, as if leading a training session, customers within earshot. " 'What are you going to do if you get [tables] fifty, fifty-five, and fifty-six down? You've got food up for table fifty-four. And fifty-six needs some more iced tea.' 'The food's more important.' 'Okay. But what are you going to do first?' 'Get the food.' "

Wrong. "You go by the other table and tell them you'll be with them in a minute. Then, as you're walking by, you get the food, you tray it up, you grab the iced tea pitcher. You put the iced tea pitcher down on an empty table, serve the food, grab the iced tea pitcher, fill it. Pre-bus as you're going back." Tamara moaned, "She *can't* get it."

Tamara can. After her anti-stress cigarette is smoked, she returns to work, reorganized and remasked. "As soon as you hit those doors, that smile better be on your face, acting like everything's fine. It's weird. It's almost like you were walking into another place, from the front of the house to the back of the house."

No smile is in evidence now. "I feel very unappreciated at this restaurant. I do everything I possibly can," from serving to managing to training, for $2.70 an hour. "Actually, I've contemplated moving over to IHOP because of it." She ate at a new branch last night with her fiancé. "I was checking it out."

Tamara glanced at the bedroom. "It's like I've got two jobs. Up on my feet all day long at work, I'm basically exercising, the stress, and then you come home and the kids are crying." She is not the sturdiest woman, either. When she gets sick, Don demands a doctor's note. "I tell him, 'You got the money? I can come up there and show you I'm sick, but there's no way I'm going to the doctor.' " Don concedes, and Tamara loses a day's pay and tips. She has no health insurance ("they say I make too much money for *me* to be on medical") but has enrolled the girls in a state medical program, without which she would be on welfare.

At home, stresses on and off the job almost made Tamara cross a feared line. "There was twice, where I . . . I didn't literally beat them, but it came *very* . . . on that fine line. Where I was spanking [Meagan] on the bottom a little bit too much. There was never any bruises or anything, but you start spanking them and you don't stop . . . Whoa, I'm not going to be my father."

As the trickle of the clay fountain in her living room helps in quieter times, louder water helps in rougher ones, as Tamara described. "I walked out of the room, went in there," she pointed to the bathroom, "turned on the shower, and let them beat on the door. If you don't hear any noise, you can calm yourself down. I get so frustrated between work and then [coming] home and Luz Maria will not stop sometimes. I feel like *screaming*. The days she has her ear infections, it's like a week to two weeks [of] nonstop screaming." Tamara cannot spank her and risk dislodging the tubes in her ears, so "I always snap on Meagan" for something minor. "But I go back and tell her, 'Look, Mommy shouldn't have done that. I'm not going to sit here and tell you I had a bad day.' She says, 'Okay, mom.' "

What Tamara really wants is a friend. "I have no friends, as far as like, girlfriends." She gets along well with two Village Inn waitresses, but one spends her leisure playing bingo, the other smoking dope. Neither activity interests Tamara. Someone suggested she make friends in coffeehouses. "I love sitting at coffeehouses. That doesn't mean anybody's going to come up to me, 'Can I be your friend?' " She looked embarrassed. The only person who comes close to being a friend is her Mary Kay consultant.

A reason Tamara likes restaurant work, in fact, is its human contact. "I love waitressing. I really do. I'm a very people person. When I go to fiestas or stuff, I'm constantly watching people. Doing the job I'm in, it's perfect. But it's such hard work for a low pay. I barely make it every month."

Later that year, on the phone, Tamara told me she had begun hemorrhaging again. Doctors found cancer cells in her uterus and evidence of an inflammatory disease, and she had a partial hysterectomy. She was having hot flashes, she joked. Those hormones again. A year and a half later came a long letter.

"I married the man I was seeing when we met." They are fixing up a house his grandfather built. Meagan is happy and doing well in school, and Luz Maria's ear infections are slowly disappearing. And "I have a lump in my breast they need to remove. After that I'll be cancer free."

She was now twenty-six and felt she was going on sixty, she wrote. She had had three major surgeries within four months and had taken off work a total of two weeks.

She also wrote that she had quit the Village Inn, four days before her fourth anniversary. She had been managing the restaurant several days a week, doing "figures and bills" and training, all for a third of what Don made. Then he "started cussing at me because of something with another server. I handed him my keys to the restaurant and walked out the door."

Now she works at a Denny's, Sundays only, while recovering her health. She feels strange not working full-time and may start again, as the manager wants her to. "I love waiting on tables and I love the restaurant business, but I think this brake [*sic*] is doing me good. I'm very happy. I just am tired a lot."

 Dolores Romero

The easiest way to find the Guiding Star is not by looking into the heavens. It is by following Highway 90 into New Iberia, Louisiana, and watching for the lights in the parking lot. This is Cajun country, where stars of multiple varieties shine. The Guiding Star, recommended as the best place around for boiled crawfish, crabs, or shrimp, depending on the season, or sausage, boiled potatoes, and corn on the cob in every season, with a fiery mash coating every morsel, is one.

The Star's dining room glows without pretension. Numbered tables of card-playing size are faced by quartets of scuffed blue wooden chairs. Each table is covered neatly with a skirt of newspaper, the *Daily Iberian* being among the publications recycled for the cause. The final touches on the table are a basket of crackers, a paper cup of mayonnaise, and an array of hot sauces bottled within the area code. The only wall decoration is a huge photograph of a customer beaming over a mountain of crawfish remains. Throughout the evening, a cash register jangles, pool balls clack from an adjoining room, murmurs of appreciation rise from steaming plates and sopping newsprint, and gusts of laughter or yippy screams punctuate the air. A young man chases a young woman into the ladies room.

The star of the Star is Dolores Romero, or Ms. Dee, as she is known and as she signs herself. At fifty-something, she is the oldest employee and unquestionably the best, at least outside the kitchen. After you have seated yourself, Ms. Dee saunters up to your table and sets down precisely the same drink you had the last time you were here, one year before. The transaction is wonderful to behold. The customer is agog and thrilled. Ms. Dee parts with a small grin and a slight raise of one eyebrow, her only acknowledgment that she does have one hell of a memory.

She also has one hell of a following. Christmas presents from her regulars the previous year included a decorative candle, a crystal candy dish, and a twenty-dollar bill in a card. When she was out for eleven days with back problems, several of her regulars went to the Guiding Star to eat, learned she was not there, and left. They did not even bother with take-out.

Dolores Romero got her job at the Guiding Star the way people get jobs in New Iberia: her ex-husband is related to the owners, Ralph and Ronda Schaubert. They live on the premises, their home and business sharing a common wall.

"I been knowing [Ralph] since he was a little bitty boy, and I had heard he needed a waitress," Ms. Dee recalled when we spoke the day after she had demonstrated her ability to remember drinks. "I just went back there and said, 'Ralph, you got your waitress.' He says, 'Okay, come to work tomorrow night.' " That was six years ago. Ms. Dee marks the anniversary by making a cake and giving slices to her regulars, a generous gesture, considering what she is commemorating.

"Hell," she called that first shift. "My feet hurt. I didn't know where anything was. Friday night is our busiest night, and that's the night he put me to work. I hadn't waitressed in maybe—" she paused, "quite a few years. In fact, I made the comment when I went to work [that] I was coming out of retirement."

Ms. Dee's voice, smoky and low, is less lively than it was yesterday at work, but her accent, a muted version of New Orleans's curled version of southern, does not waver. She seems different, too, sitting in a scrubbed kitchen in a small home on an unprepossessing city block, hard by a commercial strip several miles from work. On a wall behind her are a crucifix, porcelain knickknacks, and the inappropriate sign "Bless This Mess."

She is wearing another sign, a cartoonish T-shirt that reads "Let The Good Times Roll Louisiana." In the Guiding Star the night before, she indeed seemed to be rolling with good times, her manner dashing, friendly, and confident, her dark-complected face open and pleasant. Today, the dash is gone, and her face looks worn without its smile. She is toting up the years.

She began waitressing when she was fifteen, working weekend nights at the nearby Southern Cafe. "I was going out with this guy, my first husband, and he didn't like that too much. So I quit. Then I finished school. My first job after school was another waitress job. I've more or less been waitressing all my life." There was one major exception.

In her late thirties, Ms. Dee became disturbed by societal sting. "People look down on waitresses. It's not one of the highly prestigious jobs?" She was arch for a second. "[They'll say,] 'She's a teller at the bank, oh, *really*!' 'She's a waitress, oh, yeah.'" The "really" indicated approval; the "yeah" was dismissive. "That's how it is around here."

Her reference to bank work was intentional. That is where she set her sights after the sting stung too much and she heard about a job as a night deposit clerk. She had been out of school for twenty years but nervously had to take three weeks of bank classes as part of the application. A test followed. She aced it. "I think my lowest score was a 98."

She worked at the bank eight years, first in "a closet" off the drive-in window, then as a courier, which she enjoyed more. There was a problem, however. "When I took the job in the bank, I wanted to see if I could better myself. I bettered myself mentally, but not financially." Consequently, she reversed her steps. "I guess waitressing has always been in my heart."

The Guiding Star shone on Ms. Dee at a propitious time. The youngest of her ten children (five of them stepchildren) was nine, old enough to be alone to some extent. Ms. Dee was offered the 3 P.M. to midnight shift, which allowed her to spend much of the day with her mother, who was recovering from open-heart surgery. "My husband was here with her at night. It kind of worked itself out." The Romeros' hours remain the same—a commercial fisherman, he leaves for work in the early morning to fish, hours after she comes home. "A long-distance romance," she said dryly.

"I've come to love the job," she continued. "Well, not the job, the people." She is especially attuned to strangers. "I usually try to make them feel at home, ask where they're from, and we get a conversation going, if I'm not too busy." She recalled honeymooners from Missouri who read of the restaurant in a guidebook and liked their experience so much that they drove back several days later. Another night, "I took the time to show a man from Michigan how to eat crawfish," and paused for a photo with him.

If new customers are French-speaking, Ms. Dee is their waitress by default. She "picked up" Cajun French from her maternal grandparents when they came to live with the family in her early teens, so "all the waitresses, if they happen to go wait on some people from France or Canada [who] start speaking French, they tell them, 'Wait, hold it. That's Dee's.' A lot of people from France, if they speak slowly enough, I can pick up. But if they start rattling, forget it."

Her maiden name—Bonin—is French, but her ancestry is mixed. Her maternal grandmother was an Atakapa Indian, from a tribe based in western Louisiana. Also, "I think we have some Spanish origin there with the Indian." On her paternal side, "my dad's people from Louisiana were pure—pure Cajuns." A "pure" Cajun being an oxymoron, Ms. Dee laughed long.

If her legacy of languages does not seem likely to endure—only English is spoken at home now—the Bonin-Romero family surely will. The day she paused to talk, she had twenty-two grandchildren (half of them step-grandchildren) and anticipated another that day. By the same time the next year, she had twenty-six. In fact, she claimed that the main reason she works is so she will not have to babysit. It was her first witticism, and she did not mean it.

There certainly is nothing witty about work at the Guiding Star. "I do everything, with the exception of cooking. I'm the one that does the main cleanup. I sweep, I mop, wash the dishes, paper all the tables. Sometimes it's hell when you have to go into the bathrooms and start cleaning the toilets. I do it every day." The Star's ladies room features a curious arrangement, two toilets side by side with no divider. Ms. Dee did not know the origin of the setup but said the toilets are jointly used. "Some girls" like to go together, she supposed.

Ms. Dee was not looking forward to that night's shift. "My busgirl" is off, she reported. "I'll have to wait tables, run the register, bus tables, answer the phone," and then clean. At some point, she also tallies, for Dolores Romero is the bookkeeper, too.

"I get [Ronda's] checks ready to go to the bank. I know how to balance my register. That's a throwback from the bank." Another throwback is putting the bills in one direction, face up. When the "other girls" throw money in the register any which way, which annoys her, she gets it orderly before she begins her balance.

Even that is not all she does, she revealed in a random remark. "I like to see the crawfish come out on time, the crabs come out on time. Since I switched cooks, it's a helluva lot better." In other words, she is more or less the manager. She does not hire and fire, exactly, but "I give the suggestion, then they give me the go-ahead." Anyone who wants to wait tables at the Guiding Star best be forewarned that they must come to Ms. Dee directly. "Somebody calls on the phone, forget it. 'Take my name and number if you need me.' Or," she affected a high voice, " 'Y'all hiring?' You don't want the job bad enough if you don't come to the restaurant and see me." Three waitresses hired "on my recommendations" have "worked out pretty good," she allowed.

Asked what specific traits she looked for, Ms. Dee cut to Cajun. "Ah *know* 'em." The laugh burst from her.

Ms. Dee did fire an elderly "buslady" for stealing tips from the tables she was clearing. (She was known to have a video poker habit.) "The first time, I wasn't quite sure. The second time, I *saw* her and I confronted her with it. The third time, I saw her again and I let her go.

"Now, we had another older [buslady], she was good." When facing a table of detritus, the woman neatly separated cash from chaos. "We always had our tips, with her. But I had to let her go because she was getting ugly with the customers." Ms. Dee started breaking up. "If they ate the crackers and reached over to this table for another basket"— Ms. Dee put on a witchy voice—" 'Don't take them crackers, ax me for some.' "

Then the woman yelled at the wrong person. When someone at a table asked for beer, she relayed the message to Ms. Dee, who was "stuck at the register and had about five tables to check out." Seven minutes passed. "She hollered, 'Table three needs a goddamned waitress, right *now*.' " The Guiding Star, perhaps for the first time, went silent. Later, "I told her I didn't need her anymore. She was seventy years old and she was busing tables, but she had a mouth that wouldn't quit."

Ms. Dee does not perform her many jobs for a great salary (she disclosed only that she makes less than standard minimum wage) or for great tips. At the Guiding Star, tips are pooled, which is fine for every waitress but her. "I've seen myself in one night make up to ninety dollars and come off with fifty-three." When twice-a-year regulars "from San Anton' " came in recently, including the man photographed with the crawfish remains, he sought her out and "put a roll of money in my hand, and it was thirty dollars." She put it all in the tip can. Tipping is not Ms. Dee's favorite subject.

"I pretty much can spot the good tippers"—they include tourists—"and the not-so-good tippers, and I don't make a difference. I've had one couple that's been coming there for years and they've never left a tip, but they've always gotten the same service [as] somebody that's going to leave a twenty-dollar tip." In her experience, women are among the not-so-good tippers. "Fifteen ordinary working women," she told me months later on the phone, ran up a bill of $140 and collectively left her a $2 tip.

Her voice then lifted as she recalled a large group of customers from a company that makes an item called a car parts tray. They were so pleased with her service that they wrote a letter to Ralph, with special thanks to her. Ms. Dee put the letter in her album.

Low tippers do not "aggravate" her as much as other factors do. "I did quit once and stayed away for two weeks" because of "a bunch of things that been going on that I wasn't satisfied with." One source of aggravation was a "little cook" who was "very ugly and disrespectful. You'd ask him to come do something for you, and he'd get dirty-mouthed about it. He had been there for so long, he thought he was cock of the walk. So we pulled his drawstring in a little tighter. He's calling to come back, but we won't take him back. Everything is running real smooth now." His successor is nineteen years old.

Customers present another source of aggravation, based less on how they tip than on how they behave. Some are "very demanding. They expect to have their food on the table when they get there." She spoke slowly, as if trying to temper judgment about one man in particular: "I guess he thinks he's a pretty influential person around town. He'll call me and say, 'Dolores, this is Mr. So-and-so. Get me five orders of crawfish, we're on our way.'" She hurries to comply.

Some men pose a difficulty by coming on to her, "even at my age and my face," she laughed. "We get a lot of driftovers from the truck stop. Truck drivers, they pull up for the night and they have nothing to do, so they come in. They'll eat an order of crawfish and an order of shrimp, drink a few beers. I've had one guy point-blank ask me, 'Why don't you come go with me to Tennessee?' 'Sure, I'd love to. Can I bring my husband?'"

The greatest challenge she faces is the phenomenal pace of business. Friday nights always are busy, for reasons that probably include payday and Roman Catholic strictures about eating meat, but some go off the charts. "Last Friday night, I *knew*—I had that feeling—we were going to be super busy. These little mayonnaise cups I brought y'all last night? On Friday nights, I usually make seventy-five to a hundred. But last Friday I made a hundred and twenty and we still ran out." The night was "a killer. I didn't get home 'til one o'clock in the morning, and they still had some customers in there partying with the boss. I said, 'Bye.' I had been there since one o'clock Friday afternoon." As usual, Ms. Dee had had almost no break. "I try to eat two, three pieces of potato and a couple of pieces of sausage around four-thirty, five o'clock to hold me up."

Weekends also bring gargantuan take-out orders, which she oversees. "Last Saturday, we had to get a hundred ninety pounds of crawfish ready to go, plus ten orders of crawfish, eight orders of clams, ten orders of corn, and eight orders of potatoes." In the midst of that, eight groups of people walked in to eat. She explained the situation and mollified seven of the groups (the pool table and a poker machine helped), but the eighth, an annoyed local couple, drummed their fingers on their table the entire wait.

If Ms. Dee's mind does not respond to such stresses and order her to take time off, her body does.

One night not long before we talked, she admitted, "they picked me up off the floor. I passed out. I had been having chest pains for about three weeks, but I never told anybody anything because I'm not a complainer. My husband does enough of that for both of us," she semi-smiled. When she "went under," the staff, "very quietly so as not to disturb anybody else," carried her outside and to the Schauberts' living room. She came to, a little, but had trouble breathing, so they called an ambulance, instructing the paramedics to go to the house, not the restaurant.

The diagnosis was "just stress."

Ms. Dee went back to work as soon as possible, partly because she does not want to stay home. "I'm *not* a housekeeper."

"Could have fooled me," I said, glancing at the scoured surroundings.

She looked triumphant. "I *did* fool you! This is my mother's house." After enjoying a big laugh, she explained that her mother had made a special trip to Kmart just for this occasion. Ms. Dee lives behind her mother's home, in "the true place." We strolled to it, indeed a more appropriate site for the "Bless This Mess" sign, and chatted with her pregnant daughter, who also lives there and was overseeing her toddler.

Hours later, Ms. Dee left to earn the money that helps sustain her home, her family, and herself. "I pretty much maintain a happy-go-lucky attitude, because this is my *living*. If I don't treat my customers right, they're not going to come back. Therefore I won't have a job. I put everything I have into it. And more."

4

HIGH ENDS

*A*S ALMOST ANYONE who has worked in restaurants will testify, many different highs may be experienced behind the scenes. The women in this chapter pose a dilemma that is free of drugs (more accurately put, this was not a topic of conversation with these particular women) but full of stress. The stress, and the dilemma, involves behavior and money—and the matter of how much of both the coddled dole out to the coddlers.

Wendy Levy

Chez Panisse in Berkeley, to glean from a harvest of press clippings, may be the most influential restaurant in the United States. On the occasion of the place's thirtieth anniversary, *Newsweek* proclaimed that founder and chef Alice Waters had "revolutionized the way Americans think about food." Earlier, on the restaurant's twenty-fifth anniversary, another publication effused that Waters had "single-handedly changed the American palate." The article painted a picture of Waters or her suppliers "scouring the countryside for ingredients," from dew-fresh produce to newly slaughtered creatures, which she then transformed into what became known as California cuisine.[1] The cozily elegant, amber-hued downstairs rooms on Shattuck Avenue, where (as of this writing) a full-course dinner on Friday or Saturday costs seventy-five dollars without wine, tip, or tax,[2] remain mythically popular. One might think Chez Panisse provides the waitress job of waitress jobs. It does, in ways.

Wendy Levy, who is in her mid-thirties, with bright eyes,

black hair shaved at the back and long at the front, and tribal-looking earrings, is a booster. "The philosophy of Chez Panisse is so singular and special within the restaurant community," she said forcefully, that it transformed for her "the nature of what waitressing is. I feel like an educator half the time."

Chez Panisse has "a higher purpose," she added, relaxing in her colorful cottage kitchen one town away. "There's a definite philosophy that permeates the restaurant. Alice has changed the face of eating in America. We only serve organic produce, cooking things simply, with European influence, to bring out the flavors of what is in the food, knowing the farmers who bring the produce to the restaurant, the way the circle continues. The restaurant lives out those philosophies. You can come in and eat a plate of food that tastes like no other. It's not [the] fancy food you get in all these fancy-schmancy restaurants. It's done with care and thought and the principles she believes are important.

"[Alice] sponsored the Garden Project, which is this organic garden run out of the San Francisco County Jail. When we put radishes on people's table, many people are like, 'What are we supposed to do with these?' You tell them where they've come from, that the inmates grew them, and you can dip them in a little salt and chew them. You are educating."

Educating people how to eat a radish? Wendy sighed. "I know. It's amazing how many people still are in the frozen vegetable milieu. I identify food a *lot* to people, because we use different kinds of greens that are not available [generally]."

Thanks to California's "extraordinary produce," Wendy is very busy. "I need patience to answer these questions, but the fact I'm being asked in such a way, I feel respected. I like letting people know about the philosophy of the restaurant. I like guiding them through their meal."

Tasting precedes the tour. "We get to work at four-thirty and prep our stations out, and at four-forty we have a menu meeting. The chef verbally runs down every dish. At Chez Panisse, I know what farm and where the farm is located [for] the vegetables in each salad. Then we'll go through cooking method and all that with the food and the desserts. Then we go up to the line, four-forty-five, and the cooks prepare a sample of every item. The chef tastes it to make sure it's okay, and then we all taste it so we get to form our opinions. If someone says, 'Is the fish stew really garlicky?' there's no way I'm going to know unless I taste it, right?" (When customers ask for recommendations, however, Wendy complies only if they insist. "Most people want to hear you recommend what they wanted to order.")

Wendy feels respected economically, too. She earns fifteen dollars an hour and "extra side tips" above a 15 percent service charge (referred to by the French phrase *service compris*) included in the check. The 15 percent goes to the restaurant, which uses it in large measure to pay salaries. "Before *service compris* at Chez Panisse, the waiters were cleaning up. They were making three hundred dollars a night. Now it's a more egalitarian system."

Wendy also gets "full benefits, like a regular job," including two weeks of paid vacation, sick days, and "disability if I need it"—all a rarity in the noncorporate restaurant world. "I've got a 401(k). Thank God, I've been able to start a retirement plan. Chez Panisse has afforded me that opportunity, and it shows they value me." She has needed the disability provisions, too. "The restaurant takes care of me. When I was out—I fell downstairs here and broke my foot—they paid me extra sick time. Then they let me answer the phones for a couple of weeks while I was recuperating. It was extraordinarily humane. And the health insurance is great."

She is fortunate that it is, no thanks to parents who "let their children run wild. I was out of work for two weeks because of a run-in I had with a child." While she was carrying a heavy platter of food to a table, a six-year-old boy who had been playing underneath the table jumped up. Wendy clenched the platter so as not to burn him, while twisting to make sure he was all right. "I couldn't continue working that night. I was in spasms. The parents were clueless that anything had even happened to me."

For all her advantages, she knows that any waitress is identified less with where she works than with the work itself. "If you have a career being a cook at Chez Panisse, you've garnered already so much respect, you have a particular context. But being a waitress . . . it has a certain kind of weight on it, no matter where you're a waitress."

Wendy's "where" began in Brooklyn. As a child, she played waitress, serving her younger sisters choices from her handwritten menu. More complicated components of the work came later.

"My parents split up when I was about twelve. Every other Wednesday we'd have dinner with my father" at a steak house. She and her sisters "were all heartbroken but trying to have a good time." When "these waitresses would come up" to the table, "I would watch my father flirt with them. I remember getting flushed with embarrassment, seeing my father acting kind of sexy this way. Ew-w-w, he's *winking* at her! 'Dad, don't do that!' "

Still, the waitress got Wendy's attention, too. "What I really remember is wanting to be a waitress. I was fascinated with her. I don't know if I had a crush on her or whatever, but she looked old and sophisticated to little twelve-year-old me, with her pad. She was attractive and in control and, you know, sexy. I wanted to be her. I didn't particularly like the way my father was acting, but that's because seeing your parents become sexualized is difficult for any kid."

Wendy announced to her mother (skipping details about her father's flirtation) that she wanted to be a waitress. The job was not "part of the picture of what my parents had planned for me. Yet I planned a life as an artist very early on"—Wendy also is a filmmaker and teaches filmmaking part time—"and I thought actresses and artists wait tables. I wanted the stereotypical life I thought I could have in restaurants. I didn't think about how hard it was to garner your self-respect. I found it exciting, before I was in it." Then she was in it.

At By George Italian Cuisine in Brooklyn Heights, during her "polyester zip-up uniform days," she was "playing at being a waitress." Then a married cook, playing differently, tried to get her to go out with him. To spark her interest, he and the dishwasher "would show me dirty pictures." They did not know, however, that Wendy was gay. "I was in the closet that whole summer pretty much, and then I ran into one of the waiters at a gay bar. It all came out. The kitchen freaked. They would show me pictures of nude women and go, 'You like *dat?*' "

Yes, she did. Nevertheless, when she moved to California at age twenty-one, still a virgin in terms of experience with men, she decided it was time to try one.

At a modest Berkeley restaurant called the Buttercup, Wendy waited tables and cast about for a deflowerer. A policeman "got totally fixated on me at one point," proposed marriage, and "brought his mother in to meet me," but Wendy rejected him. Instead, she selected a cook. "I hardly had to do anything except look up," she recalled. "He started walking me home and we started talking. I was attracted to him and started to get that feeling—maybe this will be my first . . . hm-m-m." She was attracted to his mind, too. "I definitely am not about to give it up for someone who's an idiot." She also liked his hands. "I've always loved chefs' hands. Especially as you get into more fancy restaurants, their hands are so agile and expressive, the way they flip the pans and chop. He had that gentle expertise." They got together but then broke up and went their "separate ways," she as a lesbian, he as a Rajneesh (a follower of the controversial and later discredited cult leader Baghwan Rajneesh).

"It seemed natural to me that it would happen in the restaurant. Those are the people who form your immediate circle. That's your context." She smiled broadly, with very white teeth. "Waitressing is a sexual business. It just is."

To her, steam rising from a kitchen grill is a metaphor for sexual heat rising in the kitchen among staff members. "In restaurants I've worked at, before you know it, she's sleeping with him and he's sleeping with her, she's sleeping with her and he's sleeping with him. You're always in motion, you're physical, plus the heat of the stoves and everything else. Late at night, it's like you cannot be held responsible."

Before making her way to Chez Panisse, Wendy spent four years "working corporate" at tony Campton Place, off San Francisco's Union Square. Her outfit was what she calls a "Stepford waitress" look. "I wore taupe pumps, off-white pantyhose, a taupe skirt, a little white blouse with little puffs on the sleeves, a pink vest, a white apron, lipstick. We had lipstick check. I couldn't cut my hair too short. I couldn't wear the jewelry I usually wear." She got "wonderful benefits" and "a high rate of pay and great tips, but I had to turn over a bit of my, you know, soul.

"I gained a little weight at one point, and the manager took me off the floor. She said, 'What's wrong? I notice your vests are getting a little tight.' " Wendy exhaled forcefully. "I have had huge weight fluctuations in my life. During my heaviest period, I was up to about a hundred eighty pounds. But I'd been pretty thin, for *me,* for quite a long time." The manager's remark "sent me into the worst depression." Still, Wendy lost weight as instructed.

Campton Place had a major bonus, though: it was there she met Kerry Heffernan, a visiting chef from Los Angeles. "She didn't know I was gay, because I'm dressed in that Stepford uniform." Wendy could only hope that Kerry was gay, too. "I don't usually get attracted to straight women." Amid "a huge sexual tension that transformed from the restaurant," the two "developed from there" and now live together as a married couple. Having found her mate, Wendy then found her restaurant—Chez Panisse.

"Still now, there's something about the environment that *is* kind of exciting. It is like putting on a show every night. All that stuff I thought it had to offer—it did. I found my voice, in a way." She also found "a certain self-confidence," which "made stepping up in front of a classroom of forty students not scary. You don't have that same burden of feeling [that] you have to be brilliant when you're a waitress, but you feel you have to be gracious and professional and knowledgeable."

The boss at Chez Panisse furthers good waitress instincts. "If Alice is around and sees people who are feeling a little uncomfortable, she'll pull over the server and say, 'Do whatever it takes to make them feel at home.' " A free sampler of desserts has helped.

Wendy was nervous the first time she had to serve Alice and still gets "little rushes" when waiting on her own pantheon of stars, but she has little reaction to celebrities who might be heartthrobs to others. For example, while waitressing for a while at Wolfgang Puck's Chinois in Santa Monica, she often waited on Bruce Springsteen, who didn't do a thing for her, she shrugged. Madonna did not score highly, either. "Madonna once said to me . . . she was at some table with Warren Beatty and a bunch of other slobs, and she had this low-cut thing on, and I'm serving this dish in front of her, and she looks up at me and she's going like this"—Wendy reached inside her blouse—" 'I love to touch my breasts.' "

In general, "most" celebrities were "regular people. I'll never forget when Telly Savalas was in Chinois and comes up to me, and I'm like"—she shrieked—" 'What could he possibly want?' He goes, 'Excuse me, where's the bathroom?' " When she was assigned to wait on the poet Wendell Berry at Chez Panisse before a local reading, "I was all excited. I made sure they had a nice time, and I was forward. I didn't just let them have their time, but I talked about the food, I engaged with him. After the reading, he came back with a signed book for me!"

At "Chez," as she began calling it, most customers, of course, are not celebrities, nor do they rise to the level of the cuisine. Wendy estimates that 25 percent are "terrific," 60 percent are "fine," and 15 percent are "horrifying" (only a fraction of the "horrifying" percentage at Chinois). Still, the horrifying fraction makes even her job hard. "The kind of stuff you have to fend off and negotiate and mediate and mitigate all through the evening is mind-boggling. The cooks just have to cook the food. We're the ones who have to make [customers] feel decent about eating it."

What? At Chez Panisse? Yes, precisely because it *is* Chez Panisse. "A lot of people come into the restaurant with awe, and it's sort of wonderful to wait on them." Others act bent on "trying to challenge the status quo," complaining that a portion is too small, a drink too cool. "People come in with attitudes." Others tote what she calls "cluelessness." By that, she did not mean people like a recent table of "sweet" Chinese visitors who spoke virtually no English and ordered simply "bottle of wine." (Wendy managed to narrow the request.) Rather, she meant Americans. "It's more than my pleasure" to help along "inexperienced diners," but some are very trying. "You'll get Americans who have never been out to eat before and have no idea. 'Put the napkin in your lap so I can put the food down.' "

If anyone is annoyed that she does not come by to check on them (she does, though, read her tables "constantly"), a lack of hovering is company policy. "We don't normally go up to a table and say, 'How is everything?' " The assumption is that everything is wonderful.

"Some people, they're ogres to start out with, and then you feed them and they turn into little angels. You know kids who start screaming and crying when they get hungry? Adults are the same way. Ask any waitress." Other customers are simply rude, snapping their fingers to find her or engaging in more boorish behavior. "The other day, I was at a table helping another waiter out, and I was putting some food down. Someone at the other table *pulled* on my apron." Wendy gasped and turned around. "I wasn't their waitress. 'Excuse me? Did you really do that?' I couldn't hold back." The apron puller, a man, apologized. "Still, it boggles the mind. How people will infiltrate you physically and put their stuff all over *you*."

Frequently, the "stuff" is the flaunting of familiarity. A San Francisco businessman in the arts who "spends a lot of money" at Chez Panisse and "likes to be coddled over" holds his plate in the air when he has finished eating, until someone takes it. He also expects someone to be there with a new bottle of opened wine the moment the first bottle is finished.

Sometimes familiarity is friendly and blunt; this often comes from tourists. "[They'll ask,] 'What's your ethnic background?' " She laughed. "I've gotten, 'What are you? Are ya Grick? Are ya Spanish? Are ya Irish?' They're nonplussed when I tell them I'm a Romanian Jew. That wasn't in their repertoire. But they want to know about you, to *claim* you in some way."

Some ask her name. " 'Oh, I didn't get your name.' You *know* every time you come to the table, it's Wendy this, Wendy that. It's too much familiarity. I have a friend who sometimes when they say, 'What's your name?' says, 'Oh, Miss.' "

Wendy has a theory about name askers. "To be on a first-name basis with your waitress makes you feel magnanimous. I've never been asked by a woman what my name is. I don't think it's a particularly sexual thing. I think it's a power thing. *They* are the host, they want to show their friends and family and *you* who's the boss. They don't realize it's not a name-exchange relationship."

Once, the mother of a former Chez employee, who came in to eat with three other women, overstepped the bounds of familiarity spectacularly. "She was like, 'Hi, how are you?' She's showing them she's familiar with people at the restaurant. Then she looks at my hand and sees my ring. She goes"—Wendy put on a high, excited voice with a New York accent—" 'I didn't know you got married! When did this happen? Congratulations. Mazeltov, mazeltov.' Then she said, before I have a chance to answer, 'That's so wonderful! Is he Jewish?' I'm past the point of lying. I said, 'I did get married, but I didn't marry a man. I got married to a woman.' She's holding my hand, and she drops it. 'Oh-h-h-h-h.' " Wendy now laughed. "This woman's a *therapist*. At the end of the meal, she gets herself together and says"—Wendy's tone dripped with condescension—" 'I want to applaud you for the courage you had to share your situation with us.' "

Infrequently, Wendy feels an unusual connection to new customers and has become friends with regulars, but those unions mostly develop over time and are rare. "There's got to be some division."

Although she does not care to be asked anything personal by people she does not know well, she recognizes that her background comes in handy with customers who share it. "There's a certain ethnic bond. When L.A. Jews come and they're pushy and loud—'Wendy, you better take these people.' I speak their language. There is a cultural thing. I understand why [the therapist] felt a little familiar." I asked Wendy about a phenomenon several waitresses had mentioned to me: loud New Yorkers, rightly or wrongly assumed to be Jewish, infuriating the waitresses in various ways, which in turn led to anti-Semitic remarks. Wendy said, "It is a small part of the Jewish population. To me, most of the time they don't mean anything by it. It's like something out of Woody Allen. I wish it wouldn't happen, but I think there's a cultural bias to begin with. If other people came in dressed up and Waspy-looking and acted the same way, you wouldn't get [remarks like] 'those pushy' whatever."

Meanwhile, Brooklynites especially "want to claim me," she said. "My Brooklyn accent will get worse around them, because they'll be 'tawkin' like this and I'll start 'tawkin' like that.

"The only hard thing is when my students come in with their parents. 'This is my film instructor!' When I'm in school, they ask me questions, they hand in papers to me, I get a certain degree of professional respect. Taking their order is not part of that, you know? Their parents are paying for their education and their professor is a waitress."

Her silent response is a mental rundown of her resume. "I've got four films and two publications and x-y-z screenings and installations. . . . It doesn't matter, because I have to wait tables." Her verbal response is quite different. To "start getting onto the respect bandwagon, I put on this sort of thing: 'Hi! What a coincidence! Come on in and sit down!' I'll fake it the whole way and start acting like I own the place." Parent and student customers all were "fine" about their surprise server, although they had known nothing of Wendy's private life. "It's not something I share with my classes. I'll sooner come out to the class as a lesbian than as a waitress."

A year after our conversation, Wendy quit Chez Panisse. With Kerry, she opened the Autumn Moon Cafe in neighboring Oakland. Reviews have been good, and business is great. Wendy told me she has never worked harder in her life. Yet, as she strolled around (in jeans, a blouse, and many earrings) delivering food, greeting and seating people, she radiated happiness.

Nella Powell

Nella Powell's working life began in Memphis in 1933, when she was seven years old. Her mother had died that January. Her "daddy," she called him, remarried in June, to a woman who found work for Nella "ironing white shirts. Then after I got older, I babysat for one of the prominent families here." By the time Nella was a teenager, in the 1940s, she had set her sights beyond Memphis. "I told my sister I wanted to join the army."

One of the prominent Memphis women got wind of the idea, convinced Nella she would become "too tied up" with a military career, and set about finding an alternative, first in south Florida. "She had a friend that owned this Biltmore [hotel], [but] this friend told her they didn't have black maids in Florida at that time." The woman also had a friend who was moving to Atlanta and wanted household help. Nella went, becoming a private maid rather than a private in the army.

When her employers, the Stewarts, an airline executive and his wife, left Atlanta to return home to Connecticut, they invited Nella to go along as a cook. "Well, I was really young, and I had never been north. I thought that was God's country." She did not volunteer much information about what the social climate of Memphis had been like in her formative years, but her brevity spoke volumes: "Things were so bad." She added, "I grew up when you were still sitting in the back of the bus."

She cooked for the Stewart family for "twenty-something" years, in Connecticut and Hyannisport, at their summer home next door to the Kennedys. Nella (who requested a pseudonym for herself) related a stash of Kennedy anecdotes: the children of Robert and Ethel Kennedy acting self-important and trying to force her off the sidewalk ("they was some rough kids") until the man with them, Ted Kennedy, told them to get out of the way ("he was just nice"); president-elect John Kennedy's valet, Rupert, intervening with the Secret Service to let Nella and the Stewart children get close enough to watch a presidential helicopter land; Jacqueline Kennedy firing Rupert. "Miz Kennedy got somebody else," she said without warmth. Nella, a Catholic, went to mass daily in Hyannisport at the same church as Rose Kennedy, whom she did not recognize in her "socks and funny-looking shoes and an old-fashioned coat and scarf around her head."

Unquestionably, her favorite Kennedy was Ethel, who, she said, chuckling, "would go in the airport without shoes." More important, Nella liked how Ethel treated her cook, Ruby, who became Nella's long-time friend. When Ruby died, "Miz Kennedy got in touch with all of us so we could go to Boston to the funeral."

Nella knew southern money, but she is still stunned by what she saw, through back doors, of Yankee plutocracy—homes with three dining rooms, separate electric and gas kitchens "because the lights go off a lot," a boathouse with "a heater and a piano." At the home of the Paul Mellon family, one of whose maids she knew, even the higher levels of hired help had help. "They had somebody to iron their aprons." She preferred the less ostentatious Stewarts. "I had worked for them so long, I felt like it was family."

Then Nella got so sick that she thought she was going to die. A sister in Memphis begged her to return. (Actually, she begged her not to die up north because of the difficulty of bringing her body back.) Nella did return to Memphis, and her trouble was cured with a hysterectomy. Then she decided to stay. She was forty-five years old, with a wealth of experience and an experience of wealth. Word must have spread quickly that Nella Powell was again for hire.

A man she knew on the board of the Memphis Country Club called her and said he had spoken with the manager, who "wanted me to come out and talk to him because he knew I was a good cook. I went out and spoke to this manager. He said I had too much personality to be in the kitchen. He hired me as a waitress." She began laughing, her brown eyes sparkling and her black dress shaking. Nella Powell still has personality.

She is sixty-seven now. She was sitting in a small office of the city's only African American–owned high-rise window cleaning business, which she inherited from her brother. She took it over partly because she has chronic knee problems that became so severe she could not wait tables anymore. She lost some weight in the past few months, she said, and that helped—her walker is stowed in the hall—but still she is heavy and walks with a limp and a cane. All in all, she is having a hard go of things in body and business. Male employees resist doing what she wants them to, like finishing a job. Handwritten signs around the office ("Reward for 40' ladder. No questions asked") indicate other troubles.

If her current work is a burden, past work animated her and seemed to be the reason she let her phone machine pick up calls for an hour or so, enabling uninterrupted reminiscences. She has a delicate accent in the mid-southern range—"army" sounds like "ahmy." Her words at times emerge as a soft rush, with a sentence starting up for a few words like a headline, then stopping, before a regular sentence begins. Punctuation is often a laugh.

Sometimes, too, her softness swoops so low it arrived at the threshold of inaudibility. But when I later listen to the recording of our conversation, a cranked-up volume knob reveals words not to be missed, words she may have been accustomed to speaking under her breath.

The Memphis Country Club is old guard, old money, old society, with an old oak shading the parking lot where a member's day might begin. When Nella Powell began working there, she faced a sociological split. Members welcomed her. Employees did not. "There were so many [members] there who knew me and knew of me, and in a place like that they [ask] for who they know. Then they tip. Therefore, it was easy for me." Some members may have felt she was simply back home. Some had seen her up north, in the same circles where she worked and they socialized.

She appreciated their welcome, but apparently the way her co-workers received her had more impact, for she repeatedly brought it up. At first, she spoke diplomatically: "It's hard anywhere you go when people have been there longer than you."

Eventually, she painted a picture less of resentment than of subterfuge. "When I started working there, a lot of the other waitresses would tell different things, would test stuff to try to get me fired. There were a lot of people this particular girl had waited on, and they would ask for me, because they knew me from when I was small. When I first came, they would try to help me out and be friendly." Some co-workers complained to "the girl that was head of the dining room. They'd make up stuff on me. I just let it go. Then there was one waiter. I was busy waiting on somebody. Back in those days, I could carry a tray. He would try to trip me up, with the tray." Her tone did not change, but she began to pause a lot.

"At Christmas time, people give you all these envelopes. I'd be busy around there, and [envelopes] would be stuck in my pocket, and they'd steal them out of my pocket. Both of them run into bad luck," she said almost to herself, paused, and then laughed. "You run into all kinds of things. That was when I first went there. After a while, they didn't mess with me." She also worked at people's homes for parties. One family asked her to work Christmas Eve, "but I cut that out. I needed money, but I didn't need it bad enough to work on Christmas Eve."

At the club, tipping stereotypes held: men were best and women worst. The least favorable setting for Nella was the ladies bridge lunch, where "a big tip was a quarter."

Her largest tip, which became legendary at the club, came from Mr. Stewart, her former employer. He was approaching ninety and his daughter was trying to get him to stop driving. On a visit to Hartford, "I said, 'Mr. Stewart, when you stop driving, I want you to sell me your Mercedes.' He said, 'Well, I'll see about it.' His birthday is in September and mine is, too. Just before his last birthday, he called me up and told me I could come and get the Mercedes whenever I wanted. I asked him how much was it, and he said, 'I'm giving it to you.'" The car is broken down now, after one of her nephews "messed it up." For a while, though, "I really enjoyed it."

She drove it all the way from Hartford to Memphis, stopping in Charlotte to see a Stewart granddaughter. "I'm kind of short, as you can see, and I'd be down there [driving], and all you could see was the head sticking up." During recent financial troubles, she almost accepted the Stewart family's offer to move back with them, but it came just as her brother, who owned the window cleaning business, got sick. So she stayed on.

She stayed at the Memphis Country Club twenty-four years. "I didn't have a lot of problems with the members because, I guess, I have a good memory." She added, laughing, "I guess I'm neurotic, but I could remember things," including names and who ordered what. "But, always in any group, you going to find somebody. And if I found someone being nasty, I'd go along with them and continue to be as nice as I could and try to please them.

"If, for instance, something is wrong with the food, then I would try to tell [the servers] to go to the kitchen and try to get it straightened out. If I couldn't, I'd simply tell them the story. Because nothing's going to go perfect all the time.

"Sometimes some of the kids get smart when they're growing up. But if the parents were there, they would straighten them out. If I knew them, *I* would straighten them out." When she waited on children "and you ask them a question and they say yes or no, the mother would say, 'Yes, *ma'am*.' I've had some [children] yell at me, but if their parents are there, most parents don't allow their kids to talk to you like that.

"Sometimes the teenagers would come in and get smart" and "try to run you around," including asking her to get them beer and cigarettes. "They'd try to tell you they are old enough, but if you've been around the kids from the time they were born, you *know* how old they are."

Parents often acted as a safeguard. "It's when the kids would come in alone that you would have your trouble. And, uh, a lot of them try to throw their weight around." They would "speak in a way of 'Go do this.' I'd say, 'Is this the way that you talk to people? I know your mama don't know you're carrying on like this here.' I would kind of carry on in a 'mammy' sort of way." She had partly swallowed that sentence, and one word sounded odd. Had she really said "mammy"? Yes, she had. I needed the volume boost to make out her next words: "Kind of Uncle Tom, I guess, is really what you'd say."

This approach worked on children, but not on certain "older people," who "would get smart, say smart things. I would always choose to ignore it and go along." For her own mental state or for fear of a complaint costing her the job? "Oh, it was my own mental state."

"The main thing I found is when someone else is mad, it's best for you to keep smiling. That's what I tried to do when I was there. I loved it. The girls would tell me all the time . . . I'd be feeling bad, my knees are bad, they would see me walking around dragging. [But] as soon as the members would come in"—she laughed—"they said I'd be coming across the dining room like there was nothing wrong with me. It's almost like a feeling I'd get. They were teasing me and making fun of me, but I realized that was my job, and I tried to do what I could."

In Nella Powell's years at the Memphis Country Club (which she nearly always referred to with all three words), nothing much changed, she said. "The serving part of it was basically the same"—formal. "The Memphis Country Club is different than even Chickasaw," another local country club. One "girl" hired from there "didn't know how to serve the way we serve. We had a lot of fancy servings. They didn't always put the food on the tray down there. They had all the plates up and down their arm." Imagine that, her eyes said.

Service at the Memphis Country Club stayed the same, and so did its members. "A new generation" came along, "the same kind of people." She characterized them as "pleasant." Still, how did it feel to be working in a place where neither she nor anyone in her family could join, even if they had the money? "It didn't bother me, because the thing is, the only way you would ever get a black member in there [is] when you vote. . . . If one member says no, you can't join . . . there's always going to be one that says no. That part didn't bother me. It did [bother] some of the younger people."

Among the members, Nella Powell especially liked old, old Memphis: a group of men who had to be at least seventy-five to be part of their own inner circle. "None of them could hear. They would come out with these corny jokes, and they were so funny, and you really had to laugh. They call themselves the Old Goats, and one of the members said I was the nanny goat." She laughed. "It was said as a compliment. Some of them were ninety and like that, but it was nice. They met once a month, and I'd always wait on them." She recalled, smiling, "Then there is a group of men that played golf, called themselves the Saturday Morning Dogs and things like that. So it's really a lot of fun."

She gave no indication of knowing she had slipped into the present tense.

"The main thing is, you have to have patience and leave your feelings most times at the front door." Her mood had changed entirely. "You are always going to find somebody who is not going to do right. And, uh, sometimes a member will say something and then come back and apologize.

"Actually, what people don't realize is that in a country club setting, they mostly treat you like family, and most of them treat you like they would people [who work] in their homes. Some would treat you better than they would people at home."

Nella Powell's last years at the Memphis Country Club coincided with two changes. One was a new assistant manager, who antagonized many employees. He fired a legendary waiter who was accustomed to talking back to members and who had told one complaining man who wanted something to "get it yourself"—an anecdote beloved in the kitchen. Furthermore, the waiter would not rush, as the new assistant manager wished. After the waiter was fired, members got him rehired.

The assistant manager then turned his attention to Nella. He "kind of picked on me. He'd see me talking to the members, and he would think they were talking about him." If she stopped to talk with women she had known since they were little girls, "he would say I wasn't moving fast enough. The thing of it is, a lot of people don't like you to throw stuff at them," that is, to serve them too fast. "They want you to take time and wait on them."

"This new person," as she called him, did not set much stock by experience, either. "He'd give a lot of tests. He would ask you what side should you serve from, and all those different things. I had been serving a table since before I was big enough to *get* to it," she said indignantly. "When I left, a lot of members felt he was the reason." One, on behalf of the members, offered to intervene, but she said no. "I told him I was ready."

She does not mind hearing about the assistant manager's subsequent missteps, such as bringing in inexperienced help. "A lot of times when you're in a place like that, if you are dealing with people you know and you wait on all the time, they'll put up with a lot more than [they would from] somebody they don't know. Evidently, that's what happened" on a famously disastrous day. "One lady had real important guests from out of town, and one of the guys served her a bad crabmeat cocktail. [The assistant manager] jumped on the waiter and went back and got a shrimp cocktail and spilled it on the lady's lap!" Nella laughed so hard her chair shook.

The other change is that African Americans have begun to appear at the club as guests. "They have meetings and things [at the club] and black people are there, and some of the members act funny. One of the members who was an old Memphis took this black guy to the Red Room to have drinks, and the members—a lot of them were little old ladies and didn't like it." Local African American dignitaries, in Nella's later years there, also came to the club as guests. "The thing that I noticed is a lot of the members, when the black people come out, would go out of their way to try to be nice to them." Clearly she welcomes the inclusion of such guests, but she insisted she is not bothered by a lack of African American members. The reason is "the setting that, you know, I grew up in," as she called it. Another reason may be that discrimination in the Memphis Country Club membership does not affect her directly. Discrimination in the window washing business does.

"They say things are better, but . . ." She wonders how much better. She mentioned "this white girl" she had hired and then fired, who started her own window washing business and got a big contract "without a speck of insurance." Powell's company "always" has to show proof of insurance. Also, "a lot of things we bid on, we know we are not going to get."

Nella Powell well knows she does not have the workforce she needs, workers like "the best window washers my brother had," a man and woman team who left to join the circus. "You have to know how to rappel, and she and her husband were really good rappelers." Now Nella is faced with hiring people she considers slothful. "There are so many people that don't want to work, *but* they want to draw a check."

Members of the Memphis Country Club offered to help her sell the business, but she hesitates. "There are a lot of people around that said, 'You are the only black high-rise window cleaning company, and I hate for you to just give up.' But it is so hard." Old Memphis had its advantages. She spoke of members who, in addition to the 15 percent gratuity added to checks, slipped her another 10 percent in folding money. "I had a nice living and I miss it, since I'm not on salary down here. I really miss it."

Martha Shissler

The spa's brochure spells out some of the lure:

· The Golden Door® lies just six miles north of Escondido, in Southern California's loveliest countryside.
· In such an atmosphere of rare privacy, each week 39 guests individually achieve a rapport with Nature and with themselves.

"You meet a colorful group of people. You are looking at people that first of all have to be well-to-do to be here. It's not cheap. And when you figure you're paying airfare, by the time you leave, if you have anything else extra done—colorings, permanents, whatever goes on out of my area—you're looking at five thousand dollars" (closer to seven thousand dollars by early 2002).

Martha Shissler spoke in a tone of friendly frankness. She is a pretty, stoutish woman in her fifties, with dark wavy hair, clear bronze-toned skin, and lovely eyes. She wore a white smock over street clothes, an angel pin, and a brass-colored name tag reading "Marta S. Dining Room Supervisor."

Martha dropped the *h* in her name when she began working at the spa six years and seven chefs ago. Another Martha was already employed there, so Martha Rodriguez Shissler figured that because her name is pronounced "Marta" in her native Mexico, she would be Marta at work. During a walking tour through and around the spa, whose reputation rests on its ability to coddle demanding, dieting, and often famous women, Martha spoke respectfully about the Door metaphor—old one closing, new one opening—and added that the Golden Door was meant "to give you a center."

The stroll led to the guest complex, clusters of one-story buildings encircled by Japanese-style gardens. No one was to be seen. Because this week only thirty-four guests were individually achieving a rapport with Nature and with themselves, Martha was able to show me an empty guest suite. The idea is to be "very private," she whispered. The suite's peaceful feeling was alluring. (I was staying in an Escondido motel whose rooms were decorated with Broadway musical themes, mine being a claustrophobic tribute to *Cats*.)

Huffing a bit heading up a hill, she pointed out where predawn walks start. "Most of the guests get up at five in the morning to go on their little hikes," guided by spa "shepherds." Martha herself is "not a morning person. That's sad to say," she said, smiling. (She does not exercise either, which she also called "sad," while smiling.) In the home several miles away that she shares with one of her two daughters and the daughter's child, Martha's wake-up routine focuses on birds. "I have cockatiels and lovebirds. I like to talk to them in the morning."

Leading the way to a hilltop enclosure for outdoor nude massages, she mentioned that no one would be there. She was right, of course; part of her job is knowing where everyone is. She must—she feeds them. "Some people eat in the rooms, some people eat at the pool, some people might eat out here"—she gestured at the gardens—"some people eat in the dining room. I have people everywhere."

She herself arrived at the Golden Door "by quite accident," she said. (Martha speaks English confidently and without a Mexican accent but sometimes employs curious phrases.) She was born in Tecate in 1941 to a journalist father and housewife mother, who divorced when she was young. Her mother went to work in a restaurant in Tijuana, placed Martha in a convent for safekeeping, emigrated to the United States, opened a "small taco shop" with twelve tables in San Diego, and sent for her. Martha left the convent, picked up a tray, and got to work.

"At that time, I didn't like it, because I *had* to do it. I've worked ever since." Martha is the personification of work ethic. "I believe as long as you're capable of working, you should. I pay taxes, and I don't like to be taxed more to have somebody stay home and have babies after babies after babies." She shakes her head unhappily about able-bodied people, including a part-time Golden Door waitress who is a single mother, collecting welfare. "Why should we take from the government what's not ours?"

Martha headed down the hill to her dining room and kitchen domain, settled in an alcove, and went to get coffee, offering whole milk, Lactaid, nonfat, 2 percent, or half and half to go with it. At the Golden Door, they aim to please. From an adjoining room came the shouted voice of a woman guest lecturer speaking about choices: "You realize you've done it and you've done it and you've *done* it—and you don't need to *do* that anymore. You really don't."

It is not a message Martha gives the waitresses.

"What I tell my girls is, pick one person and remember what they like and what they drink and blow their mind away. . . . It's like a game." Most of the waitresses are eighteen to twenty years old, live at home, and include many students "studying a career," in Martha's phrase. "Like I told them, 'Waitressing, you can always get a job and survive. I did it, and you can. When you do it, just do it good. Take pride in it, because you never know if it's going to get you out of a jam. Even after you're married.' " She is proof positive of her own words.

At seventeen, she married a navy man in San Diego, with whom she had two daughters and a planned future. He began going to college in preparation for medical school and worked in a hospital lab, while she worked as a waitress. They bought a house. One day, while he was taking a flying lesson, his plane crashed. He was killed.

Martha, then twenty-five, soon was working two waitressing jobs. "So it was a little bit hard." Her faith (she has practiced at least four religions) helped. "God takes care of me. He really does. He's always been there, or something comes up. An opportunity. When I think, gee, what am I going to do, something happens. And it works out, and then life goes on."

Her financial redemption was alcohol. She began serving cocktails in a Mission Valley hotel to a free-spending crowd.

"We used to wear Gay Nineties outfits, a long dress with the ruffles halfway up the leg. It wasn't provocative." The mandatory high heels were a problem. So was a particular customer. A member of the hotel's board of directors, he tried to have Martha fired after "I turned him down." His offers included an apartment. "I don't think I stepped out of bounds. I wasn't rude. I was very pleasant." Her income at stake, she had to convince the manager of her propriety—and did.

She later married a midwesterner in the restaurant business. (They would eventually divorce.) She moved with him to Wisconsin and without him to Bloomington, Minnesota, where Counsel Corporation had started a chain of Mexican restaurants called Chi-Chi's. In Martha's modest assessment, she began as a hostess, and "then I became into management and training and coordinating their openings." She added with no evident irony, "I was their little mascot."

She then crossed her second northern border, into salsa-deprived Canada. "In '81, nobody knew what a tortilla really was." From Vancouver to Montreal, Martha trained staffs in the art of burrito rolling and much, much more. She also oversaw enormous opening parties, beginning at a thousand invitees, to help the staff learn volume and the customers learn tacos. "I don't know how I survived every time we opened a restaurant, on three or four hours' sleep, but we did it. For fifteen days straight."

About the time she was sent to the San Diego area to manage a Chi-

Chi's, the franchises started closing. A waiter who knew a cook at the Golden Door asked Martha her plans. She had only one: "I don't want to move back to Minnesota."

The Golden Door opened to Martha/Marta Shissler.

Her job is to "make your dining experience a pleasant one." The understatement masks much. When guests check in on Sunday for a week's stay, they are interviewed about food preferences and allergies. Martha takes it from there, diligently.

"Some people are vegetarians, which I have no problem with, because we have a regular menu and a vegetarian menu. But there's no-garlics, there's no-dairies, there's no-eggs, there's no-tomatoes, there's no-spinach, there's no-carrots . . ." She paused. "I have to make sure that whatever food is presented, for breakfast, lunch, and dinner, don't include any of those allergies or dislikes." How much of this is attributable to allergies and how much to dislikes? She narrowed her eyes ever so slightly. "Ninety percent . . . dislikes." Martha carefully notes all on a computerized diet sheet and file cards.

According to the diet sheet one January week, there was to be no cilantro for Ann, no Brussels sprouts for Lynn, no apple juice for Fifi, and no trout or red snapper for Katy. "No hot cereal!" for Karen, read a later penciled-in notation. Martha also notes portions—"small," "medium," or, in Golden Doorese, "tall." Posted in the kitchen is a notation that "tall" begins at 175 pounds.

Martha meets the week's guests when she delivers a postexercise restorative at 10:50 Monday morning. "We give them a potassium broth, which is a V-8 base. We serve it hot so it works through the bloodstream faster, for leg cramps."

She then makes announcements about lunch and dinner. The breakfast trays contain menus for both, but "half of the people haven't read it." She takes notes. She always takes notes. "I look at my menu every day, and I turn in a list of my specials. Then I make my changes. Then I talk to the guest, when possible, and double-check on those changes."

After the broth break, "I come back, I do my lunch order for the chefs, I do my individual cards for lunch. The girls prepare the trays. At twelve o'clock, I start on my dinner things. I make out my lists for dinner for the chefs, then write my individual cards."

At "about a quarter to one," she is back in the kitchen, overseeing lunch delivery. "I expedite each individual plate and put it on each tray," along with the diet card. If needed, she also helps serve, taking trays to wherever guests said they would be. "By one-thirty, basically all of my lunch is done, and I'll go out to wherever my guests are to make sure everything was okay."

From 1:30 until 2:00 or so, she is busy with paperwork or meetings. She eats lunch around 2:00, "after everybody has eaten and it's calmed down." She also snacks "all through the day. This padding"—she tapped a hip—"it's because I eat a lot."

She may not care about her weight, but guests certainly care about theirs. "I think the biggest disillusion now is our first-timers come with the idea they want to lose ten to fifteen pounds. You're not [going to do it]. You're going to lose five, six, which is your water weight. What they're trying to do is train your mind on how to eat healthier."

After lunch, Martha might do more paperwork. "I have to do my own ordering, my own inventory for all the kitchens." There are three kitchens, each with its own requirements. "I have to know how much dishware I have on hand. I order silverware, mats, uniforms. . . . I have all these little things."

She works a split shift, "according to the records," as she put it. She may not be off until 4:00 but must be back at 5:00.

The big event is dinner. Martha makes it not only as dietarily accurate but as festive as she can. She and the "lunch girls" spend effort on such details as how the napkins look, folding them differently each day. That was her idea, augmented by a book. Also, "I have different placemats and different candles and different napkins to work with," apart from scores of choices of chinaware.

Seating differs, too, thanks to Martha's forethought. "In the beginning of the week, it's long tables. You don't know everybody yet, so you feel more comfortable with a lot of people. By Friday, I have little tables of six or five. By then you've made friends." At 6:30, the dining room opens. "They come in for their mock cocktails [called 'mocktails'], they pick up their cards, and they can sit anywhere they'd like."

Early in the week, most guests are relatively undemanding, although some want last-minute changes. "They don't understand this isn't a restaurant. Everything is made special order." If they do not want the main entree, even the vegetarian one might not work. Today's vegetarian dinner is a twice-baked potato. "They bake the potato, they scoop everything out, put [in] ricotta cheese, corn, carrots, celery, onions. Somebody is no-onion—they can't have that. If somebody's no-dairy—they can't have that." With notice, Martha also alters the entree (today's lunch featured mushrooms and spinach in phyllo dough with tomato sauce), leaving out whatever ingredient offends. She must order her alterations early, though. "If you change your mind at the last minute, I can't produce it for you," not quickly, at any rate. Some guests "don't understand, sometimes, why." Martha appreciates repeat customers as much as any waitress; "they know the routine."

Some guests, furthermore, arrive with "a lot of different diets" they plan to follow. "Sometimes you can accommodate them and sometimes you can't. I have to work with *my* chef [Michel Stroot, from Brussels], and my chef is an expert on what he does. He really doesn't like people to vary from the menu."

Other guests add new requests, continued Martha, or revoke old ones. "Today, my no-spinach lady can have spinach," she laughed. "She's happy now." The no-cilantro crowd usually stays the course.

From morning to evening, Monday to Friday, Martha Shissler finesses diets, allergies, and whims. This week has been "*easy,* believe me!" she exclaimed. Nobody has pretended (let us be frank: the word is *lied*) that she ordered something she did not. No one has limited herself to little more than air. Best of all, the no-mango woman is not back.

In extensive detail, and speaking as if she were testifying before a Golden Door tribunal, Martha told of a "terrible" mistake. The sum of it is that a mango-allergic guest from New York licked a fingertip she had dipped in some mango sauce. "This was on Friday. She was due to depart on Sunday." Despite claiming that she could die, the guest refused any in-house medical help and so frightened the Golden Door management that they comped her entire stay. Martha, as supervisor, "partly" got in trouble, she said, grimly. (When I later questioned my allergist, he said that it was "a bit far-fetched" to consider mangoes fatal, especially given the woman's lack of immediate reactions. He left no doubt she was a charlatan.)

Some guests, such as the no-mango woman, are infamous, some merely famous. Celebrities, including a Hollywood crowd, have long been drawn to the Golden Door—and indeed are themselves part of the draw. As with countless other options, guests can choose whether or not to let their presence be known, whether or not to stay in their rooms the whole time. Employees sign stipulations promising that they will not reveal anyone's identity. When I visited, the list of "Your Golden Door Neighbors" revealed many prominent addresses but no prominent names: no former first ladies (Martha mentioned two who had stayed there, one liked, one disliked), no sisters of former presidents (one of whom has become friendly with Martha), and no entertainment legends. This week, everyone may have been who she said she was.

"Sometimes [a celebrity will] use a different name," mostly to keep lesser beings from bothering her. (Annoying a celebrity is among the few transgressions that can boot a guest out the golden door.) Although some stars stay in their rooms, "some of them fit right in." A talk show hostess "was wonderful. She's a great lady." Martha beamed: "She ate all her meals with the guests, didn't order any specials. She was wonderful and very thoughtful. We've had other people that are just as famous that have been very demanding and very rude.

"Most people are nice. Sometimes people have a lot on their minds and might act rude or mean because something has happened, and they don't know how to deal with it. That's what I like to tell my staff. Sometimes they intimidate the girls quite badly." She paused. "[To the point] where the girls will cry.

"We have comment sheets that people write at the end of the week. Some will say, 'One of the girls was very rude to me—she forgot what I drink.'" Others complain if their reading glasses were moved a couple of inches while the room was dusted.

The people most likely to be on the receiving end of complaints are the young Spanish-speaking women (there are some Anglos, too) who are part cook, waitress, and housekeeper and who may seek out Martha for comfort. She does more than comfort them.

"Sometimes I get very shy girls that are very timid. When I see them blossom, and see them even get aggressive sometimes, and talkative, and get involved in what they're doing—I enjoy that." She looked the most pleased I had seen her over the course of three separate talks.

She looked chagrined, however, when I asked what the "girls" were paid. "I start them at five dollars fifty cents and then up go to six dollars an hour." Barely audible, she whispered, "It's nothing." It *is* close to nothing. A part-time shift brings in as little as $16.50, minus taxes, minus gas money.

She cannot increase pay, she said, but can increase hours. She augments a three-hour dinner job by offering guests "a mini-massage at the end of the evening." It is "a little rubdown, which is from the neck or the waist up. We had a masseuse train girls on how to give these little massages." Dinner waitresses thus get "two extra hours' salary."

Guests do not dole out much help themselves. After the multi-thousand-dollar tab, most women never tip anything. (Men's weeks, which have their own challenges, are popular because men do tip.) One woman every fourth month might leave ten dollars, Martha said. If "you have twenty girls—because I have to remember the day girls that served the breakfast and the lunch and then the waitresses that served the dinner"—that comes to fifty cents a person. Instead of distributing change, Martha puts the cash in a kitty and treats the staff to a meal out. "I always include my cooks and my dishwashers."

During the upcoming weekend, the kitchen staff may be short a person. Unless Martha finds a backup, she will have to fill in herself. "That means this coming week I won't have a day off," she said, shrugging. "I think my employers are happy with my work. I try to give them ninety-nine percent or more of myself." Over the years, "I've only had one [raise], but it's okay. I like what I'm doing."

An Asian gong sounds. It is 6:30, mocktail hour. The dining room lights are flatteringly low. The tables, set this evening with square plates, are very pretty. On a sideboard, cloth napkins are artfully folded, next to the diet cards.

In the kitchen, the show is about to begin. Under a framed "A" sanitary report from the County of San Diego are the workaday detritus and tools of the trade, including a dog-eared *Fancy Folds*. The core of the room, ten times brighter than the dining room, looks spotless. The air smells clean and, somehow, low-fat. Young cooks stir and chop. Talk is in English and Spanish. Chef Stroot peers into a bubbling pot: "Beautiful."

There are two complications. It is pouring rain. Several guests have put in requests to have their meals delivered to their rooms, so room trays must be done first. Also, the owner, Deborah Szekely, is in residence and has sent word that she wants a snack of almonds, pine nuts, dried figs, and tea. Someone starts putting that together, while Martha calls out, "She likes whole milk in her tea." A waitress leaves with the completed tray, while others return from their room deliveries, drenched.

Martha and the young waitresses then set out six trays, three over three, on a stainless steel table, while she quizzes. Is the water out? "Yup." Salads out? "Yup." Candles lit? "Yup." "You guys are so good," she smiles.

She goes into the dining room and picks up the diet cards, writing down what each woman is having (or not having), returns to the kitchen, and takes up a commander's position by the trays. It is time to "expedite each table." Michel starts slicing the chicken. With low-fat cooking, he explains, one minute it's done, the next it's flat. Notes in hand, Martha recites how much of what—chicken, vegetables, and variations on the twice-baked potato—goes on which plate. "Small, no carrots" on six, upper right; "tall," no restrictions, on five, upper middle. Michel helps relay the information, in Belgian-accented Spanish, to his staff. Each waitress picks up two completed trays and goes out the swinging doors to the dining room.

Soon, food gives way to feedback. One waitress reports that a guest says her potato has red on it and she cannot have tomatoes. Answer: red chard bled onto the potato. Another guest sends back word she wants more carrots. Only two pencil-sized ones are left. Michel puts them on a plate, gussying them up with a bit of parsley, while Martha tells a new cook always to make more than ordered because if amounts are "right on the line," there could be an accident. (Also, the staff meal is the leftovers.) Next, a waitress reports that a guest is angry because she has no muffin. The cook of the insufficient carrots frantically starts putting muffin ingredients together. Michel and Martha stop him, and let the woman eat bread.

During a rare pause, I ask Martha where she sits to eat. A waitress interrupts: "She doesn't sit."

Another add-on request comes through the doors. "Martha?—wants to know if she can have a half piece of chicken."

"Half a piece of chicken and she's a vegetarian?"

The chicken is delivered.

After dessert—a flan garnished with two half slices of kiwi—goes out one door, more questions come back in.

"Are there eggs in the flan?"

"Has the kiwi been soaked in lemon juice?"

Kitchen clean-up starts at 7:15. During the staff dinner that follows, everyone eagerly eats anything available.

The spa's brochure continues:

> · You will never suspect your own body's gift for life-regenerating movement till you receive close and caring instruction under ideal conditions. You will never really know yourself till you recognize all your own potentials. The Golden Door dedicates itself to encouraging the full and individualized human potential of each guest.

Sandy Ward

Her black bow tie is askew on her white tuxedo shirt, her petite frame drags, her hair is damp around her temples, and she looks frazzled, blinking rapidly as if each blink represents something else she had better not forget. It is about 9:30 at night. The brightly lit restaurant is packed, the staff is feeling "slammed," and she is working as front waiter—the greet-the-customers, take-their-orders, and see-how-everything's-going job—in a team of two. She prefers being back waiter, the get-the-food-together and serve-it job. When customers are unhappy, the front waiter takes most of the heat.

Sandy Ward looks as if she has been taking it for hours. She is spinning, and so is the restaurant.

Welcome to the View, revolving atop the Times Square Marriott Marquis in Manhattan. While customers are treated to a leisurely 360-degree panorama of New York (and New Jersey), servers are dashing between the outside revolving restaurant wheel and the inside stationary guts of the enterprise. In addition to the job of serving, they also must literally figure where they are and where their tables went. Disorientation is par for the shift.

"When you leave the floor, you look at where you are, as far as the landscape is concerned. Like, is the Empire State Building close? People do walk [too far]. Sometimes we miss the kitchen door and we continue to walk. It's a circle, so you're going to make it eventually, you know?"

The following day, Sandy was sprawled comfortably on her living room rug in the sunny Greenwich Village apartment she shares with her husband, David, a chef, and their infant daughter, Sena, who was napping. Smiling and looking tranquil, Sandy seemed almost unrecognizable from the night before. Last night had been bad, she said.

She had earned the usual compensation, though. Sandy was getting, she believed, "probably about the highest" tips waitresses could earn in New York City.

She mulled over the evidence. Hip and expensive restaurants employ some women servers, "but I don't think they have the turnover we do. A place like the Four Seasons, [they] don't have women." That may leave the View (a place virtually unknown to locals), which a Zagat guide called "pricey" and "respectable."

Each waiter in a team of two makes up to $250 a shift and up to $300 on a Saturday night, after serving three full sittings. "On a *busy*

Saturday night, you would almost turn your tables four times," including once "during pre-theater." Sandy has earned over $400 a shift, "but those [times] are around Christmas, when you have major parties" and people are "throwing money, basically. Those are great tips." (Wary of attracting the interest of the IRS, Sandy asked that I use family pseudonyms. She has subsequently left the View.)

Last night's frazzling shift yielded no notable cash but much notable unpleasantness. At one table, a couple was arguing about the origin of a menu item. Because of the theater neighborhood, "everything [on the menu] is named after a Broadway show or an off-Broadway show." The man saw a reference to the farce *Tony 'n' Tina's Wedding* and claimed to the woman he was with that Tony and Tina were rock stars. She disagreed, so he urged Sandy to settle the argument. Sandy figured he meant Ike and Tina Turner—yet told him she was not sure. "You don't educate your guests. Ever. You can't." She takes the same stance when she asks customers whether they would like a cocktail and they say, "Okay, we'll have shrimp cocktails." She just puts in orders for shrimp cocktails.

From the arguing couple, Sandy was revolved to a family at prayer. "It was a four-top, a family, and they were very scared and angry—I don't know about what." Their tableside prayer did not put them in better spirits, nor did it help Sandy and her back waiter, Kay. To the staff of the View, prayers before meals signify fundamentalist Christians, and fundamentalist Christians signify poor tips.

"We were very busy, so we were running around. They weren't the type of people who were going to relax and love the experience. They thought they might be ripped off. You can feel that tension."

Then there was a mozzarella misunderstanding. "They expected fried mozzarella sticks. "Instead it was fresh, with tomatoes and all, and they had never seen anything like that. [Kay] said something, and they interpreted that as rude." They wrote on their check why they were not giving a tip on their $140 bill. "I didn't *care*" about the tip, said Sandy, but the note irked her. "I thought, what an awful thing to do! For *Christians*. Why are they trying to jeopardize our jobs?"

The table fit a stereotype that the staff had spotted "a mile away" and that had been confirmed by orders of iced tea. "I don't want to appear prejudiced or anything, but it's southerners. I don't know what they come up here for."

Sandy knows why she did. She was a stereotype, too: an actress-waitress.

She started working in both worlds at eighteen, selling tickets at the box office of the O'Neill Theater in Waterford, Connecticut, for twenty-five dollars a week and waiting tables at a Ground Round in Groton. At college in upstate New York, she found work at a second Round; and, following college, she clowned around. She graduated from the Ringling Brothers Clown College in Florida.

By the time she mustered the courage to move to Manhattan ("I was very scared of living here"), her resume included juggling, which helped land her "some very good auditions" and two commercials. In New York, she also joined a theater company, the Actors Theater of Manhattan, and later moved into the study of playwrighting. All the while, she faced restaurant stages.

"When I got to New York . . . in the early '80s, they had a lot of glass-front restaurants with those little lights, like Christmas lights. I'd always wanted to work in a place like that. I thought they were so beautiful." Sandy found sparkle in midtown, at Loew's Summit.

"It was a union hotel. I didn't know what that meant." She did learn that "after thirty days' probation, you automatically are part of the union and you pay them dues." She added, "No one explained what the union did or anything."

The tiny lights twinkled with bogus bonhomie. For five months, Sandy worked diligently, putting money aside for the necessities of an actor's life, such as a publicity packet. She then learned that other Summit waitresses were busy with their own project—the misuse of discount coupons.

After customers paid for meals in cash, as Sandy described the scheme, waitresses "would take cash checks, attach the coupons to the check, and pocket the remaining cash. There was this major scandal going on. I was aware of it, but I didn't know how it worked. Because it was a union house, these waitresses had been there for years. I wasn't a part of their circle at all. I heard whispers and little jokes at the employee dinner table before the shifts," but no more.

About the time she heard about the hoax, a manager implied that she was in on it. "I was really naive and stupid, so I started telling the truth: 'I think there's a scam going on. I'm not a part of it.' Of course, they were like, 'You *are* a part of it.' I was so stupid—I said [I'd] take a lie detector test. They said okay." She took the test but never saw the results.

"They said it proved deceptive, my answers. I was a *mess*. I thought, the world doesn't operate like this if you're honest, and all that crap." Her boyfriend urged her to call her union. She did.

At a meeting with management, "the union guy was like, 'She's not lying—look at her.' That's the *only* defense he could come up with." She still seems distressed.

"I didn't talk about that incident for years after. I would cry about it." She shook her head. "Maybe I was set up, because they knew if anyone would admit there was a scam, it would have been me. I don't know exactly *how* I was used, but I definitely was used. It was such an awful ordeal." She squirmed.

"Then the Marriott opened." She semi-smiled. "It was this Mormon company" and seemed the pinnacle of propriety. Leaving the Summit sleaze, Sandy walked into the Marriott Marquis as if into the enfolding wings of the Mormon Tabernacle Choir. "It was very refreshing, to tell you the truth. It felt very safe. I'm very close to the people I work with. There *are* some really nice people there." One, a young chef, she married.

When she became pregnant, she kept waiting tables, but in the latter stages of her pregnancy, the Marquis gave her work in its party planning offices. Her child's birth had an unexpected impact. "After I had her, I said I don't want to be a waitress anymore, because it wouldn't be good enough for my daughter."

The statement did not go over well with Sandy's mother, who had been, among other jobs, a part-time waitress herself. She pointed out that some of her best friends were women with whom she had worked decades ago and that they had all made good money.

After Sena's birth, Sandy went back to the Marquis offices. Soon she recognized that waiting tables paid much more than the office work. She eventually returned to the dining room. Nevertheless, her attitude remains resolute. "Today it's 'Take Your Daughter to Work Day,'" she noted, adding that even if Sena were old enough to understand, Sandy would not take her daughter to the View. Sandy wants to end the occupational lineage with herself.

She is, perhaps despite her intentions, especially well informed about restaurant work, being not only the daughter of a waitress but also the wife of a chef. "One thing my mother always taught us [when] we'd go to a restaurant: 'Try to figure out what the problem is. Is it the waitress or the waiter, or is it the kitchen? Is it management? Did they overseat them?' That's what they did to us last night. They slammed us. I wish the whole public could figure that out."

She wishes her co-servers would figure out something else: not to blame the cooks.

"They're hot behind that line, and they're trying to pump out this food. You don't fuck with them, basically. When I come back with a steak that someone says they wanted medium rare and it's medium, I *always* blame the guest and say, 'This fool, he ordered it this way. Could you . . . ' David taught me that, and I get along with the kitchen great.

"My feeling is, it's like a patriarchal society. The chef is daddy, and the managers could be daddy. Waiters are allowed, in many places, to act like kids and not take responsibility. They are able to be little brats and complain. 'We don't have enough of this,' or 'You did this wrong,' depending on who they make daddy that day. There's a lot of that stuff going on, and a lot of screaming and yelling and tantrums in the kitchen."

Besides the tendency to "blame the kitchen" for anything wrong, "they'll throw their trays down" to let off steam and "use the kitchen as that area, where other people are working and are under a lot of pressure. They don't seem to have that respect or that understanding. Meeting the guests is difficult. What the kitchen does too is difficult. I'm a good waitress when it comes to the kitchen, because of David."

She is not a good actress at the View, however. Unlike other waitresses, Sandy makes it a point not to perform tableside. "I know other waiters who *really work* the tables and charm them. I don't. I think that works to my benefit."

What works to her benefit even more is the result of a paradox. Although Sandy Ward waits tables at possibly the most lucrative restaurant in New York (for a woman), few customers are New Yorkers, who have a reputation for tipping well. Instead, many are Europeans, who have a reputation for tipping poorly.

"We have a policy in our restaurant that we can ask a foreign table [to include a tip]. We came up with a sentence: 'For your convenience, would you like us to include the gratuity?' If they agree, they have to sign the check, and you have to write all over it 'fifteen percent included.' Usually, if the service was very good, they'll say yes and leave two dollars more, sometimes five, ten dollars. That's where you can make the money."

The 15 percent solution makes the gratuities left by the customers more uniform, but their behavior nonetheless varies. In Sandy's experience, Spaniards are afraid to make mistakes, Italians and French are more confident and "very generous," Israelis are "very cheap," men from India and Egypt are "very arrogant," Germans are "wonderful" and like to sing, "Norwegians are cheap," and the Irish and English are identical: "They want their well-done meat and they don't tip."

She looked pained about another stereotype. Most African American customers, she said, undertip. "You get ten dollars on a table, on a deuce, no matter how much the check is, most of the time. I'll be honest with you. You [order] your piña coladas and your cognac and cokes, and everyone at the bar laughs at you and says, 'Oh, we know. We know.' Even the black waiters say it, 'Oh, I know. I know.' Mother's Day is coming, and that's a major black holiday at the View. Most people have requested it off. I'm a mother this year, so I get it. It's great, because you don't make any money."

She reported that African American servers fare no better from African American customers. "One of the black waiters, an older man, he can't take it. He gets a lot of attitude," including being called "boy."

Another holiday Sandy avoids at the View is New Year's Eve. While working in the offices of the Marquis, she once was involved in putting together the View's gala. "I got out of there. I saw the party I had helped plan, and I was so sickened by all these people in their tuxedos spending their money like that—five hundred dollars a couple for all you can drink and eat? I thought it was so phony. I took a subway home because I couldn't get a taxi, and I was home by quarter to twelve. David and I went in and looked at Sena, and it was like, this is *real*. Over there wasn't real."

All in all, it is a delicate balance—to be disdainful of spenders, big and small, but not of their money, and certainly not of a revolving restaurant that names its food after plays.

5

"IT WAS DESPERATION TIME"
Waitressing as Salvation

WOMEN OF LITTLE MEANS are not known for saying, "If I really get desperate, I can always run a corporation"; or, "If this keeps up, I might as well go back to being a tenured professor"; or, "I guess I'm just going to have to cut another album." To wait tables when desperate for cash—that is the common American experience. Financial need, however, is only one way that waitressing acts as a balm to desperation. As I learned over and over, it can also fulfill other wants.

Gladys Gilbert

"This wasn't an original idea. I had seen a show on Phil Donahue . . . where a woman had done this. My ears perked up. She was miserably unhappy and just left. I thought, okay, this is an option."

The idea "germinated" for years while Gladys Gilbert, a well-to-do Connecticut housewife, raised two children and lived among creature comforts and conjugal misery. One day, after her son had finished his college years and her daughter had just gone off to begin hers, Gladys's husband, a successful businessman, announced that he was leaving for a business trip. It was to be the next weekend.

Gladys gave herself a pep talk. "This is the window of opportunity. This is five minutes in which you can head for the moon. You'd better take it."

She was forty-four years old, had no money of her own, and "had never worked a day in my life." She went out and bought a one-way airline ticket, New York to Miami. She chose Miami because she knew the area, after earlier trips there with her husband, and because "I thought living in a warm climate would be less expensive."

When she came home, she hid the ticket "in a great big book in the library and walked back and forth in front of that book five million times." As soon as her husband went on his trip, Gladys Gilbert "literally fled from an abusive marriage."

"I left with practically nothing, because one of the problems with him was he was always into everything that was mine," including her journals. "I had *no* privacy. So I couldn't take any money out of the bank, I couldn't pack anything."

Now in her mid-sixties, with shoulder-length brown hair and a tan, clad in a pastel top and shorts with white tennis shoes and socks, she looks the picture of confident leisure. But, as she told her story (anonymously) over lunch in a Hilton hotel near Ft. Lauderdale, it was clear that leaving had not been easy.

"The horror set in when I walked out the door of the house. For the last time. You can always put a match to a ticket. But it was a beautiful house. I loved the house. I put so much of myself into it. I'm not sure I can . . ." She suddenly faltered and teared up, before continuing. She spoke of spending "half a lifetime" collecting antiques with which she had lovingly furnished the house. "I'm amazed it still hurts."

She left no note, in case she changed her mind on the way to the plane. She did write a letter and took it with her to the airport. Her flight was called. She had not changed her mind. She took the letter from her purse.

"I can *see* that mailbox. And as I walked through the doors to get on the plane, I dropped it in. 'Now you cannot go back. This is it.'

"I went to a hotel on Miami Beach and hid away there for a week or ten days, just deciding what to do. That first night I was there—this I'll never forget—I woke up in the middle of the night, sat up, and looked over immediately, thinking I'd see Bill. [I realized,] oh, God, I am free. I was determined I would make it, no matter what. I never took a nickel from anybody." She did contact her children during these early days, but not her husband.

Her options, she felt, were limited. She had a degree from the University of Connecticut "in English lit and philosophy. For a princess, that's fine," but not for a never-before-employed nervous wreck who was "learning to crawl. Never having earned a *penny,* never even thinking about it. [In] my background, I was always told you go to college,

get a degree, you get married, you have children, *and* you're *happy.*"
She fairly shouted the word "happy."

"As to why I decided to waitress—number one, I had no skills, no
confidence, low self-esteem." But "I was determined to prove to myself—and, I guess, God—I could do this alone. Very, very important for
me to do that. Being that I had no office skills—I took typing four
hundred years earlier and didn't have the confidence to brush up on it—
the *only* job out there is waitressing.

" 'How hard could it . . . ? Any idiot can do this,' " she recalled telling
herself. "I wanted a job I would be physically exhausted from at the end
of the day. I was feeling, this is probably all I can handle, and I need to
be exhausted so I can sleep."

Gladys made her way to a community that had "a charming Cape
Cod-y feel to it" and was on the bay. "I thought that was kind of soothing because my soul was in absolute torment." She rented "a tiny, one-
bedroom apartment in a nice, safe, clean, lovely building. It was furnished, and it was two hundred seventy dollars a month. I kept a budget.
I knew somehow I could come up with that kind of money, that I would
do anything. I also knew I had to have a safe, clean environment if I
was going to survive and not go back." She made the apartment even
safer, in case her husband—"a wild animal" at her leaving—should find
her. "I had locks and security systems. It was like a fortress."

It also was across the street from a restaurant. "I applied for a job
and lied about my experience." With her "any idiot can do this" attitude
intact, "I wound up in probably the busiest breakfast restaurant there
was"—and indeed on her own. "The waitresses were very unfriendly,
very unhelpful, young and foxy-looking, and here I am forty-four and
shaking.

"People lined up around the corner, waiting to get in. The first table,
I walk up to six people. 'I'll have eggs up,' 'I'll have eggs over,' 'I want
mine basted,' 'I'll have mine easy-over, lightly fried,' 'Whole wheat
toast,' 'White toast,' 'I don't want any toast.' I went in the kitchen and
I stood there. I spent the whole morning crying. [The owner] said,
'What's the matter?' I said, 'You know, it has been a *little* while . . . ' "

She returned to her customers with resolve and a ruse.

"All I did was walk up to the table—I don't know how it occurred
to me—and I said, 'Please forgive me. This is my first day.' Which was
true. 'Will you bear with me?' '*Oh,* yes, yes, yes.' They left a ton of
money on the table. Smart? I did that for two and a half years."

Gladys recognized that part of her psychological survival depended on feeling "good" about waitress work "in some small way. The way in which I did that was to tell myself it was a kind of mini-business. I go into my business every day and make X number of dollars" and go home. She slept well. "You bet I slept," she laughed. She worked ninety hours a week.

"I think it was mostly exhaustion. I tried not to dwell on [work] too much. Not because I was waitressing, but because I wasn't waitressing well. I can remember thinking to myself, 'Well, he always told you you couldn't do a *damn* thing. I guess he was right. You can't even wait-ress.'" Spreading her hands, she counted off finger by finger: "Lousy mother, lousy wife, lousy housekeeper, lousy drinker, lousy sex part-ner."

When she finally told the restaurant owner the truth about herself, he was "very understanding." She believes he did not fire her because "he was embarrassed to." He also, she felt, recognized that he would benefit from her commitment to independence.

"I wanted to do it on my own. The way I did smoking. Whew-w-w! And I'm comparing the two. That's how difficult smoking is to give up. Oh, my *God*. What did I do? I withdrew from the world. I had books, which I had always had, and dove into them, as I always had. I took up needlepoint; I found it very soothing. Couldn't listen to music of any kind. Nothing emotional, except books. I used to take long walks on the bay."

After her first month on the job, Gladys began to do better. "I slowly but surely learned to write little codes, because I didn't even know which table the food went to. If you ask people nicely, 'And you're get-ting . . . ?' But I never knew which table it was. Finally—*Dummkopf*, figure it out! If you write down the number of the table *on* the check, imbecile . . ." Breakfast shift "never was good. Eggs up, eggs over, scrambled, tight, loose, oh, God! This kind of toast, that kind of toast. I finally said to him, 'Look, is there any reason why I can't work lunch?' He said, 'No.'

"Once I got on to lunch and dinners, I could spend time with people. I found I had enough of a personality, and my sense of humor was returning. And I *like* people, [so] I did really, really well." She also began noticing particular quirks of the people she served. "The way some women would get up from the table—some would brush their skirts, some would pull the back of the skirt out to make sure it hadn't caught somewhere." Dinner was her favorite time to watch and work. It was "different," she smiled. "I had gone from the match girl to one of the princess's ladies in waiting."

There was, however, a cloud outside the silver linings.

Despite the owner's private moments of humanity, he "treated everyone badly," including Gladys. "He never spoke. He barked. 'Gimme a cup of coffee. Make sure you wash the cup out with hot water. Do it now.'"

He had no compassion about her long hours. Many of them she had requested, as a sleep aid. "I could not spend five minutes in my own head at that time." He also had his own requests. "I could be working from nine in the morning until we closed at midnight . . . and he'd come in with a party. Knowing the kind of hours I had put in, he would expect me to wait on his people. I did it, and I smiled. He never left a tip."

"I never spoke to him about it. I was such a *mouse*. The way I went from one abusive situation to another. This is almost as bad as what I left—I used to say that to myself. I thought I was wearing a sign that said to the world, 'Dump on me, it's okay.'"

Some customers must have read it. "Boat people" (men who lived or worked on boats or sailed for recreation) who were "rude and rough" especially upset her. "Of course, I was very sensitive to what I thought was abuse. I felt everything was, really, and wanted to get away from everyone and anyone who talked to me roughly, because I'd had it for so many years. And wound up [in] the job where you're apt to be spoken to roughly, more so than any other damn job, simply because I felt there was nothing else I could do."

Despite the treatment she received, Gladys did not give as well as she got. "When I was very young, maybe seven or eight, my father—who was a very sensitive, intellectual, wonderful, tender guy—we were at Woolworth's having lunch at the counter. And there was a waitress who was stumbling around." Gladys turned to her father and whispered, "'What is her problem?' A derogatory comment. He turned to me in a second and said, 'Don't ever criticize anyone less fortunate than you. Not verbally, not in your heart, ever.' *Burned* in my brain. Often in my life, I've felt like being rude to someone incompetent in a situation. I could never do it, because I would hear him. I hope I didn't have to work very hard at [it]. I'm just not a rude person."

Sometimes the restaurant owner assigned Gladys the job of cashier, which she found had the reward of quietude but the penalty of boredom. He also assigned her to hostess duties, which she "loved."

"You can get dressed up. It was good for my image, for my self-esteem. Because you had very foxy-looking girls on the floor, and why he stuck with me was a very, very kind thing for him to do, especially as a hostess. I was slender, and when the hair was done and the makeup was done, people didn't exactly throw up their hands. I'd like to think it wasn't awful. But it was very good for me to do that.

"And if you're not terribly busy, it's thoughtful to get the coffeepots and to walk around and make sure everything's okay. If you see the waitresses need help . . . God knows I could have used it. I never had a hostess who really cared. So I felt good about helping out and being good for the house."

Over the months, then years, Gladys's waitressing skills improved. "I enjoy bringing clean, fresh, nice plates of food out, putting them down, and looking at the reactions of the people. That pleased *me*. I felt nurturing. It felt as if I were serving dinner to my family."

Nearly one year after she fled to Florida, her husband filed for divorce. "I probably never would have. I was afraid of having to go to court and talk about personal stuff. I am a very, very private person, and there was an awful lot of garbage. There was some physical abuse, and I simply could not, at that time, talk about it. To anyone, let alone strangers. I did as *little* as possible to get his ire up."

She did return occasionally, painfully, to Connecticut, to see her children. "I could never go near the house. Because it wasn't the house, it was the destruction of the family I was going back to visit."

By now, Florida was her home, and waitressing was her work.

"I worked myself to death for very little money. No confidence. But little by little, as I began feeling better about myself, and my hours were cut down . . . I had taken a typing course in college, and I went back to brush up. I said, 'You cannot feel good about yourself if you do this forever. You're being put upon too much. Work up your office skills; put on a suit, a smile, and some lipstick; and go find a job.'"

Eventually, she got a "good" one in the federal district court in Miami. The work included jury selection. She liked the job but was infuriated when Cuban exiles pretended they did not speak English to avoid jury duty. She also became upset that she was passed over for advancement. "I was so unassertive."

She earned extra money by waiting tables on the weekends, mostly in small Italian restaurants. "I didn't feel the shame of waitressing." She did once have a boss, an older man, whom she described as "an absolute pig," who would "take a cucumber and hold it in his groin" and wink at her. Still, waitressing was "probably the only job I had that I really, in some instances, liked."

Stability returned to Gladys's life. Her Florida apartment no longer looked like a motel room, as a friend had once chided her. Gladys had responded that she had nothing of herself there because she no longer knew who she was. Also, "I can't start collecting this stuff again, because if I have to leave it again, it's going to kill me."

In the past six years, in different apartments, she has hung a few paintings and photographs but is ever wary of commitment. She rents— "and always and forever will." She does not wish to marry again, either. "I met a great guy a few years after I finally picked my head up off my navel and started looking around the world. Turned out to be my best friend for many, many years and helped me a lot, restoring confidence." Still, "if a psychiatrist were to say, 'We're going to play a word [association] game. 'Marriage . . . ' 'Bondage.' "

After more than a decade of work, Gladys "was able to stop worrying about money," as she put it delicately. The explanation came after a pause. She "inherited some money, rather unexpectedly." She quit all her jobs, with no regrets. "Working was not a good experience for me."

Linda Bolanos and Susan Donley

The Kashim, which means "meeting place" in Aleut, had a reputation as the best place to eat between Fairbanks and Anchorage, said Linda Bolanos.

Her mother, Susan Donley, agreed, but then added that was not saying much. The food! "I couldn't believe how poor it was, as far as quality, compared to the States." The service! "Alaska's so much different than the lower forty-eight. They're laid back. I don't know if they knew what the word 'service' was in Wasilla [the town where the Kashim was located] at that time. I was very efficient—boom, boom, boom. And my humor was so different, and we [had] always *dressed* in San Francisco. They would be wearing jeans and T-shirts and sweatshirts. I remember going to work and I'd always have high-heel boots on and my makeup. I looked *good*. They thought I looked like a stripper."

"These are rugged women waiting on tables," nodded Linda. "I don't think they even care if they brush their teeth."

Susan, recalling her gay customers back in San Francisco, laughed. "Those queens were good to me!" When she first arrived in Alaska, from San Francisco, "I looked like Lara from *Zhivago* going into town, by God. If I died, I was going to die looking good. That lasted about a month. I was in and out of a ditch all the time." She had never driven in snow.

She is far from the snow now. She and Linda (as well as Susan's third husband and Linda's fiancé) share a pre-fab house in the saguaro-sentried desert near Tucson. The house is lined with Alaska photographs and artifacts that pertain not to the Kashim but to Susan's father, a trapper and guide from whom her mother is gratefully separated. The Arizona neighborhood looks suburban, but, as in Alaska, the frontier is not far. A wild boar recently gored the family dog.

Mother and daughter, sitting around the kitchen table, are strikingly dissimilar. Susan, in her early sixties, is stout and medium-complected, wears a bright, loose outfit, with her gray hair cut short. She is likely to throw back her head, roar, use earthy language, and light a cigarette. Linda, thirty-four, tautly slender and dark, has luminous eyes and long, straight black hair. She wears an ironed white T-shirt tucked into ironed jeans and is disconcertingly intense. She unwinds by rock climbing.

The two have more than a half century of waitressing experience between them. When Susan started, back in 1959, however, she never expected to say, as she does now, "Waitressing was my life." Marriage, yes. Motherhood, yes. Earning? Never.

She had a ninth-grade education and was raising six children (including a young half-sister) in San Francisco when she became part of a common story. "I was desperate. I had no skills. I was left with all these children to raise." She meant "left" literally; her husband had left her for her best friend.

At the nadir of her job search, she found Foster's, a restaurant as desperate as she was.

"It was a nightmare!" she laughed. "They hated me. I had cooks *screaming* at me. I had everyone screaming at me. I thought I'd *never* learn to be a waitress. Just because they were desperate for help, day by day I learned.

"We had to memorize our orders and call them in. I wasn't a yeller. I can remember saying, 'Excuse me, please,' and they would say, 'Shout

out your damn order!' " When a blind woman insisted that Susan ask the cook, a "monster" named O'Reilly, to open her soft-boiled eggs, "he hit that slide with the big butcher knife—wham!—and said, 'I don't fix eggs for anyone except my mother, and she's dead.'

"I used to be a weeping willow. A customer would hurt my feelings, and I'd go back and I'd be crying. This old waitress got ahold of me and said, 'What the hell's wrong with you now?' " Susan put on a pitiful voice. " 'I didn't get the right order, the cooks are yelling . . .' She said, 'You're going to let *those* assholes ruin your day? You can't. You're going to be miserable the rest of your life. And we haven't got time.' "

The advice stuck. So did Susan.

"In those days, you had to have work ethics. You *had* to be there on time. You couldn't take off unless you had a priest and a surgeon there with you. These kids were left alone much too young. They were loaded down with work." Susan was trying to keep them out of trouble and also needed their labor. "I couldn't work and maintain a house, so something had to give."

Security gave, too. "I worked graveyard [shifts]. I'd leave these little kids alone at night. There's no money for babysitting, so you just pray to God the house is still there and nothing has happened." The children knew to settle any problem short of an emergency by themselves. "Don't be calling me to tell me, 'Cardo was eating all the Spaghetti-Os,' because I'll kill you when I get home."

At home, work had another impact. Susan borrowed menus to teach the children how to order. She did not want them to feel the shame she had experienced, coming from "very poor people" and not knowing how to eat out. Also, she did not want them to waste a waitress's time.

Her main concern, though, was to support them by keeping her job. In any restaurant, she said, "either you fit in or you don't." Finally she fit in at Foster's. "I had to be about thirty when I came into my own. I said, 'I'm making a hell of a living.' I found out I had a gift for waitressing and I *loved* it, and it was just bullshit. I call it 'romancing the customers.' "

Linda, her youngest and possibly most earnest child—born three years after the Foster's immersion—spoke up. "There's a lot of organizing skills," she said solemnly.

"It's mainly romance," countered Susan. "You've got to tell that cook how great he is." If he messes up, then you are in a better position to tell him what's wrong. Most romance was directed toward customers, of course. "Acknowledge they're there"—she imitated a nod to indicate presence. "The hard waitresses" also taught her how to say almost anything to customers. "If the cook is screwing up, tell them he's on drugs. Some people you don't kid with. You know when to back off and you know who to romance."

Linda looked unconvinced. Romance is not her specialty.

Susan poured coffee into a trio of mugs and proclaimed that she owes her survival to homosexuality. "In '59, I had no idea what a gay person was. We whispered about them and laughed about them and pointed at them. Then I got to know them, and all I can say is if it hadn't been for them, I don't know what I would have done. They were *my* customers. They tipped very well and followed me wherever I went."

Some followed her, post-Foster's, to a restaurant on San Francisco's Fisherman's Wharf. "This [new place] was all fishermen and longshoremen. It was my third night there, I'm working graveyard, it's Saturday night, and here come [my old customers]"—dressed as women. Concerned what the macho customers might do, she tried to get the gays to calm down. "Well, they're wild and crazy. They could care less. They're all in drag, feathers flying. It worked out, but I'm telling you, the other customers were not impressed."

In less charged situations, gay men "were the highlight of my day," she smiled. "They always made me laugh. They did my hair for me. I was like a Dora Drudge. I was guest of honor at their balls, and my goodness gracious! They would deck me out."

"She looked like Cinderella. Serious," said Linda.

Susan began taking her children to gay parades, partly out of waitress pragmatism. "This was cheap entertainment."

She got another eye-opener when antiwar hippie protestors, whom she had also laughed at, became customers: her own support for the Vietnam war eventually turned to opposition. It was fortunate that she (as opposed to Linda) "always looked at tips as a gift," for hippies tipped "absolutely nothing." When one protester asked what he could get for a dollar, Susan impetuously filled a bag with hard-boiled eggs, oatmeal cookies, and other items and rang it up: one dollar. "He walked away, and he looked in the bag, and he looked at me, and he had the biggest smile." Five years later, a conservatively dressed man came in the restaurant and gave Susan a box of candy and a thank-you card for the food. She had not recognized him, but he recognized her.

Susan got another surprise when a San Francisco newspaper included her in an article about night workers. "No one was even aware I had so many children because I never talked family. When you hit the floor, as far as I was concerned, it was always showtime." Suppliers saw the article, too, and from bread truck driver to milk deliveryperson, gave her their "leftovers. They *really* helped me. [And] they did it in such a way, it wasn't charity." Susan made a distinction, too, about poverty, reciting often, "We were broke, but we were never poor."

Besides her myriad benefactors, "the salary wasn't bad either, in San Francisco at that time. I was making twenty bucks a day. You couldn't work without being in the union." She took a swallow of coffee. "The union broke San Francisco. They had to have so many busboys, so many dishwashers, and the company couldn't afford all this. As a waitress, you weren't allowed to pick up a plate because you were hurting your brother's job. You couldn't pick up a broom." She remains ambivalent about unions.

She "thought it stunk" that employers had to keep "lousy waitresses" with union seniority and that she herself had to sacrifice hours to go vote in an election or face a big fine, even when the president was unopposed. Yet she feels that restaurant unions are "desperately" needed. Linda "makes two dollars thirteen cents an hour, and no benefits. It's too bad the unions can't work better with management, and management work with the union."

What bothered Susan more at the time were other issues. San Francisco "was getting real racial." School busing was about to take her children from their schools, all walking distance from home and from her. A series of unsolved homicides, the Zebra and Zodiac killings, semi-paralyzed the city, making life especially hard for tipped employees on night shift.

Suddenly, an alternative appeared. Susan's eldest son, Buddy, visiting from his job on the Alaska pipeline, urged her to move up near their (still squabbling) parents and bring the youngest children, who were still living with her. He promised to buy them a house and said she could retire.

Susan hesitated and hesitated. Then, in 1975, she, four teenagers, from thirteen-year-old Linda to eighteen-year-old Michael, and two dogs crammed into her packed '69 Ford, whose radio did not work, and went to Alaska. "I hated these children by the time I got there," said Susan, sweetly.

Somewhere in Canada, she got so fed up with their bickering that she began speeding. The car jumped into the air and, upon landing, broke an axle. Then a flood washed out the road. When the family—stranded, broke, ravaged by mosquitoes, and rescued—finally reached the promised house, Susan discovered it lacked features such as central heat and hot water. She also learned that Buddy's income was not enough to support them and that the nearest restaurant was fifty miles away.

The desperate woman again found a desperate restaurant.

Susan, abandoning her Lara look, "worked her way in" to the Kashim through some rough shared experiences. Two customers died in front of her, both of heart attacks.

While she worked for money, her children worked for free—feeding their grandfather's sled dogs. That meant loading slaughterhouse guts onto his truck. "He had, would I be exaggerating to say, sixty-some dogs at that time?" Susan asked Linda.

"More," said Linda, flatly.

"I'm fighting the road, we're building wood fires and heating water on a stove," and the children were hauling guts. Then, in almost comic relief, Susan's mother confided that she planned to outlive her husband just to be able to cremate him and throw his ashes over the Chickaloon Bridge. (He was terrified of missing his "parts" in what he called the Happy Hunting Ground.) In the midst of all this, another family furor bubbled up.

Buddy became a born-again Christian, scaring his younger siblings by preaching about God's vengeance. Susan told him that her God was a kind God and that his "must be an asshole."

The next day, Buddy came to the Kashim. "He said, 'I gotta talk to you. Don't ever call God an asshole again.'"

Susan asked, none too cordially, if he had come all that way to tell her that. "He says, 'Mom, *God* burned your house down.'"

The house had indeed just burned down. The cause, however, was less divine destruction than earthly ineptitude. The morning had been so cold—85 below zero—when her children left for school and she headed to work that Susan had stuffed the stove with Presto logs to keep it hot.

A few days after the fire, and after settling her family into a trailer, Susan, with Buddy, returned to the Kashim. The excited staff took her into the banquet room. "People had gathered clothing, bedding, pillows, dishes. I was astounded. I was humiliated, because I never asked for anything. Something for nothing, you always pay. They said, 'Look what we got for you!' And, 'Not only this, Sue . . . ' they had got this big mayonnaise jar and had been putting money in. They handed it to me. I was so ashamed they were giving me charity, I started to cry. They thought I was crying because I was grateful."

She took Buddy aside. " 'I don't want this shit. We don't take charity.' He said, 'Mom, that's not charity. In Alaska, we don't live alone. We need each other.' 'How the hell do you pay for this?' I was really nasty. He said, 'You don't. When someone else has a disaster, you give what you can to help them.' It was the biggest lesson in humility I ever had to learn."

Another came from her daughter.

By the age of fifteen, Linda was eager to bus tables at the Kashim. Susan was "very nervous" that Linda would "screw up." Furthermore, "I knew that once you start working, you work forever. I wanted them to still have fun." Fun, to Linda, was not hauling guts for free. Susan, by then the senior waitress, relented, with the provisions that Linda work "double hard" and never complain. " 'I can't cut you any slack. You got to make me look good.' "

While keeping a close eye on Linda, Susan realized that a customer named Wild Bill was doing the same thing. "He was a loudmouth, and he was always patting the girls on the butt and hanging on them. I was looking over, and I could see Linda was just dying. This man had his arms wrapped around her and was saying he was going to stuff her in a sea bag and take her off to Australia and kiss her all over. Of course, he's playing to this big audience of men.

"I went over, and I put my arms around Linda, and I said, 'Bill, have you met my *daughter* Linda? She's just started working here.' I thought, now he will know you don't do this. You can overreact when it's your kid, so you have to be really fair. Linda said"—Susan reported in a whisper—" 'Thank you, Mom.'

"I'll be a son of a gun, this guy is such an idiot. I looked back, and there's Wild Bill, and he's got Linda cornered again. I went back and I said, 'Bill, didn't I tell you once, this is *my daughter* Linda?' I'm laughing, and everyone's looking at him and looking at me, and I had this pot of coffee, and I'm pouring it in his lap. He sat there while I poured, then I turn around and walk away. He didn't feel it for, I guess, fifteen seconds. All of a sudden he jumped up, and he screamed, 'Son of a bitch!' Everyone was roaring."

From then on, Linda left problem customers to her mother.

She did pick up every other skill her mother had to teach. "She could tell you what made me what I am."

"They called me 'The Nazi,'" said Susan amiably, adjusting her chair and fanning her cigarette smoke away.

Linda said one lesson was not to whine.

"That's right," Susan nodded. "Don't be saying you don't feel good or you've had a bad day or it's your period. We don't care. *Get your side work done,*" she said, rapping the table with each syllable. "You can't handle your station? Give it to somebody else that can."

Another bit of pithy advice: learn borders. "There's invisible lines you don't cross over, in stations. You don't see the line, but you know what people *don't* want any help, other people [that] will appreciate *any* help. It's like little worlds in these things."

Linda was a good student, usually. "She and I locked horns a lot," said Susan. "I'd say, 'You have to be to work at least fifteen minutes early. Half an hour is good. Have a cup of coffee, get yourself going, and be ready to hit that floor.' Of course now," Susan added with a mother-knows-best look, "she's a fanatic on being on time."

Linda bused tables at the Kashim until she was old enough to be a waitress. That meant old enough to serve alcohol, which was available at breakfast. She yearned for the next step.

Susan "absolutely" understood. "She had more than earned the position of being a waitress."

"I needed to grow," Linda intoned. "I needed to come into the restaurant knowing that I was a waitress." She even took the Kashim's menu home to study it. The reason, both explained, is that Linda is dyslexic. She memorizes menus, to keep her secret.

Once Linda got the job, the two worked amiably as a team, pooling tips and skills. "My mother would be the front person, like in the higher-class restaurants. She'd be the talker . . ."

"The romancer," Susan broke in with a wink.

"I'd be the fast one, going around taking all the orders."

The team was not to last. As Susan once had been desperate to find any work, now Linda was desperate to do any work best. Her new goal was to become the best waitress. The trouble was, her mother held the title. Susan grimaced. "She got better than me. Then I got jealous. I thought, my God, am I getting too old? *No one's better than me.*"

Making the schism worse, in 1979 the Kashim installed computers. Susan, a self-proclaimed computer illiterate, kept her techno-troubles as secret as Linda kept her dyslexia. "I didn't want anyone to know, because I was the oldest waitress there. I was almost in tears. I didn't know what the hell I was going to do. I would have to get *her* to go and ring up my orders."

When Linda sometimes balked, Susan pulled rank: " 'Goddamn it, get my orders in if you want a ride home.' "

The problem also was vanity, Linda revealed. Susan could not see the computer keys without her glasses, yet she refused to wear them. Susan, looking sheepish, added with a laugh, "And I was having hot flashes on top of that!"

"All's I know," said Linda, somberly, "is I took everything she taught me, and I used it, and I embettered that."

Susan noted, "I told her—and it took me a long time to learn it—whatever I taught her, not to pass it on. When you're a waitress, don't tell new people everything you know. It's your job you're protecting. I cut my own throat with her."

Victorious, Linda decided to move on to a new challenge. It was a "great" restaurant in Anchorage called the Downtown Deli.

Susan said she herself was "delighted."

At the Deli, Linda went from fast to faster. "You've got to learn to short-talk. Say something only that you know would have a short reply, not a detailed reply." It was the highest-volume restaurant she ever worked in and the only one to give her waitress nightmares. Of the many recurrent nightmares waitresses related to me, most involved panic about some supernatural act (tables that keep doubling in number) or a quest (ketchup available only on the other side of the woods) that leaves a waitress unable to do her job. Linda's fit the genre: she cannot deliver endless plates of food because the plates are stuck to her hands.

The Deli was so jammed that people would "smash themselves into booths, people would share chairs." Linda did not have time to eat, drink, or use the bathroom. "Sitting on the toilet was like taking a break, so your brain automatically told you you weren't going to the bathroom for the day."

The only helpful person in management, she said, was the owner, Tony Knowles. He bused tables and also offered generous benefits, including profit sharing. Later, he became Anchorage's Democratic mayor, then Alaska's governor.

Susan said pridefully that her children who went into the restaurant business "have all been employee of the year, employee of the month.

How much prouder can you be? I'm not talking as a mother, I'm just saying I'm so proud of these children that *don't* have college educations. They make a great living and become legends of their own. They have followings."

Mostly gay followings, said Linda, adding that two of her brothers, including Buddy the born-again Christian, are gay.

Susan wondered whether Linda really had to reveal that.

In 1990, Linda left the Deli in a literal freefall. She had jumped on a counter to retrieve a water pitcher from a shelf where the night crew (of men) stored the pitchers. "There was ice on the counter, and I slipped." She landed on the cement floor. "I was paralyzed from the hips down." The medical horror story that followed included a botched operation on her back and a misdiagnosis from an Anchorage doctor.

A hero of the tale is Tony Knowles. Susan shook her head. "This man was *so* good. He made sure the workmen's comp was the top of the line, still was concerned about her." Early on, he visited Linda in the hospital and also invited her to sue him, giving her "names of great attorneys."

When Susan saw that Linda was "going downhill" after her blundered operation, she decided in desperation to airlift her to a hospital in Seattle. Tony Knowles arranged for the ambulance and the plane. Linda arrived "babbling. She was in terrible shape," said Susan. Hours later, the smiling staff told her Linda had had a spinal leak (which the Alaskan doctors had claimed she did not have), had been overdosed on morphine, and would recover. They later informed her that Linda had been four days from death.

Once on the mend, Linda decided Alaska's rehab program was too simple and the climate too cold. She left the forty-ninth state for the fiftieth and spent three years working "*all* day on making myself better." She fell in love with a native-born Hawaiian, an "awesome" cook and now her fiancé, and moved with him to Tucson, near some of her relatives. (Susan later left the Kashim for the cactus, too.)

When Linda was ready to work again, she decided to test herself in a corporate setting. She found one in a Tucson mall. It was a branch of the General Mills–owned Olive Garden.

To enter the garden, Linda had to pass an extensive test requiring her to memorize not only the food and drinks (including twenty cordials) but all their ingredients. Susan, shuddering, broke in to say *she* had needed to learn only lingo such as "two eggs on a raft and wreck 'em" (scrambled eggs and toast).

The Olive Garden never knew what hit it. Within four weeks, Linda received her first honor. "I couldn't wait to tell Mom I was employee of the month!" She also worked fourteen hours a day.

She enthusiastically tackled the selling of "add-ons"—"your alcohol, your desserts, and your appetizers. If you don't make this list, you can be terminated. If you can't sell, what do they need you for?" Linda was "always the top add-on [seller]," with no small effort. "I made it a habit of always eating in our restaurant, to find out what I really liked." She also ate at other Olive Gardens to learn how others sold. Then she went to work, especially on older customers. "Senior citizens want small meals. I made appetizers into small meals for them."

By the end of a shift, with other servers struggling to make the company minimum of five dollars per table in add-ons (or else spend their Saturdays in retraining classes), Linda's chit showed she had done three times that. "I didn't tell them my secrets."

"Boy!" said Susan, approvingly.

Part of the secret is this: the corporation, as fanatic about add-ons as Linda was, never noticed that she sold virtually no entrees.

Next she was promoted to corporate trainer. "That was my spot. Because, see, being dyslexic, I knew how to train people. I trained them how I thought I should have been trained."

Susan groaned, lamenting that she would never have lasted in a corporation. She made rowdy customers leave by telling them she was giving them a glass of prune juice "to hurry you on your way."

Linda indicated she would have pulled her mother off the floor for retraining. She did pull servers who merely *told* customers about dessert. "They're not *enticing* them." At home, she made her favorite dessert, tiramisu, to help her enticement powers. Soon, she became "the highest add-on person they've ever had" in the General Mills empire. She received a trophy, was promoted to manager, and began working sixteen hours a day.

She was, however, not very happy. She did like some things about corporations. "They have great sanitation." The Olive Garden's sanitation buckets scored high: "You dip your hands, the bacteria's *off.*" She liked the rewards, from trophies to pay. She did not like the practice of firing an employee because of something a customer claimed the person had done. She did not like the hours or becoming the "bad guy" to employees and upper management. "It was the lowest confidence-builder I ever had." Also, she admitted, "I missed serving." Finally she quit.

After looking around town, she homed in on a place that was as far from corporate America as one can imagine: the ultra punk and hip Cup Cafe, in the not-for-the-narrow-minded Hotel Congress.

At the Cup, Linda Bolanos stands out for her lack of tattoos, piercings, and/or neon hair and for being the only person who is efficient (she spent two weeks studying the menu and figuring out her own code for reading and writing orders) or pleasant, not to mention both. "I take my job very serious. There can't be any room for error for me, because I do have a learning disability I never want anybody to know."

Following her mother's lead, Linda arrives a half hour early, makes sure "everything is done," and is poised to pounce. Carry both regular and decaf. Put a tray under one arm, to carry things back. Along the way, see who is finishing what. "If a beer gets down about like this"—she held a thumb and forefinger an inch apart—"*ask*. 'Would you like another beer?' Because once they run out of beer, they're not going to want another." Do not take the time or energy to count tips.

There seem to be few customer situations Linda cannot control. Recently a difficult woman ("tell her it was a black lady," said Susan) asked for, and got, separate servings of salad dressing seven different times. "She was running me," said Linda, who on the seventh request told the woman to wait her turn. That earned Linda her first, and only, complaint.

This steams Susan, who has heard Linda talk of a notoriously inept and hostile Cup waiter named Snappy telling coffee-drinking hippies (still nontipping) to "get your ass up to the counter," so he can seat more affluent customers at their table.

"Can you *imagine?*" gaped Susan, her mouth open wide for extra effect.

Linda, at the Deli in Anchorage and the Cup in Tucson, has had spirited run-ins with cooks who did not attack their work with the same ferocity she did. Just last Sunday, a Cup cook "freaked" and got "real frickled" when she put up tickets faster than he liked. She was ruining his rhythm, he complained.

"To me, a ticket is a ticket," stated Susan.

Linda said nothing to him at first ("you start arguing, there's time wasted"), but she wondered why he, too, did not "like the challenge of taking on a bunch of people and pleasing them," as she did. "I end up smiling, thinking the poor guy can't handle the pressure." All such incidents pass. "Every day I come home saying what a wonderful job I have."

Susan shook her head.

As Susan and Linda sipped and talked, they learned something new. Despite differences in their own style of serving, they are in complete accord on a matter that involves discrimination against them both.

"She'll probably disagree with me," said Susan at one point, glancing at her daughter. "When you go in for fine dining, there's something about a waiter. Isn't that sexist? I don't say a woman isn't qualified to do it, but there's something elegant about that tuxedoed [male] arm coming up with the tray."

Linda's voice was grave. "I would agree with her."

"Would you? Really?" Susan looked stunned.

"As far as going to a fine dining, I would definitely prefer a guy to wait on me," continued Linda. Her reason seemed to be primarily the tray weight, for she spoke at length about heavy trays, as if unfamiliar with places where waiters do not carry them. "A woman carries the tray more down on the shoulder, so it *looks* awkward." Raising a muscled arm to demonstrate, she claimed that she was "good for the first five hours," but during the second part of a double shift, "you are definitely down on the shoulder." She looked unhappy. Being down on the shoulder is not for Linda Bolanos.

She added that she prefers working at "normal" restaurants and being waited on in them by women. "I think we're more aggressive and a lot faster, and we seem to see a lot of things. We're more organized with our time, more so than a guy."

"Yes, yes," Susan agreed.

Women such as themselves, then, are great in their place.

The important thing about waitressing, added Susan, is the "way you treat it. And it has been very good to us."

Catherine Blount

Catherine Blount appears to be living like a wealthy eco-eccentric. Her summer home is a converted wooden barn on the glorious island of Islesboro, Maine. Baccarat candlesticks and drying watercolor pictures line a large dining table in the tumble of the living room, only steps from a composting toilet behind a curtain of a door. (If it is privacy you want, use the outhouse.) She has a five-stall kitchen, the original stanchions gracefully carved. Posing where a horse once stood, with a row of cookbooks and a Cuisinart taking the place of hay, Cath-

erine mockingly held up an apron and smiled. She looked great: forty-five, slim, slightly tan, fine features, short blondish hair, T-shirt, and khakis cut so short the white pockets hung below.

Leaning back on a busted bench outside the barn, a baseball cap shielding her eyes, she spoke of growing up in Washington, D.C., and northern Virginia amid the upper-middle-class trappings of private schools and country clubs. She said that her father had owned an outer-space technology company and her mother drank. In an all but unbearable saga, she described her mother having an affair and her father being so desperate to end it that he gave up his business and moved the family to Princeton, where he had taken a job he did not like. His wife was temporarily distracted but ultimately unswayed. "He worshipped her, which is not a good way to love somebody."

For a year or so in Princeton, after her mother had returned to her lover, "we had a housekeeper and a governess. By the time I was fourteen or fifteen, my father figured out, 'Cathy can do this.' It's such a typical scenario: someone's got to be *mom* here. Guess it's me, so I became an adult"—she snapped her fingers—"overnight."

She began with cooking. "I got out the *Joy of Cooking,* knowing zip. I'd made a failure of a lemon meringue pie and Christmas cookies up to that point. I got into a *major* nurturing mode, which is sad in a way." She had been "primed" to go to Radcliffe and then become a United Nations translator. "I made this decision, that I didn't know I made back then, to sacrifice myself for the sake of this family. I was coming home every day, cleaning house, doing laundry, folding clothes, ironing, getting dinner on the table. I discovered I had a gift for cooking. The whole cooking thing, going into restaurants, that was definitely a big part of it." She especially tried to please her father, but he had an ulcer and could not eat her "perfect corn souffles."

"Psychologically, you see this setup? You're going to try *harder,* damn it. You're going to try harder to make somebody *smile.* Dead setup for a waitress. Make everybody happy. You're better off joining a monastery," she laughed. "You don't think these things consciously, but [waitressing] seemed like a comfortable thing I could segue into, from waiting on my family."

Catherine got her first waitressing job during summer break in high school. "I worked at PJ's Pancake House in Princeton" with "a couple of black women," who became mother substitutes. "Those black women taught me" how to wait tables. Their main lesson was to think on your feet. A doctor who ate at PJ's with his wife helped, too. "One day in the *middle* of a really intense rush, I'm trying to keep my wits about me and get people their food. The place was crazy, insane. This guy grabbed me by the arm. He says, 'Honey, you know what the secret of waitressing is? Good waitressing?' I said, 'What?' 'Never let 'em see you're in a hurry.' I *never* forgot that.

"I've had office jobs, too, but I've always felt waitressing was more honest. There's something inherently honest about doing a job and going home with cash at the end of the day. Maybe it's a child's view of earning money. It's instant gratification. It's definitely the American way."

She definitely needed the gratification. Her father was earning much less than he had, and the ensuing divorce cost him a great deal. Catherine and her three siblings went from private to public schools, from "living pretty high off the hog" to living much lower.

"My view of my life is that it's been a real struggle for a long time, but I've gotten everything I needed. I deserve this, now," she said, gesturing to the bucolic beauty around her and referring to the time she now has to enjoy it. "I have worked really hard. I usually have always worn about five hats at a time. Waitresses do that."

She had no idea, however, what she would do for a job when summer ended, nor where she and her two children would live. There was no winter home. Furthermore, her inherited share of the summer home, her only capital, was being contested.

After high school, Catherine went to Boston University on her own dime, saved from serving pancakes. There was no alternative. "Daddy had gone down to Nassau and come back and told me, 'I'm sorry. I gambled away all your college money.'"

She went home for Christmas and got more bad news. "My sister was distraught, the diabetic. She couldn't handle the load. My brother was smoking pot and drinking, and my little sister was lonesome, and I felt sorry for my dad." Catherine quit Boston University and took night courses at Trenton State. (She later went to George Washington University but was expelled after taking part in an antiwar demonstration, she said.) During the day, she got full-time work at "a computer office" and took care of her family. "I was raised Catholic," she said at one point, "so I always thought it was a fair world. You got what you deserved."

At about the age of twenty, she more or less hit the road and split much of her time for the next two decades between the Northeast and the Southwest as well as between kitchens and dining rooms. "Cooking and waitressing, cooking and waitressing. I'd have a kitchen job for a while, then I'd get tired of the isolation and the grueling hard work of a kitchen, especially cleanup and the heat, and I'd get a waitressing job for six months or a year. Always radically different restaurants. Then I'd get sick of catering to people, so I'd get a cooking job and hide in the kitchen. [For] somebody with my head, it's perfect. The kitchen gives me a chance to be alone to think. I'm really good in the kitchen, too.

"It got to the point where if I wanted a waitressing job, I'd have to lie and say [I'd only] waitressed. You can't tell them you've worked in the kitchen. It's much too big a threat." She added, "I'd look the owner in the eye and try to sound barely competent. It was really hard. They'd know I knew more than they did. I'm not *bragging*, 'cause I don't care." When I suggested that bosses want competent waitresses, Catherine called the assertion "one hundred percent bullshit. They want somebody that's going to do what they tell them to do.

"Most of the people in the food business don't know what the hell they're doing. You go into ninety-five percent of the restaurants in the world, the food sucks. I bet I waitressed or cooked in fifteen different restaurants in Bucks County [Pennsylvania] in the '70s. Some of the most expensive places, the kitchens were dirty, with mouse shit everywhere. There were roaches."

The source of droppings at one "high-class place" was all too evident. "We used to make vinaigrette in these old wine bottles. I come in one morning, there's a mouse in the vinaigrette bottle." The chef "took the vinaigrette, poured it into a container, threw the old bottle out with the mouse in it. I've seen him dump cigarettes in the mashed potatoes he was making. 'Potatoes duchesse,' " she scoffed.

At that restaurant, as at any, "you got to balance the pros and the cons. If you're working with great people, and the place stinks and the boss stinks—well, the great people make it okay. That's hard to find.

"Waitressing is a high-pressure job. It therefore creates a lot of insecurity among people who aren't real secure. There's a lot of people waitressing that shouldn't be."

That evening at an Islesboro restaurant, Catherine pointed out the incompetence of our waitress (not to her face): she took three trips instead of one, had not memorized the specials, did not talk and work simultaneously. "*Move* while you're talking. Get things done while you're chatting with the customer." Mention desserts *while* you clear plates, not after.

Catherine herself exuded confidence supreme. Over the course of two days, she pronounced herself a "damn good chef," a "*real good* waitress," a "damn good dancer," a "good songwriter," and a "really brainy" student. She described her "God-given gift" for playing the guitar and her "photographic memory."

Seven years earlier, she had been an insecure mess.

After becoming pregnant on purpose by a man whose gene pool she admired, she had a daughter (now fifteen). She married another man, who adopted the baby, and with him had a son. For years, the family lived in the old Bucks County town of Yardley, on the Delaware River across from Trenton. Catherine had a part-time "civic-duty kind of job" and took care of her children and home. Then came a triple blow. Her husband, who had left his first wife for Catherine, left Catherine for another woman. Next, Catherine's older sister died of diabetes. Then their father died.

"Frankly, from the fall of '88 until probably January of '91, I was a basket case." Catherine read Catholic mystics and rethought her life, miserably. "I stayed home and lived in this sort of cave of questioning." Finally, "I figured out there weren't any damn answers," she laughed, "so what am I looking for? It hit me at one point that life was in the living of it, not in the questioning of it. I felt it was God poking me— 'Go get a job.'" She obeyed. In the fall, when her son started school, she looked for waitress work.

"I knew it was something I could do without even thinking about it." After rejecting a number of places because "the vibes were so bad" or the hours so wrong (she was determined to be home by 3:30 in the afternoon to greet her children), she went to a recently opened restaurant. Luigi's was named for the chef and co-owner, Louie. His twenty-two-year-old wife, Linda, "the ice queen, ruled the roost."

"Her hair's up to here," Catherine gestured a foot above her baseball cap. "She's got more makeup on than one of those Guess ads, and she's wearing this tight-fitting spandex thing with a big, wide glittery belt and black stockings and spikes." Catherine showed up in a plain dress, no makeup, her own hair "kind of dumb, with the perm growing out. I hadn't done anything with my appearance in years. I filled out an application."

Rather than admitting that she had waitressed or cooked in some twenty-four places, she wrote that she had waitressed in two. Linda hired her. "I couldn't believe I managed to hide who I was from her."

Linda was Italian American, "from Trevose or something, some real lower-middle-class, working-class . . . I don't know. Had a degree in journalism, I found out, and still said things like, 'I shoulda went to the store.'" Catherine's disdain increased. As hostess, Linda seated people very slowly. "She'd glide through that place like Theda Bara, in her *stupid* clothes."

Catherine realized that she herself was the only non-Italian at Luigi's and the only person who neither had worked for Louie before (he had run another restaurant in Trenton) nor was related to him. She thought of herself, as did co-workers, as "the white girl."

On her first day of work, wearing a headband and acting perky, "I'm all Miss Pollyanna," she recalled. Within the day, the twenty-six-year-old in charge of training indicated that he might be interested in being her boyfriend, despite his current girlfriend. Within weeks, the other men, led by Louie, subjected Catherine Blount to some of the most flagrant sexual harassment imaginable.

She is still grateful.

"I was a babe in the woods in 1991, starting *all* over again. *Life.* All over. It was as if I'd never had a job," she said. "It didn't take long before all the guys that hung out with Louie during the day and the guys in the kitchen started asking me, 'So, you got a boyfriend?' 'No.'" Catherine tried to speak like a thug with a Jersey accent: "'Whadya do for *sex?*' I'm coming out of the *hermitage* here, and these guys are coming at me with this straight-ahead Italian stuff. 'I don't have sex.' 'Whadya tawkin' about? Whadya, crazy? I got a cousin for ya.'"

A handsome waiter "kid" named Joey was ready to help, too. "'I got this friend. He wants someone he can fuck around with.' That was their expression. Literally. I should be thrilled."

In a way, she was. "Somebody cares. *Men* care about whether I get laid or not. You know? Men care that I'm an attractive woman in the world who doesn't have a partner. Nobody'd cared about me like that in ages. All the white guys I knew," she laughed, shaking her head, "all the Waspy types, were too polite to talk about that."

Joey did not need to talk. He had, she told him, "the most beautiful face I've ever seen in my life." He "looked like a young Marlon Brando. He thought I was hot stuff, 'cause he found out that I wrote music." She made a face. "Forty-two! This kid was twenty. Not even old enough to go to bars, and he's flirting with me, and I was flirting *right* back."

Joey was working and watching the night the woman more than twice his age made her Saturday night debut.

Mostly Catherine was working lunch shifts, as she had hoped, and filling in on some dinner shifts. "I probably worked there for three weeks before they let me work a Saturday night, 'cause they were intense," she said, lighting a cigarette. "You had to know your shit. I started smoking again working there, too."

A prerequisite to getting "Saturday night money" was being able to use a tray correctly. "I got really good at it, but the first night I did it, I had two lousy plates on a tray, and I took it out to a table, flipped open the jackstand, put the tray down, and because Joey . . ." she rolled her eyes, "because I was staring at him, I didn't put the tray down properly. [It] slipped right off the jackstand, right onto my shoes, and right onto the floor. My first Saturday night. Ah-h, I died. *Everyone* in the place was laughing. It was all because of Joey. If he hadn't been there, I would have done fine—and *he* knew it. He made me give him a ride home that night and made me pull the car over and proceeded to attack me. I loved it." She laughed exuberantly. "I did."

Joey, though, was no match in her affections for Louie, a "multiple addict" of drink, drugs, gambling, and sex.

"I remember meeting Louie and looking in his eyes and loving him right away." Also, he was "one of the two most brilliant cooks [and restaurateurs] I've ever known in my life. He was so Sicilian, he loved women. What do they call it now? Sexual harassment. Harass you until he was blue in the face. But there was something about the way Louie did it. This was *so* good and healthy for me, psychologically. Coming out of this terrified place where I felt men had destroyed my life, between my father and my husband."

Louie, addictions or no, knew how to run Luigi's. "He treated his customers like *gold,* whether he liked them or not. Smart man. 'Anything you want from the kitchen, you can have it. You want to have a dinner of appetizers? It's yours. Want a free glass of wine? Here.' I learned a lot from him. I learned a lot about what *real* hospitality is."

In the kitchen, she learned more. "With those guys, it was a real heavy sexual tension *all* the time. Louie never let you go by without grabbing your butt or something. Nobody'd touched me in five *years,* you know?" He grabbed the other waitresses, too, she said, and they went through a pro forma shrieking ritual for him to stop. "They'd known Louie for years," mostly as waitresses from his Trenton restaurant.

"He'd come up behind me in the walk-in and grab me like this"— she demonstrated—"by my tits, and behind me or something like that, and I'd just laugh and poke him in the ribs. At first he scared me, but then I realized, this is nice." She added, "There was something innocent about it with Louie."

Perhaps not quite. "He offered me a hundred dollars," she whispered out of hearing range of her children, who were playing nearby, "for a blow job. 'Catherine, I gotta have some sex.' I said, 'Get it from your wife.' He pulls out a hundred dollars, puts it on the table. 'I'll bet you give a great blow job.'" She laughed. "I was *not* offended. I've been a feminist all my life, since I was a kid, in my heart, but there was something about the way Louie did it that I found absolutely charming and harmless." She said softly, "He loved them all, you know? He loved them all."

Once he did go too far, even for her. "I'm back in the kitchen, the place is real busy, and I'm stooping down to get some kind of a dish out from under a shelf. Louie's on this side of me and Joey's on this side of me, and Louie takes my head and holds it down like . . . I'm in a big hurry, right? You know what the ultimate moment of humiliation was? I had my hair up in a barrette, and the way he pushed my head, it made the barrette fall out and my hair fell down. There was something so vulnerable to me about having my hair fall down," especially between the two of them and in that situation. "I did my usual Catholic girl response of 'Oh, Louie! Stop it!'" The next day, however, she would not talk to him. Finally, she told him he had insulted her and added that he was going to lose a friend if he treated her that way. He moped. They made up.

One Saturday night, Louie outdid himself another way. The restaurant was mobbed. He was supposed to be maître d' but did not show up until after eight o'clock. And he was high. "His wife's pissed off, so he goes in the back and gets the jug, starts drinking." Soon, he was "seating people, schmoozing people, going around with a bottle of wine, pouring wine, chatting people up, drunk on his ass. His eyes were bright red. I watched him—without missing a heartbeat—make a *whole* lot of irritable customers who were waiting for tables happy. Talking to everybody like they were his best friend. He'd pop down at a table, pop up again, bang! bang! bang! He's *all* over the room. He runs back in the kitchen, he's yelling at everybody, 'Why don't you get these orders out?' He's got *thirty* orders up on the line. There's five guys behind the line trying to put this stuff out, little sauté pans, real good food. Louie jumps on the line. I've never seen a man work so fast and so expertly." Six waitresses and waiters watched in amazement. Within fifteen minutes, all their orders were done.

"It was incredible. *Thirty* orders. He jumps off the line, he goes"—

slapping his hands and shouting, as she did now—" 'That's it. Get it out while it's hot. I'm outta here.' " He goes back out front and schmoozes the room again. I was like," she whispered again, " 'I'm impressed.' "

Catherine was no slouch at Luigi's either, she allowed. "I'm *bright*. I wait on somebody a couple times, and I'll remember when they want their appetizer, how fast they eat, what kind of coffee they're going to want, whether they're going to want the Sambuca out of the closet after dinner. Little details. Whether they want me to talk to the wife first. They'll give you those kind of signals. Is he going to order for her? What's their M.O.? In better restaurants, you have to know that stuff.

"There's a *lot* of art in waitressing. A little thing like picking up a plate and seeing [that] it doesn't look quite right. A little finish here, a little finish there," rendered by "taking your waitering towel and cleaning off the edge and maybe pushing the meat to a different angle. Or that needs a little garnish. Brighten it up. Finish off that work of art. Put a frame on it. Set it down on the table in the right way, so that the entree faces them and everything sort of frames that. Little touches. Good waitressing's about little touches."

When taking an order, "the girls at Luigi's used to go, 'What did youse want?' God almighty," she laughed. At the end of a meal, they asked, " 'Are ya done?' I'd try to set an example—'May I take that for you?'—and hoped they'd hear me."

Few seemed to hear, or care. They "were all pretty much impressed by the men they were with" and "living in La-La Land, showing each other their engagement rings." One waitress was married and confided in Catherine about her husband's abuse. She also was an exception in another regard: she was friendly.

The others "all rejected me so poignantly. They never invited me to go out with them after work." Catherine sighed. "Gum chewing, perfect nails. They'll never know how much I loved working with them, because they were all very threatened by me. We never really connected." When one got married, Catherine was the only waitress not invited to the wedding.

If the women at Louie's rejected her, the men certainly did not. Some of their comments "were appropriate, some of them were inappropriate, but I didn't care. I thought it was wild, like unbridled sexuality." No one was more unbridled than Louie.

"He really was the most generous creature. When I waited on his family on Christmas Eve, before I left, he slipped a twenty-dollar bill in my pocket. I stayed a half hour late? I volunteered to stay late on Christmas Eve to wait on his family, which meant the *world* to him, to have his family in there. I'll never forget, I was on my way to midnight mass with the kids, and he says"—she did a thug shout—" 'Catherine, I'll light a candle faw ya in church.' He *meant* it. I loved Louie. I'm serious. He brought me out of myself. He let me feel like a woman again without being scared."

Bertie Halpern

Opening the door to her small memento-packed apartment overlooking the last Broadway marquee with light bulbs, Bertie Halpern appeared much younger than her seventy-four years. Her red hair was cut like a cap. She wore a fish-patterned Hawaiian shirt, slacks, and scuffed Chinese slippers. She also held a hand over her mouth. Mumbling, she explained that she could not speak well, having just lost three teeth.

Empathetic in all matters dental, I began to express sympathy, but she cut me off with a wave. "That's all right. They weren't mine."

Bertie Halpern, it would become clear, often uses a one-two punch—funny/not funny, or not funny/funny—in her repertoire. Her life is filled with enough drama for several plots, while her overlay of comedy can make a stranger double up laughing. Careful of that punch, though. "You're a good person, but conventional [people] intimidate me, because I'm such a rebel." For "conventional," read "dull." "I'll say anything for dialogue. I don't have any friends left because of that."

As midday Manhattan skies darkened to deliver a colossal window-pounding thunderstorm, Bertie poured herself a Scotch on the rocks, gestured toward a generous lunch spread, and began disclosing her own scenario. The main character eluded summarization. Who is she? She has titles for her unwritten autobiography: *The Gripes of Wrath* and *For Whom the Belles Toil.* "Another title for a book of mine was going to be *Pisces, Jewish, and Gay.*" She spoke of a woman singer with whom she used to travel out of town on "one-night stands. This is musically, not sexually." A double entendre? "I had those, too."

"My poor mother, when I think about her—my God, she had this little freak on her hands when I came into her life. This Russian peasant who hardly read a paper, didn't have any education, had very low self-esteem. 'If I'm nothing, whatever comes from me is nothing.' " She also was "always cleaning or cooking or baking or washing the dishes," Bertie said. "I don't think I saw my mother's face 'til I was twenty."

Her parents were "in business" but were rarely in any business, or any place, for long. "We moved from Brooklyn to the Bronx . . ." After falling behind on rent, "we used to have our furniture put out on the street. I thought it was a game when I was a kid."

Bertie, for Bertha ("I hate that name"), was the third of four children. A baby brother, Ralph, was born in 1930 when she was nine. "I was wild, running around in the streets. I didn't pay any attention to [my mother]. I was a disobedient child, considered a *bad* kid, you know? When Ralph was born, it was too much for her." Bertie temporarily was sent to a "home," she called it. "She got me out of the way. I figure it was a family decision."

Bertie grew up to be "a guy with a thirty-six breast."

Her gay course—"part cleverness" at taking on the male role, she said, and "part genetics"—began in childhood, she thinks, when she emulated cowboy stars. "I would stand in front of a mirror with two guns and twirl them. Now, a nice little girl doesn't behave this way."

Nice little girls do not join the Communist Party, either. Bertie joined about 1942, she said. "Everybody belonged to the Communist Party. It was the thing to *do*. We were so *poor*. What the hell did you have to lose?"

Bertie's apolitical collision with the restaurant world began when her parents tried another business: running a delicatessen. "Deli be my *destiny!*" she shouted, waving her glass. It was on Saratoga and Atlantic Avenues in Brooklyn and offered fifteen-cent sandwiches, plus serenity. "There's no tension or pressure. You're in a neighborhood on a corner where everybody knows everybody."

Bertie did not plan to spend her working days anywhere near tables. Theater was supposed to be her destiny. She took acting classes at the Berghof Studio in Greenwich Village and philosophy classes at Cooper Union. "I pick brains, and I get in trouble with that. This is another thing about being Jewish—you're considered pushy. A lot of Jewish people *are* aggressive. I went through an anti-Semitic period in my life. I couldn't stand them, but I couldn't stand any group of people together." She called herself, after a sip, "eclectic."

When she was twenty, a platonic friend named Jack inadvertently changed her direction. She and he "were very tight. We were in the Village together all the time. Many nights we slept in Central Park because I didn't want to go back to Brooklyn and he didn't want to go back to the Bronx." It was safe to sleep in the park, she said, and both were "too stoned" to care when they landed on a rock rather than a lawn. In 1947, Jack told her he was moving to Miami Beach. Bertie announced that he could not leave without her.

"I stole money from my mother to go there. I remember how much I took, and I remember how much the bus fare was. Thirty-three dollars. It was a horrible experience. They didn't have toilets on the buses. They stopped every three or four hours" for people to relieve themselves. She "felt like Groucho Marx," she laughed. "I couldn't straighten up."

In Miami Beach, Jack got work as a waiter in a Collins Avenue hotel so exclusive it did not hire waitresses. Bertie found similar employment several economic notches lower. The restaurant was a local legend called Wolf's (now Wolfie's Rascal House), and it bore no resemblance to her mother's deli. "Waiting on people at a table—my God, how scary. But it was desperation time.

"This woman [customer] asks me for grapefruit. I bring her a whole grapefruit. When we ate it in my house, we ate it like an orange. We'd cut it in fourths. I never had the experience. So she's looking at me, 'What am I supposed to do with this?'"

Bertie began yelling. "These women came at me, the waiters, like a battalion! This *army* of hostility. I ran from the diner in tears. How could I be so *stupid? Oh, God.* I'll never make that mistake again." She had no chance to at Wolf's.

After returning to New York, she found work at another legendary restaurant, Jack Dempsey's. "You'd get a lot of these guys that were half bagged, they'd come in and challenge him. Jack Dempsey always sat in the window [at a table]. It was almost like they could have had a dummy up there."

Bertie's appearance could have deceived, too. When she wore a black apron over a white uniform dress, she recalled, "That's when I became a woman, or looked like a woman. Or a waiter in drag." In her apartment, a framed photograph grabs the eye. A handsome young person in a tuxedo smiles seductively at the camera, looking like a young Eddie Fisher. It is a young Bertie, indeed in drag. She guessed the picture was taken around 1948 at the 181 Club, Manhattan's then-famous gay nightclub at 181 Second Avenue. Bertie, cross-dressing, worked there not as a waitress but as a waiter.

"It was like the homosexual Copacabana. It was a lovely club. Wedgwood walls, white and blue. It had a nice stage. They had the cream of the crop, as far as female impersonators. These weren't just drag queens.

They were guys that had talent behind their costumes. The costumes were lavish and wonderful. They had borzoi . . . with rhinestone collars. They'd make their entrances like that.

"This is the funny part. The lesbians, the dykes, were supposed to take the boys' part. When I think about it! We were doing 'On The Town' . . ." She began singing, " 'New York, New York, it's a wonderful town . . . ' Okay. We're very uptight, we're too busy being *men* to be able to relax and let loose and sing and dance and have a good time. You couldn't get out of this rigidity of the male role. The female impersonators were wonderful, but *we* were dreadful." The lesbians also worked harder. When they finished their act, they, unlike the female impersonators, went back to waiting tables.

The clientele included gays and straights. "It was like a slumming place to go to. Anybody could come in there. Anybody *would* come in there. One night, party of six is headed toward my table. I'm looking like that." She pointed to the photograph. "*Guess* who's one of the customers? My sister Helen, who didn't know about that side of my life." I gasped. "Right. I go to another lesbian and I say, '*Please* take this party. My sister just came in with her boyfriend. I can't face her.' Whoever it was wouldn't do that for me, so I was forced to take them.

"I didn't acknowledge my sister. She didn't acknowledge me. She never saw me in drag. This is the kicker. You know how there's a wiseacre in every crowd? My sister's boyfriend [whom Bertie had never met] says, 'C'mere, I wanna tell you something.'

"I bend down, and he says, pointing to my sister on his right, 'She goes for you.'

"I said, 'Oh yeah, that's nice,' and I walked away from him. I would have *loved* to blow the whole thing up by saying, 'Listen, you asshole. She's my sister.' But I couldn't do it to *her*."

Bertie and Helen never talked about the incident.

In Bertie's continuing desperation to earn money, and as part of her mélange of sex roles (a 181 Club customer once admiringly called her "bizarre," for it was not clear to him—nor to staring people on the street—what sex she was), she "went to bed with men. I did that. I . . . I was a prostitute. I'd find these women who were prostitutes. Very attractive. They didn't stand on street corners—they worked at a house, through a madam. Like a hundred bucks, two hundred. I would be some of their lovers, and through them I got acquainted with some men. I [didn't] think any man would pay a hundred bucks for me. Maybe twenty-five, fifty. So I made a mistake—I didn't get the money up front once. I had an appointment with this man and I went, and he fucked me, and he screwed me twice because he didn't pay me." She poured another round of drinks.

Bertie's opinion of men did not improve when she returned to waiting tables. Some asked, " 'Where's that young waitress that waited on me yesterday?' Or, 'Where's the pretty one that waited on me yesterday?' Don't you love that?"

Her eyes suddenly sparkled.

"This is the *best* thing that happened to me. There was this guy that came in, he said, 'Just give me a check, miss. I'm on a diet.' " She laughed loudly. "I come out with the humor of all these places. The thing is, everyone was playing a part. I couldn't believe these people were *serious*: the role of customer, the role of waiter. I'd think you've got to be reading *scripts*."

A role she played opposite one customer, Lucille Ball, whom she did not recognize at first, was that of nervous fan. "I was in the kitchen, maybe having a cigarette, and they said to me, 'Do you know who's at your table? Lucille Ball.' I turned into a different person. I didn't know who I was anymore, and I wish they hadn't told me who it was. I could have been more relaxed, and she, probably, would have gotten rid of this pain in the ass, who turned out to me." Bertie imitated her anxious questions: "Is everything okay? Would you like a little more of this?"

Bertie is indeed starstruck. "I've written to a lot of celebrities, and I've gotten answers. You know who I like? Quentin Crisp." She called the writer/performer "brilliant."

"He responded to my letter. He called me. He's *listed*. When we met, I said, 'You've got to be kidding. Even my plumber has an unlisted number.' He said"—she imitated a delicate fey tone—" 'Bertie, if you have an unlisted number, you are stuck with your friends.' "

Some stars struck no positive tones. "Liza Minelli stiffed me. Nothing." It was a long time ago, she added.

Arthur Miller was little better. Bertie waited on him at The Gaiety, at Lexington and 56th. "It was a deli, owned by three Jewish men. They were *terrible*, these guys. They'd bounce you around like a ping pong ball. 'I have some overtime coming, Harry.' 'See Lou.' 'Lou, I have some overtime . . . ' 'See Bill.' 'Bill, am I getting paid for Thanksgiving Day?' 'See Harry.' "

Miller came to the deli to visit Harry; "they were chummy." Afterward, he "left a quarter or something. It was ridiculous. They don't care, you know? The best tippers are the working man." To Bertie, Miller did not attain that level of respect.

She found even poorer tippers out of town, at an Atlantic City hotel. "I worked Haddon Hall, and they'd have conventions. They'd have doctors. They were the worst. They would have champagne breakfasts, champagne coming out of the spout of a metal lion, and scrambled eggs."

She moved from job to job to job. "When I was out of work, I would go to an agency on Fourteenth Street or down around [Warren] Street, which was very, very depressing. They were dirty; there were empty booze bottles in the hallways. People coming there for dishwashing jobs, anything pertaining to the restaurant business. You'd sit, waiting for people to call needing whatever, [for the day]. It was the pits. It was like being stranded and falling into an unfamiliar world again. So many times I would go to the address—I would get a little slip of paper, [like] 423 Eighth Avenue—[and] if the place would horrify me, I wouldn't go in. But I had a wonderful feeling of freedom when I didn't go in. It was great, like playing hooky." With her freedom, she often bought a movie ticket.

As the decades went by, Bertie learned to cope. At a seafood restaurant where fish identification was casual ("if they ran out of snapper, they used striped bass, and vice versa"), she waited until other waitresses' orders were picked up. "Whatever was left I'd figure was mine. I couldn't tell one fish from another. I hung back. That's another way of dealing with something that's unfamiliar to you."

She preferred the familiar: New York delicatessens. She liked the ease of the orders, the frenzy of the lunchtime crush, and she fit in just fine with the famously brusque service. She told people at noisy tables to quiet down or be thrown out. To her surprise, they quieted down. "I would push myself as far as I could go without getting fired."

At one well-known deli, the owner, "a crass and vulgar man," also pushed the behavioral envelope. "To impress the waitresses when they were having a coffee break, also to drive them back to their stations, he would stir a cup of coffee with his penis." She added that the coffee must have been lukewarm.

She was no fan of co-workers, either. "I find waiters and waitresses horrendous, most of them." She estimated that "two out of ten are nice. Now, the fact that I'm much older makes me less tolerant of things. Maybe I'm looking for a fight. Older people are, to an extent, invisible.

That's why I insist upon keeping my hair red. If I go gray, I'll really get lost."

Bertie's hostility took her only to the edge. She was merely "threatened" with losing jobs. "Belonging to the union, Local One, they can't fire you, which I think is a detriment now." She said the only fireable offenses were getting into a fight or being drunk.

When Bertie Halpern was sixty-something, her age suddenly seemed not to matter. A "sweetheart" at an employment agency called her for an interview at a new restaurant, a global phenomenon then hiring for its Manhattan debut on West 57th Street.

It was the Hard Rock Cafe.

"My immediate reaction was, Hard Rock? This new thing that's happening? They're going to hire me? Like I'm a female Lindy waiter? No *way*. She said, 'No, it's okay.' I said, she's got to know what she's talking about; I'll give it a shot. I was excited about it, in a way. This was *young,* this was *vibrant*, this was *in*. And I was a hip kid.

"There were three other women about my age waiting. Everybody else was like from eighteen to twenty-two. I was interviewed by this man. He's a gem. He was very ecology-oriented. I'm selling myself. I said to him, 'You know, I'm hip, I'm hip.' He said, 'I know you are, Bertie.'

"He hires me! I am thrilled. But you have to come in for two days to learn the computer. I never saw a computer in my life. I am frightened. I am having agita"—New Yorkese for "heart palpitations"—"Man, I'm not going to make it. This is like the grapefruit all over again."

She began laughing, remembering the frustration of trying to place orders for drinks. "What if you have a party of six with different drinks? Won't I be there forever, at this computer? I'm looking for the number of the *olive*."

On opening day, Bertie was temporarily saved: the computers broke down. "It was kind of grace time. I could collect my thoughts or maybe become acquainted with it a little better." She never did. "The computer was so frightening."

Then there was, of course, the hard rock. "The music was deafening. Deafening, deafening. 'What??? Did you say rare? How did you want that?'" It was a wonderful shtick, Bertie in her cap of red hair, leaning over, a hand cupping her ear. "'What did you say, honey?' Then when things broke down, nobody was getting their orders, and that would make them angry. 'Where's my food? I've been here half an hour . . .'

'You're poifectly right, lady, but the computer is down.' 'A likely story.' "

She had trouble communicating with colleagues, too. "I veered toward the women my age, but they weren't very friendly. I think everyone was extremely nervous. I never know whether it's them or me, anyway, when I have this problem with people. What am I projecting here?" She reached out to young workers. "I'd try to let them know I was younger than I appeared, but it didn't work."

The Hard Rock Cafe was not Bertie's destiny. "This wonderful couple, this manager and manageress, they were very gentle people. The man that interviewed me, it was like," she whispered, " 'Everything's going to be all right, my child.' I said to them [after a month], 'I don't think I can do this.' They said, 'We understand.' "

When she was much younger, Bertie worked a gig that was harder than the Hard Rock Cafe. It was a restaurant named Traders, around 31st Street and Seventh Avenue, she recalled, and was a fur industry hangout. Most customers were men, who treated the place like their private club. "A lot of them were very arrogant. They had a very bad attitude. They were equivalent to the Jewish princess—'I'm here, you take care of me. I want what I want, and I don't want to hear about waiting.' "

Bertie was growing angry. By now, the afternoon was drawing late, and the Scotch was having an effect. A certain familiarity had been established, and many painful memories had been aired. But nothing was preparation for what she recounted about Traders.

The best-known customer of all, "Big John," Bertie loathed. He had a seal fur business in the Hudson Bay and once a year made a trip to Manhattan, the fur district, and Traders.

"Big John used to come in, and he'd always remark, 'Ah, your tits are bigger today than they were last year. Did they grow?' To me and to everybody. And touch some of them. Yeah. But they accepted it, because you do. You *do*, you do. You want to make money, Big John was *very* generous. After our shift, 'Sit down, Big John will buy you a drink.' 'Give us a drink, give us a drink,' " she lilted sarcastically. "Everybody loved Big John. I didn't love Big John, because I was a guy. I was a guy with tits." She laughed harshly.

"My boss loved Big John. He spent a lot of money there. If John wanted to screw one of the waitresses in the booth, it would be okay with my boss."

Bertie was uncomfortable at Traders, not only because of Big John and the other customers. She hid her homosexuality from everyone. The other waitresses "kind of knew there was something different with me, maybe, because a lot of them would talk about their children or their husbands. I never came forth with those stories. So what was *my* story?" Her voice became louder. "You know what I did once? You want to hear something crazy?" She took a breath. "I had had it with Big John, with his 'big tits' and 'How are your tits?' You know what I did?"

Bertie shouted now, as she well may have then. "He was sitting down. I got on *my* knees, spread his legs, and I said, 'How are your *balls* today, John?' and I went for his balls," grabbing them.

"He turned into a sixteen-year-old girl and closed his legs real tight. What *satisfaction* that gave me! I had been wanting to do that for a century. I think it's retribution. Because the men's balls are hidden. Are they hanging? Are they dangling? Women's breasts are out there, and I've had it. I'm getting drunk. I'm getting angry just thinking about it."

Silence filled her apartment.

Her action "astonished" the other waitresses. "Some of them laughed. What are you going to do? It was a combination of joke and tragedy almost, because you don't *do* this to a man."

Big John "made it a joke," too, and returned to Hudson Bay.

As for Bertie, she kept her job. "It was a union place. I couldn't get fired. I wasn't drunk."

◼◼◼ Hilde Meck

In the Los Angeles suburb of Van Nuys, Hilde Meck grew up serious and became more so. Her sister was often in psychiatric hospitals. Her father was in jail at least twice, to sober up, after her mother got a friendly judge to sentence him. "I used to go to jail and visit him and give him money. I was trying to be like a little social worker, help my family, help my mom solve her problems. . . . She called and asked me for advice. In a way, I felt like I didn't have a childhood."

Hilde went to UCLA, inclinations intact. She worked in a "nuclear medicine radiation biology laboratory," where cats had "isotopes in their heads. It was like top-secret. Heavy." After college, "I got a job working in south central Los Angeles, right after the Watts riots. Very heavy, very depressing."

Her voice is as flat as the facade of the Los Angeles high-rise where she helps coordinate a small nonprofit organization. As we left the Wilshire Boulevard lobby, which was lined with marble and filled with plants, Hilde told me that the restaurant where we were heading was the only one she knew in Westwood that serves brown rice. In a black skirt, bright blouse, and heels (she is the only current or former waitress I met who wore heels), with her wispy blonde hair, Hilde did not fit the brown rice stereotype. Soon, dipping a plastic fork into a styrofoam plate of shaved carrots, a few kidney beans, and brown rice (but foregoing a hit of wheat grass juice), she admitted that she had not always been health conscious.

"I had this split life, where I worked very hard—I was kind of a crusader—and then I let loose with drinking and drugs." She pulled out the *u* in drugs, giving the word two syllables. The "letting loose" is the reason she appears under a pseudonym here, one meant to reflect her German heritage.

All the while she worked at her jobs, she said, her girlfriends seemed to be having a lark of a life—they waitressed. "I always felt envious of them. Like, oh, wow, it's so neat to have fun, have a drink after work. I was just very serious."

Her next job was evaluating patients who had been sent involuntarily to Los Angeles psychiatric hospitals. Again, "I chose to work with the poorest, the sickest, the people that have the least."

By then, she was getting psychiatric help herself. "I was in therapy because I was drinking a lot. I was having a lot of blackouts. Not at work, of course. I was always together at work, I *thought*. I thought I did a really good job."

Then, while she was on assignment at Camarillo state hospital, a patient tried to rape her. Soon thereafter, another of her patients killed his grandmother, thought to be the only person he loved. Hilde concluded that some people had problems beyond even her abilities to solve.

"I stopped working. I stayed home, and I did art." The art she did was painting, mostly abstract oils.

After six months of living on savings, Hilde had to look for work. This time, she sought something that might be her salvation rather than her destruction. She decided to wait tables.

"That was my wish, to do something very simple, something, in a way, very clean. You just, like, give what you give. You put something beautiful in front of someone. You give something they want. It's a very simple, clean act. In the moment. That's very Zen. They're hungry. You bring them food. They eat." She laughed, a very little. "That basic."

Some of her friends were aghast that she left a white-collar career with so much responsibility in order to be a waitress. She did not care, she said. She liked going home knowing that her day was done. Clients no longer hitched rides in her mind. Tips symbolized the difference: "It's like a completion. You pick up the tip off the table, and now it's on to the next customer."

Waitressing was all she hoped it would be. "I loved serving food. I loved the people in the kitchen, watching them make it. It was fascinating to me. I never got tired of it. I thought of it as something beautiful and creative."

As she deliberately chose her work, she also deliberately chose her restaurants. She excluded fancy, expensive ones. "I never wanted that kind of fanfare." She also rejected those that seemed frantic. She selected by sense: "I would go into restaurants as a customer, and just go by my feeling."

Her goal was to be the farthest from zombie and the closest to Zen. "A lot about meditation is practicing being in the moment, where you just are where you are. For me, serving food was a way to practice. Because if you get distracted, you make mistakes."

For a while, she worked in a variety of places. One she liked for its "authentic" food. But she disliked how the owner, whose staff was largely illegal immigrants, expected all his employees to do whatever he wanted, such as climb ladders to wash the chandelier. It was difficult to say no, especially when the immigrant workers said yes.

Hilde described her favorite restaurant, where she worked two and a half years, in terms of an environmental womb. It had "a lot of really big pictures on the wall, big photographs of nature, some very beautiful pictures. Sunsets," she breathed. It was named Earth, Wind, and Flour.

The pictured calm reflected careful management. "It's very well organized, the way the system is, the way you put your order in, and the way the kitchen is set up. It works, even when it's very busy, [when] every single table is taken and there's a line. It can appear to be chaotic and crazy, but actually it's functioning very well.

"I felt people there cared about each other. When you are super busy in a restaurant, one little thing can completely overwhelm you; and when someone helps you, it's such a gift. It's so incredible. That's something I especially loved about working in a restaurant. It puts things into kind of a strange perspective, where little things are very, very precious."

Hilde developed a fan club of customers. "I had people there tell me I was their favorite waitress in the city. Like, they would drive out of their way to see me, to be at one of my tables, because I really cared a *lot* what they ate, [that they tried] something new, that they enjoyed their dinner. It sounds funny, but it's true. I really cared. It's almost like a sacrament. I mean, it is."

In a sense, she still was the child trying to make everything better. "I think what motivated my suggestions would be if people could eat a lot of vegetables and pasta—say, something with no meat—and feel, like, light when they left and say they could enjoy it more than a meat dish. That to me is profound. I believe that not eating meat will help save the planet. It's *true*. If we eat a lot of meat, it uses a lot of resources. It's not good for people."

While customers ate healthily, the staff often was famished. Many, including Hilde, tended to rush to work at the last minute. "I'd bring protein powder or a drink in a thermos, or [go] in the bathroom [and] eat rolls really fast, because my metabolism is such that I have to eat sometimes quickly. It's kind of an irony that you're serving all this food and a lot of people serving it are *very* hungry."

Some servers also, for whatever reasons, often were upset. While they went into the steaming kitchen and "would be really hot-headed and angry and carrying on about how much they hated this customer or the manager, I always had a pretty good attitude, because I actually enjoyed being there. I would try to share it with other people I worked with, about trying to see it from a different point of view."

Hilde's attitude was so unusual that "they gave me an award at that restaurant." She smiled over her fragments of food. "For being outstanding, for being something special. It was nice. They said we had never done this before."

In comparison to watching over radiated cats, working in the rubble of Watts, or evaluating involuntary psychiatric patients, waiting tables at Earth, Wind, and Flour became a sanctuary for Hilde. She even got sober there.

"The therapist I was seeing kept telling me she thought I should seriously consider that my drinking and taking drugs was a problem. So I went to one [AA] meeting, and after that I never drank again. It was like, I got it." Hilde had "felt something in the room. I think I'm very spiritual, and I have a sense of presence at times? The way I described the restaurant [to you], I had never thought of it quite like that—where it looks like it's chaotic, but actually there's a deeper working order. Like the workings of a universe, where sometimes things look like they're falling apart, but underneath it all there's something that's just so smooth, that's just so right. A restaurant isn't that, but it's a *reminder* of that."

Hilde waited tables for close to a decade. Rested and revitalized, she then returned to white-collar life.

She does not want to waitress again. "Absolutely not. No way. I do a lot of writing where I am, I have a lot of skills I use. I make a much better salary, I'm fifty-one, I have medical insurance." She also feels that waitress work involves "closing options rather than opening options."

The last thought we discussed was on a list that Hilde Meck, ever serious despite herself, had drawn up in anticipation of our meeting. She planned later, she admitted, to compare the negatives and positives of what waitressing work entailed in her experience with what I had asked her about. "Little challenges," as she called them, had long influenced her life. After running down her list of negatives—nothing unusual there—she let me see her list of positives. They included the "element of [the] forbidden" (that is, waitressing being socially forbidden for a career person), "place to heal," and "*ritualized* interaction." In the number one spot was "movement."

"If someone gently puts something down, it's got a gentle energy to the motion, to that inner action, the movement around the person. I felt very, very conscious of it, the way I put things down. It gave me a lot of pleasure to do it in a way I thought was beautiful. I felt that all of us working together in the restaurant, it was like a big dance, like the cosmic dance."

▪▪▪ *Lorraine Talcove*

She is almost seventy-three years old, and she washes dishes at a Pizza Hut on Staten Island.

"Tomorrow, I go in from twelve o'clock to two, two-thirty. If it's going to be busy—say, the kids are off from school—they will say, 'Lorraine, you're coming in at five tomorrow, right?' I'd say, 'Yeah, all right.' Sometimes I work five to closing, to nine o'clock." She washes "a *lot* of dishes—you have no idea—and glasses and cups and pitchers, uh! And silver, *uh!*" She moves "every minute," for "I've got two big bins about this big," she said, stretching her arms wide. "I do work very hard. Look what I've got," she said, now holding up her hands. "Arthritis from picking up all the dishes and the heavy pots and all." The work brings her $5.95 an hour, she said, adding sarcastically, "Isn't that a lot of money?"

Lorraine Talcove was not really upset about her pay. She was upset about her hours. She wanted more. The reason is woven within her life, a life that she said began with Lou.

In her home on the southern end of Staten Island (not far from New York City's famous landfill), a seemingly endless collection of memorabilia celebrates Lou. Before telling me about him, and the connection to Pizza Hut, however, she agreed to begin at the beginning: her childhood in a French-speaking Catholic family in New England.

"Papa was French, mama wasn't. Mama spoke it, but she did a mean job of it." Her parents "started out" in Minnesota. "My father used to log, the big logs on the river. Mama, she used to teach school. Then they moved to Vermont and became farmers, and they did very well." And they begot.

Lorraine was one of thirteen children, she said, laughing loudly, and showing a gap-toothed grin. Her eyes look as impudent as they may always have been, her hair is a mass of reddish curls, and her voice is young: deep, firm, and rapid. "In those days, there was no such thing as birth control and all that stuff. Didn't talk about it. Isn't it silly, huh?"

Thanks to the farm and her mother's canning, the family "ate everything we ever wanted." Grandparents, parents, children, and hired hands sat together at a huge dining room table. "We would have a roast beef here and a roast beef there"—one at each end, she gestured—"then you had to have at least six pies for supper. Pies! We always had dessert. That's why we're all nice and, you know?"

She grinned and patted a stout hip. Her pink, green, and white flowered dress applauds every inch. "I have a couple of sisters that are pretty thin, but they work at it."

The family eventually left the farm "because things weren't going so well" and the children were reluctant to continue their parents' lives. While "Papa and the boys" got work at a trucking firm in town, World War II determined Lorraine's job. She and a sister went to Pittsfield, Massachusetts, to work for General Electric. Lorraine became a machine operator and made capacitors. "What they were used for, I don't know."

One rainy day in 1941, she met Lou. She was eighteen, he was thirty. "I always say that's when my life began. It's true. Childhood is all right, but it was hard with all of those kids, always fighting for your place in the sun. 'Mama, he did this,' 'Yes, darling, I know.' They gave us a lot of attention, don't get me wrong. They were *very* good parents, but there wasn't a case of, 'Come here, Lorraine, I love you,' like they do today." She had marveled this morning at her daughter Lois holding her child simply because he asked her to.

The first person who really held Lorraine was Lou.

Their first meeting took place on a weekend, when Lorraine, known to her co-workers as "Frenchy," was about to take a bus to visit a sick colleague and meet up with her work friend Frannie. "She calls me up and says, 'Listen, Frenchy, don't come out, it is *pouring*.' I says, 'I know, I'm looking for my umbrella.' " Many, many such details later, Frenchy heard that Frannie's brother Lou had just come home from military training in South Carolina and was going to pick Frannie up and give her a ride to the sick friend's house.

The meeting was affable, then Lou returned to military maneuvers, Frannie leaned on Frenchy to write him. Lorraine finally sent a few lines. "He wrote me back the nicest card. I can show it to you. It was very casual. But, come to find out, he was telling them how cute I was, what a nice girl. That's why in all of my letters, a lot of cards and all, I always put, 'You were always the nicest guy/the nicest in the world. And that's why I'll thank God forever/for letting me be your girl.' "

When Lou returned from maneuvers, he and Lorraine started dating. "His mother didn't mind, but his [other] sister didn't like it that I'm a goy and her brother was a Jew." (Lou's father had died.) The courtship lasted three and a half years while Lou was away at war, as a medic in North Africa and Sicily.

Although at his urging Lorraine went out with other men, she and he wrote each other almost every day, letters now stuffed in and spilling out of drawers and albums. When the war ended, Lorraine and Lou reunited in Boston. They were as chaste as always.

"What a jerk I was. We were walking around, and we had breakfast, and he said, 'Lorraine, I've got to get you a room.' We went to the Commodore, and he gets me a nice room. Then he turns to me and says, 'Now I have to get myself a room.' I said, 'Not *here* you don't! You better go across the street.' " She almost choked, laughing. "I was twenty-three years old. If you told that to anyone today, they would say, 'What are you, crazy?' "

Lou went across the street and got himself a room.

"That was one reason Lou always said, 'Lorraine, I've always re-spected you. I always knew you were a good woman.' It was worth it. I had a good marriage out of it." Before Lorraine and I met face to face, she had sputtered on the phone that some people had warned her this "mixed marriage" would never last. It lasted almost forty-three years, she said indignantly. It lasted until Lou's death.

They had a life rich in everything but money. He was a printer and worked for the father of Jeb Magruder (of the Nixon Watergate scandal) more than thirty years, she said. He also did part-time work of other kinds. Lorraine worked, too, at various jobs, but stopped when she started having children to care for.

She and Lou had three: Freddy (as she always called him), who made a career with a pipeline company; Gloria, who worked her way through college, graduating Phi Beta Kappa from the University of Texas, earned a master's degree from the University of South Carolina, and became a teacher; and Lois, who was "never motivated" in that regard and "wanted to be a hairdresser, so that's what she does. Right now mine is a mess." Lorraine will be seeing Lois later again today for a wash and set.

The first time around, Lorraine approached waitressing matter-of-factly. "Lou wasn't making that much in those days, right after the war. One day, I realized I had to go to work because there was no two ways of doing it on one salary. I worked all over, all over"—that is, all over Staten Island. The restaurants, Italian and grandly named, included the Riviera Chateau, run by her brother-in-law Frank; the Esquire Club; and the Plaza Casino, "which was banquets."

When Lorraine began waiting tables, she exhibited a rare behavior. "My brother-in-law comes over and says, 'Lorraine, get your ass in there and stop that. The guys say, is she crazy? She doesn't want to take a tip.' I wouldn't take the tip."

In many ways, she had a lot to learn. Her sister told the head waiter to turn Lorraine into " 'the best waitress going. I don't care how tough you are.' He says, 'Remember one thing, Lorraine. I could literally make you cry.' I said, 'Good, you try it.' I started following him around. He'd say, 'You set that table. What else do you put on when you serve soup?' 'I don't know.' He said, 'Really? People eat soup without cheese here?' " Lorraine would get the cheese. So it went.

She did whatever her brother-in-law Frank wanted, including a phase of serving Italian food in "French" style. "You take a fork and a spoon and you'd get the stuff like this," she showed me, indifferently. So much for "French" style. "I wasn't crazy about it, but as long as it brought in the money, that's all I cared about."

Frank, she added, was "rough for a boss." She "always" swallowed any retorts to him. "That's why I'm so mouthy now. A boss is a boss."

She was, let us face the evidence, mouthy then. A woman of prideful fidelity, she told off one customer who "played around" and put the make on her, challenging him to complain to Frank. He did not. She also told off a potential boss. He had made the mistake of warning her, " 'We don't want a girl that's going to sit at the bar after working hours.' I said, 'I've got news for you. I don't drink. I don't need *anything* you have to give me. Number one, you're not my type. Number two, there's *nothing* you can give me I don't get at home.' "

That reminded her of another incident. She all but fell off her kitchen chair, howling, when she told me what happened after she accidentally spilled a Gibson on the rocks on a woman's lap. Lorraine apologized profusely, until the woman's husband stopped her. " 'Don't get excited,' he says"—Lorraine could barely speak for laughing—" 'It's the first time anybody's been able to cool her box off.' "

Lorraine has a raunchy side, but she was one devoted family woman. "I always made sure I had a job at night, so Lou or I were with the children. I would go to work at five and Lou would be coming in about quarter to five, and we would kiss at the door, and I'd go out. I had supper all made, the house was clean, the kids' homework was all done. This is how we lived for years and years." She often worked several jobs, like at a "big, big diner" part of the week, the Esquire Club another part, and on weekends the Plaza Casino.

A gruff old man who owned it gave her a nickname that stuck. "He said, 'What's your name again?' I said, 'Lorraine.' He said, 'Lorraine, from now on it's Sam. You're one of the boys.' " She worked like one, toting "heavy, great big trays. I could carry eighteen *dinners* in those things. I worked there, oh, gosh, about five or six years. It was nice. That was where I had my first heart attack."

It happened after Lorraine/Frenchy/Sam served breakfast to a group of forty men, helped by one busboy. She got "a little tired," drank some soda to burp, and "felt a little better. Then I said, 'Ah, let me get to work, I'm feeling sorry for myself.' " She kept trying to work but finally went home.

In the middle of the night, unable to breathe, she got up, clutching at furniture. "Pretty soon I see Lois [then twelve] and Lou up. He said, 'The dog woke me up. What's the matter?' Imagine, a little terrier." The dog had gone to both bedrooms and licked Lou and Lois in the face to wake them.

At the hospital, "they didn't expect me to live," she now laughed. "They" probably did not expect her to go back to work, either.

They did not know Lorraine. "I couldn't do the heavy lifting no more, I couldn't do the banquets no more," so she did "just plain waitressing. You know, arm service. I wasn't supposed to, but I was all right."

Over the years, she never did become tip-oriented and never considered low tips an insult. "I always felt maybe they didn't know any better. You know what I said? 'Whether they leave me a dollar or ten dollars, they're a customer. If it wasn't for them, I wouldn't have a job.'"

She left "arm service" waitressing too, "when I got sick again. Coronary insufficiency. It wasn't pumping the blood right." She then began working in a Kmart lunchroom. "I made all the sandwiches for ten girls. I mean *busy,* oh! They never waited a minute for it. They couldn't get over it. *Never* waited. Anything that keeps me moving, like dishes, I love it."

One day, her co-workers were marveling at a man they kept seeing outside. "They'd say, 'We need this guy, Lorraine. Does he walk *fast!* We call him the Radio Man. He's got his radio on, and he swings his arms.'" She knew. It was Lou. He had "an extra heart beat" and was on his daily ten-mile walk. He walked until the day he died. His heart problems finally killed him.

Seven years later, she misses him palpably. The loss is apparent in every embroidered pillow, every photograph of the sweet-looking brown-haired man, every framed poem they wrote each other. At the time, his death left her desolate. Furthermore, she had retired from Kmart and was jobless. Lorraine never had been desperate for money, but after Lou's death she was desperate for something to fill her hours.

One day, she was on her way home from a daily visit to Lou's grave. "I was really in bad shape, and I'm praying, saying, 'Lou, please help me out, I can't make it without you.' I'm coming down a little hill, and I noticed the red roof. I said, 'Gee, I heard that was Pizza Hut. Let me try. They won't want me. I'm too old.' I looked horrible at the time, because I was always very within myself. He had just been dead a year. I stop by, and I went to the builders. They had the corner posts up, and they were just starting the red roof."

Lorraine was directed to a trailer to get an application. "I straightened up and I flew right," she said, sitting taller in her chair. "Make believe

I was quite happy to be there. They don't know what a broken heart I have. With that I walked in and said, 'Should I go to confession to anybody? It looks like a confessional in here.' [One] said, 'You come on, I'll hear your confession.' I said, 'You'd *never* want to hear mine.' They laughed. This George came over—he was our first boss, what a doll he was." She pointed out his and his wife's snapshot on her refrigerator door, a veritable gallery, and then fumed that he had been fired on trumped-up charges rather than being given a raise he had earned.

Lorraine applied to work in the kitchen, but George thought the huge pizza-making machines too difficult for her. "He wanted me to take register, and I don't like register." A restaurant owner had once implied that Lorraine was the reason forty dollars was missing from his register. After a sleepless night and much prayer, and with Lou saying to quit if anyone dared accuse her, she recalled seeing the owner himself taking the money and told him so. He acknowledged she was right. Still, Lorraine had avoided cash registers ever since.

George put her to work washing dishes.

"I'm not the cleanest person in the world, but I like things to be orderly. And *oh,* it was awful. Say we had the rack to put dirty dishes on. The girls would come in, and garbage goes all over the floor. It *still* does, and I holler—*oh,* do I holler! Now they're used to me." The system improved. "They're doing it the clean way," with a big strainer on top of the sink. "That's where they throw their soda." It used to be tossed in a big pail and "was going all over the place. I couldn't *stand* it."

Days became years at Pizza Hut. "I'm past the fancy stage," she confided.

She is not past the opinion stage, though. She grew to dislike the company's middle managers, "little pipsqueaks" half her age. "You know what happens in a place like Pizza Hut? They become almost—how can I say it without being nasty?—almost like ass wipes."

Pipsqueaks do not know much about customer service, in Lorraine's unvarnished view. "People like a lot of attention. They really do. But it's hard to give it at Pizza Hut, because they're trying to keep expenses down all the time" and want employees to meet, greet, and seat customers as well as serve them and "then answer the phone."

Her opinion of many of the waitresses is not much better. "You live like a pig, you act like a pig, you've got to expect to be treated like a pig," she told one.

Between grumbles, Lorraine Talcove washes dishes for the same reason she wants more hours and for the same reason that during off-

hours—despite her often testy relationships with bosses and colleagues—
she returns to visit the restaurant. It is the same reason that when she
was seventy-two and had an operation on her carotid arteries and was
off work eight weeks, she returned to washing dishes. At home, she
misses Lou.

After "I met my Louie, I worked all over, [but] waitressing seemed
to be the most satisfying to me. In fact, restaurant work seems to be the
most satisfying. My husband wouldn't be at all surprised to get up now
and see me doing dishes. He'd say, 'Lorraine, some day when I go, I
hope you don't work too hard.' I'd say, 'Lou, you know what? If I'm
ever amongst the missing while you're living, look for me in a *big* kitchen
working.' I kept saying that. He'd say, 'What are you going to do in a
kitchen?' I'd tell him, 'I'm going to be washing dishes.' "

Or, she could have told him, she might be adding to her collection of
poems to him.

> My dreaming days are over, now that you've gone away.
> I'll always love you, Louie, and for you will always pray,
> Some day we'll be together and together we'll always dream.
> Again we'll gaze upon the moon. Once more we'll be a team.

Two and a half years after my visit, Gloria wrote: "I am sorry to tell
you that my mother died on January 16th. She was 75 years old. She
hadn't been feeling well, kind of tired, for months." On Christmas Day,
Lorraine had felt so weak that her family had rushed her to the hospital.
"They did an angiogram, which freaked my mother out, and she had a
major heart attack." To "humor" her children, Lorraine agreed to un-
dergo high-risk surgery. It "was a disaster." She died without regaining
consciousness.

"That Sunday, we had a wake for her. All the relatives who could
make it from out of town and her many friends from Staten Island and
her co-workers from Pizza Hut were all there."

Gloria mused about her mother's work. "Waitresses are usually overlooked for their contributions and suffering, but having grown up
around restaurant people, I have long appreciated their hard-gained wis-
dom and insight into human nature." Her mother "always knew that
what she did for a living was so much more than just bringing people
what they had ordered.

"By the way, she worked at Pizza Hut washing dishes right up until
she went into the hospital on Christmas. She loved that job."

6

DINERS AND DOWNWARD

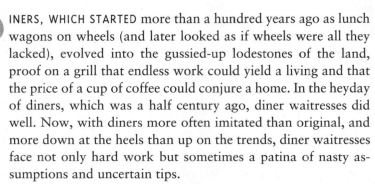

INERS, WHICH STARTED more than a hundred years ago as lunch wagons on wheels (and later looked as if wheels were all they lacked), evolved into the gussied-up lodestones of the land, proof on a grill that endless work could yield a living and that the price of a cup of coffee could conjure a home. In the heyday of diners, which was a half century ago, diner waitresses did well. Now, with diners more often imitated than original, and more down at the heels than up on the trends, diner waitresses face not only hard work but sometimes a patina of nasty assumptions and uncertain tips.

In comparison to other downscale places where waitresses work, though, diners still are looking good. Some of them.

▩▩▩ Rose Marie Willie

It is mid-morning. Rose Marie Willie approaches, dourly. She is in her early thirties. Her body, eyebrows, and lips are thin, her crimped brown hair streaked, her eye makeup dark and heavy. She wears a Route 66 theme T-shirt, black pants, black running shoes, and two gold necklaces, one of which spells out "Rose" in script. A well-tailored woman having breakfast at the counter reads aloud to Al the grill cook from her copy of *USA Today* that waitresses who draw happy faces on their checks get better tips.[1] Al shouts the information to Rose, who in response conveys the impression that few happy faces of any kind issue from her.

She turns to me. I give her my order of coffee, scrambled eggs, and toast, but pause on the home fries. I yearn for some

and know, simply know, that they are homemade, not a slab of de-
frosted shreds. On the other hand, if the helping is large, I'd best refrain.
I am waitress putty.

"Are the home fries a big size?" I ask Rose, "or small?"

The question, I learn later, catapults me into a category: Customers
Who Ask Stupid Questions.

Rose says flatly, "They're just normal size."

The Tastee Diner in Bethesda, Maryland, blocks from the Washington,
D.C., border, is a dinosaur, a single-story building amid a sprawl of
glassy, brassy office buildings and department store branches into which
one can imagine money being vacuumed from their origins in downtown
D.C. The squeaky Tastee door opens to old wooden booths, the smell
of hot breakfasts, and a sense of hanging on. A counter stool lacks its
seat; upside-down Coca-Cola cups on the stool's pole are meant to cush-
ion mistakes.

The diner's past is part of its present. A photo montage of customers
lines a wall. Carved panels over the grill advertise the reach of the Tastee
empire into two other Maryland suburbs, Silver Spring and Laurel.

Even after breakfast rush, the place buzzes. A fireman with a walkie-
talkie is getting a to-go order. A waitress shouts her order. The code is
"Take one, Al," to get Al's attention. He says one waitress, who is off
today, has shouted orders at the Tastee so long—thirty-three years at
least—that she lost her voice. Now she whispers them in his ear.

"That would be Kay," Rose informed me. "She works Thursday,
Friday, Saturday, and Sunday." It puzzled me that Rose did not simply
say "Thursday through Sunday," until I realized why. Her basic unit of
measurement is a shift.

We are sitting over coffee in a booth that afternoon in the Tastee's
less charming, newer extension. Rose, now Rosie—everyone calls her
that, she said—is thawing faster than frozen home fries. Only yesterday,
she all but smiled, she and some of the other girls had been joking about
starting Waitresses Anonymous. "I guess you'd have to be a waitress to
understand it, but it seems when people are in the public they go stupid
when it comes to ordering food." We clear *that* up, and Rosie goes on
to the transgressions of others.

"We have on our menu Cheeseburger Royal—a cheeseburger that's
got everything on it and comes with French fries and cole slaw. On the
other side of the menu, we'll have a cheeseburger listed. They'll say,
"What's the difference between a cheeseburger and the Cheeseburger

Royal?' '*Probably* the fact that the Royal comes with French fries and cole slaw.'" She issued a laugh so abrupt and rough, it sounded close to a cough. Rosie, who grew up and lives in Laurel, Maryland, speaks with a scraping voice and the hint of an accent from Baltimore, some twenty-five miles away.

"You'll ask somebody, 'What do you want on your cheeseburger?' They'll say, 'What do you have?'" After she delivers the extensive answer, "they'll start telling you, 'I want lettuce, I don't want no mayonnaise, I want tomato, I don't want no pickles.' You literally gotta tell them, 'Don't tell me what you don't want.'" She looked mightily annoyed. One bad cheeseburger order can throw off Rosie's day.

It starts at 4 A.M. "I like to have my coffee and my cigarette when I wake up in the mornings. Get ready for that day, you know? I psyche myself up: 'I'm gonna have a good day.' I get my shower and everything and usually leave my house around a quarter after five. I *try* to leave around five. I get here about five-thirty, when I don't push the snooze button. I've started doing that. Bad habit, don't do it."

The first thing Rosie does at the Tastee is determine Al's state of mind after she says good morning. A response such as "Good morning, honeypie" is a good sign. "Hey. Howya doin'?" is not. "I know somebody's already made him mad."

Next she notes whether the waitresses on the shift before her did their side work. "When you come in and everything's empty and you got to refill everything, it kind of changes your mood a little bit." Rosie indicated the cluster of condiments and the napkin dispenser on our table. "I call these fill-ups. Like somebody didn't do, obviously. *This* drives me crazy," she said, grabbing the dispenser. Napkins were packed so tightly on one side that they were hard to remove, but the other side was empty. "They do that a lot and I hate it."

Then come her next challenges, customers. "'How do you want your eggs?' 'We want them fried.' 'Okay. Fried *how?*' You've gotta ask them every tiny question. It's like crossing the *t*'s and dotting the *i*'s to get this order. I probably shouldn't even say this . . ." her rimmed eyes narrowed. "Sometimes you play into it. I mean, what would *you* think if you asked what they wanted to drink and they say, 'I'll take a juice.' 'Okay. Would you like me to surprise you? Pick one out I feel that you should have?' Or they don't say 'large' or 'small.' We automatically take them large. Then they get mad because they wanted a small." Other customers order the Egg Beaters mix just like they would order regular eggs. "'Egg Beaters, sunny side up!'" Rosie almost choked.

"It's a lot of patience . . . involved, I think, a lot of times," she mused, thanking another waitress who stopped by our booth with a pot of coffee.

"You always want to greet people in a friendly, nice manner," said Rosie. "It's aggravating when you go to the table and you say, 'Good morning' or 'Hi, how you doin'?' and they're like, 'I want coffee and eggs over easy and bacon.' You're like, 'Okay, good morning to you, too.' They don't care how you are or what you're doing, just 'Give me my food and get out of my way.'

"Very few people anymore are, 'Good morning.' Especially the older guys that come in by themselves, the more business-type men. We've got some guys that won't even look you in your face when they ask you for more coffee. They do one of these numbers." Rosie dropped her head, pretending to read, raised an arm high, and pointed her forefinger down to her coffee cup. One man who does that—and also pushes his silver-ware to one side and "messes up the whole table"—she forces to talk. "I make him work for his coffee now." He, in turn, makes Rosie work in another way. "When he leaves the table, his paper's laid open, and his tip's laying on top of the paper." She gets the message: you can grub for your tip.

Once, a regular inspired her to step farther out of line. "I asked him how he was. He's like, 'Over easy. Bacon.' I was like, 'I've never known anyone to be that way before.' 'What do you mean?' 'I asked you how you were, and you said you were over easy and bacon.' He said, 'I'm just hungry.' I said, 'Oh, well, from now on I'll just quit the small talk and we'll get right down to business.'

"The way I feel about it, I think waitressing takes multiple person-alities, in a certain sense. You have to be able to greet the ones that do want that sort of greeting when they come in. You also have to have the personality to be able to overlook the ones that don't want no kind of social contact with you whatsoever." She shook her head. "Believe me, it only takes one person to ruin your entire day.

"We have a lot of regulars that come in all the time, and it's a friendly home-type atmosphere. A lot of people know you by your name, you know a lot of customers by their name. I've got customers I call by their *food*. Their order's already in before they get in the door, if I see them outside. 'My over easy weekdays is here.' "

If, for whatever unfathomable reason, Mr. Poached Eggs decides while pulling into a parking space to have French toast instead, he knows to set things right quickly; "as soon as they come in the door, they'll get our attention immediately." Rosie gladly accommodates such rebels. "Ev-er-y single day there are people that eat and drink the same thing. One particular person, I do believe, is every breakfast, every lunch, every dinner, the same thing."

Of her regulars, "ninety percent of them, I'd say, they're grateful. They like comin' here because of the service. They feel welcome. They feel, 'I don't have to tell this person every day what I want. She's paying enough attention to me that she knows.' "

Long-time regulars would do well to heed Rosie's ways, too. When she delivers menus to people who have been eating the same thing at the Tastee for decades and are ready to have it again, what she really means is calm down and wait. "They don't understand I'm doing it to get a minute, to where I can get somethin' else done and then get back to them. Some of them get offended."

When she is walking through her station, coffeepot in hand, do not ask her for more coffee. She is bringing it. When she is carrying "a handful of creamers" while pouring the coffee, do not ask her for cream. "It's in my *hand*."

Do not, ever, ask her to smile. "People expect you to smile all the time, but they don't realize when *they're* at work they're not smiling *all day* long. When you're dealing with the public, you try to have a pleas-ant greeting about yourself at all times, as much as you can. But my whole eight-hour shift, I'm sorry, I'm not smiling. I am *not*."

Some customers, in her opinion, should never eat out, at least not at the Tastee Diner. "They act like us being a waitress, we're not supposed to make mistakes. They almost expect us to be robots, I think. Have everything there, perfect, because they got it set in their head they're going out to a restaurant, they're gonna be waited on. *That's* supposed to make it as perfect as if they were able to get up and walk around and do everything themselves. We're perfect, we don't forget nothin', we're Speedy Gonzalezes. They forget sometimes we are human, even though they don't look at us as being.

"They want us perfect, in one manner, to wait on them and be at their every beck and call, but then not perfect in a way that, I think, they belittle us for *being* waitresses.

"People, ninety percent of the time they come into a restaurant is because they *do* want another *person* waiting on them. They literally want someone coming back constantly checking on 'em, giving 'em more coffee, seeing how everything is. Personally, myself, I *live* once in a while just to go out to a restaurant to have the tables turned. Have them waiting on *me* for a change."

Rosie made her way into waitress work on the apron strings of her mother, who "short-order cooked for a long time" at the Tastee Diner in Laurel. (Rosie never mentioned her father except by implication, saying she comes from Irish and German heritage.)

Rosie waited tables on the night shift at the Laurel Tastee when she was sixteen, "and when I come back the second time, I started at the one in Silver Spring. Then I ended up over here workin' nights." There was more to her start than that. Rosie became pregnant in high school, dropped out, had a baby boy, and months later was "in the middle of separating from his father and trying to find a job." That was when she began night shift.

"Before I come back to here, I had other jobs doing different things, but I always end up back waitressing for some reason." All the jobs were manual labor. "I did construction work, like had-to-have-a-job type of thing. Personally, I'm a survivor. I'll do whatever it takes to pay my bills. I was doing construction for this company—they weren't union or nothing, I was just doing grading and picking up trash and different kind of things."

Even when she joined a union to do the same work and received better benefits and pay, Rosie was one unhappy apprentice. "Women were very few and far between. They were out there, I'm sure, but they weren't where I was, and I wasn't where they were."

Sexual harassment she could handle. "There was this guy that got mouthy with me, saying he wants me to have his baby, followed me out to my car after work. I went to my boss and said, 'I don't want to complain, but get him off my back, or I'll go to the hall and write him up.'" The harassment stopped.

Rosie's main problem was aesthetic. "I was all dirty all the time. When I'm coming home, I was like, somebody's going to see me like this, you know? I felt it wasn't feminine enough or somethin'. I felt really *weird,* like it took something away from me. When *I* go to work, I want to look nice. When I come home, I want to feel good about myself. I don't want to be all greasy and dirty." Diner grease did not compare. She quit.

Then, one Friday night, while she was visiting employee friends at the Laurel Tastee, the Bethesda Tastee called with a typical restaurant emergency. "They had a girl that didn't show up. Everybody there knows who I am, so they asked me would I be interested in coming here to help them out." Rosie rushed from the known of Laurel to the unknown of Bethesda.

"We were really busy. I picked up on it, though—fast. It was different because you get certain things, [supplies,] here and get certain things *there*. I've been here ever since, except a time or two I left." She raised a thin eyebrow. "I think all of us here have quit at some point in time and come back."

Many stay at least a decade. "We're like lifers." Asked how the waitresses get along, Rosie paused. "When we get busy, we all get on each other's nerves, too. When it's over with, it's over with. If I get into an argument over toast . . ."

Toast! The waitress's crucible, the diner's downfall, the most argued-over and fought-over of all food items. Why? Because waitresses must often make it themselves, thereby stopping everything else, and because it is ripe for stealing. Passing the test of toast can take years.

"Toast is awful!" Rosie all but screamed, before confiding that "big-time" toast fights take place at the Silver Spring Tastee. "We've even got girls that mark their toast, the corners. If somebody says, 'I didn't take your toast,' they'll say, 'Look, the corners are torn off. It is *mine*.' Toast is such a pain. If you don't take it with the food right then, it throws you off. It will throw your whole entire day off."

At the Bethesda Tastee, there are unwritten rules of toast. "If my food's ready and their food's not, I'll take their toast and put more in, and by the time their food's ready, their toast will be up. I don't intentionally take someone else's toast." (She did at the Silver Spring Tastee, though, "just to aggravate them.")

"I like this place," she said, looking around while a busboy mopped the floor. She likes the owner, too. "If we're really busy, he's not above helping us make coffees or hot chocolates. This is a small establishment, and I don't think anybody here is above anybody. No matter where your standings are."

She also likes that she can speak her mind about Tastee food she finds less than tasty. "The other day, there was this regular customer. She says, 'I want something new. What's good? How about this barbecue?' She was asking the cook. He says, 'It's good.' I said, 'Na-a-ah, I don't know about that. I think you better let her taste it first.' She tasted it, and it turned out she didn't like it.

"When I'm waitressin', I am myself. I don't think formal waitresses or waiters can work as at ease as we can. We have one-to-one conversations with our customers. It's not strictly 'sir' and 'ma'am' and 'I know you're so very fragile and I won't get too close to you.' It's like we're us and I'm me."

Rosie stays herself no matter the shift and no matter the situation, including working graveyard shift on weekends, which can mean serving customers who have been drinking excessively. "There's been a few times a ruckus will break out. But ninety percent of the time, you're waitressing, but you're also paying attention to what's going on around you. You can tell if this table's having problems with the table next to 'em. You can pretty much catch on that something's going to happen unless something's done. We'll say to one of 'em, 'Let's calm it down, just enjoy our meal. We don't want no trouble.' "

Sometimes she is too late. "I've been in situations where a fight has broken out, and I've been cornered to where I can't move because of the guys fighting back and forth."

Day work is different. Rosie has had, she smiled widely and unexpectedly, some "really good days." They would include "a big tipping customer." Some leave as much as 30 percent. Some, however, would "dig in their pocket and give you all their change before they'd give you a dollar."

Rosie and the other waitresses also perform a fair amount of nontipped work. About ten in the morning, after breakfast rush, she starts doing her "fill-ups" for the next shift. "By two o'clock, when I'm ready to leave, I'll look around and if I have a sugar that's been really used, I'll refill it. Right before I leave, I'll change the ice in my creamers and butters and fill up the jelly holders and make sure they have tea and lemons. Then you got your ketchup and syrups. Your basic wiping down. We try to do the windows every day." Inside only, she amended. Also "we clean the coffeepots and the coffee machine."

Cleaning is constant, even if business is not. She makes from forty dollars a day to sometimes more than one hundred. "We could have a whole week of nothing—no tips, no business. But you got to keep yourself going and say next week's gonna be better. You have to keep faith." One day of the week is never good. "For some reason, Tuesdays weren't my day. I started making a joke. I was telling everybody Tuesdays don't exist anymore. We'll call it that day after Monday and the day before Wednesday."

Rosie Willie's day used to include taking care of her son (the tiny ring on the chain she wears next to the scripted Rose is his baby ring), but recently he decided to live with his father, a steamfitter in West Virginia. (The three meet at a halfway point in Hancock, Maryland, every other weekend.) Rosie said, several different times, that she no longer worries as much about the boy getting involved in drugs and gangs as she used to.

These days, instead of being with him after work, "I'll take a shower or bath, then I do it all over again—the hair and the makeup thing all over again, but in a different mood. Then I'm going out and looking for something to do. I'm going grocery shopping or I'm going visiting. It's nice."

She seemed blasé about the future of the Tastee, not even knowing whether her boss owns the building. Rumors about installing computers concern her, because she has found that when using them, "you don't even talk to the cook. I like knowing that my food *has* been ordered and it's getting prepared."

If she were to ever leave the Tastee (again), Rosie vowed she would not work at another restaurant. She was thinking of trying to be a police officer, her inspiration strictly "adrenaline," she said, not a wish to change society. "I've never been very politically educated. *My* life revolves around things I'm doing physically. I don't have no idea what's going on in this world. I honestly do not. I don't watch the news, I don't read the paper. You could say I don't care about what's going on except for myself, you know? Maybe that's why I'm a waitress." She laughed, some. "There I go."

Joanne Mulcahy

"I know how much I loved waitressing, because I chose it. And because I'm middle-class and educated, I didn't have to choose it." After starting as a teenager in suburban Philadelphia and waiting tables in some ten cities for some twenty years in some thirty restaurants, she still loved it. Even after finishing her doctorate and moving to Portland, Oregon, to become the state folklorist—that is, even with a Ph.D. and a full-time professional job—she waited tables.

"Because it was so much a part of my identity, I couldn't let go of doing it. It got me through graduate school, not just because of money. It was also a world that made me feel whole. I didn't really feel that way as a graduate student. I didn't feel I belonged there. But in restaurants, I always felt like I belonged."

Joanne Mulcahy, a slender, chestnut-haired, stunning woman of forty, camouflaged in the flannel and boots of the Oregon dress code, grew up near Pennsylvania's old-moneyed Main Line and did not feel she "belonged" there, either. "That whole enclave of the Main Line [had] tremendous class division. There's all [these other] people who shore up the wealthier segment of that population. There were a lot of Irish people that came as landscapers, waitresses, in places like the [Merion] Cricket Club." Her family was no exception. "My parents were from New England, both Irish on both sides."

Both, furthermore, had worked in restaurants. "Even though they were educated and eventually got college degrees, my father came from a very working-class background. For him, it was a tremendous sense of pride to get a college degree and move out of that world, but he instilled in us very young that working in a restaurant was a source of pride." Her mother had been a waitress when she met Joanne's father. "I grew up thinking it was perfectly honorable to wait on people. I later [met] people whose parents had not let them wait on tables because they thought it would be demeaning. I remember being *so* shocked."

At fifteen, as her family expected, Joanne got a waitressing job. It was at the Dolley Madison Ice Cream Parlor in Wynnewood, where her sister had worked. The place stays in her mind, however, for another reason. "I remember my sister telling me there was a man who came in alone and he lived with his mother." Joanne got the implication: the man was lonely, and she should take care of him. "Afterward, I've thought there's something destructive about that. When I hear about men doing something very violent, I go back to that first instance of her telling me about that. I remember thinking, what does loneliness drive people to?" Before Joanne was out of her teens, she learned more about male violence and she found a place that cemented her trust in women.

The Mari-Nay Diner, which she recalled affectionately and often, was on the pre-Revolutionary trail now known as Lancaster Pike—the main drag of the Main Line. (Mari-Nay stood for the owners' military service in the marines and navy.) "I loved the people there. That was a restaurant that taught me how people come to restaurants for community. People go every day, and they want you to know them and to pay attention to them."

In exchange, Joanne has written, customers brought an array of flowers and other gifts to the waitresses.[2] She came to believe that the most meaningful jobs "are the ones where the gift exchange outweighs the market exchange." She believes teaching is that way, too. She teaches gender studies at Lewis and Clark College in Portland and also teaches writing in a graduate program.

"But even though restaurants would seem like a world where the market exchange was pretty straightforward—leave you a tip, you get a certain wage—it's *never* that. People come to waitresses for all the assorted stereotypes and clichés, of telling their troubles and being heard. I think that's part of the gift of what waitresses give to their clients."

While driving to a trendy Portland restaurant that was upscale for her tastes (it offers sweet-potato chips), Joanne said that she remembers the Mari-Nay not for the customers but for the other waitresses. One was a beautiful woman named Marie. "She had red hair, and she would sing 'Amazing Grace' in the kitchen—and if I even think about it now, I can start crying. I don't know what her story was. I think she had a really hard life. Had come from Ireland." And she had "ended up at the diner. She was very sexy. People told me she was a prostitute. I remember even as a teenager thinking, 'So what?' "

Joanne worked at the Mari-Nay throughout high school. After her shift, she rewarded herself with a ritual. "I remember going home on hot summer nights and sneaking upstairs, when I was a teenager. I had smoked from the time I was thirteen, and that was part of waitressing too, for me. Going home and going upstairs and blowing smoke out the window and counting my cash. It's *such* a sweet memory." She tilted her head back and laughed. "All this cash, it was hot, and I was smoking."

She went to college in New Hampshire, dropped out after one "futile and confused" semester, and returned to her womb of work. This time, the Mari-Nay assigned her a full-time job at the core of the operation. "I worked on the five A.M. shift with all these older women, who at first I was very afraid of. Bea, who was an amazing woman." Joanne's written account describes her this way: "Bea had finesse. She balanced ten plates to an arm, hurling them across the counter along with sharp words for meager tips."[3]

"I think they still knew that I was not a working-class woman who would choose that for my life," she said, "that I had options they didn't have. But they still treated me very much like one of them. There is a sense—if a woman is sixty years old and she's done this her whole life and she doesn't even have a high school degree, she knows it's something she had to do. And you had choices that she didn't have. But I've always found that, after a certain point, whatever resentment or whatever there may have been was at least temporarily transcended. I try not to romanticize it, because to romanticize it denies the class divisions that are very real. But I found that I never worked in a place where if I worked hard enough and worked well, people didn't respect me for who I was."

The Mari-Nay put Joanne literally, and figuratively, back on her feet. Before long, she returned to her studies, this time at the University of Pennsylvania. In the course of getting an undergraduate degree in comparative literature and a doctorate in anthropology from Penn, Joanne moved on to what usually is not regarded as the best of all waitressing worlds: summers in Philly. "There's a kind of sultriness to that heat and humidity. But what I mainly remember is sitting out on the back steps, drinking beer after shift." Beer and cigarettes were not her only opiates. "How did you get through a double shift? I don't know what people use now, but from as early as when I was in high school, people got diet pills. A lot of places, in bars, customers would give you cocaine. The waitresses were always snorting cocaine. That was less for me than taking diet pills. Double shifts were," she sighed, "inhumane. It was such long hours.

"There were some places where if you worked a lunch shift, you'd get there at least by ten to set up. Maybe you could finish [first shift] by two or two-thirty and do side work until three or three-thirty. Then you'd have to be back at five to set up for dinner. If the dinner hour ran from seven till ten, you'd have side work after that." In other words, she had a thirteen-hour work day with a ninety-minute break.

And it was not her only job. At the time she also served cocktails at the Windjammer Lounge, on the edge of Philadelphia. It featured a disc jockey who played Frank Sinatra songs on Sunday nights for a couple who fascinated Joanne. "The woman was like Blanche Dubois out of *Streetcar Named Desire*. She wore taffeta dresses and had a southern accent and was kind of fallen glamour. And this younger man obviously adored her.

"I have a strong memory of that place because I had so many waitress jobs [going] at one time when I worked there." Each job required a different costume. The Windjammer made her wear "a sailor outfit," which she kept in her locker in the basement of the lounge. "You had stockings and shorts and this red, white, and blue thing with a white collar. One time I was so tired, I went to work and put on my stockings and my top and I forgot the shorts. I went through the kitchen. It was all men, and I think they were all from different ethnic backgrounds, so they were very polite and didn't want to point out to me I forgot to put my shorts on." She laughed, shaking her head. "Everything stopped when I walked through the kitchen. I went into the Windjammer Lounge and started putting out the ashtrays and everything. No one could bring themselves to tell me I had forgotten to put my shorts on." She laughed again. "It was this waitressing identity crisis. I had too many jobs, too many outfits."

Another of the Philadelphia restaurants in which she worked was distinguished by its miserly owner. It was "the only restaurant I ever worked at where we weren't allowed to eat. Eating well is one of the perks of working in a restaurant, especially if it's a good restaurant. This was a French restaurant in Philadelphia, which will go unnamed. The woman who owned it had a truly monstrous reputation." Employees, hungry and angry, figured out a ruse. While carrying food upstairs from the basement kitchen, they balanced a tray on one shoulder and snacked quickly and adroitly from the plates by pinging the bottom of the tray with the free hand. The desired morsel, such as a "tiny bay scallop," would fly into the air and drop into the server's open mouth. "The plate's really close to your mouth," Joanne explained, laughing more.

"I was trying to eat while I was carrying a tray up the stairs when I slipped and fell down the stairs. I wasn't carrying all that much, but I hurt my back badly." She began taking painkillers, quit (as she had long planned) to travel in Europe, and figured she would relax and get better there. About one week later, at the British Museum, she twisted to see something and felt "such excruciating pain that I ended up in the hospital in London for a week." A country with nationalized health care is "a good place to have a medical disaster."

Her disaster was a slipped disc. Back in the United States, she got better slowly, with exercise and acupuncture, but never tried to get workers' compensation from her former employer. "I probably thought I was responsible, for trying to eat. Maybe I felt terribly guilty and that's why I never sought any compensation. But I have had other injuries; waitressing is hard on your body. And I'm small-boned, I'm not very strong physically and never have been." (Among her other injuries is a "shattered" arm she got from falling off her bike to avoid a truck. It healed, with a "railroad track scar all up my arm," but it is not up to toting heavy trays.)

She did, once, almost take a corporate job—waiting tables at the

International House of Pancakes in the Philadelphia suburb of Ardmore. She winced at the memory. "I don't know what it was that put me over the edge. The *training* was so intense. One of the things I liked about restaurants was how informal things were. That could work both ways. When you got fired, your name just got crossed off the schedule. I remember the first time that happened [to a co-worker]. It was terrifying. I thought, 'God, that's it—all of a sudden you don't exist anymore.' But the good part was, you walked in and were hired and you filled out an application. There was *some* formality, but then you [just] went around with somebody and followed what they did.

"But the Pancake House was too much for me. You had to learn all the pancakes and all the kinds of syrup. Then they had tests, and they had films they showed you. I don't think I ever worked a shift. I trailed, and then I was supposed to do my quiz on syrups, and I flipped out and walked out." (Today, training remains tough at the IHOP organization. When I visited San Francisco's Lombard Street branch, the most popular syrups—butter pecan, old-fashioned, strawberry, and blueberry, their dyes seemingly undiminishable—sat on every table, ready for use. But waitresses also had to learn eighteen "Pancakes, Waffles & French Toast Specialties," not to mention thirteen other "Pancake Originals," several separate menus for the elderly or children, and knowledge of "what's in all the ingredients," as an employee put it during her cigarette break.)

Joanne, recognizing that "something in me" did not lead to jobs "in mainstream places that try to make you conform," left pancakes for the opposite end of the social scale: the Merion Cricket Club. There she learned formal serving techniques unused at IHOP or the Mari-Nay. "You had vegetables that came in a big dish, and—I think this is considered French style—you had two large spoons and had to lean in between people and use the spoons . . . You pick up from the bowl—the vegetables—and serve them on the plate. I wasn't all that adept at it. A lot of times," she laughed over her trendy Portland meal, "I would flub it. The peas would fall onto the table."

Also at the Cricket Club, "I learned you set up the silverware the proper distance from the edge of the table. The silver was polished every day, and then you wiped it off and shined it. The restaurant I worked in in Seattle was like that. Everything had to be spotless. We used to use vinegar and water to make sure the glasses were crystally clear. And you learned how to serve and how to pick up the dishes correctly, so your presence is almost imperceptible."

Joanne absorbed mostly by observing. "As a folklorist, I know you learn most of what you know in a job from informal instruction and watching. I don't think anyone ever said to me, 'Serve from the left, clear from the right.' I saw somebody do it and picked up on it." In the same way, she learned not to clear plates until everyone was finished. (She also learned that she would rather serve than be served in "higher-class restaurants," she said. "I'm much more comfortable doing it. I don't really enjoy being the recipient. In ways, that's not right, because everyone's playing their role. I realize I have a tendency—when I'm in a nice restaurant, I feel apologetic being waited on.")

She got some training at serving by working at a new restaurant school in Philadelphia and then working for two of its graduates. "This older Jewish couple were simply wonderful, wonderful people. She had been a theater teacher, and he had been something in the business world. He used to say, 'I was a whore before I went into the restaurant industry.' They started this place called Under the Blue Moon, which was small. They called it international home cooking." Joanne worked for them, happily. "*There* the class division didn't exist, because we were all young, educated women who had chosen to be in a restaurant."

During the decades of her waitress itinerary, Joanne worked in Washington, D.C. (while studying at Georgetown's language school and while working at the Smithsonian); in Newport, Rhode Island; in San Francisco; in Kodiak, Alaska; in Seattle; and in Portland. But her heart remained at the Mari-Nay. "The style of waitressing I enjoyed the most was working in a diner." Bea had eventually taught Joanne her plate-carrying trick: "You put two plates together with your thumb. When you hook them with your thumb, you can pile a third one that sits on your wrist, and then you can pile all the way up. There was a tremendous kind of theatrical flair to doing that and doing it well."

No matter where she worked, Joanne liked one constant about waitressing: the tipping system. She found it "much more stabilizing" and "democratic" than pay structures in other professions, where "there are all kinds of perks and hidden exchanges of money." As for the mercurial nature of tips, "I *liked* that element of waitressing. It was always unexpected and unpredictable. And I loved *cash*. I never felt as rich as I did as a waitress. There was a real lethalness about having that *money*. The first time I had a job where I got a paycheck, [it] did not feel like real money." Her boyfriend jokes that a home she owns means nothing to her financially, but a hundred dollars in tips makes her feel rich.

The bigger the tips, the better. "I like extravagance. My mom told me stories when I was young about when she was a waitress and tips she remembered. These big tippers [at] the Lake Champlain resort in upstate New York. I loved it when people left huge tips." She added that tips are in a sense both meaningful and meaningless.

"What's the right tip? At the diner, people would drink coffee all morning and leave me five dollars. It was probably fifty cents for coffee, but they took your table all morning, and they knew that. It was the same when I went to work in Alaska. I was there for the five A.M. shift, and all these fishermen would come in and hang out and drink coffee before they went fishing. Their whole bill would probably be two or three dollars for coffee, and everybody would throw ones on the table. I loved coming up to a table with"—she fluttered her fingers in the air—"piles of money."

Any tip depended, of course, on getting the job in the first place. Joanne more than once felt like a second-class worker in a lower-class world. When she worked for a caterer in Washington, D.C., in 1986, she recalled, "people would call and say they wanted all men." A decade earlier in Newport, she had obtained work at a French restaurant only because sex-discrimination lawsuits were pending against local restaurants. She was hired merely as a back waiter, "more like being a glorified busperson."

Sexism affected her wages, but racism affected her conscience. When she waited tables at the University of Pennsylvania faculty club, she began to feel a rare self-consciousness about the work. "There was some gathering of military personnel. They were very condescending toward me and were overtly racist toward a black woman I was working with. She didn't seem disturbed by it at all, and I was incensed. I wondered afterward if maybe my reaction on her behalf had to do with my own sense of outrage at not being treated like an equal."

At most restaurants where Joanne worked, "black middle-class people . . . were treated as nicely as white middle-class people would have been." But in Alaska, "some of the waitresses were really racist toward native people. They wouldn't wait on them. They tried to put them in somebody else's station, or they'd treat them badly. Even in Oregon recently, I've seen Hispanic people treated badly. There's a *lot* of overt racism in restaurants. The Denny's case really broke it open."[4]

Sexism and racism in the restaurant industry, however prevalent, are talked about openly. To Joanne, the "huge taboo to talk about" is class. "It's there with waitressing, in your face. There's no way to get around it." The serving staff, of course, tried.

"Secretly you develop all these strategies for keeping your self-esteem intact when they treat you like you're a piece of the furniture or [like] you don't matter. You can go wait on people hand and foot and pretend you're humbling yourself and bowing and scraping, but there's so many counterstrategies. Humor among them is the most important, making jokes about people." She recalled behind-the-scenes speculation about "what they would be like having sex with their wife, or why it was they were so bent out of shape they had to abuse *you* to feel good about themselves." One drawback of diners, she noted, was the lack of behind-the-scenes privacy.

Joanne found that the more education she accumulated, the more being treated like furniture began to bother her. "I started to feel resentful. I'd never had that experience before. Once, there was a cultural conference going on at the University of Washington, and there were a bunch of people in the restaurant ordering their food and treating me the way people treat waitresses. They were having a conversation about something I knew something about, and I stood thinking, 'I know as much or more about this than they do, and they are treating me like shit.'" She laughed. "I thought, 'If you don't have any options, you accept the fact that people treat you like you know nothing.' I remember feeling furious."

She also noticed that condescension emanated not only from customers toward the waitstaff but also from the waitstaff toward customers. "If people came in that were kind of overweight, dressed in polyester, and coming off the ferry, like in Seattle, or if it were in Newport, and they were coming to town to go to the beach and were considered poor folk from Providence, the *waiters*—this is what used to outrage me— would start acting scornful. 'Oh, God, who wants to wait on these people? They're going to leave a lousy tip.' They'd come to the kitchen and laugh at them if they couldn't pronounce the French on the menu correctly. If you're working as a waiter or waitress, you may not be from a working background, but you are a working person. Here you are ridiculing other people. What you're doing is everything you can to elevate your own class status at the expense of somebody else."

The issue of classism within the world of restaurants had come up recently from yet another point of view, one that shocked her. Her boyfriend had decided to open a "very unpretentious Italian deli." Joanne's friends, asking in vain about foccacia or whether he would serve cappuccino, "couldn't hear this was not going to be a fancy restaurant. It was a working person's . . . diner. I found myself having to cover this sense of *shame*. I thought, 'Where is that coming from?' These are the kind of places I worked in for many years. I grew up with a sense this was perfectly good work. But there is so much baggage now about the association of certain kinds of restaurants and class. There's not only working in places like that but even *dining* in one. I thought back to my father and [how] he almost transmitted to us a certain ambivalence. I think he felt [that in] giving up that kind of work, somehow there was a price that was paid.

"I [had] the same ambivalence when *I* left waitressing. I had thought many, many times, this was enough. Why did people keep telling me it's not enough? I loved waitressing, and I would go back to it—I really would." She loves teaching, she later said, and feels "that's what I need to be doing, but [even by teaching summer courses], I don't make enough money."

She knows that her own waitressing options are more limited than they used to be. "There's lots of places that wouldn't hire me, that want twenty- to thirty-year-old women." Managers would not tell her that directly, she said. They simply decide she is too over the hill to waitress well. "Or they justify it by a kind of code. 'We have a certain look here to cultivate. That's why we can't hire . . . '—fill in the blank: poor women, black women, Hispanic women, women over thirty-five. It's so pervasive as to be unconscious." The message: go work in a diner. She added, "I can't think of any place else where you would make good money and have a measure of respect for your work."

Joanne's dilemma is not only looking older but also feeling it. "Where I started to feel physical limitations—and I was only in my early thirties—was one job I had in Seattle doing banquets at a big hotel, the Four Seasons." She did recall two pluses of that job. It had a break room, although that was not as cozy as "hanging around the kitchen, trying to keep track of your cigarette in a pile of embers." It also hosted her best New Year's Eve ever, "waiting on the Black Firemen's Association and dancing my way into the new year." The heavy Four Seasons trays, though, were a strain. After hauling "tons and tons of plates [that] have these silver covers to keep the food hot, and you pile them on," she felt "worn."

Her last spate of waitress work coincided with a personal emergency. In 1987, she had been driving through Portland en route to Seattle, when she stopped at Powell's bookstore and parked outside. Thieves broke into her car and stole "everything I owned." Virtually penniless, she drove to Seattle and learned that a "medium-range" waterfront restaurant was doing a mass hiring. Also applying for work were "all kinds of young blonde waitresses in their twenties. I was in my early thirties or mid-thirties then. It was like a cattle call. There must have been a hundred people on this Saturday afternoon. They gave us all applications to fill out, and then you broke down into groups of three or four and had a [group] interviewer. What they were doing was setting up this competitive environment, pitting people against one another.

"I was in a little circle of people. I think we were all women. One woman started talking about how much this job meant to her. I almost lost it. I thought, I will not humiliate myself in this fashion. The job meant something to me, too. I had been robbed, I didn't have a cent to my name, but I refused to be reduced to sitting there trying to outwit and compete with these other women. I walked out.

"It was horrible. But it was also all about age and how you looked. You could see everyone sizing everyone up. There was an implicit message: you had to present yourself, you had to look a certain way and be a certain way to people to be hired." Plus "it's a way of ensuring conformity from the very beginning. You won't get any uppity types when they had to beg for employment."

She next applied at "a very nice French restaurant called Campagne, [which] gets written up sometimes as among the best restaurants in Seattle." The owner "asked me about a couple of kinds of wines and *beurre blanc* and various kinds of sauces, and I was screwing up all over the place. I could never remember wines. Then I started talking about anthropology. It turned out he had studied anthropology in graduate school and [had] even been interested in the same thing that I was— ethnopoetics, which is kind of a poetic patterning within native American speech patterns. All of a sudden, we're talking about ethnopoetics and I was hired. He saved my *life* by hiring me, because I was so broke."

She had "complex feelings" about Campagne. "Lots of regulars with plenty of money" wanted to be waited on only by "their" waiter. "It's more like having a personalized servant than the motherly diner waitress who listens to all your problems." Servers included men and women. She said she "loved" both, "but it wasn't the same *feeling* that I had of safety among waitresses." At Campagne, she also had an odd "sense of not quite belonging, because I didn't feel *something* enough—hip enough, wine-knowledgeable enough, classy enough. Odd, huh? Not upper-crust enough to *wait* on people! Hierarchies hidden within hierarchies . . ."

Campagne also was the only restaurant where Joanne cried on the job. "I had been going through . . ." she hesitated. "Ah, I was going frequently to . . ." she paused again, "a support group. This was something that happened to me years before. I was raped as a teenager. I can talk about it very easily, in part because I've written about it." The "it," she explained briefly, had taken place in the countryside outside Philadelphia. Only decades later, in Seattle, did she seek help.

"I started going to Seattle Rape Relief. They had a wonderful program that ran for about three months. But during that time, I got in touch with a kind of fear I never felt before. When I was going to Georgetown, I worked at night in a place on M Street. I think the bars closed at four. So you were walking home between four and five in the morning. I never thought a thing about it. In Philadelphia, some of the neighborhoods I lived in . . . There was a horrific gang murder in the neighborhood where I lived. They found somebody's head under the sidewalk. This was blocks from where I was living, where I used to walk home." Still, even carrying hidden tips, "I don't remember feeling a lot of fear. But after I went through this rape relief session, it allowed me to feel that fear I had denied for so many years. And it was terrifying. Also a lot of grief and anger. I went to a pawn shop in Seattle to buy Mace, and the guy almost talked me into buying a gun.

"During this period, I was very emotionally fragile. I was working lunches [at Campagne], and there was this really wonderful hostess, very funny woman and very warm, also named Marie. I told her what was happening, 'cause I was feeling kind of, you know, not like myself at work. I had a table of women one day who started to bicker with me about a Perrier water. They said I put this charge, like a dollar, on the bill, and they claimed they hadn't had it. And I lost it. I went in this stairwell and started to sob hysterically. I was inconsolable. I didn't think I was going to be able to walk out there again and face them.

"Marie took care of that. She went and got the charge card and put it through. I . . . I was a mess. I remember thinking the thing [that] distressed me the most was that [I'd] felt I was a feminist from a very early age and always felt a great deal of solidarity with women. . . . I've worked in so many places where men harassed me. There were a couple of places where the managers were complete jerks and sexual harassment was part of the job. I worked in places where you wore hot pants. But it had never gotten to me before. [Now] I felt betrayed by women, who were always the people I could count on to back me up. Maybe it had nothing to do with gender. Maybe it was just my emotionally fragile circumstance, but that's the only time I ever remember getting upset and crying and going over the edge like that.

"I always felt like waitressing taught me, more than anything in the world, how to not let things get to you. I felt I had an invisible shield. I still sometimes can recapture that feeling. When I was the director of the folk arts program [in Oregon], I would go out and do field work in communities around the state. Sometimes they'd be small places where I still don't think it's very common for a woman to go into a bar at night. But I felt my job was to scope out the community, so that's what you do as an anthropologist. I would go into a bar, and that invisible shield would come back. I learned that waitressing. You get somebody in your face, pointing their finger at you, turning red, and the veins standing out on their neck because their steak was overdone. I remember the first time that happened to me, thinking, 'They can't touch me.' I have used that *so* much in my life. I think it all came from waitressing."

"One of the classic patterns that people say about anthropology is that you go into another culture and then you come to a cycle and come back to study your own. I often wondered what that meant for me." Joanne speculated that perhaps she "could look at Irish Americans in an urban enclave" but realizes that is not the topic she would choose.

Instead, Joanne would choose waitresses. "I've never felt there was any other group of people in the world that I had an immediate affinity with. It doesn't mean they would all like me. It doesn't mean I could work everywhere with all waitresses. But I respect and admire and feel an affinity toward women who work in restaurants, and that covers a huge terrain. That's how I would describe it, as my tribe."

Sally Merlo

Sally Merlo steamed. Even by letter—ballpointed fulminations on paper torn from composition notebooks—she steamed. She steamed about her ex-husband, to be sure, but mostly she steamed about the status of waitresses. The written steams were vented around three in the morning, after she finished her shift and came home to the dreary Long Island basement apartment she shared with the youngest of her two daughters.

In one letter, Sally steamed about poor and dangerous working conditions, including "roach infested kitchens and wet floors." In another, she wrote that employers do not think much of the job of waiting tables and therefore do not think much of waitresses. The attitude from the boss "somehow carries over" to both server and served; waitresses feel "low self-esteem," while customers feel "arrogance."

Boiling as Sally Merlo's written words were, they had no punch at all in comparison to her spoken ones. Raised in Valley Stream, Long Island, which all but abuts Queens, she has a strong Nassau County accent ("for her" is pronounced "fuh huh")—grating or endearing to some, utterly unremarkable to those who share it. Years of smoking have also put a rasp on the grate, making her bursts of disgust—and there are many—sound like small explosions. She developed a throat polyp from "smoking and yelling too much."

"Let's face it, you have to do things for survival, and it's what waitressing is. There isn't any security. You can be gone like this," she said with a snap of her fingers. "Just as it has been my sad experience, and you never know. It's very, very tenuous. The jobs are basically a dime a dozen. They want bodies who can take the orders. If it works, it works. If it doesn't, so what? Someone else can take your place. Most of the women who go into it are probably in my situation. They're divorced. How I got back into it is that my husband took every single penny out of our bank accounts and left me with nothing. Three years ago. He was a stockbroker."

He not only emptied the bank accounts then and left her with "tremendous bills," but he also gives her no financial help now, she said. "I just filed with the Department of Social Services [for] child support. My older one is living with him because she feels she wants a dad. He feels because he has one [child] and I have one, he does not have to give me any money. And he's living with a twenty-six-year-old."

Not long ago, the family had shared a Victorian house. "I had a nanny and a housekeeper and a gardener. We were doing very well." Sally moved to the cellar after the split. "The thirty-thousand mortgage had never been paid, so the house was lost. Basically, he took the money and ran. I threw him out, so this was his reasoning behind doing what he did.

"I didn't know a lot of the things my husband did, because Italian men tend to be very, very secretive. Whatever he did was his thing, I shouldn't be involved. 'As long as I'm doing for you what I should be doing, what do you care what I'm doing outside to make my money?' That's southern Italian thinking." Her ex-husband, she often pointed out, is "southern Italian," whereas she, she pointed out equally often, is "northern Italian."

Sally has had a life of changed directions. "I was seventeen when I graduated. I didn't know what I wanted to do. I knew I didn't want to be a secretary. That was the trap they pushed everyone into." While trying to decide her next move, she worked at a Walgreens drugstore, then panicked. "I could see women who were in their late sixties, seventies. I looked at this poor woman hustling for this dollar, and in my mind was, do I want to do this all my life? No. That's when I decided to go back to school. I couldn't see being that age and still working like a dog for the same dollar I was making as a seventeen-year-old. It didn't seem fair. At her age, she should have more in her life."

With the encouragement of her parents, who had little money but "pushed" education (it "was always a big thing" to northern Italians), Sally went to Adelphi College, helping to support herself by waiting tables. "I never thought I'd go back into it again [later], but," as she put it, "never say never."

Certain aspects seemed not to faze her. When she was about nineteen, she related, "I had gone into a walk-in refrigerator to get something, and a [busboy] followed me. He tried to kiss me and all, but I found a knife. I said, 'If you do anything to me, I would slit you, and you'll be sorry.' He got scared. I never reported it." It was "not that big of a deal in my mind."

What a "Greek cook" once did "I wouldn't even call . . . being harassed. Every time I went up to get prices, he's like, 'Oh, I could do this to you, and that in your butt.' I said, 'You wouldn't last a minute.' Just walked away. I leave him with something to think about. Why should I fight with him? This acknowledged he has an attraction for me. He doesn't know of a nicer way to put it, because he's a low-life." (In a silent code for disliked customers, she rubs her chin in "an Italian gesture that says you're a jerk.")

Sally graduated with a triple major in marketing, business administration, and sociology. "I worked at the radio station as a business manager. Also I worked at [the National Organization for Women]—I was on the political action committee. I'm into all that stuff. Before I got married, I had been accepted to law school." Her goal was to go from law to politics. "I would like to change the world."

Law school was an option, but "I was tired of school, and so I got married instead. Now I'm kicking myself."

She did volunteer work for former Democratic vice presidential candidate Geraldine Ferraro for a time and then entered the retail clothing business. Sally was helped by a woman buyer who "guided me in the right direction" toward "so-called men's jobs," including being a floor manager at Lord & Taylor in Manhattan. "I stayed there a while, then— I don't know why, I wanted to have children, so that's what I did." At the time, she left without regrets.

"I didn't follow up on a lot of things. I kind of attributed it to the confusion of the time. What is it I really want? I feel women have a lack of focus in their lives. We know we can get married, which is like a little safety hatch, not thinking these things will happen because 'you are going to be different.' I think this is why we don't focus on our careers. Men know they will always have to work, no matter what. Whatever strides have been made in the so-called liberation of women haven't done it—because now we're liberated, but to do what? Work two jobs? Kill ourselves raising kids and work?"

Her musings came in the middle of an acrimonious divorce. "I was basically a stay-at-home housewife. I felt if I were to have children, it's not fair to have someone else raise them," nanny or no. Thus "I kind of fell into a traditional marriage." It ended, she said, when she threw her husband out. "He was a binge alcoholic on the weekends. He was abusive. He'd go on Friday nights and not show up until Saturday, and vomit. Really, at a certain age you just don't do that anymore.

"I said, 'This is it, you're out.' *He,* being of southern Italian extraction, said, 'Okay, now I'm going to . . . ' " she raised her middle finger. "We had achieved the so-called American dream. And he kind of blew it."

"Anyway, what questions do you have?" The sudden sharpness may have been a jolt from the obvious. Sally was midway in age between the searching teenager she had been and the drugstore woman she did not want to be, and at this minute she was an unemployed diner waitress.

The reason for her current unemployment lies in a how-not-to-run-a-business tale of the Great American Waffle House in Oceanside, in Nassau County. A dandified diner with a red, white, and blue metal awning, on a bleak corner across from a gas station and a funeral home, it did not invite, even at lunch hour. It was nearly empty as I entered for my first appointment with Sally, which had been set up the week before. A black-haired woman in a waitress uniform, sitting on a stool and smoking, shot up and hurried over to me. Clearly disappointed that I was seeking Sally and did not want a seat in her smoking section, she told me Sally had called and was on her way. I sat at a woodgrain formica table, bought a limp salad, and wondered what was going on.

The side door opened and in rushed a woman about five feet tall with reddish hair cut swooping at the forehead and short in the back, a heart-shaped face, and an energized manner. Sally Merlo introduced herself, bustled me into her car, announced that she was not working at the Great American Waffle House anymore, and sped off.

Later, in her darkish apartment (she sleeps on the couch, her daughter in the bedroom), she said the black-haired woman had "secured her position by sucking up, because she is kind of a mediocre waitress, in my opinion. I happen to be good." Sally described herself as not being like "a lot" of waitresses who come from "a lot of dysfunction" and hang out with "the Pagans, the biker gangs."

After her college waitressing and before her post-breakup waitressing, Sally revealed, the job had also played a role in her marriage. She had waitressed on weekends to earn money while she and her husband were trying to buy a house. She had also found that waitress experience helped when she gave dinner parties. "You learn how to carry things" and set them down gracefully. "It makes it a lot easier to serve people. You don't get flustered when you have a lot of people for dinner. You learn to organize" and "to pace yourself to get everything done at the same time."

After her tips helped to secure the house, her husband began objecting to the work. "As he started doing better in his job, it was like a big deal [that] he didn't *want* this. It's a reflection of your own ego. My husband felt it was beneath him to have a wife as a waitress." The conflict led to a marriage counselor, a woman. "The marriage counselor says, 'You can see why he feels that way, don't you?' I'm like, what kind of a marriage counselor is *she?* Any work you do has some dignity to it."

Yet Sally knew she had lost. "There's a certain value system placed on jobs. Sally the neurosurgeon is treated differently than Sally the wait-ress." Sally the waitress parted with both the marriage counselor and the marriage in the reluctant dawn of her new working life.

To her parents, who had some restaurant experience, waiting tables "was a job like any other," she said, pouring me more coffee. "You're quite welcome. Let's not forget age discrimination, too. I think this has a lot to do with my not finding a so-called real job. I'm now forty. All you have to do is look at my resume and say, 'She graduated in '78, a little bit of arithmetic. Let's get a couple of twenty-two-year-olds, pay them twelve thousand a year.' "

When Sally set out for a full-time position "that maybe is not what I'm about," she said with an especially laughless laugh, "my stomach was all knotted up" at the prospect of interviewing. To ease the strain, she targeted the world she knew best.

"I walked into all the little restaurants up and down Sunrise Highway. I dress like this, neatly. They know I'm not a drug addict, I don't have tattoos on my shoulder. You're taking a chance with anybody who walks into the door. But . . . I don't have that big coke jewelry, I don't say 'yo bro,' walking in. They think this is a nice middle-class woman who will probably be a pretty good waitress." (At another point, Sally mentioned, "I always made more money. I don't know why. I'll speak to you as a human being. I don't sound like a waitress.")

The Little Southshore Diner hired Sally immediately. Her first day there "was like riding a bike, getting back on," but she did not stay long. It was too slow to provide the money she needed.

The Great American Waffle House opened at just the right time, if not just the right way. The owner brought to the enterprise a love of waffles, but little experience, Sally said.

On opening day, the cooks did not know where the waffle ingredients were. "I'm serious." The owner did not think the day would be busy. "People were waiting literally two hours for waffles."

By the third day, Sally's old waitress nightmare was back: customers are "yelling and screaming" at her to serve them, but her feet are stuck to the floor. "It's like being paralyzed."

Still, business was hot. "We were making a hundred a day. My rent was made in one week. We killed ourselves, but we made the money. Then it just died."

The death was fast, dumb, and almost comical. When business slowed, the bosses printed coupons on the reverse of supermarket receipts. Two waffles for the price of one! The idea backfired spectacularly. Someone forgot to limit the free waffle to a second customer. Many large, hungry Long Islanders showed up with only their coupons for companionship.

The bosses responded by arguing with the customers. Business slowed more. Sally was fired. The reason, she said, was not only because of business but also the result of "politicking" by the black-haired woman, who was chosen by the boss to deliver the news.

Sally was disdainful. "Most people don't want to fire somebody, even if they don't want them anymore. I guess he couldn't look me in the eye and give me a good reason for firing me. I've had to fire people, but I don't knock them down.

"Do I feel bitter? No. As a matter of fact, I do have another job already. The guy has to get back to me. It'll be in a diner with Greeks again. They're remodeling the restaurant. From each experience, I learn." Her new job, she added with a look, "will take a little more skill than throwing out waffles."

Chastened she is not. With "so-called managers, I cut right through the fat to the bone. That's why I'm having problems sometimes in this work. I hate stupidity. Maybe I will tell you in such a way, you will get your back up. If I'm doing something wrong, you can tell me. 'Sally, you're an ass. You fucked up,'" she discharged her laugh. "I'd say, 'Okay, how?'"

She knows she does not represent power. "For some reason, they always mop the floors when it's busy. I'm surprised there aren't a lot more lawsuits. They truly do not watch out for the waitress. On the hierarchies, the cooks are at the top, your busboys and dishwashers. They'll fire a waitress before they'll fire any of them. Because we're *women*." (Sally cited a perfectly horrible example from years later. A "ditzy" waitress at another Greek diner accidentally hit her in the head with a tray, hard. The boss told Sally, "You shouldn't have been in her way." He also told her to keep working. She did but then went to the hospital.)

What matters much more to her than the behavior of bosses is that of customers. When men snap their fingers in her face, "I go, 'This is not traffic school. You can put your hands down.'" It is "the American disease," she said, of people being focused only on themselves. She recalled asking a male customer if he wanted something to drink. His reply was, "Hamburger, rare."

She greeted another man, who was wearing some kind of I've-been-to-the-Galapagos sweatshirt, by commenting, "Oh, you went to the Galapagos. How interesting."

His response stunned her: "How did *you* know about the Galapagos?"

Knowing the man was addressing not Sally the neurosurgeon but Sally the waitress, she stood there, pad in hand, half laughed, then half steamed, in outraged Nassau County-ese, "How do *I* know about the Galapagos? How do *I* know about evolution and Darwin? How do *I* know about the HMS *Beagle*?"

The man knew to shut up

She leaned over her dining room/kitchen table, by an album of balloon bouquets she and a waitress friend make to try to bring in more money. "I don't like being thought of as stupid. It rankles me. It doesn't matter what level you are, you have respect as a human being. Basically, we do have a class society." She shook her head. "You get people that pretend they're so sophisticated. They're really not. For me, sophistication is the ability to get along with all kinds of different people."

Sally waits on peers—"mothers around my age [who] have smaller kids"—with empathy. "I *know* how harried they are and know what they go through just to get out. I always take extra special time with them. I give them extra napkins and make sure the kids get their food first. This way they can relax."

Fathers do not fare as well with her, especially on weekends. "That is 'divorced dad time.' They come in with their daughters," she said, tellingly, "and they're trying to pick me up with their *kids*. I'm like, how dare you?"

"Sort of friction" also emanates from wives when "husbands are flirting. That's not my fault he's doing this, but, of course, it *is*, because," she said suddenly softly, "I'm the waitress."

Several years later, her divorce final, Sally had other major concerns in addition to the status of waitresses. One was the September 11 terrorist attacks on the United States. She has unpopular opinions, she warned me on the phone. Like? The United States "was asleep at the switch!" she fairly shouted. All this money spent on fancy defense and espionage, and nobody knew? She has been reading a lot about Islam and rues that it is not better known. "People don't have the basis of comparison." She also expressed concern that if the United States caused the death of Osama bin Laden, he would become a martyr.

In the meantime, Sally Merlo was also busy with something else. She had acted on a longstanding concern about the state of public education. One prompt had come back in her mercantile days, when she asked "a group of my sales associates" what galaxy we were in, and their answers ranged from "New York City" to "Long Island." Another had come from overhearing the statement that "Jesus was Catholic." The concern led to a decision to become a teacher. She foresaw "2 years + loads of money" to get her degree, she wrote at the time. To finance it, she was working at the Apollo, get another Greek diner.

Diana Candee

What would be, for her, a perfect day as a waitress? The answer came quickly: "Breakfast shift." Diana Candee smiled.

"I'd forgotten about that. Because breakfast, you didn't have any desserts, you didn't have fountain drinks. Everything was cooked. You didn't have to do salads first. All you were responsible for was the toast. You usually had two or three cooks on the line. Pancakes and eggs are fast. People got in and they got out. People don't drink tea at breakfast. They drink coffee. Tea was always such a hassle. You had to do a teakettle *and* a saucer *and* a cup *and* a lemon *and* a tea bag. And you were supposed to warm up the teapot first so the water would stay hot for a while. With coffee, the cup's already on the table. You pour it and you're gone. All these things I haven't thought about for twenty years."

Diana eventually became, as far as she knows, California's first female installer of solar panels, which, she laughed, could be considered "more significant work" than waiting tables. Nevertheless, her experiences as a waitress stuck with her longer and in a deeper way. No wonder. Consider what happened during one graveyard shift at a Sacramento branch of Denny's.

"There was a guy who came in about three o'clock in the morning, and he was a weirdo. He set his key chain on the counter, and it had a little toy gun and a toy cannon on it. He ordered something and stayed there for about three hours. He was sliding around, sort of sleeping on the counter, and he hadn't paid his bill." He also was "getting real obnoxious verbally."

The other waitress, Louise, who "had been there for a hundred million years" and "was a bitch" did not intervene. The "weirdo" (who Diana learned had been recently released from the state mental hospital in Napa) was Diana's customer, so Diana had to ask him to leave.

"He didn't want to. I took his plate, coffee cup away, started wiping down the counter, and I picked up his key chain to wipe underneath it. He said, 'Don't touch *my* fucking key chain,' and he hit me and knocked my glasses off, and they ended up down at the other end of the counter."

Louise, who "didn't take any shit off of anybody," finally came over. "He hit *her* in the face, and he broke four bones. And the cook—I hadn't been particularly fond of the cook up until that point, he was this tall, mangy, rangy guy—came out from behind the counter with a butcher knife. The busboy got a pot of coffee. The cook put this guy down, *on* the ground, with his knee in his throat, with the butcher knife. The busboy stood on the counter with this coffee pot ready to crash on his head if he so much as moved, while I called 911, or whatever it was then. And we had maybe eight to ten customers."

Diana's laugh started to build.

With Louise crying loudly and the cook and busboy poised to deliver death or dismemberment, business continued. "People were coming into the restaurant, and I was *seating* these people, giving them their menus and saying, 'I'm sorry, our cook is busy at the moment. The grill isn't available. Would you like a cup of soup?'"

Connecting solar panels on a roof was never as dramatic.

Diana Candee now lives with her husband and their two young children in a sunny home in a development that all but overlooks San Francisco airport. Planes taking off and landing are such a familiar sight from the house that her son's first word was "airplane." The Candee home has a fair scattering of children's things inside, while the outside shows evidence of a number of ongoing projects instigated by her husband, a heavy-equipment operator. Diana, who runs a photograph album business from her home, is more of a full-time mother than she thought she might be. On a frantic but blissful morning (the first day of school), she cheerfully disregarded a sinkful of dishes and sprawled on the couch.

She has told me over the years I have known her that she was not always terribly happy in her youth, for reasons that seemed to do with having more weight and less romance than she desired, but she seemed happy now. Her short blonde hair was shiny, and her blue eyes sparkled as she let loose with a glorious smile. It came as she explained to me that, to her, a "dinner house" means a kind of place with "steak and three-course meals and fifty-dollar tickets" and thus higher tips than coffee shops. "You wear a nicer dress, and you have to do your makeup a little better, but if you're being subservient, you may as well be well-paid for being subservient."

Diana first attempted subservience when she spent the summer with her father, who lived in the northern California town of Yreka. "I wanted a summer job. My older sister had waitressed the previous two years, so she knew what it was about. She taught me how to carry plates." Ambling to her kitchen, Diana talked over her shoulder about how restaurant plates must be weighted, with wide rims, "or they don't work." She spread out her right hand and put a dinner plate on every finger but her pinkie. "You should be able to serve four or five people at once." A waitress also should be able to handle seven glasses, she said, building an imaginary pyramid three glasses tall on one hand. And, "if you're a good waitress, your hands are never empty. I worked in one restaurant where you got fined if you put your hands in your apron pockets."

In Yreka, all four restaurants said no to her because she did not have experience. She went back every week until one said yes. She almost wished it had been otherwise: "I remember it being *very* stressful." The manager's wife "watched me a lot," while Diana made a lot of mistakes, such as dropping several plates simultaneously. When she improved, the wife "got nicer," and Diana was launched.

"I had fun that year. I was sixteen years old, I was away from home, I was losing weight, I was going out with the cook, I was trying out a new personality, I was wearing makeup for the first time in my life, I was getting a fair amount of attention. I particularly liked the regulars who'd come in and sit at the counters. There was a father and son who were loggers, and they used to come in all dirty and sit down to dinner, and the son flirted with me a lot." One weekend, the son cleaned himself up and came in alone. Diana did not recognize him.

"My dad used to come and get me, every night. He didn't want me walking home at ten o'clock at night with an apron full of tips." First, though, he had dinner. She remembered his order, as she did that of all her regulars. "He used to have a hamburger steak and a salad with roquefort dressing, every night."

They also shared another ritual. "My feet *really* hurt. I remember going home to my dad's house. He was actually quite sweet, I'd forgotten. He'd do a big pot of hot water and Epsom salts for my feet. [And] he was really good at getting all the junk out of my uniform. I'd take off my uniform and sit in my slip with my feet in the pot, and he'd squirt [my uniform] with whatever he squirted it with and put it in the wash. Then I'd go to bed, and he'd hang it on the clothesline, and I'd get up the next morning and iron it and go off to work."

The following summer, Diana went to live with her mother, in Ashland, Oregon, and opted to keep waitressing. The town hosts a Shakespeare festival and had "lots and lots" of restaurants, which Diana checked out and then wrote on a list. "My mother helped me print up this sort of a resume with my name and address and phone number and references on it. She told me to put it on an index card that was colored, so when the manager was thumbing through all these pieces of paper, it would stand out. I decided since it had taken me three or four weeks to get a job last year, that at the beginning of the list [I'd] put the restaurants I didn't want to work at, [to help] get my answers down.

"I went to a restaurant at the top of my list, which really was on the *bottom* of my list, and handed them my little card. And they said, 'Oh, you've waitressed before. Do you have a boyfriend?' 'No.' They said, '*Good*. We don't want any boyfriends hanging around here while you're working. Come to work tonight.'

"I went home in tears. I'd only been gone twenty minutes. And my mother says, 'Honey, don't get discouraged *yet*.' I said"—Diana began a mock wail—" 'I'm not. I got a job.' "

The restaurant was well-suited to being at the bottom of anyone's list. It was "so dirty, I wouldn't let my family eat there." Diana did not eat there either and could barely work there. "They had a jukebox, and the plug was upholstered into the wall, so you couldn't unplug it. If nobody put money in, it got stuck on Tony Orlando and Dawn's song 'Tie a Yellow Ribbon 'Round the Old Oak Tree.' I *hate* to this day that song. We could turn it down but couldn't turn it off. *Now* I think I should have taken a pair of line pliers and cut the cord, but [then] it never occurred to me.

"About halfway through the summer, new owners took over. I came in one day and thought we had new glasses, because they were so shiny. I said to the manager, 'Did you buy new glasses?' He goes, 'No, we fixed the dishwasher so the soap dispenser works.' "

In Ashland, as in Yreka, Diana learned a basic fact of restaurant life: "The cooks can make your life miserable if they don't like you." A good cook, she smiled, "changes the oil in their grease thing, like they're supposed to do. Everyone hates to do it, so a lot of 'em cheat and just pour more oil in. You want a hamburger and French fries, and the cook throws the burger on the grill, throws the buns on the grill. The lettuce is cold, the tomato is sliced, the grease is fresh, they get the French fries perfect, and you deliver a piping hot hamburger and French fries to a table. People dig in, and it's good—they're totally happy." A bad cook delivers oily French fries tasting like fish, does not heat the buns, and overcooks the meat. "They start with the same raw materials, and what do you get? It makes all the difference in terms of how much money you make."

Much greater differences were to come. Lured by a favorite aunt's offer of a free place to stay, Diana moved to Sacramento after graduating from high school. "I wanted to be a carpenter. That was my goal." She also applied to a project that had been set up to train solar technicians. "I registered with the carpenters union and was looking for a job and couldn't find one. Built fences on the side and ran out of money, so [I] went back to waitressing." She sighed.

The job was at a Denny's franchise owned and managed by a "really, really awful" husband and wife team of "slimeballs," who fought a lot. He "was a jerk, and he used to beat her up. She'd wear turtleneck sweaters in the middle of the summer to hide the marks on her neck." The restaurant was in "a vortex where three neighborhoods would come together. There was a fairly respectable Asian neighborhood, and an upper-middle-class white neighborhood, and a red-light district. That was what we drew from. We would get 'nice clientele' in the afternoon and evening. At ten and eleven, you'd get families after a movie. At two, you'd get the bar closings. About three, you'd get the bar owners, after they'd shut everything down, who were wonderful."

One night, she found out how wonderful.

"There was a woman who came up to the counter and was supposed to pay her bill, and she was all pissed off the steak wasn't right." Sitting nearby were Ted and Bill, the owners of a gay bar down the street. "They'd come in with their friends, and they had this guy named Kenny"—their bouncer. He was a "great big black guy. I think he used to play football, and he used to come in in a wedding dress. *Huge.* A huge guy, with a beard and full-voiced—I mean, he wasn't effeminate at *all,* which surprised me. They always tipped really well.

"Anyway, they had a radar for trouble. They sat at this big table which wasn't very far from the register. I was taking this woman's money, and she was getting all weirded out. She pulled a gun out of her purse and was complaining about her 'fucking steak.' I remember having the drawer open and seeing the gun and thinking . . . I tend to react more slowly than I should."

Diana took a breath. "Kenny, who was six feet away, was up like *this*"—she snapped her fingers—"he had her hand behind her back, he had the gun out of her hand. He said, 'Pay the lady and leave.' In his *wedding* dress. He knew I was in trouble before *I* knew I was in trouble. He kicked her out of the restaurant and didn't give her her gun back. I said, 'Let's call the cops,' and he says, 'No, I want to keep the gun.'" He did.

"At four," she continued, "you'd get the pimps and the hookers, because they'd pick up the bar traffic and they'd do their thing, and when they were done, they'd come in for breakfast." There would usually be a group of one pimp and several women. Diana recalled one pimp in particular, a tall, slender, African American man who "usually wore those *Saturday Night Fever* kind of suits and lots of jewelry. The hookers were usually white, and there were usually two or three of 'em, and they'd sit in a big table. It would take 'em forever to order. They would ask him what they could have."

Whatever he allowed them to order cost less than what he ordered for himself. "They changed their mind over and over and over again. 'I don't want it medium rare, I want it rare.' They'd send things back and send them back. *He'd* send them back. I hated them. I had some sympathy for the women. It took me a while to figure out who they were and what they were doing. I was pretty naive." The pimp handled all the money, including a tip fashioned of small change.

Diana paused, recalling the contrast with other African American customers she cherished, including a firefighter who wrote out his "tip" and left it under his coffee cup. "Like 'Clean your windows with vinegar and water.' I loved him. He wasn't cheap, he was just idiosyncratic."

As morning approached, other favorite customers arrived. "Somewhere in the middle of the night, about four-thirty, the cops would come in for breakfast. We always gave the cops free breakfasts. I developed a real fondness for the cops in that job, because you had so much trouble. We used to write a [breakfast] ticket and put it up on the wheel and write 'no charge' on it. I don't recall their taking advantage of it, ordering steak and eggs." Then the owners decided the police had to pay half. "We were so embarrassed, we wouldn't do it. We stopped writing tickets and just told the cook what to fix."

The owners also instituted a more dangerous cost-saving measure. "I was told if people left without paying, I had to go after them in the parking lot. Like the naive young thing I was, I did. You were supposed to get the car license number and all this stuff. These owners, they went to Europe every summer, they had a big mansion filled with antiques. They worked their tails off, but they were the ones that fined you if you had your hands in your pockets. And they fined you if you made a mistake adding up the bill. If you undercharged, it was bad for them, because they lost money. If you overcharged, it was bad for business."

Diana's first "runners" were four men, "b-i-i-g black guys, and they got up and walked. That's one of the reasons restaurants don't like you to give separate checks. If everybody at a table wants separate checks and they all leave at the same time, it's real easy for a couple of people to scoot out the door while someone else is paying." That is precisely what happened. "I figured it out, and I followed them into the parking lot.

"They were getting into their car. 'You didn't pay. Come on back in and pay.' The guy looks at me and said, 'You've got to be kiddin'.' 'No, this is stupid, come on back in and pay.' He says, 'Honey, I've got a gun in my back pocket. You want to *see* it?' I said, 'No, I just want you to come in and pay your bill.' He took it out and showed it to me. He didn't *point* it at me. He just says, 'See? I got a piece here.' That was the last time I followed anybody in the parking lot."

The owners made Diana pay the man's check herself.

They were consistently tight. "They trained us without paying us. They trained us for two or three days, which was unheard-of. And they used to keep me after my shift. It was sort of a hazing thing. They'd make you wait and wait and wait outside the office, then they'd go through your tickets with you and tell you how you'd written the scrambled egg order wrong. I'd get off at ten at night and wouldn't get home until one or two in the morning." The owners noticed everything, except the little notebook Diana was carrying.

She kept working, mostly on graveyard shift, for little money. The reason for both the undesirable shift and the low wages, she learned, had much to do with "the queen of the night shift," Louise. "I'd run my legs off and go home with six or seven dollars in tips. I just thought it was night shift. The owners kept telling me how Louise was crazy about me, and I kept saying I want to get off the night shift.

"Well, after she got her bones broken in her face, I ended up working her station, and I started *seating* people, and I realized she'd been skimming from the very beginning." Louise had been putting the good tippers in her section and the bad ones in Diana's. "I started making a good twenty, twenty-five bucks a night more." She diverted the conversation to recite an old restaurant joke about territory. A customer asks a passing waitress what time it is. Sorry, she replies, it's not my station.

Even with better graveyard tips, Diana yearned for breakfast shift, which she had pulled a few times. The tips were better and the time went faster. "But you had to have worked there six or seven years before you had enough seniority to get breakfast." It was a popular shift in part because of motherhood. "If you work in an upscale restaurant and have [school-age] kids and you go on at five in the afternoon, you don't get home until midnight. You don't see them. And you have to work weekends. A lot of those women had husbands who worked shifts, too. So they worked six [in the morning] to two, and the husband at the shipyard or the army depot worked two [in the afternoon] to ten. They didn't have to pay for child care, because one of them would be home. A lot of women stay in coffeehouses for those reasons."

Why did Diana herself stay at Denny's? Partly because she was biding her time. Also "I knew I didn't have the personality" for fancier places and "didn't think I had the body for a dinner house. Slender, petite." She well knew what had happened to her sister. A restaurant had hired her for the upcoming summer, but when she gained weight at college and showed up at the restaurant as scheduled, she was told, "We don't have room for fat waitresses."

Diana, in a way, did not have the body or personality for Denny's, either. "I wasn't a really good waitress" in terms of garnering tips. "It used to make me really mad when people thought I was working for tips. I [felt] damned if you did and damned if you didn't." She shifted on the couch. "I don't really like tipping. It's a system that allows management not to have to discipline their employees. If I had been a real kiss-ass, I might have made ten, fifteen." Instead, she averaged 6 percent.

One reason is that she did not laugh at customers' dirty jokes, which often centered on her breasts. One customer called her Betty Boob, a pun on the cartoon character Betty Boop. "Everyone in the restaurant called me Betty after that. I *never* liked that." She winced. "I guess I'm just an old fuddy-duddy. I never had a body that conformed to society to start with, so when people commented on my body, I never liked it."

While customers fantasized about her, she fantasized, too. She dreamed about owning a restaurant so good and so popular that she could afford to kick out anyone who harassed the waitresses.

Some harassment came with the shift. "People who sleep in the day and work at night, they're a different breed. There were some people I adored. Some firemen and ambulance drivers and janitors who were just quiet. They liked the night shift because you don't have the same supervision. But that was such a tough neighborhood. The red-light district dragged the common denominator down. I went home just exhausted."

After nine months, Diana traded her waitress shoes for work boots. She had been accepted into the solar technician training project. Her contentious connection with the owners of Denny's was not over, however. Because other restaurants had made her stay past the time she was paid for, she had been prepared when she began working at Denny's. "I went out and got a spiral notebook on the first day, and I wrote down from the very beginning the hours I worked and the hours I got paid for. It was minimum wage. So when I left, I went to the labor commissioner and I complained."

The owners somehow knew "I was going to do something. I went in for my last check and [one of them] made me wait two hours. And he wrote on the back, 'Endorsement of this check constitutes payment in full for all services rendered.' I *needed* the money. I called the labor commissioner, who I'd already been to see." The commissioner knew that the "owners hired lots of illegal aliens as busboys and they couldn't wait to snag them on something."

When Diana asked what to do about her check, she was advised to try to deposit it unendorsed. "I took it down to my savings and loan and told them what was going on. They said, 'We'll run it through, and if it bounces back, we'll let you know.' " A bank clerk photocopied both sides of the unendorsed check for her.

"When we went out to the labor commission [hearing], the owner was there and he walked in and [shouted], 'She doesn't have a case because I wrote on the back of her check . . . ' The hearing officer says, 'Can you produce the check?' He's fumbling through his check file and I said I deposited it unendorsed and here are the photocopies. The hearing officer said, 'Well, let's proceed.' So. That was scary, but it was also satisfying."

Diana was awarded three hundred dollars in punitive damages.

She never waitressed again.

Jennifer de Haro

"It went downhill from there," she said, close to a laugh.

Jennifer de Haro was reminiscing about one of her many dramatic walkouts. Her three strapping teenaged sons were babies, and she was head waitress at a Mexican restaurant in her hometown of Portland, Oregon. It had "great" food, she said—not that her Mexican-born husband liked any Mexican food Oregon offered.

The walkout involved "this little Cuban gal" for whom Jenny had found a job at the restaurant. "She didn't have much going for her, and I wanted to help her." Before long, the owner got involved with her, and his wife told Jenny he was going to give her Jenny's shift and section.

"I walked out right there. Tore up the ticket and threw it in the garbage. Part of it was I was unhappy in that kind of work, and I was in a bad marriage. I was on edge most of the time anyway."

Jenny then headed downhill, starting at Lung Fung. It was a "rock 'n' roll lounge"/bar/Chinese restaurant its owner had carved from an old bowling alley and hoped to turn into a kind of concert hall with egg rolls. The food was good "if you ordered off the Chinese side, but you never knew what you were getting."

The restaurant could seat fifteen hundred people, but when the Coasters came to perform, "there were *thirteen* people that showed up. He did not even publicize it. The guys were *so* mad. It was terrible. Well, they couldn't get black people to come very much to that lounge because they treated them so horrible, basically."

Jenny's job was to serve cocktails. "You had to wear a black skirt and a red blouse. Some of these gals would have tight, almost rubber skirts, with slits up the side. I usually wore a longer skirt and a rayon blouse or something like that. I had one you could tie at the side that was kind of provocative. It wasn't low or anything. Some of these gals would get really rank, I'm not kidding you."

Jenny still has a conservative shell. Tonight it is manifested in a dark, inexpensive-looking outfit of blouse, jacket, and slacks, possibly bought for her "bureaucratic job," which she is not fond of. She has black hair and a pretty face, with some puffiness around her eyes. She seems thoughtful, compassionate, and unaccustomed either to an evening out without her boys or to a dinner with cloth napkins.

"Especially in cocktails," she continued, tipping "adds to the sleaze aspect or the carnival-type atmosphere. I had a horrible time. You'd have this bank of twenty-five bucks" for making change. As the night progressed, "you didn't want to carry five hundred dollars around on your tray, so you'd turn [about a hundred] in to the bartender. Well, you'd have to have a bartender you could trust. Cheryl [more or less a prostitute, in Jenny's description] was about the only bartender I could trust to not go"—Jenny whined—" 'I don't know where your hundred dollars is.' Or you'd get it back, it would only be seventy-five. I had times I had to *pay* to get out of that place, because people stole my tips. 'Can you watch my tray while I go serve this food?' 'Yeah, sure.' *Forget* it.

"When I worked at Lung Fung, I actually tried to go back to college. I just couldn't do it. My kids were all small. I was pregnant with my third, and I already had two little ones. One of the things that bothered me the most was that I would go to work and I would wait on these people forty hours a week and be nice. Then I'd come home and I'd be worthless. To my own kids. I didn't have any energy to feed them, to do anything—and if I did have energy, it was because I was, ah, using drugs [to] get me going.

"I know for a fact it goes on with a lot of these women. Because it's an easy job to *get,* if you can comb your hair straight. And some of 'em aren't even clean. It was pathetic. That's why they have uniforms," she laughed and laughed, and added that certain restaurants provide showers for the same reason. "Oh, some of the kitchen help is awful. Awful! Chaucer's *The Canterbury Tales,* it's kind of like that," she laughed again. "The cooks have boils and horrible . . ." she trailed off.

She figured that health inspectors never entered many restaurants where she worked because of various payoffs. The only reason food was edible at all, she grinned, was that the staff had to eat it.

Alcohol was eminently potable, though.

At Lung Fung, Jenny happily helped drink up the profits. "We'd say we had a backache, and that meant 'the backache special.' It was Bailey's and Grand Marnier and coffee and all this really good stuff. It's just so *boring.* You want to get into the music, and unless you're feeling high, it's very difficult to enjoy seeing the same drunks every night."

Another reason she scammed drinks was retaliation. "A lot of these owners figure they're going to get ripped off, so they're not going to pay anybody anything." Consequently, a "huge turnover" brings in new ill-paid employees, who repeat the cycle, thirstily.

Jenny's own weekly cycle was more than the "forty hours a week" she first mentioned. She described working from 6:00 P.M. to about 2:30 A.M. "because that's what you work in a lounge." Those hours already topped forty. She added offhandedly, "You'd have to get there early, count your money, do this and do that, so you'd get there by five-thirty." The hours now are close to forty-five. And, after the 2:30 A.M. closing, "you'd have to clean everything up, which took an hour and a half or so. You'd just get paid for an eight-hour shift. Then you get home at three o'clock or four sometimes."

In other words, Jenny worked more than fifty hours a week, standing. "I really learned to take care of my feet. Some of these women would be in total pain the whole time, to have nice high heels. But I would get the rubber sole stuff, or huaraches with the nice thicker sole. I kept my weight down," too, from exercise at the bar. "You were back and forth and up and down, deep knee bends."

Lung Fung's owner eventually got a Jenny de Haro walkout, too. He yelled at her for his own mistake in scheduling, and "I just left."

She smiled. "Come to think [of it], I don't think I ever got fired." That would not have mattered anyway, she said. In the restaurant business, one could do anything but steal from the owner and "probably get a job anywhere." She certainly did.

Jenny did not start off life amid raunchiness and sleaze. She in fact comes from a distinguished Portland family. "My mother's side of the family has been here since the mid-1800s. Her grandfather founded the public library in Portland. That was kind of neat—a pioneer, an early state legislator." (Jenny has kept an appreciation of good books and recommended, to my gratitude, Denise Chavez's *Face of an Angel,* a novel about a waitress.)[5] Jenny's father's family came to the United States later, from Switzerland.

Jenny's three sons, José, Andy, and Mario, about whom she speaks with great affection, are less comfortable in their Oregon hometown. Some people call them "beaners." She is relieved that they go to schools with children from mixed cultures; black students welcome them more than do whites.

When Jenny herself was in high school, she got her first job, at a Safeway snack bar. She was "thrilled" to be hired. "Actually, it was one of the better jobs" she ever landed, she smiled. "I had benefits at sixteen. They paid you to wash your uniform and all kinds of little perks. As time went on, the union got weaker." She added, "What do you need a union for? Five bucks an hour?" She had "the best benefits I've had of any place" in a nonunion restaurant. The union did intervene, however, after one restaurant tried to fire her for being pregnant. "I was able to get back on the job."

She was adrift early. "It was when I started drinking, when I was twenty-one, I decided I wanted to do that kind of work"—serving something to somebody—"again. So I got to working in bars. Then I wanted to do food because my husband kept coming into the bar, drinking up all my tips, and making a big nuisance of himself."

He said he came in to keep an eye on her, " 'cause he was the one who needed an eye kept on him, you know what I'm saying?" (After the hours she worked, she also had to get up at 7:00 A.M. and drive him to work—that is, when he had work.)

"There were relationships way worse than my marriage, stuff that went on in the bars. I didn't mess around. Even though I didn't like my husband, I knew that wasn't the right thing to do for the kids. But there were a lot of [women] bartenders who had boyfriends and affairs, and then their husbands would come in, there'd be a big fight. It was really something."

Jenny's first downhill slide place had set the standard. She tended bar at a Chinese cocktail lounge and restaurant in a shopping center in her old neighborhood. It had been the first establishment in the neighborhood to serve hard liquor. "I used to sneak in there and peek in the doorway when I was a little girl. Then I ended up *working* in that place."

A later dive was so "horrible" it made her shudder. "One of the bartender's sons came in and vandalized some of the poker machines on my shift. I saw him do it. Everybody told me to keep my mouth shut and not tell. I wouldn't do it—I didn't want the slug in there on *my* shift. I basically turned him in to the owner, and he got in trouble. Her mother, the bartender, was after me, and I told her off. She set me up one night. I left the place clean, she came in and trashed the place, and said I had left it that way. Awful people."

The restaurant, Jenny added, was a hangout for contractors and construction workers who used it to "do all their drug deals" and "enforce their rules on each other. I mean, they would beat each other up with baseball bats," within the restaurant. "It was 'anything goes' in this place."

The experience even made her stop drinking. "I got so sick of the way people act when they're drunk, and the repetitive behavior. You can predict what everybody was going to do in any given situation. The games they would play with each other, hitting on people—it got to be sickening. A lot of women I worked with [had] bad drinking and drug problems. That was how they supported their habits. They would sell drugs while they were working" as well as using them. "People shooting up drugs in the bathroom, drugs going around the place the whole time."

Some customers sidelined as short-change artists. "The guy gives you money, you give him change, and he says it was a twenty, it wasn't a five. When he tries it again about an hour later, you get a little bit suspicious." Others told her she had not made the right drink—after they finished it. Some accused her of watering their drinks. They were right. "These people were so shit-faced, you couldn't with a good conscience give them another drink."

Customers also hit on her "a lot," she said. "I always felt I was out in the meat block. They'll look at you, and they judge your figure and the way you look and the way you walk and the way you carry yourself." She was "pretty cold" in response. "It's weird because when I quit that business, I noticed I missed the attention. 'Cause you're always getting," she put on a mocking tone, " 'Oh, you're so pretty.' You do miss it." She paused a beat. "Not enough to go back."

Jenny quit bar work after realizing "I had worked in so many different places, I'm just working in any place I hadn't worked." She also realized she was harming not only herself. "I finally got to the point . . . this horrible existence. I've got to do something for my kids."

Soon, she was waiting tables across town in a Swiss restaurant called the Matterhorn, wearing dirndls that "push up your, you know," serving cheese fondue dinners to ministers, and singing folk songs. She also was snorting cocaine in the back office.

One difference in going from cocktail to food waitressing was that the hours were even longer. "You work lunch shift, you'd come home, and then you'd work the dinner shift. Your whole day was tied up from eleven [in the morning] 'til eight or nine at night."

One similarity was that customers still tried to get more than they paid for. Instead of dealing with short-change artists and drunks conniving for money or booze, Jenny faced a scrubbed white-collar crowd besieging her for "extra sodas, extra bread, extra whatever they could get out of you. Extra ice cream."

Now it was customers, not co-workers, who stole her tips. "Walk by your table and you'd have a tip there, and they'd pick it up." She rolled her eyes and laughed. "One guy that did that, we chased him out and ran him down and got the money back from him. There were certain things that would rally the troops." Toward the end of another dinner hour, when a man walked in carrying "a sawed-off shotgun [and] emptied the register," the troops were too scared to rally.

The biggest difference at the Matterhorn was the owners. "They wanted to run a very respectable place. They were not flaky at all." Co-workers were cooperative, too. A cook made it his business to feed her well, for Jenny was pregnant again. (The timeline of where she worked during which pregnancy is fuzzy, as is which substances she used when.) The waitresses were friendly—apart, that is, from the avaricious Irena from Romania.

Irena wore a button that read "Tipping is not a city in China." If one of her regulars sat in someone else's station because hers was full, Irena went over, muscled aside the other waitress, and waited on the person herself.

"Oh, this woman was terrible. This was what I was up against all the time. I was good at it—I was good with the people, I had a good memory, and I was real reliable, so I would get to the point where they would want to make me the head waitress. There would always be one of these Irenas." This one apparently was convinced Jenny was going to get her job. Little did she know. "I *hate* this work."

Jenny then made a mistake in her sideline, dealing drugs. She had "passed through cocaine" for Matterhorn co-workers, among them a hostess, servers, bartenders, and young relatives of one of the owners. She also sold marijuana. One day, she brought in a larger than usual stash, about four ounces. Irena reported her. An owner summoned Jenny to his office.

"I said, 'If you want bust me, that's fine, but I sat right where you're sitting and snorted cocaine with your son, which he provided.'" The man was so upset that he threw a pencil and blurted, "What the hell am I supposed to do?"

He did not fire Jenny but let her punish herself with her conscience. "Obviously what I did was wrong. Even if everybody else was doing it, so what?"

Irena, meanwhile, miffed that Jenny had not been fired, stole her custom-made dirndl. Jenny later spotted it in the dressing room and snatched it from Irena, pointing out to everyone her initials in it, which Irena had tried to wash out.

There were also wholesome moments at the Matterhorn, when waitresses put down their jealousies and their drugs. "We'd sing Swiss songs and German songs. Some I knew because my dad used to make me sing this stuff." She happily named the tunes, from "The Happy Wanderer" to "The Lonely Goatherd" and "*Sound of Music*–type stuff. That was really fun."

The pull and tug with Irena took its toll, though. Jenny eventually quit the Matterhorn. Then she quit drugs. Then she quit waitressing.

It is a great job for some, she said. "These gals would come in at fifteen or sixteen years old and you'd see them transform, kids that came from broken homes and felt crappy about themselves. They fixed their hair better and [learned social skills]. You *have* to be social with people, or you can't do the job. They'd get that attention, and some would mature and get something out of it. A bumpkin came off as somebody who actually can help somebody."

Jenny recalled a high school friend who lost both parents as a teenager and then waitressed for fifteen years at a local seafood restaurant. "She liked the attention, because she didn't have anybody at home anymore, and she was a very good waitress." Waiting tables "worked for her. I don't want it to sound like [a] horrible, horrible thing. It just wasn't for me."

WORLDS WITHIN WORLDS

*N*O WAITRESS IS AN ISLAND, to paraphrase the old line. Instead, she represents worlds that may be out of the realm of our notion of serving, and out of the realm of how much we know of the self-contained worlds within restaurants.

Somewhere I read that integration, when it takes place in America, most often takes place at work. Schools, neighborhoods, places of worship, places of recreation often remain, for various reasons, more segregated than not. Work is where we meet and spend time with people who are different from ourselves, whether in hue or, indeed, in view. Our commonality lies in what we do.

Some waitresses celebrate the worlds exposed by their colleagues, some embrace various factions to form separate worlds, and some are in worlds that were separate in the first place. Yet all, finally, share the knowledge that serving is not always a simple act and that merely standing at a table of the seated constitutes its own world.

Mary Ellen Foster McEvily

A petite woman of fifty-five in a plain skirt and blouse, her nails clean and buffed, her hair short, her scrubbed face bearing only a hint of makeup, sitting up straight in her spotless and organized modern apartment high above Manhattan's Upper East Side, Mary Ellen Foster McEvily looked like purity incarnate. She had been.

At a monastic Roman Catholic cloister in Beacon, New York, the duties of then Sister Mary Brian of Jesus included the

ritual of serving food. "I was. Yes, I definitely was" a waitress, she recalled.

She grew up in Delaware, attended parochial grammar school and high
school taught by the order of Ursulines, and, in her second year at her
parents' alma mater, the University of Delaware, decided to become an
Ursuline herself.

"I did not want to follow the pattern of marrying right after college.
I wanted a broader experience of the world. I also felt very inclined to
serve people in some way, and my experience with the Ursulines had
been wonderful."

Although "it was not that unusual a thing" for young women in 1960
to enter religious life, her decision surprised everyone. "One of my closest friends said to me, 'I don't understand. You seem so *normal*. The
only way I can deal with it is, I'm just going to think of you as dead.' I
never heard another word from her."

Mary Ellen laughed heartily. Her voice, as she is well aware, has a
marked animation that is in startling contrast to her demure appearance.
It also was startling in the cloister.

Her decision to enter a religious order left her college boyfriend baf-
fled, although she had earlier sensed a divide. "I distinctly remember we
were at a dance and falling all over each other, and I looked up across
his shoulder and thought, I'm in love with the idea of being in love and
not [with] this person. I felt terrified."

Her parents also were surprised at her decision to leave the secular
world, but they did not object. Her father, who was and remained a
Presbyterian, and who witnessed another pivotal change in his daughter's life much later, "was one of those wonderfully good, direct, honest
men" about whose soul she used to worry as a girl. It was a "time when
Catholics thought if you did not belong to the church, that was it—all
over for you. My mother said to me very wisely, 'Don't you *ever* worry
about your father. There's not a better man on the planet.' "

While becoming an Ursuline, Mary Ellen continued her education,
getting a B.A. with a double major in English and history and an M.A.
in medieval literature. She then settled into novitiate training and life at
the secluded cloister in the mountains of Beacon.

"I have one picture I must show you that will put things in perspective." She got up and returned shortly (nothing is misplaced in Mary
Ellen's realm) with a black-and-white photograph. A pleasant-looking
older couple in rattan chairs on a sun porch look at a squeezed-cheeked

woman in full habit sitting between them. Mary Ellen has to point out that she is that woman.

She lived at the cloister two and a half years. It was "*extremely* isolated" and structured. "Every minute was planned," including meals. Memories of them "set me thinking about the history of one person serving another and how that got formalized and ritualized. It became part of the structure of monastic life and another way of teaching. Here is a way of perfection, a way to live, even when serving something as simple as a meal. There is a holiness in doing that, a sacredness to eating.

"At dinner, at all meals, the refectory was set up so that you had two long tables where the individual novices and nuns sat. The superior and the assistant would sit at a head table. They were bare tables like this," she gestured to the one in front of her, "no tablecloth or anything. Every place had a drawer in which you had a knife, fork, and spoon; a starched linen napkin that was changed once a week; a steel bowl; and a small enamel pan in which you washed your dishes. At the end of the meal, a huge pitcher of soapy water was passed down the table. You poured what you needed, washed your own dishes, and put them back." No, dishes were not rinsed.

The nuns ate in silence, save for a single voice. "One person read to us during the meal. In the beginning, in the novitiate, it would have been things of a spiritual nature."

When the time came for Mary Ellen to serve her first table, ceremony and scrutiny were intense. She gestured to her own body as she recounted the steps involved.

"There was this elaborate pinning back of that big veil, because it flapped down here and really got in your way. The long sleeves, which are more like [the sleeves of] an academic gown, had to be pinned up here so they would not drag in the food. You put on something called an inner sleeve, which was a starched white sleeve, over your black sleeves, to serve. A full-length white, probably starched cotton, and gored apron, very formal, and cuffs which were made of pyroline, which is a kind of plastic. When you finally were a server, it was quite a big deal. The first time you did it, the older novices would check to see that you were exactly pinned and the apron [was] on correctly. You're very nervous. Out of proportion so, but keep in mind that it was such a small world—you want to do everything *perfectly*."

Once she had passed inspection, she picked up the food, in bowls or on serving plates, and took it to the head table. "The food was formally offered to the superior. She bowed to receive it, you bowed when you

gave it to her"—Mary Ellen bent at a generous incline to demonstrate—
"and then went on to the next person.

"The person sitting at the head [of the other tables] received the first
plate of whatever it was, took what she wanted, always remembering it
had to last until the end of the line. That was hardly ever a problem. It
was worse if you were seated in front, because you were afraid if you
took too much, the person at the bottom of the table would not get
anything."

Nuns served in small "teams," with the senior member of each team
serving the mother superior and her assistant. The best "waitress" was
"the quietest, most discreet, most attentive." A not-so-good one might
"drop a plate, trip, be very noisy. Because if someone is reading to a
large group of people, to put a plate down like that"—she let one clatter
a fraction of an inch—"was not good form. The whole idea of great
control and great peace was very obvious."

A related idea, from sixth- and seventh-century monasteries, she said,
was that "food was to be used because it had to be. Don't give it too
much attention, and certainly do not allow yourself to be tempted to
take great pleasure in it." Salt and pepper were provided in Beacon, but
no one could break silence and ask for them. "If it was in front of you,
you could use it and pass it to either side. Since you really didn't know
whether somebody else wanted it or not, the server could move it along.

"When all the dishes were finished, the people who served that meal
would then in turn be served [at] something we called 'second table.'
There was no reading at second table; it was all silence. But you did
have the same kind of service, so it was never a case of just being a
waitress and then being dumped. The same kind of civility and grace
was extended to everyone."

The core Christian idea of food service, she said, was in the Benedic-
tine rule book, "which has many, many rules of hospitality. The point
being that God, and specifically Christ, is to be seen in the guest and so
served." She did not always succeed in this. "The reality was much more
inclined toward the petty. Even though you're not speaking during the
day, there are still ways of communicating. If somebody really ticked
you off for some reason, it was very tempting to think, I could just dump
the mashed potatoes," she smiled. "It wasn't always holy at all."

At points in her cloistered life, Mary Ellen found some strictures trying and difficult, including the headdress. "It was very hot, because it
was made of pyroline [and] the pieces up here"—she touched her temples—"were starched linen. Of course, in the summer you perspired.

They began to melt." One windy day, in a field by herself on the property, she debated taking the headdress off, to let the wind blow in her hair. "I argued with myself. And I took it off. I remember crying and thinking, I'm not even disciplined enough to withstand this. But," now she laughed, "it was such a wonderful feeling!"

As she progressed to being a full member of the Ursuline order and then a teacher out in the world of students, that feeling of freedom returned. "I was one of the first people to go into ordinary clothes." Times and garb were changing, but the way of serving meals was not.

"I was in a college community, I was teaching—did all of this as well as serve a table. Even the president of the college served a table. Nobody was exempted," except the mother superior. "Only on Holy Thursday did the superior serve, and that was an imitation of the gospel."

During Mary Ellen's teaching years, her thoughts before and during mealtimes strayed even farther from those of a novice. "I would be more likely to be thinking, 'Okay, I'm going to eat at the second table. I have to get [to] a meeting at ten of one. How am I going to get this all done?' Much more concerned with some more real-world pressures."

There was another change at table, too: talk was no longer taboo. "I think the superiors realized that people doing very important jobs and busy all day *needed* some time of recreation" to talk. A server, for example, might address the nun being served, or two nuns sitting together might have a seemly conversation. "None of this was too hilarious, I have to assure you. It was all quite formal. You talked to the person next to you; you did not lean across and talk to people four feet down."

Served and server still bowed their heads to each other.

To get a cross-country comparison to Mary Ellen's experiences, I visited Sister Dianne Baumunk, the effervescent and robust principal of Ursuline High School in Santa Rosa, north of San Francisco. Her former novitiate adjoins the school.

To her, every aspect of meals there had made for "nerve-wracking" tension, she said, especially the silence. "I didn't expect that." She laughed ruefully. "No one mentions the little *fact* that you have a rule of *silence* when you get there. I'm like, what?" She is only about a decade younger than Mary Ellen, but her vocabulary is younger still.

She hooted at Mary Ellen's description of meal readings having "a spiritual nature." In her case, they began with a selection from the *Roman Martyrology*. "This saint who was *dying*, they were *beheaded*, they were *scourged*. It wasn't really appetizing kind of *reading!*" If laughter is good for digestion, one reader provided it. In a passage about Pope Pius X, she repeatedly read "X" as "ex." The nuns were "all holding ourselves trying not to laugh, because you're not supposed to respond. It's breaking silence." Finally, they exploded.

When Sister Dianne moved up from being a postulant to a novice, she and other novices took delight in tricking the postulants, who were seated across from them and were supposed to learn table manners by copying. The novices cut up and ate plums with a knife and fork, then watched postulants do the same. "We were terrible!"

Members of the Santa Rosa Ursulines usually served meals for a week at a time, although some were too clumsy to serve the head table. One server, whose nervousness was legendary, dropped an entire tureen of soup in the mother superior's lap. Sister Dianne empathized. "Well, you were always nervous around the superior [and her assistant] because you knew they were going to correct you. They corrected the way you walked, they corrected the way you talked, they corrected the way you bowed, if you bowed too much, if you walked too fast, if you walked too slow, stooped your shoulders, whatever." That included not seeing the superior glance at the salt.

Ursulines practiced "modesty of the eyes," she said, which meant keeping one's eyes lowered. "You didn't have a lot of eye contact with people, but you were still supposed to be *aware*. The persons on your right and left, if they needed the salt, couldn't ask for it, because you were keeping silence. You couldn't reach for it, because that would be impolite. You were supposed to be *aware* they might need it and put it there for them, which is probably good training." She added, "If no one saw to your needs, you were supposed to do without.

"The fact that conversation doesn't go on in normal things, like at any time we're eating, or working even, makes the atmosphere different. Like at breakfast, it's just silent." At that meal, there was not even a reader. "We used to get up at five o'clock in the morning and had an hour's meditation in silence in the chapel, all together, and then mass, and then you were *dying* for a cup of coffee." Not being "a morning person," she especially craved coffee. "You were pretty contemplative at breakfast, if you were still awake."

Breakfast often featured bread with a dry crumbling cheese she figured someone had donated. Someone else donated the legendary case of Hachiya persimmons.

"Even the superior didn't know anything about persimmons. They served them like a bowl of fruit for dessert. Some were mushy and some were firm. Well, those of us who are from here know the mushy ones are the ones that are ripe. If they were firm, you didn't eat them," for they taste like alum. Because of the rule of silence, however, no one could warn anyone.

"I saw this bowl come down, and I was the first one. I picked up a mushy one. *I'm* no dummy." The others, thinking good Sister Dianne was taking the worst for herself, took firm ones. "That was pretty funny"—she made a dramatically puckering face—"and they have to eat the whole thing! That was gross!" Another rule was no leftovers.

For a longer view of cloister serving, she walked me over to visit a group of elderly nuns at the nearby Ursuline home. In a living room area, several sat talking or doing needlework, awaiting a signal for lunch. Sister Dianne brought up the issue of no leftovers being allowed and the scrap plate that was passed around for such items as pits. "I have actually seen people eat their egg shells because they missed the scrap bowl. They thought they were supposed to eat everything, so they did."

Her remark caused Sister Cecilia, who had entered the Ursulines in 1923, to look up from the lace tablecloth she was making. "I would call that true grit."

The room became so merry with memories of food disasters that Sister Bernadette told of being at a poor mission where "Sister Stella from Ireland" decided to make "potato wine"—that is, vodka. "It was a deep, dark secret. Nobody knew it but us nuns." Everything was fine until Sister Stella decided to hide the evidence (the pulp) by sneaking it to the pigs. "The pigs all got drunk, and they squealed, and they bit one another!" The noise alarmed the priests, who rushed down to investigate. "They never found out we had made the potato wine."

A bell rang for lunch. The old nuns, drying their eyes from laughter, walked to the adjoining kitchen, picked up plates, and circled a modest buffet of leftovers and salads.

Sister Mary Brian of Jesus never meant to leave the Ursulines. In a very abbreviated summary of an extraordinary change in her life, she described how in 1977 she asked to live alone in an apartment, near the high school where she taught in New York's Westchester County. She was granted the provisional right to do so for two years but then was summoned back to the convent and told to return there to live.

"It was one of those rules from Rome. I said, 'It's not going to work for me.'" A rule that "has *nothing* to do with faith or the deepening of an interior life in *any* event—that, to me, is a much more arbitrary thing, like my father and mother not being able to be married in the church. What good did that do?"

Mary Ellen decided, reluctantly, to leave the Ursulines. She was forty and "terrified" about the financial insecurity of leaving, with only a teaching job for income, but she was certain her choice was right.

The next year, the husband of a new teacher at the high school invited her to a family birthday party. She went hesitantly ("I had a thousand papers to correct") and met a man named Tom McEvily, a widower with six children, who was older than she was. "I called him Mr. McEvily all evening." A romance began. Mary Ellen's concerned father, unused to this role, asked whether the suitor was financially stable. She assured him that he need not worry. McEvily was president of an insurance company.

She and he married the year they met. Mary Ellen moved into her new husband's huge suburban house, where some of his children (the youngest was seventeen) still lived, and where again the matter of serving food assumed great importance. At first, she was overwhelmed, less by keeping a full-time teaching job while becoming a wife and helping oversee an enormous home than by the "unresolved grief" of the children. She found her way slowly, by focusing back on the ceremony and respect she saw in serving a table. She did not wait on the children, although she did cook for them and learned to negotiate the loaded emotional terrain of a dead mother's kitchen.

Mary Ellen decided to make evening meals a celebration. "I set the table as beautifully as I possibly could. Placemats with flower arrangements. We had candles every night." She encouraged the children who were still living at home to bring friends to dinner, and they did. "It was the only thing I could do to create an experience." The experience expanded. For St. Patrick's Day, she planted shamrocks in potatoes she had carved out. "That was the centerpiece, with green candles. It became something that was specifically me." She prepared themed birthday dinners. Her actions, she laughed, were based on "intuition and terror." She also recognized "the importance of food in making a connection."

Eventually, the children moved out and had families of their own. The McEvilys sold the house and rented their current apartment. If they like living in the city, and so far they do, they plan to buy a place. Meanwhile, between lavish trips abroad, he plays tennis and she, no longer teaching, pursues the writing of poems. Her poems mark a time in which she returns, with rueful wit and too loud a voice, to the cloister.

UN BECOMING

I used to dress in voluminous
black and small bits of starched white.
I used to sing like a nun, notes
sprung pure and mint with ease.
After some practice,
I walked like a nun,
a kind of Indian glide unrustling,
but they said I never spoke like a nun.
Ruby and gold words dangled
jewel questions like earrings,
unbecoming
my paragraphs danced,
unveiled arabesques
sentencing me one
by one un becoming.

Melissa Mason

Here in the Everglades, said Melissa Mason, giving a tour of the tattered trailer park where she lives, it is not polite to go to someone's door, knock, and wait to be let in. Instead, doors being unlocked anyway, you should barge in unannounced and slam the door behind you.

This does not allow her to sit naked in her living room next to the air conditioner as she would like, she giggled, but proper behavior does help keep mosquitoes out. Melissa puts great stock in proper behavior. A blonde, blue-eyed thirty-eight-year-old with a comfortable figure and a girlish, southern-accented voice, she went to charm school three times. "It finally took!"

Her trailer, which she shares with a roommate half her age (who is now away with one of Melissa's ex-boyfriends), is home also to two birds, flying free in her newspaper-carpeted bedroom, and to any number of uninvited swamp creatures, including newts and lizards. Melissa feels "pretty proud" of having made the trailer habitable, from the condemned wreck it once was. Her journey to it twists like a canoe ride through the mangrove-lined lagoons of the Wilderness Waterway, only steps away.

"I had such a Beaver Cleaver upbringing," she sighed. "My dad was an engineer who worked for the highway department. My mom," she giggled again, "was a domestic engineer." Melissa grew up in a southern New Mexico town her grandparents helped found, near Roswell. Speaking of Roswell's famous/infamous UFO incident, Melissa intoned, "*Something* happened out there." She hopes it was a UFO, she said, peeking at the sky (she is also ready for "visitation" from aliens), for that would be romantic. "Romance not being lace and flowers and frilly—it's romance as a whole way of life. That's the way I live my life, why I work here. Because it's romantic."

"Here" is the Flamingo Visitor Center of Everglades National Park. The 1950s cement complex on the Gulf of Mexico has a certain architectural spiritlessness, but the center's restaurant, the Flamingo, is appealing. Its picture windows face the water, and a number of eating nooks, stairs, and banisters offer a sense of intimacy. What is pleasant for the customers, however, is a struggle for the staff. "There are not good wide places to carry your trays. You have to go up and down the stairs; there's slippery spots."

Neither tourist nor "parkie" (as employees call themselves) is here to focus on human design, however—not in the company of such stunning natural wonders. One can see alligators *and* crocodiles, mahogany hammocks and butterfly orchids, a treasure of birds from anhingas and egrets and cormorants to, if one is lucky and looking, roseate spoonbills. (Rarely does a flamingo alight.)

Melissa is among the stunned. As she delights in reaching for a drawer handle in her trailer's patched-up kitchen and feeling a green tree frog instead, so is she thrilled to venture outdoors. "There are ibis in the yard. There's 'gators walkin' through all the time." Glancing past a pile of trash by a neighboring trailer where her boss lives ("she doesn't keep her yard too well"), Melissa preferred focusing on the tree by her front porch, a sea hibiscus which in the morning has "blooms that are yellow, and by evening they've turned red, and they drop off." The gulf is "basically in my backyard." Forget swimming, of course. The water is "full of sharks and 'gators and mud."

Melissa may live in a place whose charm is partly in the eye of the beholder (witness the snake skeleton she brings out from a closet to be admired) and she may own nothing more than her car, Goodwill furniture, some savings, and culled swamp finds, but her paternal ancestors came over on the Mayflower, she told me, and include presidents—"the Adams brothers" in her nomenclature—and "the poet Longfellow." She has "always been proud of my heritage." On her mother's side, she said, her tone less cheery, were slave owners. "I like having my heritage from the South for every reason but the slavery part." She added, continuing a line of romantic fantasies, "There were few and far between real cruelties, physical cruelty of slavery, I think."

After the "Beaver Cleaver upbringing," Melissa went to Eastern New Mexico University, focused on fraternity parties, got a business degree (because it was easy, she claimed), and continued drinking and partying in Virginia Beach, where her sister's husband was stationed with the navy. "I hung around with navy flyers and the whole *Top Gun* thing." She also waitressed, with less enthusiasm. She did like working in a "beautiful" beach hotel whose clientele included Muhammad Ali. The descendant of slave owners thus served the descendant of slaves. "He had a bagel and coffee and orange juice every morning and left a five-dollar tip."

After returning to New Mexico, she worked "for the oil and gas industry off and on for ten years," got laid off, and on a whim began working at Yellowstone National Park. There, after a carefree stint cleaning cabins (she especially liked finding sex toys in wastebaskets), she later waited tables, was eventually promoted, and became a most unhappy assistant dining room manager.

"I like seeing things done the right way." Her co-workers, mostly college students from the East Coast, she said, apparently did not. "They have no work ethic," she added, pursing her lips. Furthermore, despite her frequent admonitions, they continued swiping food off customers' plates in the pick-up area "against health regulations first and foremost, and then company rules as well." A mutual geyser of discontent erupted. Melissa left.

Having admired a Floridian's tan in Yellowstone, she headed to Flamingo. The job she got was clearing tables, since no waitress jobs were open. She arrived December 1, 1992, only months after Hurricane Andrew whammed into southern Florida. "It was still so bad that when I drove through Homestead, I started crying at the edge of it and was hysterical by the time I got to the park. Pictures, TV, media did not do it justice." She saw "piles of debris, couple hundred feet high, of people's lives. You saw couches and toys and picture frames and everything, pile after pile after pile. Then I get to the park, and the air conditioning went out in my car, and the mosquitoes were horrible. I get here after dark and I'm like"—she screeched—" 'What have I done?!' "

To her own surprise, she stayed the season. She left at season's end to other romantic places that beckoned, including North Africa, but returned to Flamingo again, and again. After three years, a waitress position opened up. She took it and stayed and for two years has waited tables at the park year-round.

Late one evening, she relaxed by the center's mosquito-net–domed swimming pool and gestured toward her environs. "Our situation here is a lot different than in what we call the 'real world.' You have people come and stay a week, so you may see them breakfast, lunch, and/or dinner. We usually work two meals. There are some people who come in from the Keys regularly, or from Homestead. Come out birding. We have one couple, the five years I've been here, they've been here every single Sunday.

"We have one little couple now, probably well into their eighties, they've been here three weeks. Everybody will mention 'the couple,' and we all know who they're talking about, because they're just *cute* as they can be!" They are "romancing each other. They have to sit right beside each other and touch each other, and they talk and smile to each other. He's so solicitous of her. It pepped us all up. I told them tonight, 'My mom and dad are about your age, and seeing you here has made me so homesick, I've planned to go home earlier than I intended to.' " Melissa is certain the couple will make a point of saying goodbye. Most do.

"Here we can't just serve the guests and then they go away," as she put it. "We have to be *really* particular about customer service and have to play tour guide. We have to know a tremendous amount of details about the park, because we get asked every single question you can imagine. 'Why don't you just go out there and get your fish?' Then you have to explain about the national park thing." The explanation, of course, is that a national park is meant to preserve species, not kill them.

Fresh fish, involving a 120-mile round trip, are offered only on weekends. "We have a fish called snook. It is heaven on a plate! But they're in danger of not being there anymore because the bay is clogged with algae it's not supposed to have, and it's *too* salty, and on and on and on. We have to know all this."

She heaved a chesty sigh. "The windows in that restaurant are the greatest draw. They're so beautiful, but they lead to *so* many questions." They also prompt visitors to ask for a window table for dinner, especially in high winter season. The request "makes us all laugh," but the customers are accommodated. Their usual view is of blackness.

Customers pump the waitstaff about personal matters, too. "The most common one, 'Do you all live here, or do you drive from town?' Almost *every* table asks that, without fail. My line is, 'We all work here so we can live here, not vice versa.' " If she expands on that, some customers still continue to question rather than placing their order. And, because federal park employees must wear a name tag that also bears the name of their home state, customers ask Melissa about it as well. Or they did.

"New Mexico is a very popular state for tourists. Two years ago, about Christmas time, I had a six- or seven-table section, which was too many, but it was just one of those things. Everybody [says], 'Oh, you're from New Mexico! I've been to Santa Fe. Where do you live?' When six or seven tables do that to you . . . I was in tears by the end of the night. So I changed it to Florida." Nobody asks her a thing about Florida.

For Melissa, charm school has its uses. Customers comment so often about the friendly service, in comparison with the rudeness they and she encounter in other parts of south Florida, that she wonders whether people still are upset by Hurricane Andrew. If customers "from back East, particularly New York," are rude themselves, however, charm school is no help. "I take it personally, quite often. I have to tell myself that's just their way."

"Ninety-five percent of the people are not rude," she said in a sing-song voice, as though she had repeated the statistic before. "But the five percent stick in your mind. They treat you like you are a servant, that you are stupid, uneducated." She added with pride, "A good fifty percent of our waitresses are educated with completed degrees."

How customers treat her is one thing; how they tip another. "Men get *much* better tips than women." Waiter-waitress couples at the Flamingo confirm it: men get 10 to 20 percent more. "I don't know if it comes from the old stereotype, 'Well, men need to support their family' kind of thing." Melissa believes "women give better service than men do, normally. We're a little more attentive, a little more warm." Waitresses are "the ultimate mothers," she said more than once.

In the Flamingo, her bone of maternal contention is not with co-workers but rather with cooks. If customers do not get "the service they deserve," which includes lemon on the fish, or a piece of meat the size the menu said it was, "I convey that frustration to the cooks. I try to do it as nicely as possible. They are typical cooks. They don't take it well." In response, neither does she. After the apparently common blow-ups, those involved do not go their separate ways after a shift to cool off. There are no separate ways.

As waitresses see the same customers virtually all day long for weeks, co-workers see each other virtually all day long for years. "You meet, greet, and mate quickly," Melissa laughed. "A month is like a year on the 'outside,' as we call it, because it's intense living. You form relationships much faster here."

If and when those relationships unform, "you can't get away from that person," she said cheerfully. "You have to learn how to deal with feelings. I've seen some people not do very good jobs of it. I try not to ever have a really bad ending. Melodramatic? I don't go in for that. If there is some problem, it's more of a not speaking kind of thing or keep it very formal. 'Hi, how are you today?'" She and her last boyfriend ended their relationship in the proper Flamingo manner. "I said, 'I don't think this is working out. You're a jerk, and I can't deal with being with you.' He says, 'Well, I feel the same way.' We had a couple weeks where we didn't speak a lot. After that, we were all right. You just go on. Your only other choice is to leave."

Her "current boyfriend" may not last long, in this place where a common joke is "I love you, honey, but the season's over." He is "very easy to get along with. We have the same etiquette, everything. But he eventually wants to settle down and I don't."

The work/live/play setting also affects nonsexual relationships. "Tempers flare and people take sides. Our supervisors know us extremely well. They probably know, in a lot of circumstances, our personal life better than our work life." Melissa is no exception. She is friends with the food and beverage manager (the neighbor who has trash in her yard). "You come home and go next door to the boss's house, and you have a few drinks or sit around griping. Then that gripe can come over into work."

Tonight, she said, all employees did their jobs well. "Tonight was a *great* night. Very smooth. The seating was smooth, the customers were excellent, the kitchen was perfect, the food was great." When she asked me how my dinner had been and pressed for an honest answer, I confessed that the vegetable pasta dish was bland. She admitted that it was on the menu "basically to appease vegetarians" (which tasted true), urged me to fill out a "comment card," and soon acknowledged that most food is not "great."

"There's only so much they can and will do for so much money, and our facilities are not conducive to real high-quality food. It's just a restaurant in the middle of a national park. A lot of times, we get managers who will say, 'I'm going to make this a five-star restaurant.' Why? This is for the people."

It might not be for Melissa, for long. "When you're here for a long time, people view each other differently, and you get to be too involved with the whole process, you know? I care too much about the little things. About this manager got to do that or this was done this way. I feel I should have a say in it, because I've been here forever. In this family."

As stars sparkled over the honeylike air, she smiled. "I *really* like it here. It's very easy to live here. I don't have a lot of responsibilities. Not that I avoid responsibility, but the things I find useless in life, like paying a lot of bills and keeping up with this and that social thing, and *driving* [are gone]. I don't ever want to drive to get to work more than five minutes. That is a waste of a person's life."

She "probably" could stay in the Everglades, living in her trailer, indefinitely. "I know my background and my education and my upbringing. I grew up in a home full of antiques and beautiful furniture and china and crystal, all those really nice things, and I'm tickled by my little find." Seed pod or chipped dish, it makes little difference. "I call my style 'trailer trash,' " she giggled one more time. "That's what we call ourselves over here."

On Halloween "two years ago, I got a huge plastic bag, put it on, put my legs through it, and I got cereal boxes and beer cans and put it all in there, tied it around my neck and went as 'trailer trash.' I won the prize."

Suz Kling

"I felt waitress work could go one of two ways. Either it would build confidence, if you were the kind of person who needed confidence building, because if you worked at it hard and long enough, you [would] come to the conclusion you could fix, change, or remedy anything with a free piece of cheesecake. The other thing, though, for a person like me, . . . a type A control freak who probably had too much confidence and aggression and chutzpah and needed maybe a few lessons in the opposite direction, it was good because I had to accept I couldn't change everything. You have to surrender. 'It's *caca*. It's *awful*. You're right. I did ruin your outfit. You did get the wrong meal. I'm *so* sorry.' "

Suz Kling—SUZ, as she signs her letters in neon magic marker—is off and going and going and going, a kewpie doll with attitude, much mascara surrounding huge eyes, her hair hennaed, her red sneakers high-topped (she is a leather-rejecting vegetarian). From her red-lipsticked mouth issue blazing campy, vampy voices and lingo one deduces from context—"doing Bertha" means cleaning, while " 'tron," from the non-sexist yet mocking term "waitron," means waitress—for why interrupt the show?

She has been vocalizing about Andrea's Old Time Cafe in Bandon, Oregon. The cafe, which attracts locals all year and tourists in the summer, looks inviting, with handwritten "For Sale/Wanted/Guitar Lesson" signs at the door and a sense inside that the ceiling has supported its share of macramé plant hangers. Suz had probably dusted them. "I started out cleaning the restaurant, not 'tronning." Neither occupation had been her intention.

In 1977, she was part of "a busload of New York hippies in search of someplace to live." After stopping "in Oklahoma once by mistake," where she briefly acted as a cocktail waitress in a dry state—do not get her started on *that*—the group left sooner rather than later for Oregon, lured by mild weather and progressive politics. They happened upon the coastal village of Bandon.

"Knew I would live and die here. But what are you going to do in a tiny little town to make money? I had the philosophy degree [from Columbia], but that's not exactly preparation for a long-term career. I begged and whined and got myself in at the library for part-time. Libraries are *not* well funded even in the best of times, and I still needed more money. I went to Andrea and said, 'I could clean this place. I could do Bertha once a week, you could pay me forty dollars. We could trade in food also.' I loved it. My mind was to myself, and nobody bothered me."

Suz commuted by motorcycle, strapping a rented rug cleaning machine and opera records on her bike with bungee cords, then scrubbed to arias when the cafe was closed. Knowing that Suz worked without gloves ("a true anal retentive has to feel the grit and get it off with their fingernails"), the pastry chef once snuck a surprise into her pail. "You've never had a shock in your life until you've touched a peeled banana in Spic 'n' Span underneath the bubbles. 'Oh, my God, she *did* cut it off his body, finally.'"

In ways, Suz was best suited as "Bertha." Even now, working full-time in the library, every lunch hour she drives to her one-room circular house (picture a Japanese inn with a psychedelic decorator) to clean it. "I sort of view this scene as a stage set, so when I come home, I want it to be perfect. I wash all the dishes, possibly even scrub out the sink, vacuum, Mop & Glo the bricks. That's what makes them shiny. Wipe the surfaces. Surface wipe is important to a type A personality."

Unfortunately for some of the public, this type A needed more income. Suz became a waitress, too.

"It's a very hard job to leave, because they always need you. They'll call you at midnight. 'So-and-so didn't show up. We're desperate. We're *begging.* Please!' What are you going to do? If you're the slightest bit co-dependent, you're going to show up. Women are perfect for this job because we are trained to be co-dependent. 'Oh, you *need* me! I'll be right there.' Of course, I had this co-dependent relationship with this alcoholic [ex-husband]. My life melded.

"Anything's an opportunity to inquire into yourself or study people, and certainly waitressing is the prime opportunity. I was very conscious of, how much can I push myself there? I used to be in theater when I was 'tronning. I stopped. I wanted to do *The Vampire Lesbians.* I'm not doing *The Sound of Mucus,* no."

At Andrea's of Bandon, Suz of New York had center stage.

"The entire time I waitressed, my goal was to establish equality." When "the '50s" guys called out, " 'Hey, honey, babe,' I would do it right back to them. If somebody was treating me in what I thought was a servile way or abusive, my goal was to get us equal so we can face each other and do our necessary exchange." Name exchanges were not part of it. "I'm here in a servile server position, and that's how we're going to have a relationship." It was hands-off as well. She told customers who touched her that they could die if they did that again.

"The more years I worked there, the more edgy my humor got. I used to think, I need to open up an S&M bar and do dominatrix Suzie, because these people seem to think this is funny." If someone across the room signaled her, she signaled back, as if playing charades. " 'What does it mean? A plate? It looks like a plate? It's a *glass.* It's half empty!'

"You can say *anything* if you do it in such a way where it's not a direct jab." One frenzied night, a local German-born woman got impatient with how long her food was taking—" 'Vair is my salad? I ordered it sirty seconds ago' "—and Suz told her to chill. She and her husband were stunned, but they returned. "*They* would come into my S&M bar," Suz thought.

"I had to allow myself to exercise the theater, the personality, the bizarre behavior." She wanted to see what people "could bear, what I could change, and how I could get what *I* wanted, which was the most amount of money out of the situation.

"I can remember one Sunday brunch. I was going to be the diner 'tron. I wanted to see how many pieces of gum it would take where I could get the wad big enough to have an impact and still be able to talk." She got a three-gum wad working and sauntered over to her first victims. "I'm trying it out, snapping. 'Right. A good choice. You will be very happy with that, darlink.' This guy doesn't see this is a theater performance." After the meal, he pulled Suz aside.

" 'I just want to tell you something. You look great, your clothes are good, you're pretty efficient, and I liked my meal. But the gum has got to go.'

" 'Sweetie, did you think this was for you? I'm trying something out here. It's a *prop*, okay?' " The man fled.

"There were certain prejudices I had, and I entertained them freely." Suz could "not tolerate Ken and Barbie"—read: self-important man with google-eyed woman. "My goal would be to get Barbie to talk to me. Ken has already done the salad order. I'd say [to Barbie], 'What would *you* like for your salad dressing? You *will* tell me.' She would. It became apparent it was sort of a game."

The game included calculation. "You're a woman. You psyche out what the people want. We're raised to do that, I think. I put people on my screen when they walked in the door." The screen told her that women tipped the men more and the women less, while men tipped the men less and the women more.

"Men are used to paying women for their services in this culture. Even 'trons I worked with would joke about being whores: 'We're all whores on this bus.' Women, however, give it away every day. They go *home* and give it away. Why should they pay you for something they do for free? I understand it. I resented it tremendously, because 'Hey, I'm your sister, I'm working hard here. Can't we bond on that level?' " The answer usually was no.

If a group of women came in and it was Suz's turn, she handed them to a waiter named Spencer, who slipped Suz a few dollars as thanks. "They're paying him for his charm services, not his food delivery services." To Spencer, "four professional men would say, 'Look at you. You're a waiter, you're nothing. Your dick is *much* smaller than ours, and the way I'm going to tell you is that I'm going to leave you a dollar fifty.' It's all very subtle. No one is standing on the table screaming their position."

If Suz, however, served the men, "easy cash, no problem." They tipped not her work, she felt, but her "stand-up comedy. I am merely there at their disposal. I could be sent off the scene should they have something important to decide. I'm only being allowed in the court to entertain. But they're willing to pay for it, so I'm willing to do it. It's a contract."

Suz's most successful scenarios involved men who liked her act so much that they joined in. "My favorites were the gays from the Bay Area. I *loved* the men. They were amusing, sophisticated. We were able to exchange snappy dialogue and do Nick and Nora [from *The Thin Man*]. It was like a stage performance. And they would leave ten dollars, and I was very happy. And I knew they would." Also high on her list were African American tourists. "Here I am [in] this white enclave. Wall of plaid. I'd go"—she put on Camille-like angst—" '*Please* move here, and bring your friends. I'm dying.' They were great."

When "I did my salad dressing cassette" for a couple in their seventies, and the wife declined to answer her husband's question about what kind of salad dressing he liked, Suz promised her a free dessert. The woman laughed. "It was like sisters."

Not everyone was appreciative. One woman got "very irritated" when Suz explained that sautéed cod meant the cod was sautéed. The woman "wanted servile. With fun, I could do servile." An irritated yuppie man left "a very snotty note" calling Suz "cavalier." "I said, o-o-oh, that's such a cute word, I *love* it." And she could be just that. "I had mice run across the room. 'Look, it's our pet! It's Mickey!' "

One party escaped her reaction. "I went to clear the table, and here is this folded thing made to look like a five-dollar bill. I open it up, and it actually says on the inside, 'You thought this was real money. We have a better tip for you: the gift of Christ!' " The customers had left quickly, "which was wise." (Suz's background is Dutch Reform Protestant, but she is not, in a word, practicing.)

Suz's fire took in everyone, including fellow local vegetarians. When they asked whether the pasta was eggless, "I would say, 'Yes, it's egg-free, and fiber-free as well. In fact, it's invisible.' "

Child customers, a.k.a. "Bam-Bams," were prey, too. "I would go up to two-year-olds and say, 'You'll never see your parents again unless you sit. In that chair. Right now.' " She cut Bam-Bam ordering time short by saying they had two choices of juice, not more, and avoided taking meal orders from children directly. They "know if they can delay all the adults"—they will if encouraged. When Suz saw such scenarios develop, She'd say, " 'When Bam-Bam knows what Bam-Bam really wants, I'll be back. You guys talk about it. You got like ten hours here, and possibly overnight. We could have breakfast.' " (She used the same technique on people who frantically waved her over to order but had not decided what they wanted: "This was a dress rehearsal. We'll do the real performance half an hour from now. You have thirty minutes you didn't think you had.")

"New Age parents" were the most oblivious to their children's behavior. While Suz was serving a party of fifteen, a "Bam-Bam got up and went to the bathroom. Flushed an entire roll of toilet paper down the toilet. It's August. I have eight thousand things to do, and water is flowing underneath the door into the room. I said to myself, this is not acceptable. I got the plunger and brought it to the table. Very quietly. I went up to the lead father and said, 'Do you see this? You need to use it right now. Come with me.' " He did.

"The majority of people want to be told what to do," she said. She certainly told her current husband. He "used to be a nightmare to wait on," bringing in favored ingredients for the staff to put on his pizza. If he wanted to be with her, she told him, "You will sit very quietly. You will give your order completely, clearly, succinctly. You will *never* harass the waitron and will be very grateful and tip twenty percent even if she forgot your order completely. Maybe she's having a bad day."

Dominatrix Suz and the 'Trons issued similar rules to Bandon residents: "This is how you behave, this is what you tip, don't beg for free desserts. We know you."

Unfortunately, they also knew her. Some asked her about library books she had put on hold for them. Others put their overdue books in her car. "I had to lock my car to stop it from happening, because I wouldn't always see the pile of books sitting there, and they'd get an overdue notice, and it would be *my* fault because I didn't return them. How was I to know? I'm *'tronning* here."

Having two jobs gave Suz freedom to "push the envelope" more than others could, but a price was extracted. After working in the library, then at the restaurant, "I'd think, I have nothing left to give. If somebody asks me *anything*, like what is the weather going to be tomorrow, I might burst into tears. Everybody has sucked out all the juice. I've given crayons to the kid, I've cleaned up the kiddie litter on the floor. 'Cinderella will be out in a minute.' I'm going to crack. I'm going to primal right here. R. D. Laing. Throw up, spew chunks, and smear it. But. . . ."

The "but" made all the difference. It was her connection to the drama of another world: backstage.

One cool off-season April evening at mostly empty Andrea's, a young self-conscious waitress happily greeted Suz, who was playing the role of customer this evening, and then grinned at her usual order for house wine: "A glass of swill, please." Suz empathized with a recent account of insolence from customers, told about a drunken cook who she thought surpassed her in attitude, and then spoke of how backstage bonds deepened.

"Being behind the scenes of anything is like being in on an inside joke. It's the ultimate observational stance." The joke, she paused to add, entailed much work. " 'Tronning" was "the hardest job I ever did. In July and August, it's like any restaurant during hell week. You have to have the patience of a saint, a mind like a steel trap. You have to multitask like you've never multitasked before. You're a sycophant, a co-dependent, you're entertaining everybody. You're balancing the kitchen, who's ringing the bell constantly. You're entertaining [Andrea], who was like intermittent random management."

There often was not even enough cash in the register to open. "I'd have to get in the car—my *own* car, my own gas—drive to the bank, get change, come back here, do my opening balance . . . it was insane." Andrea (the owner, and "the Red Queen" to Suz) exacerbated the problem by "imperiously ordering things from the kitchen" before it opened. Then she did "her employee as prop thing by calling me over and using me as a display item" to impress people. " 'Here's *Suzie!* '" Suz trilled. " 'She's really a librarian, but she chooses to work for *me* as a waitress!' "

Suz's response was furious, but silent and calculating: " 'Keep talking, because every minute will cost you either chocolate cake, free pizza, free pasta. I'm taking home two coffee mugs.' I kept an absolute balance in my mind. I didn't think I was scamming. If you're going to make me angry and I have to suffer angst, that's a big, ugly chunk."

Andrea also ignored the "living chaos" in the cafe. Suz could not. "We had supplies we had no idea where they were. My biggest fear is that someone would order a bottle of wine. We kept white wine in one refrigerator by the 'tron station. This repeatedly happened to me. I'd open up the door and the *bottles* would fall out on the floor." Suz upped her hysteria act. "I got twenty-two people screaming at me, plus a kitchen, and I have ten bottles of wine bouncing around on the floor I have to put back in some semblance of order? You must be *joking*.

"You're trying to prioritize all your tasks, everybody is making demands. The water glasses come back from the dishwasher, hot, of course. I don't have time to be *thinking*. I take the glass and go into the ice thing. It shatters. I'm going"—a breathless soprano—" 'Fuck! This can't be happening!' The bullets are coming in. They could come in from anywhere. You're hyperventilating, and you're deep breathing. You *have* no alternative; you have to clean out the ice maker right now because some other 'tron could come in and start putting glass in somebody's water."

The breaker switches, located in a far corner of the dining room, would go off. "They would scream at us. We're in the *middle,* mind you . . . I'm not doing my nails out there. 'Suzie! Turn the switch on!' " She now became a harridan: " '*You* do it!' "

During one dinner rush, smoke from the featured special, a Cajun fish entree, triggered a fire extinguishing system to start dripping foam on the stove. "Do we say, 'I'm sorry, we're closed'? Or do we attempt to salvage this? 'Trons always attempt to salvage the situation." Suz began talking faster. "We're clearing off the surfaces, wiping it down, all these toxic chemicals are being flushed into the garbage, and we're trying to reset up. We did salvage the situation. I was never more astounded in my entire life." She took a breath.

Another time, "somebody placed an order for leg of lamb, of all things . . ."—lamb orders appalled Suz, especially if customers said they had just seen lambies cavorting nearby and decided to eat some—"and there were fifteen tickets up on the stove. [The chef] got to my order and he said, 'You're not going to believe this, but I don't have any left.' " Suz made him tell the customers himself. "I mean, fifty percent of my tip is the food."

One frenzied night, she raced into the kitchen to grab a plate of substitute food for a man who had engaged in her "number one pet peeve": ordering a dish, maybe named for a chef's aunt, without asking what was in it and then complaining it was not what he wanted. "I watched it happen in slow motion. The food *slid* off of the plate and went ka-blammo into the opposite wall. Wow, this is a Jackson Pollack happening. The veneer is gone. What am I going to do? Usually, if the chef was at all close to you, and this is where they would exercise a certain degree of power, they would say"—she held up a hand—" 'Don't panic' " and fix a new plate of food. He did. "This happened several times, usually *before* I left the kitchen, thank you, goddess.

"I'm near tears here, and this person I'm not involved with, who isn't even potentially my friend, is going to save my ass. That bonding moment is going to be very deeply meaningful because it's going to allow me to function."

The moment is "*intimate.* Having intimacy in your life is such a rarity anyway. Here you are in this high-stress situation where all emotions are to the fore. You're screaming and yelling, 'Fuck you!' I'd get in the back of the kitchen, and we'd go, 'Can you *believe* Ken and Barbie in B2?' All this high-intense stuff is going on, and the people you work with, you develop an intimacy with them. Stress does that." Conversely, the winding-down, end-of-shift slow times offered more intimacy still.

"This must be a universal experience. Even the men I worked with, I think it was their one opportunity to talk in a real way. You can't go anywhere. What are you doing to do? You *talk* about your life, your relationships, what you're doing and where you're going and where you've come from. That contributes to the sense of intimacy you ulti-mately feel with one another. We used to talk about it frequently, how working in the restaurant was a form of therapy. It pulled me out of a lot of dark moments."

Suz's were so dark—getting a divorce, working two jobs sixty hours a week to make ends meet, "going insane"—that her much-needed free restaurant therapy was all she could afford.

At some point, even intimacy was not enough. Suz began losing the other major component that had kept her going: her sense of humor. When she no longer could summon reserves of "banter and wit," as she called them, "I was dead." Her audiences did not care. " 'We're coming here for Suzie, and she needs to be onstage right *now*!' I definitely set myself up." Suz went from "strain" to "drain." After sixteen years, she took a final bow.

"I always wanted to leave the restaurant, even though I had attach-ments. I had attachments to the people I worked with. I had attachments to the theater and the experience of it. But I never really wanted to do it. I wanted to lead the contemplative life."

What? Yes, even when eating out, Suz Kling craves quiet and distance. "I am not somebody who wants to be entertained by a 'tron in my face." Not even someone like herself? "*Never.* I would be so irritated if some-body did what I did. 'I didn't come in here to talk to you. I just want my food.' "

About a year after our conversation, Suz got cancer. She said she had been misdiagnosed as having ovarian cancer that had metastasized. In terror, she stayed late at the library, hauled medical volumes off the shelves to the floor, read up on her symptoms, diagnosed herself, and found a doctor who confirmed that her suspicions were right: she had "dual primaries"—ovarian and endometrial cancers. Had she followed her first doctor's misdiagnosis and accepted his treatment, she thinks she would be dead by now.

Instead, she is on the other side of chemotherapy, and her lost hair is growing back. She calls it her fifty-thousand-dollar haircut.

▩▩▩▩ Cynthia Shearer

Oxford, Mississippi, delicately poking the sky midway between Clarksdale and Tupelo, has a reputation as a literary oasis within a region of supposed rubes and rednecks. One reason is the University of Mississippi, known as Ole Miss. A second reason stands on a rise up another road: it is Rowan Oak, the home of William Faulkner. Although the university is also known for its once-violent stand against integration, and although the novelist may not have been as noble as he is sometimes perceived to have been, the town's twin touchstones are nonetheless accorded great respect. Writer Cynthia Shearer is connected to both. She was a Ph.D. candidate in Ole Miss's English department and then became curator of Rowan Oak. Neither is the reason she became a writer.

After pointing out details of Faulkner's gracefully proportioned 1848 frame house, she strolled out back, through scents and sounds that in seconds conjure the South to a Yankee, and sat on the porch steps of an old cabin on the property. Sun filtered through lilac leaves, making a pattern on her plain cotton clothes. Cynthia is fortyish, with blunt-cut blonde hair, pale skin and eyes. Her accent and voice are soft, her words strong.

She grew up in Alapaha, Georgia, a rural town whose populace she invokes with exquisite sadness in her first and luxuriously praised novel, _The Wonder Book of the Air_.[1] When she was three years old, her father left the family. The divorce did not set the family apart, but her parents' social differences did. Her father was an air force officer, her mother an English teacher and the town's "only white liberal woman with a college degree."

Despite such differences, on nearly every school night throughout much of the 1960s, the mother took her children to the local truck stop, the sole place to eat out in Alapaha. It offered Cynthia an "extended, surrogate kind of family."

"My first impression of a waitress was these big, country, uneducated, very warm, open, friendly women who would smack their gum and sing along with the jukebox. *But* you had the sense they were professionals, because they wore white uniforms and white shoes." Schoolgirl Cynthia was especially drawn to Lurleen, who had left Alapaha but returned with a hard-luck story and a baby, and to Mabel. (For discretion's sake, Cynthia asked that the names of everyone except William Faulkner and herself be changed.)

Her captivation with Mabel came from watching what happened when a certain truck driver parked his rig. "This man walks in the door, she goes over, puts the quarter in the jukebox, and plays the song"—it began with "Hello darling, it's been a long time," she recalled—"and goes to sit down with him, which is something a waitress would *never* do. And of course, *she* was married to someone else and *he* was married to someone else."

While Cynthia was still wide-eyed, the truck stop closed, an event that spelled opportunity to some neighbors, former Mississippi farmers. Led by their matriarch, a pistol named Lynn, that family decided to build a new place. "There was something about watching them throw up a restaurant out of cinder blocks with their own hands and order the meat and the vegetables. My mother's take on the world was [that] you kind of withdraw in your cloistered superiority and endure what the world deals out to you. These people just joked it off."

Cynthia craved their company. "Because my family was so isolated from most of the white racists because of our views on integration, most of my contact with the people in my town came through being in this little restaurant." She babysat Lynn's grandchild and then helped serve food. "I would do things like take the hamburger out of the window and give it to the person I knew it went to." Before long, Cynthia got hooked on self-sufficiency.

"I wanted my own freedom. Babysitting was okay, but you were at the mercy of some child, really. Waitressing, you always know there will be jobs like that. At eleven years old, you learn you can make your way in the world, that young. That there is income, and that it's just a matter of talking to people and getting the order right. I can remember being told at that age I had a knack for it. The big deal was when you could figure out what needed to be done without having to be told."

The idyll ended around 1969, "when things started integrating." Lynn's family, "the most notorious racists in town," was terrified, said Cynthia, by "any thought of an up-and-coming black middle class," because of their own lack of education. Their opposite was Cynthia's mother, "the only white teacher in this county who believed in integration." The clash hurt. "We went for a period of about two years where the other people in the town really didn't talk to us." Cynthia's socializing was limited to the cafe. One afternoon, she lost that, too.

She and an older brother were in the restaurant when Lynn suddenly "jumped up and said, 'Lock the door, lock the door.' I didn't know what they were talking about and looked out. There was this black family, a man, a woman, and some children, trying to come in. I was twelve, thirteen. I just locked the door. They told me to lock the door, I did it. My brother got furious and said, 'I'm going to open the door.'" He and Lynn "got into this little standoff, and my brother kind of grabbed me, and we both walked out the kitchen. I still had no clue as to what the standoff was about. Walking home, my brother said, 'I'm never going in there again, and I don't want you to go in there either.' He explained to me that they were trying to keep the restaurant from being integrated."

Cynthia did as she was told then, too, and stayed away. The following years were especially lonely. "I was never good at the kind of isolation my mother enjoyed. She had kind of a martyrdom about it. [For me,] even though they were racists, they were so interesting. I'm still interested in that kind of people, because they *were* overlooked."

When high school and the Alapaha Cafe finally were behind her, Cynthia moved on to nearby Valdosta State University and a Western Sizzler. The former was a compromise (her mother did not want her going to the more worldly University of Georgia), but the latter was a goal. The Sizzler, on a highway near the air force base, had a reputation as a place where waitresses could make a lot of money. Because of a long waiting list for waitress applicants, Cynthia accepted a job working at the salad bar.

Again, she was lonely. "Most of the other people working there were high school dropouts and were very hostile toward university students." The most hostile waitresses were "the two main doyennes," both married and both nearly three times her age.

"Tillie was tall and red-haired and almost mannish. Helen was very feminine and pretty and Lebanese and mother-earthy and absolutely adored men." Both were "serious waitresses. They had never been anything in their lives but waitresses, so they had their certain amount of contempt for me, because they knew that [the Sizzler] was not the end of the line with me."

Cynthia worked the salad bar and then the cash register, and (with the help of a grant) she barely was able to support herself. "I was financially on a shoestring, but I was independent of my mother when I was eighteen." She paused. "The big break for me was one Saturday, when one of the waitresses had been beaten up by her husband."

Trudi, like many other waitresses, was married to a mechanic at the base. Yet she was different. She was only in her twenties and "absolutely beautiful. That was one reason the rest of the waitresses hated her." Cynthia became acutely aware of the role of looks among women, herself included.

"In my case, I was not . . . I was not pretty. [My] youth elicited responses from men, but the waitresses who were pretty, they *really* had it rough. Not meaning to elicit these responses from men, and also incurring the hatred of the older waitresses. A man being waited on by a twenty-three-year-old, it figures, will leave a better tip than a man being waited on by Tillie the battle-ax with her dyed red hair. People would come in and say, 'I want Trudi to be my waitress.' For somebody like Tillie, who was a super waitress . . . she could take twenty plates, ten on each arm, and be perfectly charming while she was doing it and make sure everyone has enough coffee. I think that was the first introduction I had to the physical-female, and the double-edged thing," of being beautiful.

One edge got Trudi. "It was a Saturday, it was crazy busy. Her husband had come home and had found her in bed with another man and had broken a sliding glass window to get in. She had cut her feet so badly on glass, running to get away from him, she couldn't work. This is what the manager was explaining to me. He came up to me and said, 'Do you think you could do this?' This *is* what I'd wanted to do."

With news of Cynthia's trial promotion, the waitresses' wrath increased. "They were totally contemptuous of me. I could feel it. But they were willing to help me, because they knew it would make their night go a little easier. The big deal was, were my arms long enough to stack the plates on them? This kind of stuff. I realized I would have to prove to these women that even though I was at the university, I was willing to work."

That night, Cynthia made more than fifty dollars, "a colossal amount of money. I could hardly move the next day." She did, though. "I worked there the better part of three years. That was the time I realized I wanted to be a writer.

"I knew I was putting myself in a culture I was kind of alien to and wanted to see if I could crack it. I wanted to see if I could get their respect." In trying to get the respect of Tillie and Helen, her primary challenges, Cynthia messed up badly.

When it was her turn to take a large group, which meant a large tip, Cynthia ceded the customers to her elders. "I felt they needed the money more than I did. I had what I needed, and this is their profession." Later, she learned that her action, far from being appreciated, made Tillie and Helen even more contemptuous. It also caused a conflict between Tillie and Helen.

"Helen was a real operator and would somehow arrange to be behind me in the order so she could get any big groups I didn't want. Tillie thought that was horrible and finally took me aside and explained I was being taken advantage of." Cynthia got the cooks to "smooth it over."

A Mr. Clarence, who "would cook all week, get drunk on Saturday night, be hung over on Sunday, come in Monday morning, cook all week," was someone whose respect she especially wanted, too. Also "I wanted to learn things about cooking from him. He was making a big bread pudding one time, and I watched him put it in this enormous oven, with burn marks all over his arms." Cynthia asked him how long he left it in. "He kind of looked at me and said, 'Until it's done.' " She laughed. "It was very kind, the way he did it." She learned the advice was sound. "It depended, I realize—this was a gas oven—on what else was in the oven. I know this now because I'm a middle-aged woman and I know about variables. When you're in your twenties, you want absolutes. Even now I find myself saying to my daughter, 'How long is it going to take? Until it takes.' "

Cynthia's infatuation with her new world intensified. One day, Carmen "showed up and started working there. She was somebody who had traveled 'round the country, mostly in the South, all her life. She'd always been a waitress, but she would do things like go rattlesnake hunting in the fall. She had black hair and blue eyes and was as redneck as you could be, but absolutely full of life. She'd had children and abandoned 'em to her own parents and followed men around. Here I am, the voyeur. '*Talk* to me, Carmen.' I was an English major, and they would try to pick my brains about what I did. Why did I read books? I'd work at the steak house until midnight or one in the morning and then go home and write papers on Yeats or Shakespeare."

The restaurant staff's "whole little community" was a "microcosm," she said, allowing her "to see how these people had subsisted and existed, and how they'd gotten through their lives, and the ways they would try to interpret what was going on around 'em." She added, "It was some of the most valuable experience I ever got in understanding human relationships."

At some point, Sizzler management offered to make Cynthia one of them. She declined. For one thing, some practices, such as charging waitresses a nickel for each pat of butter they put on their baked potato, "almost made a Marxist out of me." For another, she could not stand more alienation from co-workers. She was already "low woman on the totem pole" for going to college and having a father they learned was an officer, even if he had left the family. It was a good thing for all he was not a customer. "I've seen my father do things like trying to get a waiter fired because he fills a glass of wine more than half full."

Within the world of the Sizzler, Cynthia also observed herself. "This is one of those things I use a lot in my novel, this kind of detachment from what's going on around you. Waitressing was probably the first time I ever got conscious about it." She offered this example: "When you're leaning over a guy's plate to pour him another cup of coffee, and he's some backwater cash register salesman, and he puts his hand on your rear end to see what kind of response he's going to get out of you . . . I was the kind of person, 'Hm-m, so this is what goes on.' I always felt like I had kind of infiltrated this world, because the other side of my life was so vicarious. I was such a reader and I grew up in such a small town, there were all kinds of things I just never, never knew." She talks calmly now, but she was not calm when the cash register salesman put his hand on her.

"It surprised me so, I ended up splashing the coffee in his lap. The reaction of the other waitresses was another thing. It was like an initiation. They would look at you and see how you would handle stuff like that. I was so naive, I was concerned 'cause I had probably burned him."

Tillie and Helen were not. "I can remember how funny Helen thought it was, and she said something to me like, 'You could have turned that into a big, big tip.' Just a total cynic. Tillie was, 'Let's castrate him.'" Cynthia laughed. "You have this event happen, and then you have these different interpretations. It's the kind of thing I would never have been exposed to unless I had read about it in a book."

During her Sizzler years, "I began to delineate between the types of women who were victims and the types of women who would refuse to be victims. One of the women I got really close to [was] named Kathy, another waitress. When I first met her, she was married to an air force man, a Vietnam veteran. He was an abuser." Cynthia learned such things after she passed another kind of test and co-workers finally accepted her.

"The big deal, when you were in with these women, would be when they would invite you to go have a beer with them after work on Saturday night. I wasn't much of a drinker, and I would just go and hold my beer and be with them. That was when I learned what beer is. It's what makes your legs stop hurting after Saturday night." She smiled, rocking a little on the cabin step.

One night after work, Cynthia and Kathy sat in Kathy's car outside a package store, drinking beer, when Kathy began talking about her marriage. "I don't know why she trusted me to tell me these things, but she told me, for example, that her husband could only make love to her after she had dressed up and pretended to be a Vietnamese woman and that she found it totally humiliating. And he would come home and reenact the same kinds of humiliating and degrading types of authority he had been exposed to at work. He would put on white gloves and do the military white glove thing—was there dust on the shelf?"

In contrast to other waitresses, who considered Cynthia's college studies "totally useless," Kathy confided that she wanted to get more education herself. She did not do that, but she did leave the Vietnam veteran and "ended up living in a trailer. It was really traumatic, but she was happier to be away from him, not being beaten up, not being humiliated. Then the predators came out of the woodwork in her life. She would start talking about it and mention a particular customer or something, and I would be like, ew-w-w-w. I was pretty naive." Cynthia later realized Kathy also was trying to tell her that the married owner of the steak house, whose wife soon died under peculiar circumstances, was coming on to her.

"I had the same boyfriend all through college, and they thought that was very strange. My senior year, my boyfriend showed up at Christmas time with an engagement ring, which caught me totally off guard. I didn't know what to do, so I wore it." Her voice became a whisper. "The other waitresses . . . it was like I had been anointed. It was the most wonderful thing in the world to them. He was about to graduate, he was going to be a biologist, and they thought, okay, she's out of here, she's taken care of, she can have babies, she can have all the things we never had. They would say this to me."

By then, Cynthia recognized that her chances in life always had been far better than those of the other women. "Straight out of the chute, the limitations of the lives they'd been born into. That was a very sobering thing for me, because my mother had brought us up to blame my father's defection from the marriage for whatever limitations we had in our lives. She didn't remarry somebody who would beat her or require her to dress up like a Vietnamese woman. It gave me this whole different perspective on human life. That was my introduction to the knowledge that making your way in the world is contingent upon being able to execute a task. To see these women age, to know my advancement came when a woman's feet were cut to ribbons."

At the time, Cynthia was not paying such close attention to the others but was "totally absorbed in my own life." She and her boyfriend had broken up, and she had become involved with her history professor, "which was another thing they were totally contemptuous of.

"I remember reaching a point where I was very self-conscious about being a waitress, because he was dating women who were professors. He had this kind of bemused interest in me." He liked her to "entertain" him with "your waitress stories."

The most skeptical about him was man-loving Helen. When Cynthia and she were standing around the Sizzler in their black aprons, Cynthia told her that the man did not want children. "I can remember Helen looking at me and saying, 'If he doesn't want a child, it's because he wants to be the child. Remember what I'm telling you.' In those years . . . they were not just telling me everything they knew about waitressing, but everything they knew about everything. Because you impart this information.

"During that period in my life, these other waitresses were the women I could talk to about what was happening between me and this professor. I was too young to know it, but they knew that this was a bad thing. They had nothing kind to say about him."

Finally, with Helen's warning in her head and a cherished goodbye from Mr. Clarence, who "came out of the kitchen to speak to me on my last night," Cynthia graduated from Valdosta in 1977 and moved to the University of Mississippi to attend graduate school. There she married the professor. "Because I was a waitress and because I knew my way around the kitchen, he perceived that kind of talent, to look at a table and see whose glass needs filling, as the perfect requisite for a faculty wife."

The marriage lasted six years. "When I divorced the guy, I wanted to call [Helen] up and say, 'You were absolutely right.'"

Cynthia said her second husband, although also a professor (and the chair of the English department), is different in many ways, including being closer to her in political outlook. She said he was upset when she dropped out of the Ph.D. program after becoming pregnant with their daughter, but the waitresses had decided her; she wanted to write, not critique others' writings. She gave birth and stayed home two years "being a mother. I was profoundly depressed. I *have* to have something. It goes back to the time I had to have financial independence from my mother. I have to have financial independence from everyone, including my husband. It's something I learned from those other waitresses. Helen used to say, 'If somebody else is your meal ticket, then they make you dance.' "

During Cynthia's unhappy unemployment, she persuaded the owner of Oxford's Harvest Cafe to hire her to wait tables. "I was *so* excited, I went to my husband's office to tell him." She paused again. "It really surprised me, because he would not hear of it. Could not talk, he was so outraged. For me, it was just a matter of easy money and being around people, and I was lunching every day at Harvest Cafe anyway, with the other unemployed wives. Why not just stay?" She laughed. There was another reason she wanted to waitress again. "It was one of the most positive nurturing experiences of my life."

She later understood her husband's response as part bewilderment about why she had done all this studying only to be a waitress and as "a little bit of, 'My God, he's the chair of the department and his [wife] is waiting tables.' I was so angry at not being able to work and sort of angry about this thing that once your family achieves a certain socioeconomic status, you virtually are an indentured servant. The world perceives you this way. Even your own husband will."

So, on the eve of the publication of her first novel, she was overseeing the domain of William Faulkner and was not entirely enthralled with what she had learned about him. She has "tremendous respect for how *hard* he worked and for what he did," but has "contempt for a lot of things about his life," such as how he treated certain people.

"I taught a black woman who grew up as a child near here, who told me a story one time about passing Faulkner on the sidewalk. [He] pushed her off, and he said, 'Get out of the way, nigger.' " There is another clincher. "Somebody told me that the waitresses hated him here because he would go into a restaurant and sit for hours, drink coffee, leave his pipe ashes all over the table, and be a slob, and leave no tip. Somebody told me, somebody who was a waitress."

Mary-Lyons Mouton Ochsner Bruna

One sunny afternoon, thirty-four-year-old Mary-Lyons Mouton Ochsner Bruna got out of her beat-up pickup and strolled down a New Orleans street, turning heads. She wore a trim white T-shirt and jeans over a knockout figure, her arms buff from carrying heavy trays. She is shorter than not, but she walks tall, with a curvy stride.

Entering her favorite off-the-beaten-path restaurant, she smiled. Every time she did, which was often, her lower eyelids turned up, too, and her eyes also smiled. She is adorable. Speaking in the New Orleans accent that baffles newcomers (she pronounces her name "mare-lines"), she placed a lunch order with the waitress in a respectful manner and then launched into heavy dishing. Within minutes, it occurred to me that Mary-Lyons represents an unusual weave of worlds. Before lunch was over, the irony of this weave also became clear.

For nine years, she has worked at Brennan's, a pink-roomed French Quarter landmark popular with out-of-towners ready for a splurge. Famously gargantuan breakfasts include such items as crawfish Sardou and turtle soup. Breakfast at Brennan's "is not meant to be done every day. It's just meant to be done," Mary-Lyons declared, twice. "It's thirty-five dollars. You get appetizer, entree, dessert, and coffee, and," she crinkled a smile, "really good service, I might add. I *hope*. I *hope*."

She gushed on, describing some of the city's well-known restaurateurs as "all alcoholics," adding, "What do you call 'em, reborn alcoholics?" The phrase proved to be not the only striking way Mary-Lyons expresses herself. When she worked as a dishwasher when she was thirteen, she said, it "just broke my mother's back." When she is tipped precisely 15 percent no matter what kind of time was had, "it makes me wonder how people reward people. It *is* a gratuitous business."

She has a striking and cheerful sense of logic, too. Of the eight dogs she and her husband own, she said that during the day she puts seven in the backyard and keeps one inside, "so it looks like we only have seven." Of one of her four sisters, she commented, "She's smaller than me, even though she's older."

At lunch that sunny day, Mary-Lyons went on chattily about the owners of Brennan's. "There are three brothers. They'll have Diet Coke all year round, but during Mardi Gras, where it's such a party town here," they "get so polluted." She said that because they "are Irish" they were not able to be part of Rex (one of the most prestigious Mardi Gras clubs, or krewes) "because Rex was so discriminatory. They wouldn't allow anybody into their club unless they were old family from Louisiana." She talked about the Brennans "making so much money" that, in response to the discrimination, they started their own krewe and Mardi Gras parade, Bacchus, named for the god of wine. She also spoke about the brothers commissioning her—"I'm an artist"—to paint a four-paneled mural, a depiction of enormous wine bottles, in one dining room as a testament to Bacchus; about the deal souring over their charges for food at her wedding reception; about her keeping the last panel until the dispute is resolved; about "how ball-less these men are," that they "never asked *me* once" when she is installing it.

She paused a second. Sometimes Brennan's "just fries me to death." But, "for my lifestyle, it's the best job."

Mary-Lyons did not begin at Brennan's easily, either. "I was the third female hired. I had to put up with a lot of stuff when I first came. Oh, I had old waiters that had been there for forty years, and they weren't about to have women. They would steal stuff from you. You go to your station and you'd have nothing." She remembered a man angrily pointing out that he had no silverware, which she had just placed on his table. She recalled "salt and peppers or even water pitchers" being swiped from her station.

Her chat raced on, as if there were nothing unusual about her. (There was, I would soon learn.) "A big stealing thing" used to go on at Brennan's, she continued. Waiters "in cahoots" with chefs used invisible ink to rewrite orders of a party of fifteen as a party of two and split the take. The old manager "used to take home sirloin steaks."

And fighting! There was "so much blood shed at Brennan's," she said enthusiastically. People hid knives. One kitchen combatant "had to walk out of three dining rooms with blood all over him. Stabbings, that was common. That happened while I was there. A dishwasher got mad, broke a glass, and stabbed one of the pantry chefs. Then they started to find needles in the back." Cocaine was common, too, she said. "I used to do cocaine, matter of fact, when I started. I realized, what the hell was I doing, to work your ass off and make *all* this money, and then the money to be gone the next day on drugs—it had no sense or logic."

Staff drinking, she rushed on, involved "torpedoes": taking a coffee-pot to the bar, putting a drink inside, and "inhaling" the contents. The current vice also involves inhaling. "We have one little hole in the back where we can smoke. So smoking in another part of the restaurant is our big sneak thing now."

She crinkled again, before launching another riff. "Why I love waiting tables is I always fall in love with the cooks. The kitchen crew. Oh, I mean, I got to tell you, it brings tears to my eyes." Her blues did indeed water. "They're the good guys, the lower-class good guys. They're the ones that are coming up through all this horrible New Orleans society which doesn't give anybody a chance and kind of classifies you as a bad person if you're from the projects. They're the ones that are trying. They're the *truest*. I'm sure I've worked with a criminal or two that . . ." She burst into a laugh and touched my arm. "Oh, I have. One guy one time, he was a busboy, and I had a little trouble with him" and a female employee who "was spunkin' with me" for telling someone they were dealing drugs. Then he killed someone, she added. She saw the news on television.

"It's always amazing. You get a good busboy, and you just love him to death. You'll give him thirty-five [percent of your tips] if he's really good." She stopped for a millisecond to chew a hunk of bread. "What I do to help these guys that work as dishwashers or as prep kitchens," as she put it, "I have them save me the meat" rejected by chef or customer, "and I pay them five dollars at the end of the day for my dogs."

Her relationships with fellow waiters are downright daffy. "We're constantly joking. Sergio's attaching parsley to your hair or signs that say 'Kick Me,' 'My First Day.' Or I'll have escargot clamps coming off of my uniform or hot bread coming out of my apron and I don't know it. I always wear my hair up in a bun with a chopstick, so he'll hang doilies from my chopstick." She learns of her accessories only later, in the dining room.

Then there are hands-on relationships. "All the chefs, when they come in, I'm like their baby doll, and I got to give them that little, you know, admiration, 'Yes, papa, yes, papa.' 'Oh, it's good to see you.' They *love* me, the black men I work with. 'Cause I'm not prejudiced and I love them. I get hugs and kisses every morning. I think the black women see that and think, enough already, with the black men dating the white women—and then to see me flirting with them, which I do. They're old and fat and I love 'em."

She has, she added, a "sexist kind of job. There's a lot of hands on your butt. Oh, you would die. My husband sees me being touched all the time, but half of 'em are gay. . . . Every restaurant I've ever been, it's very touchy. There's a line that's drawn, you follow me?" She called it "a *fi-i-i-ne* line. For Setchie to do it to me, it's okay. It's like my sister doing it." Grabbing goes both ways and is color-blind. "Lucien has got the biggest butt in the world. We always grabbing it. 'Lucien, that thing you can put a tray on, that a shelf?' Lucien's like, 'You like it, don't you?' I'm going, 'Lord, Lu!'

"I became a waitress when I was only fifteen. I always loved it. It's funny. I come from . . . not so much of a wealthy family. My last name's Ochsner, there's a hospital started after my grandfather . . ."

I looked puzzled, although later realized that my reaction was like going to Boston, hearing the name Kennedy, and looking puzzled there. "O-C-H-S-N-E-R," she spelled without an ounce of offense—as in, the phone book revealed, the Ochsner Foundation Hospital, the Alton Ochsner Medical Foundation, a half dozen Ochsner clinics, and the Ochsner Health Plan. Stature in the medical world, however, is only the iceberg. The tip is society.

"New Orleans society is kind of, you know. I made my debut, and here I am working in a restaurant with a different class of people. I've always had trouble with some people, to put it lightly."

It began to dawn on me that Mary-Lyons was part of what she called "horrible" New Orleans society. She also understated her family's role in it, I discovered. Rex, the Mardi Gras krewe that had excluded the Brennans, not only included the Ochsners but also had made Mary-Lyons's grandfather *the* Rex: king of the whole Mardi Gras. To those who care, one ascends no higher in New Orleans society. Nor, to those who care, does one descend much lower than being a waitress.

Mary-Lyons makes matters worse by sticking even more outrages in the social craw of the krewe. She not only waits tables, but she does so at a declassé, Irish-rooted, mostly tourist restaurant. Worse still, she did not marry a pampered uptowner who waves from an elite float. She married a Cuban American, Juan Bruna, who is clearly her heart's delight. "You would think he's had years of education, the way his whole thought process is." Worse still, Juan is also a waiter at Brennan's. Worse than any of these transgressions, however, is Mary-Lyons's attitude: she enjoys waiting tables.

It is more than New Orleans society can bear.

Her co-workers at Brennan's, especially the women, were not pleased either, when they learned "an Ochsner" was waiting tables. She often heard: " 'What are you doing here?' [Also] I think I might have been a spoiled rotten brat when I first got there? Then it changed me a lot."

Everyone at Brennan's accepts her now, she said. New Orleans society, however, has not yet come around.

"Locals give me a lot of attitude because I look just like my sisters," two of whom are doctors. Although "locals" do not usually go to Brennan's as couples, she said, they do for parties. "People have thought I was my sister and was moonlighting as a waitress. They won't say anything to my face, but they whisper. Oh, it happens all the time. 'That's Isabelle Ochsner. What is she doing there?' Do you understand? I get looked down on.

"I actually have to justify my job. I can't tell you how many times I've had to explain. 'Why do you do this job?' 'Do your parents know?' I say, 'Yes they know, and they love it.'

"One time when [another waiter] and I were working teams, I went up to a table, and it was a bunch of doctors, and they knew my sisters. One of these women must have had a big problem with my sister. The guy says, 'Are you an Ochsner?' I said, 'Yes, I am.' He goes, 'God, you look so much like Missy.' But I'm the artist kind. My sister's got matching bows in her hair. She drives an Acura, I drive a truck. I don't do her justice, let's put it that way, that poor thing. Anyway, I detected all this attitude from this woman, and she ended up being really rude and so nasty to me." The woman called Mary-Lyons "Little Missy" in a "derogatory" way. "She was so out-and-out nasty that her husband, at the end of the meal, came up and held my hand. He said, 'I'm very sorry.' I was trembling."

Mary-Lyons's sisters, who also waited tables, are "very supportive" of her. Another relative is another story.

"I have an aunt that paints. She's very good, but she definitely sells a lot because of her last name, Ochsner," her name by marriage. (Mary-Lyons signs her paintings "Mary-Lyons.") The aunt came to a large outdoor party at Brennan's, which Mary-Lyons was serving. Having felt the aunt's coolness before, she wanted to avoid her, but a fellow waiter urged her to say hello. Mary-Lyons started to. "She just cut off, like that." The aunt left "right after the appetizer, 'cause I was waiting on the first three tables, and one was hers. She never said a word to me. It was truly, truly because I was waiting on her, and she was embarrassed. This is my own *aunt*.

"Locals are very snobby. The fact that I'm an Ochsner and work as a waitress just upsets people. Like during Mardi Gras, when all these locals go to Antoine's or Galatoire's, and they see my husband and I in a bow tie, walking right past them while they're all dressed up in their line, and I used to be a part of that? I see the looks I get. It's funny. I mean, I'm happy as can be, and, God bless their souls, it's not a dishonest job. I'm not robbing a bank, you know."

One of her worst experiences came from a "local" who did not realize her lineage. At Brennan's only days before we met, "they had the Rex party. Rex is the king, the major parade that goes down Mardi Gras day, and approximately ninety men in the Rex parade come." Mary-Lyons never mentioned her or her family's connection to it. "They always get so drunk they won't let women work the party, which is fine with me. I was walking up the stairs, and these two guys were helping this old man down the stairs. This old man stopped and looked at me and said, 'O-oh baby, I want to take you home and do the nasty with you.' I just looked at him. He must have been eighty-seven years old. I didn't say anything. I kept walking." Just behind the group was the boyfriend of one of her sisters. "That was the one time I wanted to use my name, you know what I mean? To embarrass him."

Mary-Lyons was so boiling mad that she called her mother. "I said, 'If they would have known I was an Ochsner, they would have never said that. Second of all, whatever happened to treating me like a lady? Because I'm a servant, I'm not a lady?' *That* comes from locals. These men go out and get drunk, and they treat *my* status like garbage. What makes me so different from their wife? Because I'm in black and white with a bow tie on? It amazes me."

Her mother must have an especially sympathetic ear. She "came from a very poor family" in Lafayette and put herself through nursing school by painting pictures of Jackson Square. "Her father was a caboose man for the Southern Pacific Railroad, and he was real proud of it." Mary-Lyons's father, conversely, "was raised on a plantation. His father wore a white linen suit with a top hat."

Mary-Lyons may be Rex's debutante granddaughter, but because of the society that spawned and then spurned her, she is dependent on the kindness of strangers: customers.

"I generally wait on people in a great party atmosphere. I would not want to be an emergency room doctor," as one sister is, nor would she want to be her sister the dermatologist, "who waits on people just like I do, by the way. She's a servant, too."

Mary-Lyons certainly acknowledges her own on-the-job problems, like a table of "conservative men" asking, " 'Is our waiter coming?' To *me*. 'Yes, he is. I'll go get him.' " More frequently, men tip a maître d' a hundred dollars to get a good table and then stiff her, or they might stiff her because the prices are high. "We'll get people that come, see the menu, and don't want to eat there because of the price," but they do it anyway. She wishes they would be "very graceful about it" and accept her friendly suggestion of a cheaper place nearby. "Don't stay and be miserable and make everybody else miserable with you."

If she believes people "don't have enough money, and they're with other people" who do, she will "throw in" something. "I'm not doing it saying, 'I'm giving you this free. Give me money.' The fact they get a little lagniappe when they were disturbed about something makes them much more at ease."

She tries to put people at ease even after the meal. If a credit card is denied, "I usually make up an excuse. 'Sir, for some reason, this card's not going through the machine.' I'll do it very discreet, just with him. If it's American Express, 'We always have trouble with American Express.' " After her delicacy toward them, she is stunned if they are indelicate toward her, leaving a low tip. "You get this real flush, kind of ill feeling. You don't want to tell them goodbye. You don't want to be *mean,* but you're so hurt."

Mary-Lyons is her own favorite kind of customer. When Juan's extended family visited from Miami, the couple treated them to a meal at Brennan's, an event they still are paying off. "We just bought a house. We owe everybody. We're knocking out windows and putting up French doors and building porches. Here I am, can't afford it, but the minute we got there, and before, when I was getting dressed, that was out of my mind. We had the best time of our life. That didn't stop me from what I ordered. That didn't stop me from my tip at the end of the meal.

"At the plumbers' convention, they are the best tippers. They have a *ball.*" In general, she enjoys all her customers, even grumps. "It's really fun to conquer people. First I apologize. 'I'm so sorry for you-all's wait, but if you're hungry, let me take care of that. And I'm going to get you your food as fast as I can.' Once I get them to vent, I start humoring with them. I always offer them a cocktail for their wait. Then I pamper 'em." She tells them to keep any pampering treats secret. " 'Sh-h-h, don't tell anybody.' I've learned, the first time I ever did [take extra] care of one table, how it pissed off the other two tables. If you have friends or a call party or somebody you haven't seen," like a returning table of tourists, "as joking and as much fun as you're having with that, you got to turn around and do it to the other tables, too. You got to include them."

If they are in a good mood, she smiled, using her favorite expression, "I have a ball with them."

This, then, is the irony in the worlds of Mary-Lyons Mouton Ochsner Bruna. She gets along much better with tourists, who have no idea who she is, than she does with the locals, who do.

AFTER SHIFT

*J*UST ABOUT EVERY KIND OF JOB, I have learned from both first-hand and secondhand experience, offers an after-shift ritual, especially for workers young in heart and slim in commitments. For many waitresses, after shift was, and remains, a sometimes fragile but buoyant time of both weariness and connection.

It also can be a time of reassessing one's life.

Kathy Anderson

Kathy's Old Townhouse Cafe in Sunol, California, a couple of hours and trends southeast of San Francisco, has just closed for the day. The plain wooden building that houses the cafe stands on block-long Main Street, perpendicular to freight railroad tracks. The cafe looks so much like a scene from Norman Rockwell—although Edward Hopper might pause at the huge windows framed by cracked white paint—that a few low-budget films have been shot here. Kitschy salt and pepper shakers on the tables were originally movie props. So were the curtains. Accordingly, thanks in part to doo-dahed fiction fantasy, the cafe looks like what it really is: a cozy hub of a rural village.

This late afternoon, Kathy Anderson, Prop., is beat. She has been going since dawn. A fair-skinned woman in her fifties, with light, curly hair, rosy cheeks, and a bit of plumpness, she semi-collapses at a table in the dining room, a few strides from the kitchen.

Seconds later, an old brass bell on the opening front door jangles. Kathy turns her head a fraction. The man who climbed the three bouncy wooden steps and walked in is a regular, a ranch hand from the looks of him, not some after-hours stranger who might expect her to stand. Kathy keeps her seat.

"Hi, Robert," she says.

"Hi, Kathy," he says.

At the Old Townhouse Cafe, there is closed and not-so-closed.

The man, an inadvertent fashion plate in a worn cowboy hat, jeans, and boots, goes to the refrigerator, gets himself a beer, opens it, and sits down. Over the next few minutes, several other men follow his precise steps. They talk and drink, but they also look over at Kathy and seem unsure what to make of not having her complete attention. One fellow, behind Kathy's back, picks up a large jar containing donations for the cafe's Halloween decorations and pretends to steal it. Kathy does not bother turning around at the laughter. She certainly is not concerned that a regular would steal anything.

As she knows them, they know her. They know that she is owner, manager, cook, and waitress here. They also know that she is fine at the first three jobs and a failure at the fourth.

New customers advertise their ignorance by insults. "They'll be looking at the menu, and they'll say, 'Is this good?' 'Is this *good*,'" she grumbled, shifting in her chair. "It's almost like it implies a partnership between the customer and the waitress, a secret society. Of course, a lot of people don't realize they're speaking to the owner. They *should*." No one, she announces, would have hired a waitress as poor at the job as she is. "I couldn't have gotten a job as a waitress if I hadn't bought a restaurant."

A good waitress, Kathy realizes, knows who ordered what. "I have run out of that kitchen and yelled, 'Don't eat that!' The fork will be halfway to the mouth. 'It's not your order!'"

A good waitress, she also realizes, is coordinated. "I'm a klutz for one thing, and klutzes should never wait tables. For several years, I would pick up the breakfast orders, the toast is on a separate plate, [and] by the time I turned around, the toast was across the room. It happened over and over and over again. Just fly off the plate, like little Frisbees."

More important than logistics, though, is realizing she has to let her regulars treat the place as theirs. That she does expertly.

"I'll be sitting here in the morning when I open, I have a cup of coffee, I have a book or the newspaper, and I have my cigarettes. The rest of California can't smoke. I can," she smiled mischievously. (State law prohibits smoking in most restaurants.) When Kathy lights a morning cigarette, regulars light up, too. "If someone we don't know comes in . . ." she mimicked a frantic stubbing out. "Just like kids," she laughed.

In the morning, "this crew" comes in, says hi, tells her not to get up, pours their own coffee, and then comes over and pours her some. "They'll bring me the exact change or something where they don't need it back. Life is good. I like this."

The help-yourself-to-coffee tradition began when the former owner, a woman named Addie, slept in one morning, and a regular named Maury grew ever more impatient and caffeine-deprived as he waited. He finally climbed in through an unlocked window and made the coffee himself. When Addie arrived, she told him he might get all dirty doing that again, so she had a key made for him.

Kathy smiled while describing the origin of the custom, but then her face turned serious. "If I were ever to stand up and say, 'Please don't do that,' or 'I really can't have you behind the counter . . . '—probably that would be the 'smart' thing to do—they'd be crushed. I may make the payments and, if there is any, I may make the profits. But it's their place, too."

In fact, if "these guys," indicated by a head gesture, want to stay later than she does, especially on weekends, they do. "They'll get caught up on whatever happened that week. If I'm really tired, I'll go home and just tell them, 'Lock it up.' When I come in the next day, because I'll take the money when I go, there will be a list, how many beers they bought. The next day they'll come in and pay for them. I've never had a problem. I have never had a check bounce. I've never been stuck."

Although theft is not a big issue in Sunol, maybe she should be more careful, she admits, when alone in the cafe before sunrise or after dark. Once or twice, a new customer has made her uneasy. "There are times when I'm extremely casual around here and times when I think about that, because it probably isn't too smart to be the only one in here, filling out my bank deposit slip. I have locked the back door but left the front door [unlocked], that kind of thing. You do get lulled into that 'safe place' kind of feeling." Usually, in the early mornings, she leaves the front door unlocked and works alone in the kitchen.

"I might get here at five. It depends on what I have to do to set up for that day. If I'm in pretty good shape, six o'clock is fine. On Saturday mornings, I'm usually here at four, because I do a big breakfast." She certainly does. The menu lists six varieties of egg dishes, nine types of omelets (many named after customers), plus biscuits and country gravy and, in the "Sweets for the Sweet!" section, French toast, pancakes, and sweet rolls.

"I would unlock the door when I came in, because I know people are going to get a cup of coffee to go. I'm in the kitchen, they come in, pour it, leave the money on the register, and I'm not interrupted." Reports of crime (there was a killing across the freeway) made her lock the doors for a while, but she has left the "back door wide open I don't know how many times. I always figure, if they want a tuna fish sandwich that bad . . ."

Kathy, joking or not, often brought up the subject of safety. The lack of safety, in fact, is what led her here.

She was, at the age of seventeen, "just a housewife," living in southern California with her husband and baby daughter. When her in-laws decided to move to peaceful Sunol, after a peripatetic and occasionally dangerous life working in the oil fields of the world (sometimes leaving a foreign country with twenty-four hours' notice when oil was nationalized, she said), Kathy's husband moved their family up, too. In time, she had two more daughters with him and gained an appreciation of Sunol as a good place to raise children.

"Our kids grew up in [probably] one of the safest places . . . in California that you could be." They played in the woods and the street, moved about on horses and bicycles and skateboards, and "camped out on the hillsides overnight."

She and her husband eventually divorced; incompatibility seemed to have been the reason. She left town with the three girls and for a while made her way in the northern California white-collar workforce, often doing marketing for software firms. "I never got child support."

The beer-drinking men are looking petulant.

Eventually Kathy remarried, had a fourth girl, and returned to Sunol with her second husband. Her daughters indeed played day and night in streets and on hillsides with safety. That was not where the danger was.

"I found myself in the middle of . . . it was a very bad divorce—very, very, bad. He was a very controlling individual, which I realized. But what I didn't realize was that he was also molesting my oldest daughter."

She said the molestation began, along with attendant warnings not to tell, when the girl was about fifteen. It lasted well over a year, until the teenager sensed that her stepfather was about to molest her next oldest sister. That is when she told her mother. Kathy confronted him with her daughter's account.

When I asked whether he had admitted it, Kathy leaned forward, answering too softly for the regulars to hear: "Actually, he said, 'Jesus Christ, Kathy, it's not like I went out with another woman.'"

Reeling from her discovery and his reaction, Kathy "came undone." About the same time, another one of her daughters and the daughter of Addie, owner of the cafe, "kept saying to both of us they wanted us to meet, they thought we'd really get along. Finally we did, and that led to a group of single women" of different backgrounds and ages, who "probably saved my sanity and maybe even my life. It was the most fantastic support group I ever stumbled across." The women helped Kathy follow through on her resolve, to prosecute her husband in the full light of Sunol.

"I knew it was the only way to keep him away. This is a dirty little secret that most always gets hidden away, until the last few years. When I exposed him to his family, to his mother, to others, I took away his power."

Complicating the situation, he was so "hateful and violent" that police advised Kathy to hide herself and her children, which she did, until they were able to make the arrest. Her face was grim, her voice grimmer, as she summed up his sentencing: "He got two weeks for the 'misdemeanor' of child molesting."

With the encouragement of her "magical" circle of women, Kathy resumed work in a number of jobs. Each time one ended (some of the companies went bankrupt), she returned to her friends and to the Townhouse for coffee and sympathy. She sometimes helped cook on Saturdays, but that was mostly to gather material for a weekly newspaper column she began writing, called "Around Sunol."

Then Addie "met someone who asked her to get married, and she said, 'Do you want the cafe?'

"I said, 'Okay.'"

Kathy was, in a word, unprepared.

The financial transactions between her and Addie were easy. "We didn't open an escrow or anything." The ninety-one-year-old Sunol woman who owned the building and whose "word is her bond," did not increase the rent, either. A verbal handshake held. Tradition held, too. Addie "wanted to make sure it stayed the way it was. I guess she felt I could do that."

Kathy did collect the many keys Addie had had made—for Maury the coffee maker and various repair people, among others. "Everybody brought their keys to me. I didn't have to ask anyone or fool around getting the locks changed."

So finances were no problem, keys were no problem, cooking was no problem. Waitress work was.

Kathy knew she was not good at it. She knew by comparison. "My mother was a waitress. My mother was a great person to never go to a restaurant with, because she was so critical of service. There wasn't a waitress alive that could match my mother, and she would be pointing that out to us very shortly." Kathy's laugh was rueful. "Not only us, but the waitress."

The main reason Kathy had no waitressing experience was her mother's insistence that she avoid the job. "She always said it was terribly hard work. She didn't want any of us to have to work that hard. 'Use your head, not your feet.' Heard that, heard that, heard that." Kathy saw the results herself. "My mother had horrendous varicose veins, and many times she had blood clots."

This cafe venture was supposed to be easier, but Kathy's perception of what it took to run a simple little cafe changed almost as soon as "Okay" was out of her mouth. "I knew I would be tired. I didn't know how tired I would be at the beginning. I was coming off primarily years of a desk job at the computer, and now I'm running and racing." She was cooking the food from which the toast flew as she went to serve it and, on top of that, was, and is, buying it herself.

"I have to do all the shopping. I'm too small for them to deliver to, much. The ones who *will* come out have a minimum buy, which is too large for me to handle. So I go to Costco and all these places, and I lug it in and I put it away. Then I do laundry of the towels and the potholders. When I have dinners, I have cotton tablecloths I iron. I *knew* there was a lot more to it, but until I got into it, I didn't know what it felt like."

Because there is no automatic dishwasher (the cafe's septic system cannot accommodate one), Kathy washes the dishes by hand—that is, if she has time. If her regulars see she is overwhelmed, they get up from their tables and help wash, too. Also, two of her daughters work part-time at the cafe.

She has developed a number of ways to keep it marginally successful. She does a good take-out business at lunch. She hosts a "guest chef" program. "People have a favorite recipe, come in, and fix dinner." According to a folksy flyer she wrote, soon "Pat and Bob return for their third annual Jambalaya fest!"

Still, she said in a whisper, out of earshot of the increasingly nettled-looking men, the cafe is far from lucrative. The guys nursing their beers point to a reason. Tables turn very, very slowly. Even dinner turns into "a gab fest and getting caught up," and nobody gets up.

They stay in part because, although she never became the waitress her mother was, "I do have other skills." She knows how to make customers feel "welcome," "happy," and "comfortable." For one thing, she listens to them, if partly to gather tidbits for her "Around Sunol" column. "This is a natural gathering place for information." Whether customers are having a 4-H meeting or talking about a neighbor's stolen wooden cows, "I eavesdrop. Everybody knows this is a given. You sit in here, you get it."

Over the years, Kathy's waitressing technique has improved. Toast flies with less frequency. She can carry three plates at once. "I think that's a major step up from two plates, which is what I could carry when I started. That's pretty exciting."

She does not joke at all, though, about what really matters to her. She does not joke about the sense of safety and trust that returned to her in and around the Old Townhouse Cafe or about the group of women who led her to owning it. She does not joke about her ability to make her regulars feel at home.

"It seems to be quite important," she wrote to me, "that they be allowed to pour not only their own coffee, but refills for strangers as well. This simple act defines who belongs and who is passing through."

After more than an hour of neglect from Kathy, the restive regulars, who had been limited to pouring beer for themselves, watched with evident interest as the stranger started putting her tape recorder away. Kathy, still looking more than a little spent, turned and greeted those she had not greeted before.

Said one, "Oh, sure, *now* you have time for us."

"Well," she smiled a touch wearily, "maybe, maybe not."

"Can I smoke?" asked the same man.

"We're closed," she said. "You can smoke."

Lucy Rienzo and Co-workers

It is midnight Friday in the Four Farthings, a casually urbane restaurant in the prosperous Lincoln Park area of Chicago. Nothing farthing-esque stands out; the decor is made up more of etched glass than dartboards or corset ads. (Actually, the name is from a reference in J. R. R. Tolkien and came with the place, which was gentrified decades ago, as was the neighborhood.) A few remaining customers linger over coffee. Open windows let in a warm spring breeze.

Lucy Rienzo, Aileen Cassidy, and Karol Shewmaker, their shifts over and aprons shed, claim a table near the wine racks and open a fine choice. The after-shift downshift has begun.

Traditionally, a change of scene is required for the psychological cleansing rite, but experienced waitresses like these women know that tradition can be modified if opportunity presents itself. Here, it does. The bosses, "Bill" and "Joe," who have left, encourage the staff to know what wines to recommend. How better to know than to uncork?

The women in the Farthings trio all are in their late twenties, have the pale complexion of people who spend almost every minute indoors, and look simply cute. Appearances deceive.

Blue-eyed Lucy, whose curly hair is tied back from her round-cheeked face, has a voice so deep she sounds like a man. She also has more cares than she did a while back—a baby at home. Aileen, who works part-time at the Farthings and full-time as an administrative assistant at the University of Illinois, is often trenchant in her comments. Between them sits Karol, the only one still in her work clothes. A full-time student and full-time waitress, she is too serious, and tired, to act cute.

"You can take anything for three months," proclaimed Aileen, a red-head with a hearty laugh, pouring the first glasses. "After three months, people start getting on your nerves."

Lucy's baritone sounded. "I don't really mind it. I'll complain the whole time, I mean, that's waiter and waitress attitude. It's just part of the job for me. I'm a born complainer."

She pointed to a room divider separating the dining room and a service area and said that behind the divider virtually all customers get taken apart. "There are people that come and go unscathed, I suppose. People who are pleasant enough, who don't cause problems, and you seem to get along with them, and everything works out nicely at the table. They made a special request, but they were nice about asking. That's all the difference in the world, somebody who says to you"—she affected a pleasant voice—" 'Would it be all right if I get that on the side?' " Others demand, she snapped nastily, " 'I want that on the side.' "

Karol, glancing at the divider, said in a voice more muted than the other's, "If you don't release it back here, you're going to end up releasing it at the table, and that costs you money." She added, as if to herself, "One thing waiting tables has taught me more than anything is what amazingly poor social skills most of the American public have."

"Do you think people get this trouble in Europe?" Aileen asked. "I don't think they do."

Karol remembered working at a restaurant that "pampered" its customers. "This woman actually called and complained because the waiter was only *trying* to be nice. He wasn't really happy." The others gasped.

The owners had daily employee meetings, continued Karol, and all were "negative, negative, negative." After a year, she began believing everything negative about herself. "A girl had to be hospitalized because of the stress she endured there."

Lucy calculated that she had never worked for a restaurant owner or manager who was not an alcoholic or a cocaine addict. "There isn't *one,*" she said, slapping the cloth-covered table and shaking its diminutive basket of flowers. "The one in San Francisco was a coke addict, the one in Montauk [Long Island] was definitely a functioning alcoholic, these two are functioning alcoholics . . ."

"Bill," said Aileen, pausing, "is not so functioning."

The others grimaced.

"Brian, why don't you pull your chair over?" invited Lucy. "Brian's been waiting tables a long time, too." A tall, good-looking young man with wavy brown hair and a dark complexion set off by his white shirt sat down between her and Karol. "I might be still working," he said, looking over his shoulder to a table of late diners. A certain shift of attention could be felt.

Lucy asked why he was not wearing shorts, as the employee manual allows. Brian said he had not done his laundry, so all his shorts are dirty. The others nodded. Laundry.

"Once the summer gets in," Aileen explained, "everyone's in shorts." She added that the manual requires only a "clean-cut" look.

"*I've* read it," stated Lucy. " 'Make sure you answer the phone politely, know all of the directions, 'The Customer Who Never Comes Back . . . ' "

Aileen and Karol groaned.

" 'I didn't complain when my food was late, I didn't complain when the waitress was rude about taking my food back, I just didn't say anything,' " continued Lucy.

Brian took up the beat. " 'But I got my revenge. I told ten of my friends and I never came back.' "

" 'If you make one person mad,' " recited Karol, " 'they'll tell ten of their friends who'll tell ten of their friends and . . . ' "

" 'You've lost one hundred potential customers,' " Lucy finished.

" 'Don't touch your nose in the dining room,' " mimicked Aileen.

"It doesn't say that in the manual," said Lucy.

"Oh, yes. Absolutely."

"I always touch my face. Always." Lucy looked troubled.

Nose touching aside, she and Aileen maintained that some unnamed co-workers crossed over the behavioral and hygienic line. "You'd be amazed at what some people will do," said Aileen.

"What people will wear," added Lucy. "They'll come in to work just looking a mess. They're not thinking about it from a customer's point of view and what it's like to see somebody who looks completely disheveled serving food."

She is less understanding about the customer's point of view on another matter. There is one main thing they do not grasp, she said. "That you have other tables. They don't seem to understand that they're not the only ones you're waiting on. Because you're not at their table bringing them something doesn't mean you're standing behind there, you know, with your finger up your nose." She looked annoyed.

Karol wondered why the Farthings customers do not understand "that you don't control all the forces of the universe. I always say, if I could control all the forces of the universe, I wouldn't be waiting tables."

Lucy figured that from the time she punches an order into the computer, "it's ten to fifteen minutes of uncontrol. Sometimes it's a half an hour, because something got screwed up back there. Not even with your order, but with somebody else's."

Aileen began fuming about one of her sisters, a "big-money, big-everything" lawyer in a national firm, who was eating out with other "high-level" professional women. "Yet when the check came, 'Okay, subtract the bar bill. You never tip on the bar.' Where the *hell* that comes from I have no idea. Then, 'Subtract the tax. You don't want to tip on the tax.' What is the waiter going to do with that?"

Karol claimed that her favorite customers praise her to management. "[Usually] all your manager and owner ever hear is that you messed up an order in the kitchen or you forgot to bring somebody a glass of wine. When somebody takes the extra two minutes . . ."

"To find the manager and tell them," interjected Lucy.

"How nice you were," said Aileen, now softly.

"But then you get a little worried when they compliment you," Brian went on, "because you think . . ."

Lucy could not wait. "They're going to gyp you in the end."

"Verbal tip," offered Aileen.

Lucy had another theory. "Sometimes people who are very rude leave good tips, like it gives them a *right* to talk to you that way."

Aileen sighed. "The last thing they're out for is a decent meal, you know what I mean?"

"You gotta hear this," Lucy said, waving her hands. "I was out in Montauk. I was twenty-seven, but I know I look pretty young. There were eight of them sitting at a table, real New Yorkers from like Nassau County with their guinea T-shirts on, you know?"

The others semi-laughed at their Italian American co-worker.

She put down her wine glass and mimed one woman, "with this big hair" and "nails this long." Inches were indicated. "I bring their drinks, and this guy says to me, 'I tell you what. I'm gonna tell you [a] joke, and if at the end of the meal you can repeat the joke exactly the way I told it to you, there's an extra twenty percent in it for you.' 'All right, what's the joke?' He proceeds to tell me this joke that is incredibly foul, like he thought I was going to be embarrassed.

"The end of the meal comes, I bring them their check, and I was about to skate out of it. The guy goes, 'Hey, c'mere, c'mere. You gotta tell me that joke I told you.' I sort of hesitated, and one of the girls with him said, 'Oh, come on, Jimmy. Why do you make all the waitresses do this?' I looked at him and said, 'Do you mean to tell me that I'm going to run into other waitresses in Montauk who are going to say, Have you waited on that asshole who makes you tell that disgusting joke?' "

"You *said* that?" asked Aileen, wide-eyed with admiration.

"Everybody at the table burst out laughing. He was mortified. He went, 'Well, I'm the asshole who's paying the check.'"

Nobody asked about the tip.

As the Four Farthings' wine collection was being diminished by another bottle, a crash came from one side of the dining room. The few customers who remained jumped out of their seats but calmed when the reason became clear: someone had opened a door between the dining room and the bar. The Farthings bar, the only route to the bathroom, features hundreds of people drinking and smoking, packed together and shouting over Frank Sinatra songs turned up so loud that sound seems to merge with smoke.

At the after-shift table, though, the burst of babel caused no noticeable effect whatever on Lucy, Karol, Aileen, or Brian. They might as well have been sitting by a whispering brook.

Lucy's first job at the Four Farthings was in the bar. "I had to start as a cocktail waitress. We all did. And we all," she paused, "*hated* it. You have to do this whole routine, go 'Hi!' and bat your eyelashes and be real nice and, 'Do you want to do some shots?' This"—she gestured at the dining room—"is like a process. This is 'Hi-how-are-you?' [and] establish a relationship. You talk to the people through the course of the evening. Cocktailing, they may come in, have one drink and leave. 'Can I bring you another one?' 'No, I'm fine. Leave me alone.'"

Not everyone had to serve cocktails. Most male waiters, including Brian, went right to the dining room. Now, however, he scoffed at the idea of any sexual component in serving cocktails in the bar. "I've been groped enough in *this* room."

"Yeah," Aileen laughed, "but that's by your co-workers."

More wine flowed.

"The idea of sexual harassment, by the way," she added, "has not come to the restaurant industry."

"I don't see it here at all," Lucy countered.

"The kitchen help? Are you kidding? There's a *lot* of that stuff. They grab you, say things. There's constant sexual innuendo. When I first started here, for about the first eight months, José was a real problem."

"Little *José?*" Lucy was agog.

"He turns out to be harmless and everything. But the point was, I was inordinately, incredibly uncomfortable, and I couldn't get him to stop, and I couldn't get anyone to make him stop." He would "walk by and pinch your ass, rubbing your rib cage like this." She demonstrated a slippery move. "This isn't your elbow here, you know? I know what's not the right place to touch. Even if you don't agree, if I say no, you stop, right? *No*. Nada. Back off. I-N-S."

She laughed with the others.

Brian, wincing, remembered the night he was "waiting on a bachelorette party, a group of twelve women. They said they were going to supply their own cake." It was shaped like a penis. "It was pretty disgusting, it really was," he said. "An anatomically correct cake. We have to like march out with this." He raised his arm above his shoulder, his hand flattened back.

Lucy looked glum. "I missed that."

"Oh, I was dying!" said Aileen, gleefully. "They walked through this dining room with all these respectable Lincoln Park couples with a giant phallus on a tray."

"It was kind of funny, but . . ." said Brian, pausing for effect, then vamping, "I felt so cheap."

Everyone was laughing now.

The conversation turned serious, with talk about how most restaurant staff members look out for each other. Aileen added sweetly, "It's like when you're trapped in an elevator for hours with people." She then voiced waitresses' common mantra: "I think everyone should wait tables at some point in their lives."

Lucy nodded. "It's also good for developing a certain amount of interpersonal skills. I always had a hard time introducing myself to people when I was in school, even when I was in college. 'Hi, my name's Lucy. What's your name and where are you from?' I never could do that. Waiting tables, you have to walk up to strangers every five minutes: 'Hi, how are you guys doing tonight?'"

Karol does not even hear herself greet her customers. "I have to admit I don't really care how they're doing. I'm thinking about something else. I got to mop my floors, I got to go to the grocery store, I got a final tomorrow—'Hi, how are you?'—then, let's see, I want to organize my files . . ."

Brian says that when he is "on" reciting the specials, the customer sometimes interrupts to introduce himself and ask Brian his name. "They completely downshift into this ridiculous kind of small talk. Meanwhile, you have people sitting around."

Aileen is reminded of a former boyfriend, years ago, whose service as a waiter was so fast and so bad that when a customer told him he had asked for a cheeseburger, not a hamburger, the boyfriend peeled the slice of cheese from the bottom of another plate, where it had stuck, slapped it on the hamburger, and kept going.

"You were on Long Island?" asked Lucy.

"Long Island, yeah."

"Well, that's all the difference."

Another bottle of wine was opened. "They still make a killing, these guys," said Aileen, pouring. "Don't you think this is such a street business? I think it's such a street business."

"I assume they must pay off health inspectors," said Brian.

Along with the subject of people on the periphery of the restaurant business came the subject of parents and other problems. Lucy lamented that her mother, despite having three children in "the service industry," changes her personality in restaurants. "She gets condescending to the waitress."

Brian wondered whether "a lot of older women" feel "a little bit threatened by their server. They think they're going to try to pull a fast one on them."

"If the waiter tries to upsell anything," Lucy went on, "that's the worst thing you could do to my mother. 'Would you like a salad?' 'No, no, no. That *won't* be necessary.'"

"Sometimes you'll get a table," said Brian, where customers say, "'Oh, we're not eating.' Hello? What are you doing here then? Can I come to your office tomorrow and use your typewriter for two hours?"

Aileen waxed philosophical. "In the best of all possible worlds," she would wait tables "as a supplemental thing," because "I think waiting tables is a terrific way to get some balance."

"Some balance I could do without," mumbled Karol.

Aileen remarked that one thing she likes about waiting tables is "the *people* you meet." She clarified that she meant co-workers, not customers. "Not even remotely."

When they go out to eat together, Brian said, "We're the professionals. If you ever go out to dinner with a group of fellow servers, you have the best time, and you know how to order great" and "tip the best."

"It's sort of a weird concept, isn't it?" ventured Lucy. "The whole tipping idea. Why shouldn't it be like any other job? Say the restaurant owners decided to pay us [ten dollars an hour], why wouldn't we give as good service?"

"I want my tips," declared Aileen. A ten-dollar-an-hour salary "would take away some effort at really working hard. When everyone leaves and there's only one waiter on, and all of a sudden you get slammed, in a way you're psyched, because you know you're going to make a lot of money."

Brian said he did well the night before, mostly because "one guy just proposed . . . gave her a huge hunk of diamond, had a couple bottles of nice champagne, and tipped me probably thirty percent, because it was *his* big night and he had to make a big show of it. After all that, she had like this much Cobb salad left"—he held his thumb and forefinger an inch apart—"and she wanted it *wrapped*."

Aileen and Lucy exploded.

"That's what I said: 'This marriage will not last.' "

Nobody at the table was looking forward to tomorrow's shift.

"Saturday night is suburban night in Chicago," said Aileen. It meant "low tips" and "loud people" from blue-collar suburbs.

Brian claimed they act "snooty" to him. "You're thinking to yourself, I make more per hour than you do."

Lucy wondered whether "it's some kind of role thing. They're coming into the city, and it's their big night out. It's their chance to be . . . it sounds ridiculous, but sort of a fantasy thing. They're going to treat the waiter like shit because it's going to change their status."

Aileen maintained that some suburban customers tip well. "They might be defensive because they feel they're looked down upon by city people."

"But wait staff?" asked Lucy. "Everybody's above a *waiter*."

Aileen recalled a Farthings' cocktail waitress who had dated a lawyer with political aspirations. "He stopped dating her because he was annoyed she wouldn't stop waiting tables, even though she was an assistant to a trader. She said, 'What are you talking about? It's fun. The cash is good.' He said, 'Because it doesn't *look* good.' Well, she dropped him, and then he felt very bad after that. He probably realized the error of his ways. Not that he wants to go back out with her."

Lucy commented that her parents disapproved of her choice of job, especially in light of the college degree they had paid for, but that they were even more upset about her brother, who was a waiter, because his future seems more important.

Brian said now that he manages the Four Farthings one night a week, his mother tells people he is a manager. He tells her, "No, I'm not. I'm a waiter that manages once a week."

The future kept hovering.

So did the past.

Lucy described life before her baby was born: "You don't have to get up in the morning. People who are working all night, who cares? You get up at three in the afternoon. You had a great time, you have no money left."

"This is the reason nobody here is a doctor," pronounced Aileen, sitting up straight. "Let's face it. What it takes to be a doctor or a lawyer or a captain of industry is probably more discipline than intelligence."

Waiting tables is "very hard to get out of," Lucy shrugged. "I feel I've been doing it because the pluses outweigh the minuses *so* much that you get sucked into it, and all of a sudden you don't want to look for another job. One of these days God is going to come down and strike me, and I'm going to have this *great* idea about what I'm supposed to be doing with my life."

Karol, whose idea is to finish school, has wound down enough for one shift. She leaves to study for a final.

"Bye, Karol," Aileen waved, adding afterward, "Karol just got a great apartment in a bad neighborhood."

"It's not that bad," Lucy protested.

" 'It's not that bad.' It's just people couldn't hear your screams for miles."

The subject turned to Chicago's neighborhoods, how some rough ones were getting upscale malls. Aileen mused, "Laura Ashley sheets on sale near Cabrini Green."

The Four Farthings' neighborhood is white, as are the restaurant's staff and clientele. Aileen estimated that she has waited on African Americans three times at most. "One black couple walked in, and you could tell they felt uncomfortable, but they were here. They were as middle-class as everybody else, but the place is just so white. They stayed, they ate, they had a fine time. They tipped as well as anybody else and everything like that, but I don't think I ever saw them again."

"It's changing a little bit," Brian said. "My roommate is black, and he got a job here [waiting tables] about three years ago and was the very first black they had ever hired here."

"But he didn't leave under very good terms, wasn't that the story?" asked Lucy.

Brian nodded. "The old manager here was very racist, and they didn't get along at all." He remembered one example of acrimony. It sufficed. The manager called the roommate a "dick-smoking nigger."

That comment prompted the roommate to throw a drink in the manager's face and, consequently, to be fired. Brian shrugged, "The attitude is, what's more disposable, a waiter or manager?"

A newcomer alighted in Karol's chair for a fast visit. Introduced simply as Jane, she looked disconcertingly like a spring flower. She was a Farthings cocktail waitress. Lucy asked her whether she was "makin' some dough, or what?" and then asked how she could stand the bar.

"You get used to it," Jane said. She, too, proved tougher than her sweet looks and light voice may have indicated. "If they don't tip me a dollar every time I get them a drink, then they have to go to the bar and get it themselves."

Brian and Lucy pushed her to reveal the bottom line. "Come on, Jane," said Lucy. "Spill it."

"Well, it was a weird night tonight." Jane said that she was on medication and not feeling well, so she had had only four shots of Jagermeister, and "I haven't been drinking anything else." The last six Fridays, she finally disclosed, she made $250.

Her colleagues fell respectfully silent.

"Tonight I only made 175," she said, looking modest.

"Some people don't make that in a *week*," commented Lucy.

"Then again," Brian argued, "they don't have to deal with that crowd." He asked Jane whether she has problems "with people who are overserved." She said she cuts off at least three people every shift. Her biggest problem, though, is being so short that she cannot see over her customers. Her second biggest problem is having to serve food. "I *hate* food in the bar." She has to get everything, from food to forks to napkins, for people who are standing and "think you're going to hold it for them while they eat." She far prefers serving drinks.

"I've been working here for five years, so I know everybody there. I like the people, I know who to go to, I know who *not* to go to, I know who doesn't tip. And they know damn well I'm not going to serve them because they don't tip. A lot of customers will even joke about it. They'll say, 'Jane, how about fifty cents?' I'm like, 'No, damn it. I want my dollar.'"

"You are ballsy," sighed Lucy.

"I am ballsy, and I grab guys' balls occasionally. They give me too much trouble, I grab 'em. 'Hey, I got control here.'" She grabs "at *least* once a night." Some guys like it, she added. "You can feel a little fluffer coming on sometimes."

Lucy and Aileen laughed and laughed.

"A *fluffer?*" asked Brian, reddening.

"A boner. Then some guys, I don't know, they could be cross-dressers." Once, she says, she was grabbed. "This guy grabbed my chest, and I got the doorman [to] have him kicked out. That's one time I got grabbed when I didn't want to be grabbed."

" 'When I didn't want to be grabbed,' " repeated Lucy happily.

It is 2:30 A.M. Jane has returned to the bar. The others decide the time has come to go home. That means facing a common dangerous moment: being tired, and loaded with drinks and cash. Brian mentions that a waiter friend of his was recently robbed of about five hundred dollars "and beat up badly." There have been muggings in this neighborhood, he adds. The women say nothing as they get to their feet.

It seems that together they can confront anything or anyone inside the Four Farthings, including the realization that the work itself has become a major part of their lives. Outside is a different story.

Oi Yee Lai

Oi Yee Lai is working hard to make money on Wall Street. That is, she is working hard to make money at Kelly's Sports Bar and restaurant, just off Wall Street.

She is an anomaly among the other waitresses, who are all Irish or Irish Americans. Her name (pronounced "oy yee lie") is hardly common here, and she lacks her co-workers' polished, self-assured appearance. The boss, one Tommy McGuire, yells at her, as he did at me when I telephoned her; and by her account he confers an inferior status upon her—not to mention inferior shifts.

She is thirty-two and looks older, with rough skin, anxious eyes, and darting moves. The day we met, she was wearing cheap-looking baggy clothes and a beeper, for keeping track of various relatives with whom she lives in various parts of the city.

When, as planned, I arrived at the end of lunch shift to meet her, she acknowledged me almost angrily, told another waitress I was her travel agent, and propelled me out the door. Minutes later, inside a mostly empty cafeteria where floors were being slopped and chairs banged out of the way, she sat down with a mug of tea, and she became a different woman.

The gruffness and travel agent story were covers. McGuire had yelled at her, too, for my call. She did not want him to yell again for thinking she might talk about him.

Oi Yee Lai is a minority, scrambling. In her home country of Malaysia, she was a minority, scrambling. There, she was an ethnic Chinese in a state whose ruling majority is made up of Muslim Malays.

"It's not a democratic country as the United States are." The "first positions" go to "the Muslim people, not for the Chinese. No matter how smart you are, how [intelligent] you are, they always pick the people of them to be the first.

"I came from a very . . . not a good life. My husband's mentally ill." She said he was diagnosed as having "schizophrenia illness, mental retardation," who got a "violence reaction" when he heard certain noises. "I [have] three children. Before I decided to come to United States, I called for advice from my husband's doctor. I asked my doctor, what happened to him? When he got money, he's okay. When he doesn't have money, he beat everything up."

The doctor advised her to go earn as much money as she could and send it home. She agreed and has been sending back her earnings for five years now. "Maybe the money calm him down. He's not in *any* way hit the children or beat up anything. That's why I'm working as a waitress. It's fast turning money." The phrase was new, but its meaning was not: she can earn money quickly, especially by turning her tables quickly.

Oi Yee Lai has never known easy times. "I'm an orphan. I don't even know what my parents look like. I was brought up by my guardian. She adopted me as a granddaughter. She passed away by a stroke."

Oi Yee finished high school and then "got a college teacher's training and started my career" as a school teacher. When I ventured that that had been quite an accomplishment, she replied, "I think so."

Teaching did not bring in enough money, however, as her family grew and her husband's mental state worsened. So she tutored at home seven evenings a week. To make the most money from the time, she ran simultaneous classes, giving one group work to do while she taught the other.

When teaching and tutoring still did not bring in enough money, she became especially concerned about her children's education. "I can't make a living as a woman in my country to support them. How much I could make? Three hundred dollars? Even my [husband's] medicine. Every month he needs injection twice. They cost eighty dollars Malaysian money."

Leaving Malaysia out of necessity, Oi Yee Lai came to the United

States partly because of language. She grew up speaking Malay and Cantonese, but "I'm English-educated." Nonetheless, her English is challenging. Pronunciation often is off, emphasis is misplaced, pronouns are switched, key words omitted. Still, it works.

The main reason she chose the United States as her destination is that a sister and brother live in New York. She has many siblings, some in the United States and some in Malaysia. All are adopted. "But we treat each other as a true brothers, sisters. We take care of each other very good." She has needed their care.

"The first waitress job I had is five years ago. I came here. I knew nothing. I was looking at Chinese newspaper, by my nephew. I do not know how to read Chinese. I got a job as a cashier. It was in Philadelphia, took about three hours' trip. I was not as I am now. I look very like . . . from my country. My sister taught me to take a contact lens and change my hairstyle and everything. Then I went there. I don't even know what's a quarter, what's a dime. I just arrived two days, I'm already working as a cashier.

"My boss lady had a black, black face on me. Seems like she's not happy I'm working. But my boss give me a chance. I work hard on it, I try to consider the quarter, dime, nickel, and a dollar, five dollars, and everything. I got accustomed with it. My boss trained me that since I don't know how to read Chinese, write by the menu numbers, like number one combination is chicken with broccoli. The kitchen will read by the numbers."

There was good reason the "the boss lady doesn't really likes me. The boss does like me. He is like he's in love with me.

"The following month, my boss came to like me more and more, and his eyes always are on me. He always sit at the back by the kitchen, and the counter is up front. He always look at me. And I stay at his home, his family home, because we are all from New York." Several members of the New York–based staff lived in the house with the boss and his wife. Soon, he tried to have the rest of the staff stay at work an hour later than Oi Yee and then drive her home.

"When he took me home two nights . . . , first he come to my bedroom, try to kiss me. I said, 'No, why are you doing this?' 'Don't you feel that I'm in love with you?' I threw him out. I said, 'No, please, this is not right, where you had a wife here and you're not my husband. I'm here for a living.' 'Oh, I'm so in love with you. I don't love my wife. My wife is stupid,' this and that. This is twenty years of marriage, I don't know how long was it. They were always fighting." (The boss, a Mandarin-speaking Taiwanese, and Oi Yee spoke by default in English.)

The boss was not only spurned; he also soon learned he had a rival. "The kitchen man in the same restaurant also in love with me. It's a triangle love affair. One night, the boss is counting his business [money] with the wife, in the bedroom," while the kitchen man, Oi Yee, and another waitress sat in the living room watching television. Oi Yee and the kitchen man stayed up late "still talking and talking."

The boss appeared about midnight, saw them, and fired the kitchen man. "The kitchen man was so mad. He came back to New York and talked to my family that he saw the boss has been loving me, and he asked my sister-in-law to send me back here before I was trapped by the boss. My sister-in-law called me, 'Better quick, come back here.'" Oi Yee did as she was told.

Through another family connection, with a "boss lady from Hong Kong," Oi Yee for the first time began waiting tables. The site was a Chinese restaurant in "Huntington town" on Long Island. "I did not know much about waitress. I learned quick. How to carry trays. The restaurant was newly opened, by a Germany owner." The owner, whom she liked, rented a three-bedroom house for the staff and told them that they could arrange it however they wanted.

"I'm the only lady waitress there. They're all waiters and kitchen men. Do you know where I am sleep? I sleep in the kitchen." The men came to the kitchen constantly, she said, "midnight time or whatever time they like" to get drinks. "They play mah jong or they cuss. I'm not a gambler. I like to make phone calls back to New York to talk with my friends—and that I would not be allowed. I got to do it secretly, hiding me." For some reason, the "boss lady" did not want her to use the phone.

Although Oi Yee gave this boss credit for letting her have "a chance as a waitress," the woman extracted her own reward. "I had to do a lot side work. I got to cut up the cardboard for her to do the packing [for] pick-up orders, the cardboard they put underneath the shopping bag so it will not turn up. This is not a waitress job. She been taking *too* much advantage from me. I do a lot duck sauce, mustard sauce. Tell you, I do a lot things. But I'm a very patient girl. I know I come here for money— it's not for argument and it's not for trouble."

For relief, Oi Yee walked to the nearby harbor. "I go there, sit down, and think." Why, she wondered, did the "very kind" owner from Germany "let us use it freely, the phone calls," but the boss objected. "I do not know why this boss lady always against me. I do not have a privacy [for] myself. Like this boss"—she gestured in the direction of the sports bar—"controlling me. Of all the place I work, it's like every boss is controlling me. The more I respect them, the more they control on me. It gets so hard. I'm a hard-working . . . I run fast, I turn tables fast, and usually I'm doing the right way. Still they like to take *more* control of you."

Very softly, amid the clang of cafeteria cleanup, Oi Yee Lai cried. She then apologized and wiped her eyes with a napkin.

Oi Yee Lai made her way to Manhattan, with mixed results. Fired, for reasons she still does not understand, for making phone calls, she found a job at a restaurant on 14th Street and Tenth Avenue "run by Taiwanese people. That is terrible. They pay us ten dollars a day" for more than a twelve-hour day and for side work that included cleaning windows, mirrors, "ceiling glass," and the bathroom. With tips, she netted a maximum of three dollars an hour in 1990s New York.

That was not all Oi Yee Lai netted. The owner's father, "an *old* man," she frowned, "grabbed me when I get ice, during morning shift. He's trying to play with me. I pull off, I say, 'Please, be respectful, I'm only here for a job.' He say, 'I don't care. You work for me.'"

After she quit, her luck suddenly improved. She found Lun Chung restaurant, "run by Hong Kong people," a block away. "I love that job. Everybody's friendly, even the boss are friendly. I learned a lot of things there. I learned how to make drinks, cocktails. I met a good boss, Mr. Tang. Everything is computerized. This is the most happiest restaurant I ever worked." She almost smiled. "We are like a family." When Lun Chung went out of business, she moved ten blocks away to a Szechuan restaurant, where "the kitchen man" tried to grab her. "I was yelling. Nobody help me, because it was in the walk-in fridge. No matter how big you yell, nobody heard." She managed to free herself.

In retrospect, Oi Yee showed much empathy for her countless grabbers. "Restaurant job is a long hours. Early the morning and late at night. Maybe it seems [they only have] a long hours job, and they are tired, and they feel they're really in need of some womans. So whenever they think you got opportunity, like you walk in the fridge or whatever you do in the basement, they take advantage of you. Just to *feel* you. What I'm thinking. I've been thinking and thinking, 'Why are men be acting like this?' Some, like the kitchen man, they're from China. They come to the United States by themself, they left family in their country. To feel need for a woman, they take up a chance. I had experience a lot when I was working in Chinese restaurant. Not in this Kelly's Sports Bar, thanks God."

In Oi Yee's next job, it seemed she had finally made it. Thanks to her bartending experience, she began tending bar at a Chinese restaurant a stroll from the United Nations. "I'm happy there, too. A lot of customers like me. I make a lot of money. I got thirty-five dollars, paid, a day." She also got whopper gratuities. "I got tips around a hundred dollars, a hundred-fifty dollars, and good customers that pay me good, huge tips. I knew a lot of famous people there."

The name that stood out was Jake LaMotta, the boxer portrayed in the movie *Raging Bull*. She also named other favored customers, including diplomats from the Nigerian embassy. "I got good tips from them. It's a hard work though, because they do not hire Spanish people." Chinese "kitchen men" do not do as much work, she said.

At the bar, "I got bigger tips than their own bar business, the register. Maybe that is why the jealousy happen. I suspect." A young manager, a brother of the "boss lady," now was "always against me. It seems that we have so much misunderstanding. He used to yell at me. Maybe he *like* to, I do not know why." The more he yelled, "the more nervous I am," and the more she had to do, including being in charge of take-out orders, which meant learning to write in Chinese. "I pick up fast."

This new responsibility meant that in addition to lugging up cases of beer from the basement and the "buckets of ice I got to get prepared, clean up the shelves, clean up the bottles, the glasses," and serving her customers ("you got to talk with them; that's what they're coming in for"), she now had to answer the phone. "It's so busy with the take-out orders, especially lunch time. I've got one phone . . . under my neck and my head, other phone calls, and either making drinks or collecting money. I'm doing two or three jobs all at same time. I never complain. As long as the boss happy, I'm happy. I try to help them as much as I can. But the *more* I help, it seems the more they are expecting from you. Eventually, it happen to be your job now."

When that place too was sold, Oi Yee went farther downtown, to another Taiwanese-owned restaurant that, when business slowed, seemed to pit one employee against the other to see who generated the most business. To her rescue this time came a customer who knew Tommy McGuire. "That is how I [came to] work in Kelly's Sports Bar."

Oi Yee knew from the start, two years ago, that she would have to prove herself in her first non-Asian work setting. "The boss lady, Mrs. McGuire, says they like to hire Irish people. But the way I'm working, how fast I turn, how fast I run the staircase, and I do not ask for more, I do not talk much—maybe that is why Mrs. McGuire feel it's all right, even though I'm not Irish. I get ten dollars paid for eleven to three."

On slow days, Oi Yee makes about twenty-five dollars in tips, but during "quick business, I make sixty dollars. The job is not hard. It's only hamburgers, shrimp in a basket. It's not that heavy. And it's not so much side work as we had in the Chinese restaurant." Also, Kelly's does have "Spanish people working the kitchen."

"I treat all customers good, and I like respectful customers. We talk nice, be friendly, not touching, not taking opportunity of you—that's the customer I like. Most of my customers, if they know about me, they know that I've got high morality."

Kelly's customers are one factor, McGuire apparently is another. Oi Yee became visibly annoyed in talking about him, describing how he casually passed on phone messages and allowed calls for male employees but chewed her out when Citibank, unbeknownst to her, called to confirm her employment, in regard to a credit card application.

"I just swallow my survival. I do my job. Sometimes I feel like I want to quit," although "I don't feel like changing jobs very often. This is not my characters. If I'm happy here, I know the system, I'd like to keep on working."

In fact, she wanted to take over the lucrative Friday evening shift of a waitress who was going back to Ireland. Instead, Oi Yee was assigned Mondays, a slow day easily managed by one person, and had to share it and split tips with a McGuire nephew who had just arrived from Ireland, with no serving experience.

Now, by her own choice, Oi Yee works only lunches. That way, "I can do evening part-time job, answering phone calls for people, and I can do some studies by myself." She is taking a course in medical billing. She looked worried. "I . . . I been thinking, is this restaurant job suitable for me? I feel like I'm lost interest in it." Yet she realized that she makes the same for three hours as she would in an office for eight hours.

She was concerned about something else, too. After her last class in medical billing, she is finally going back to visit Malaysia. "Five years, long time," she said softly. "I always have dream about that. I do not [know] if they ever recognize me, especially my younger son." He was four then and nine now. "Maybe another few more years, I'm finished with responsibility."

She used the same word about waitressing. "I can't complain. I know serving is my responsibility." She repeated, as if loathe to criticize what kept her husband sane and her children safe, "I don't have any bad feelings about my job."

We stood to leave. Oi Yee Lai, seemingly unaware of her actions, grabbed a clean napkin in one hand, picked up the salt and pepper shakers and ketchup bottle in the other, and quickly wiped the table.

EPILOGUE

Toward the end of my listening, observing, and reading, I decided I should see the view from the other side of the tray again myself. I did not aspire to be a real waitress—I knew that a single customer neglecting to say "Please" would send me packing. Instead, I cast about for a mini-immersion and was offered one by a friend. Ann Walker, of the wondrous Ann Walker Catering company near San Francisco, hired me to be part of a crew serving lunch in the city to high-tech conventioneers.

Because the job entailed only a shared group gratuity rather than individual tips, I understood that it would lack a central element of waitress work, but I believed it might offer me an overall sense of the experience. Ann said she could tell from the evenings I hosted our all-women's poker group that I had the necessary amiability to serve. Buoyed by the compliment, I began outfitting myself as instructed, in black and white. I was fine at adapting my own clothes but felt a surge of strangeness at having to buy a bow tie. It was not, well, me. So *this* is what they mean about uniforms, I thought.

I got to the convention center, bow-tied but buoyed up, and helped to assemble and then set the acre of tables our crew later would dismantle. One waitress whispered to me that she felt "off," as if she might "drop a creamer or something." I felt flattered. So *this* is what they mean about connection with co-workers, I thought.

Lunch started amiably enough. Serving a huge catered sit-down meal is easy, especially if there are no people like my customer self, inquiring about a meatless entree or other alternatives. Gradually, though, the lack of acknowledgment from almost everyone in front of whom I placed a plate of food wore amiability away.

Silent snarls formed in my head. Hey, buster, mind moving your *elbow* so I can put your meal down? Say, lady, how about *thanks?* Amid the chewing throng emerged a few cherished humanitarians. A man worried that my wrist might hurt from carrying such an awfully big, heavy coffeepot. I nearly hugged him. Actually, dear sir, darling sir, it *has* begun to ache.

Toward the end of dessert service, another waitress snapped at me—me! her sister for the shift!—for pouring coffee outside my station. My mouth flapped open. But, but . . .

Then, as I was about to leave the floor, having served a last round of coffee in both correct and incorrect locales, I felt a jab to my left hip. Stunned, I turned. At the other end of a pointed finger was a well-dressed blonde woman, about thirty, who coolly told me she wished to have more decaf.

In a daze, I got it. In a daze, I poured it into her cup, not on her head. Bitch! I finally seethed first to myself, then to the first waitress I collared on my way back to the kitchen. She empathized, as by now I knew she would.

In the kitchen, over background sounds of the program—high-techies applauding their shining futures—we learned that the woman catering the lunch event (Ann Walker had merely arranged staffing), in addition to denying us any break or any food—some mix-up with a meal truck—had now decided that we were not getting the promised tip. (Ann later fixed *that*.) All these variables, I thought, all these uncertainties.

On the way home, as the hours' experiences rolled through my mind like movie credits, the jab stood out. I am now, as then, appalled at my meekness. What if the jabber were a tipper and my tip depended on staying meek? I cannot bear to imagine it.

The women in these pages, and nearly as many who were omitted for reasons of space, did more than imagine it. They are sturdier souls than I, nurturers with nerve. Yet, I asked myself, why do they need such traits? Waitresses deliver *food* to the *hungry*. What is the big deal? Does the act of serving another, an act encouraged in all religions I know of, cut too close to conscience? Do the servers remind the served of what they are not doing? Or what they could be doing tomorrow? Waiting tables, most women know, is the singular job they have had, or might have, sometime in their lives.

From the point of view of waitresses, the big deal is self-evident.

The big deal is the toting of heavy symbolism—never mind the trays—while facing assumptions from those on the receiving end that they could do the work equally well. The big deal is not knowing how one will be treated and whether one will be paid. The big deal is the toll of the toil, the complexity of performing logistically demanding, hard, and nimble work at an often tense fulcrum between wildly varying cooks and customers.

Almost all of this had been news to me.

When I first started interviewing waitresses, I had not known that so many cooks were lascivious or vengeful. I had not known how much their mood could affect their food.

I had not known that so many customers, even if a minority, were so insulting. Nor had I calculated the effect they have well beyond their percentage. (Obviously, the jab has not been forgotten.)

I had not known that bosses could get away with what they do.

I had not known that waitresses' pay was often some two dollars an hour, *legally*.

I had not known that the work could be so dangerous.

I had not even known about the turmoil of toast.

There was more on-the-job drinking and drug use than I had expected. There was, with notable exceptions, far less talk about food than I had expected; some waitresses barely referred to it. (In the course of years of interviewing, not one recipe was exchanged.) There were far more behind-the-scenes put-downs of problematic customers than I had anticipated. Few women admitted putting down those who did not *deserve* it, but one can assume that Albert Einstein might have been dissed for not wearing socks or speaking with an accent, that the winner of the Nobel Peace Prize might have been stuck in a corner for being a woman or an African American. Despite the stereotyping that waitresses abhor when it is directed against them, they are not immune to engaging in it themselves.

Waitresses, after all, are of us.

Angels they might not all be, but hard-working women they are. Their loads need lightening. Stories they told made me want to wing through restaurants as Avenger Waitress, waving banners for reform. In my fantasy, I printed up cards to give to troublesome customers. "The management and staff are terribly sorry, but the waitress who accepts rude behavior is off today." Or, "If you leave quietly now, we will not call the police."

Next in my flight of fantasy, I plastered notices at front doors stating that each party would be allowed one free change of order or one plate of food sent back; the second would cost double. Another notice informed customers that dressing is served only in the middle, not on the side. I then flew into kitchens and walk-in refrigerators and hung more signs: "The videotape being made of your behavior will be sent to the person you most respect and the waitresses' pro bono lawyers." Then I flew into the boss's office and insisted that the wearing of uniforms, including high heels, as well as the choice of uniform must be voluntary. Customers can find their waitresses or waiters, I announced, simply by looking for people who are standing.

Triumphant from my successes, I was set to tackle tips. Oh, dear. Avenger Waitress had to pause to ponder.

Tips started out, supposedly, as coinage customers dropped into a jar marked "To Insure Promptness." (Was promptness or pittance of pay the real impetus?) Tips do more than ensure promptness now, however. They usually represent all the money waitresses and waiters earn. And they also serve other purposes.

They can, if generous, bestow a feeling of appreciation.

They can, if adequate, impart a sense of independence within a setting of dependence.

Most of all, though, they can act as a wild card, just as undercover waitress Frances Donovan reported at the beginning of the twentieth century. Tips are the gamble in an often predictable routine, with waitresses the players primed for payoff. The seduction of the gamble, plus the sense of individual entrepreneurship, plus the reluctance of restaurant owners to figure out another form of payment, all give the tipping system staying power.

I started this project with few opinions about tips. I end by thinking tips are unfair, soul-robbing, or, as social workers of past generations said, "pernicious." Alcohol and proximity to men who drank it may have begun waitresses' fall from social grace, but tips ensure it.

Tips make waitresses the most financially vulnerable women among this country's legal and illegal laborers. Even prostitutes, with whom some waitresses ruefully identify, get the money first. Waitresses may not get it at all. Whim, thy name is tip. Cheapskate, thy name is tip. Show-off big spender, arithmetic failure, happy clueless muncher, thy name is tip. Expense-account binger, thy name is tip. Rejected flirter, disgruntled steak eater, peeved water drinker, thy name is tip.

Tips, I am convinced, should not be used as carrots or as sticks. Whether or not they ensure promptness, they do ensure abuse.

The major trouble with tips is that they turn each of us from customer into employer, whether we want the job or not. The "shame of the tipping system is that the customer thinks he is paying your salary, so he can treat you any way he feels."[1] He, or she, may not be deft at figuring a proper pay scale anyway. Why, then, should eaters hold the power of the purse any more than customers buying any other commodity or service?

The pause over, Avenger Waitress did away with tips and in their place added an across-the-board service charge—varying it by region, restaurant, and/or the server's experience or ability to push the pies. With the cash, salaries were paid, as well as a percentage of health insurance. Avenger Waitress announced that the big wins would now be less likely, unless customers wanted to show appreciation in the same way they do toward other professionals who serve them, but waitresses would no longer have to fawn or flirt to earn a living.

There was a drawback.

Many waitresses were miffed at Avenger Waitress and told her to fly off. The fantasy ended.

Despite the obvious importance of tips, they are, I inferred from the waitresses, not the major factor in this very American job. Rather, something incalculable is the linchpin, something I hoped I would be wrong about—and was not. It is class.

When I began this project, it was with the aim, to paraphrase the seventeenth-century poet John Milton, of serving those who only stand and wait. I end with a stew of emotions at waitresses' attempts to hurdle the barriers not only to a decent and secure income but also to self-esteem. Even though the United States is much more socially flexible than other countries (or at least any other countries I know), and even though character is supposed to count more than, say, being in the social register, and even though being snooty or stuck-up is not meant as a compliment, and even though, thanks to constitutional amendments, we are all equal in the eyes of society and its laws, classism lives. I already knew how riven my country is by sexism and racism, but I had repressed an awareness of classism. I can no longer. The great American melting pot may be in the kitchen, but—to strain the metaphor—it certainly is not present in the dining room.

Waitresses, of course, know all about class. No matter how much they differ in almost every way, they know in which class they are expected to reside as long as they are waiting tables. Some resent the designation, some blow it off, and some seem to accept it—but all, surely, would be better off without it. It is awful, plain old awful, what they feel they must accept to get paid, as it is incalculable what they internalize. (Surely behind-the-scenes put-downs of customers are a means to get even.) Not all waitresses may sense the collective jabs to their self-esteem, but I can think of few who feel immune. Classism is as inherent to the job as sore feet.

Knowing well the women's hurdles, what surprised me most of all were the glows.

I did not expect waitresses to speak with so much affection about the job itself, whether it involved friendship with co-workers, connection with customers, or the act of serving an appreciated meal. Mostly, though, I did not expect so much pride.

Almost every waitress, even (omitted) ones who loathed everything about waiting tables or who delivered a third remade latte embellished with spit, bragged about a skill. I know how to turn a customer's frown into a smile. I memorize orders. (What a fraught word "orders" is!) I get along with cooks. I keep children happy, read my tables, work the computer well, promote teamwork. I make my plates look nice.

All the evidence points to a painful paradox: American waitresses, so intrinsic to American life, are proud of doing well what they know they are dismissed for doing at all.

ACKNOWLEDGMENTS

Above all, I thank each woman who so generously took the time and often emotional effort to tell me her waitress story. Each story, of course, was unique, each insight breathtaking. Many women who do not appear in these pages—whose stories were set aside, with reluctance, only for reasons of space and organization—will, I hope, appear in another volume.

Thank you, too, to everyone who helped me find these women, including the more than one hundred people who answered my "Reader's Query" in the *New York Times Book Review* and offered either their own stories or those of others. Thanks to other strangers met along the way, in person or not, who helped me track down the women I sought.

In the years it took me to research and write this book, I availed myself of friends, too, who helped in countless ways, from showering me with newspaper clippings, photographs, and assorted waitressiana to bestowing sundry other offerings. For putting me up while I was en route, gourmet breakfasts, please, for Kathy and Bill Wahl, Mary Brown, Susan Brownmiller, Ellen Conley, Tallulah Owings Guadagnino, Carol Morse Sibley, Paula Harper, Julie Smith, Stanley Dry, Susan Spiegel, and Stewart Halperin. Margie Watson and Catherine Blount offered not only their stories but also their guest bedrooms. For various other kindnesses, described or not, extravagant beverages of choice for Linda Connor, Gordon Craig, Karen Furey, Frances Goldin, Barbara Hall (and tablemates), Ella Leffland, Laura Merlo, Lindsay Miller, Kay and Bill Raftery, and Evelyn White. For writing letters of recommendations for grants, if with zilch success, endless trips to the salad bar for Elena Danielson, Earl Frounfelter, Leah Garchik, Elaine Maimon, and Agnes Peterson, among others. Charlie Curley urged me late in the writing to apply to the Marin Arts Council for a grant. Thanks to him for the nudge, and thanks to MAC for the award. Margie's story made the difference.

Once each interview was finished, I treated myself to the necessary luxury of having it transcribed. A raft of terrific practitioners came my way (and thank you, Lew Litzky, for the loan of your transcribing machine), none more diligent, finicky, and perfect than Amy Smith. When I proofed her work (my method is to relisten to each tape while reading the transcript on the computer screen), I mostly did stretching exercises.

To help me get my waitress facts of life straight, I thank the staff of the National Restaurant Association, the assiduous query answerers at the U.S. Department of Labor, and the staff at Colonial Williamsburg. Thanks also to Grace Kemp at the Susan B. Anthony House for the story she provided and to Kate Toll at the University of California Press for pinning down a classical waitress for me.

After researching came writing and, in the nick of time, the formation of the world's best writing group. For careful listening over years and drafts, for hosannas and nitpicks, I send, along with thanks and love, rivers of herbal tea and crates of popcorn to the women who made this a better book: Whitney Chadwick, Mary Felstiner, Carol Field, Diana Ketcham, Cyra McFadden, Jean McMann, Carol Monpere, Annegret Ogden, and Diana O'Hehir. A barrel of spicy taco chips for helping me cut my behemoth manuscript down to a svelter profile goes to Cyra "The Slasher" McFadden.

Special thanks and free desserts to the University of California Press—viz., to my editor Naomi Schneider and Press director Jim Clark for understanding immediately what, and for whom, I wanted this book to be and to Sue Heinemann and Mary Renaud for their scrutiny.

Ellen Levine, my agent, understood immediately, too, and worked to make the idea a reality.

There are two people I wish I could thank for their cheer and support. The late Charles Kuralt gave me years of encouragement, packed with waitress-related newspaper clippings. My late father-in-law, the Rev. William M. Perdue, not only offered loving assumptions but also set the family standard for generous tipping and an appreciation of working women, related or not.

Much as I am indebted to all the above, Jonathan Brittain Perdue deserves my full course of gratitude, among other nouns. Here, finally, words fail.

NOTES

Prologue

1. The Labor Department's report of occupational employment statistics for the year 2000 cites a total of 2,008,760 restaurant waiters and waitresses (a total that excludes "counter attendants, cafeteria, food concession, and coffee shop" workers); see U.S. Department of Labor, Bureau of Labor Statistics, "2000 National Occupational Employment and Wage Estimates," news release, November 15, 2001. The National Restaurant Association foraged through unpublished Labor Department tabulations for me to figure that 78 percent of these workers are female.

Chapter 1. A Brief, and Subjective, History of Waitressing

1. Marquis de Chastellux, *Travelers in North America in the Years 1780, 1781, and 1782,* ed. Howard C. Rice Jr. (Chapel Hill: University of North Carolina Press, 1963), vol. 2, p. 404; cited in Patricia A. Gibbs, "Taverns in Tidewater Virginia, 1700–1774" (master's thesis, William and Mary College, 1968).

2. Kym S. Rice, *Early American Taverns* (Chicago: Regnery Gateway, 1983), pp. 51, 88.

3. J. M. Fenster, "The Taste of Time," *American Heritage,* April 1997, p. 40.

4. Rice, *Early American Taverns,* p. 33.

5. Ibid., p. 55.

6. Heather R. Wainwright, "Inns and Outs: Anne Pattison's Tavern Account Book, 1744–1749" (master's thesis, Armstrong Atlanta State University, 1998), pp. 1, 11, 14, 15, 47, 60, 105.

7. Fenster, "The Taste of Time," p. 40.

8. Ibid., p. 39.

9. Lynn Sherr, *Failure Is Impossible: Susan B. Anthony in Her Own Words* (New York: Times Books, 1995), p. 59.

10. Anne Frances Springsteed, *The Expert Waitress: A Manual for the Pantry, Kitchen, and Dining-Room* (New York: Harper and Brothers, 1894); Janet McKenzie Hill, *The Up-to-Date Waitress* (Boston: Little, Brown, 1914 [1906]).

11. Springsteed, *The Expert Waitress,* pp. 12, 81; Hill, *The Up-to-Date Waitress,* p. 21.

12. Springsteed, *The Expert Waitress,* p. 90; Hill, *The Up-to-Date Waitress,* p. vii.

13. Hill, *The Up-to-Date-Waitress,* p. vi.

14. Frances Donovan, *The Woman Who Waits* (1920; reprint North Stratford, N.H.: Ayer Company Publishers, 1974), pp. 11, 14, 173. All quotations used by permission of the publisher.

15. Ibid., p. 16.

16. Ibid., p. 18.

17. Ibid., pp. 27, 28.

18. Ibid., p. 115.

19. Ibid., pp. 50, 51.

20. Ibid., pp. 55, 56.

21. Ibid., pp. 57, 83, 84, 101.

22. Dorothy Sue Cobble, *Dishing It Out: Waitresses and Their Unions in the Twentieth Century* (Urbana: University of Illinois Press, 1991), p. 116.

23. Louise de Koven Bowen, "The Girl Employed in Hotels and Restaurants" (Chicago: Juvenile Protective Association of Chicago, 1912).

24. Donovan, *The Woman Who Waits,* pp. 211, 218.

25. Ibid., p. 94.

26. Bowen, "The Girl Employed in Hotels and Restaurants."

27. Donovan, *The Woman Who Waits,* pp. 219, 220, 223.

28. Bowen, "The Girl Employed in Hotels and Restaurants."

29. Donovan, *The Woman Who Waits,* pp. 138, 139.

30. Ibid., pp. 95, 227.

31. Ibid., pp. 63, 64.

32. Ibid., pp. 68, 69.

33. Ibid., pp. 71, 72, 215.

34. Ibid., pp. 80, 81.

35. Ibid., pp. 102, 196.

36. Ibid., pp. 70, 198.

37. Ibid., pp. 201, 202.

38. Ibid., pp. 140, 145, 128.

39. Ibid., pp. 129, 130, 131, 225.

40. Ibid., pp. 134, 131, 132, 222.

41. William H. Whyte, *Human Relations in the Restaurant Industry* (New York: McGraw-Hill, 1948), p. 2.

42. Ibid., pp. 93, 94, 97.

43. Ibid., pp. 369, 370.

44. Ibid., pp. 99, 100. Whyte also suggested doing away with the job of checker, the person who checked every meal on its way to a customer to ensure that portions and other aspects of the order were correct: "Anyone who administers only punishment must inevitably be a source of friction" (p. 88).

45. Ibid., pp. 120, 121.

46. Ibid., pp. 70, 71.

47. Ibid., p. 74.

48. Ibid., pp. 104, 107.

49. Ibid., pp. 273, 110, 111.

50. Ibid., p. 126.

51. Ibid., p. 147.

52. Ibid., pp. 282, 283, 284, 285, 286.

53. Erving Goffman, *The Presentation of Self in Everyday Life* (New York: Anchor Books, 1959), p. 206.

54. Greta Foff Paules, *Dishing It Out: Power and Resistance Among Waitresses in a New Jersey Restaurant* (Philadelphia: Temple University Press, 1991), pp. 137–138, 132.

55. Ibid., pp. 133, 135, 138.

56. Ibid., p. 138.

57. Ibid., p. 173.

58. Joanne Finkelstein, *Dining Out: A Sociology of Modern Manners* (New York: New York University Press, 1989), p. 122.

59. W. Somerset Maugham, *Of Human Bondage* (New York: Garden City Publishing, 1939); Dorothy Allison, *Bastard Out of Carolina* (New York: Dutton, 1993); Denise Chavez, *Face of an Angel* (New York: Farrar, Straus and Giroux, 1994). For an example of Carver's writing about waitresses, see Raymond Carver, "Fat," in *Where I'm Calling From* (New York: Atlantic Monthly Press, 1986).

60. Erle Stanley Gardner, *The Case of the Worried Waitress* (New York: Pocket Books, 1967).

61. James M. Cain, *Mildred Pierce,* in *Cain X 3* (New York: Knopf, 1969), p. 143.

62. Ibid., p. 166.

63. See Studs Terkel's interview with waitress Dolores Dante in *Working: People Talk About What They Do All Day and How They Feel About What They Do* (New York: Pantheon, 1974), pp. 293–298.

64. Linda Montano, comp., *Performance Artists Talking in the Eighties* (Berkeley: University of California Press, 2000), p. 155.

65. Donovan, *The Woman Who Waits,* p. 15.

Chapter 2. Slices of American History

1. Bernard L. Fontana, *Of Earth and Little Rain* (Flagstaff: Northland Press, 1981; Tucson: University of Arizona Press, 1989), p. 118.

2. Ibid., p. 113.

3. Peter Blaine Sr., with Michael S. Adams, *Papagos and Politics* (Tucson: Arizona Historical Society, 1981), p. 2.

4. Ibid., pp. 49–50.

5. For a firsthand description of the ceremony (from the 1930s) and the texts of the songs, see anthropologist Ruth Murray Underhill's *Singing for Power: The Song Magic of the Papago Indians of Southern Arizona* (Tucson: University of Arizona Press, 1993).

6. Fontana, *Of Earth and Little Rain,* p. 50.

7. No, it was coffee and doughnuts, recalled Franklin McCain, one of the

students, who is quoted in Howell Raines, *My Soul Is Rested: The Story of the Civil Rights Movement in the Deep South* (New York: Putnam, 1977; New York: Viking 1983), p. 76.

8. Such comments are also cited in ibid., pp. 77–78.

9. According to Franklin McCain, one of the four students, they had chosen Woolworth's because it was well known to *them* for advertising so much and accepting their money but not allowing them to sit down and eat (ibid., p. 76). McCain clearly was pleased that the protest spread throughout the South, but he implied in an interview with Raines that the group's initial focus had simply been Woolworth's (ibid., p. 81).

10. Dorothy Sue Cobble, *Dishing It Out: Waitresses and Their Unions in the Twentieth Century* (Urbana: University of Illinois Press, 1991), pp. 62, 193.

11. In contrast to Beulah Compton, Jackie Walsh was much less responsive when I interviewed her. She was also interviewed by Lucy Kendall in 1980 for the California Historical Society; see "Oral History of Jackie Walsh," 1980, California Historical Society, North Baker Research Library, San Francisco, MS 3587, pp. 172, 173. In both interviews, Walsh was notable for countenancing not a word of criticism about the international, for which she had worked, although she did occasionally mention shoddy work by individual local officers.

12. In 1995, the U.S. government put HERE, which at the time had 350,000 members, under federal supervision. The *New York Times* reported that the move ended "more than a decade of investigations that had repeatedly found that the union was a bastion of organized crime," mentioning that a decade earlier a presidential commission had named HERE "one of the most corrupt in the nation" (Clifford J. Levy, "Federal Monitor to Oversee Hotel Employees' Union," *New York Times,* September 7, 1995, sec. B., p. 6). A former FBI official, who had spent his career investigating organized crime in the United States, testified to a House Judiciary subcommittee in 1996 that organized crime was alive and well in four unions, including the restaurant workers. He contended that a staff job with the restaurant union "transforms an ugly criminal caterpillar into a very dangerous but beautiful butterfly. It gave instant legitimacy, an unlimited expense account, legitimate income for income tax purposes, plus all the money you could steal from union dues, an entree into the business community and an entree to those aspiring for political office" (statement of Jim Moody, former deputy assistant director, Criminal Investigations Division, FBI, in testimony before the House Judiciary Subcommittee on Crime, Hearings on the Administration's Efforts Against the Influence of Organized Crime in the Laborers International Union of North America, 104th Cong., 2d sess., July 24, 1996).

One example of corruption was the case of Ray Lane, head of what became Local 2850 in Oakland, California, who was imprisoned in 1980 on numerous charges, including racketeering and embezzlement. Two union waitresses charged that Lane's egregious behavior included trying to turn them into prostitutes (unpublished interview with Karen Seritis and Terry DeLoache, conducted by Robert Kubey, ca. 1980). (When I interviewed him in 1999, Jim du Pont, who was then president of the local, groaned into his car phone when I mentioned Lane. "I live with his legacy," he said [telephone interview, January 26, 1999].)

13. Cobble, *Dishing It Out*, p. 78.

14. Ibid., p. 134.

15. The record of HERE and various locals toward African American members or potential members was erratic, reflecting the racism of the era as well as the employers' tactic of playing off minority groups against one another, especially during strikes (ibid., pp. 12, 67, 77, 78, 169).

16. Sweet is portrayed only positively in the pages of Cobble's *Dishing It Out* (see especially pp. 64 and 65), with no mention of this incident.

17. Beulah Compton also described how HERE had commissioned Matthew Josephson to write the book *Union House, Union Bar: A History of the Hotel and Restaurant Employees and Bartenders International Union*. She said that he met with her for several days "to get all the skinny" about the Seattle local and knew "all about the contract trouble." She further said that the international would not accept his initial manuscript and refused to pay him unless he edited it to their liking and that she "persuaded him to go along" because of the years he had spent on the work. The AFL-CIO published the book in 1956.

18. Former FBI official Jim Moody testified that because restaurant workers are often transient, they could exercise "little oversight of union operations" (statement before the House Judiciary Subcommittee on Crime, July 24, 1996).

19. San Francisco's Jackie Walsh opposed tips as well, in part because if waitresses did not report them as taxable earnings, the money would not count toward future Social Security benefits (Kendall, "Oral History of Jackie Walsh," pp. 80, 170).

20. Cobble, *Dishing It Out*, pp. 192–203.

21. Lesley Poling-Kempes, *The Harvey Girls: Women Who Opened the West* (New York: Paragon, 1989; New York: Marlowe, 1991), pp. 35, 36.

22. Text from the Harvey exhibit at the Arizona Hall of Fame, Maxine T. Edwards, curator, Phoenix, 1996, p. 33.

23. Ibid., p. 83.

24. Ibid., p. 189.

25. Ibid., p. 195.

26. The buyer was AMFAC Corporation, in 1968 (ibid., p. 209).

27. Peratis, who focused her career on employment discrimination, said in a phone interview, "We were all very young." She described herself as being "so green" that she did not know that Jeanne and Cathryn would make such good plaintiffs (interview with the author, May 28, 1996).

28. Andrew Feinberg, "Checking Out Waitresses," *Cosmopolitan*, July 1981, p. 225.

Chapter 3. "We Should Be Respected": Professionals

1. Clyde Watson's ship was taking part in "Exercise Tiger" in preparation for D-Day when a German torpedo hit it and killed more than 700 men. Despite being thrown in the water, his back broken, he was rescued. After a government

cover-up to hide the death toll, his unit was finally recognized in 1995 by President Clinton.

Chapter 4. High Ends

1. Tara Weingarten, "Alice's Wonderland," *Newsweek,* August 27, 2001; Michele Anna Jordan, "Serving Werner Herzog's Shoe," *San Francisco Focus,* August 1996, p. 58.

2. As of early 2002, the tab for one person's meal with tax and a 15 percent added-on gratuity is $93.15. That excludes any drinks.

Chapter 6. Diners and Downward

1. The newspaper article cited a Cornell University study reporting that waitresses who sketched happy faces on their checks increased their tips an average of 18 percent. Waiters who added the same sketch lost 3 percent. See "Smile!" *USA Today,* November 4, 1996, p. 1.

2. Joanne Mulcahy, "Waiting for What?" *Hurricane Alice: A Feminist Quarterly* 9, no. 3 (Winter 1993): pp. 1–3.

3. Ibid., p. 1.

4. Several cases of racial discrimination at Denny's restaurants received widespread publicity. In 1993, on the same day a federal court in California had ordered the national chain of restaurants to stop discriminating against African American customers, six African American Secret Service agents at a Denny's in Annapolis, Maryland, claimed they waited so long for their food that they in effect were denied service, while their white colleagues were served (Lynne Duke, "Secret Service Agents Allege Racial Bias at Denny's; Six Blacks to File Lawsuit Saying They Were Denied Service at Annapolis Restaurant," *Washington Post,* May 24, 1993, p. 4). In 1994, Denny's paid nearly $46 million to settle what had become two class-action lawsuits, stemming from incidents in California and Maryland (Retha Hill, "Plaintiffs Enjoy an Anti-Bias Victory: Secret Service Agents Hope Denny's Multimillion-Dollar Settlement Will Teach Lesson," *Washington Post,* May 25, 1994, p. D1).

5. Denise Chavez, *Face of an Angel* (New York: Farrar, Straus and Giroux, 1994).

Chapter 7. Worlds Within Worlds

1. Cynthia Shearer, *The Wonder Book of the Air* (New York: Pantheon, 1996).

Epilogue

1. Louise Kapp Howe, *Pink Collar Workers: Inside the World of Women's Work* (New York: G. P. Putnam, 1977), p. 132.